About the authors

WALDEN BELLO is professor of sociology and public administration at the University of the Philippines and co-director of Focus on the Global South, a policy research institute based in Bangkok, Thailand. Prior to that he was executive director of the Institute for Food and Development Policy (Food First) in Oakland, California. Educated at Princeton University, where he obtained his doctorate in sociology in 1975, he has taught at the University of California, Berkeley, where he was also a research associate with the Center for South East Asian Studies. He is the author of numerous books, including (with Shea Cunningham) *Dark Victory: The United States, Structural Adjustment and Global Poverty* (1994); *People and Power in the Pacific: The Struggle for the Post-Cold War Order* (1992); (co-authored with Stephanie Rosenfeld) *Dragons in Distress: Asia's Miracle Economies in Crisis* (1991); *Brave New World? Strategies for Survival in the Global Economy* (1990) and *Development Débâcle: The World Bank in the Philippines* (1982).

SHEA CUNNINGHAM was educated at San Francisco State University and is now pursuing graduate studies at the University of California and Los Angeles (UCLA). She is a former research associate at Food First and Focus on the Global South, and co-author (with Walden Bello) of *Dark Victory: The United States, Structural Adjustment and Global Poverty* (1994).

LI KHENG POH was educated at Cornell University. She is currently a research associate at Focus on the Global South.

A SIAMESE TRAGEDY
Development and Disintegration in Modern Thailand

WALDEN BELLO, SHEA CUNNINGHAM
AND LI KHENG POH

Food First
OAKLAND, CA

White Lotus
BANGKOK

Z

Zed Books Ltd
LONDON & NEW YORK

A Siamese Tragedy: Development and Disintegration in Modern Thailand was first published in 1998 by Zed Books Ltd, 7 Cynthia Street, London N1 9JF, UK and Room 400, 175 Fifth Avenue, New York, NY 10010, USA.

US paperback edition published by Food First Books, Institute for Food and Development Policy, 398 60th Street, Oakland, CA 94618, USA in 1998

Distributed in its cased edition in the USA exclusively by St. Martin's Press Inc., 175 Fifth Avenue, New York, NY 10010, USA

Published in Thailand by White Lotus Company Ltd, GPO Box 1141, Bangkok, 100501, Thailand

Cover by Ad Lib Design, London N19
Set in Monotype Garamond by Ewan Smith
Printed and bound in the United Kingdom
by Biddles Ltd, Guildford and King's Lynn

A catalogue record for this book is available from the British Library

Library of Congress Cataloging-in-Publication Data

Walden Bello
    A Siamese Tragedy: Development and Disintegration in
    Modern Thailand
    First Edition
      288 p.   cm.
    A Food First book
    ISBN 0-935028-74-9
    1. Nonfiction. 2. Asia. 3. Economics. 4. Social Sciences.
    5. Human rights. 6. Aids. 7. Labor. 8. Agriculture. 9. Environ-
    -ment.   I. Shea Cunningham II. Li Kheng Poh III. Title.
        SD   1998

ISBN 1 85649 663 5 cased
ISBN 1 85649 664 3 limp
US pb ISBN 0 935028 74 9
Thai pb ISBN 974 843 62 1

Contents

Tables and Figures

Tables

Figures

Acknowledgements

Research for this book began in the years when Thailand was an economic miracle, and the writing was completed in the months that the economy crashed.

The insights of many friends and associates into the Thai economic boom (and collapse) and the so-called Asian Miracle were of immense assistance to us as we negotiated our way through the different dimensions of Thailand's development path. That their ideas and opinions were often imparted with typical Thai hospitality, grace, and friendship was a bonus.

We are grateful to the following for giving us so much of their precious time in interviews: Nikhom Chandravithun, Sulak Sivaraksa, Suthy Prasartsert, Naruemon Thaubchumpon, Oranut Supaphanwadee, Chokchai Suttawet, John Ungpakorn, Witoon Permpongsacharoen, Banthorn Ondam, Larry Lohmann, Chris Beyrer, Paiboon Wattanasiritham, Chris Borden, Julie Otterbein, Bundit Thanachaisethavut, Alec Bamford, David Thomas, Ranee Hassarungsee, Khunying Chodchoy Sophonpanich, Srisuwan Kuankajorn, Thanes Kongprasert, Alec Gordon, Somyot Pruksakasemuk, Mayuli Tewiya, Bill Callahan, Leo Alting Von Geusau, Utai Sonluksub, Pasuk Phongphaichit, Panno Suttiwiriya, Sampahn Ratanaswasad, Somlak Wongrat, Surasith Hemtasilpa, Kriengdej Akaraskul, Bernard Meyhoefer, Uthaiwan Kanchanakamol, Chayan Vaddhanaputi, Andrew Turton, Nunchob Ongtanasin, Chuchchana Hanrittee, Pisarn Manoleehagul, Sirithan Boriboon, Kiyomi Nishikawa, Sathaporn Nada, David Wang, Wirun Chivapuntusri, Dhana Rachusanti, Narong Pakadet, Suthas Noonoi, Damrong Chawawiwat, Joseph Merle, Vachiravuth Toomkong, Jittrakorn Tanapoomichai, Hidetada Suda, Toshiaki Hayashi, Suteera Thompson, Somrudee Nicro, Seri Phongphit, Taweekiat Prasertcharoensuk, Teeranat Karnjana-Uksorn, Nils Ramm-Ericson, Prasert Trakansuphakorn, Sumeth Srisangthaisuk, Anthony Zola, Joseph Maier, Michelle Weldon, Precha Vudhivai, Anders Paludan-Miller, Panus Thailuan, Anupap Tiralap, Waranya Patarasuk, Deputy Minister Suthep Thaugsuban, Varunee Purisinsit, Anek Laothamatas, Vute Wangwacharakul, Roy Archer, Nongyao Nawarat, Somkiat Pongpaiboon, Ukrist Pathamanand, Governor Somchet Thinaphong, Preeda Prapertchob, Chayan Vaddhanaputi, Chatthip Narsupha, Lae Dilokvidhyarat, John Medeiros, Nikorn Weesapen, Arunee Srito, Prateep Ungsongtham, Sompong Patpui, Peter Cox, Anan Ganjanapan, Phra Prajak Kutthajito, Uraivan Tan-Kim-Yong, Kaulaya Todrabum, Veerasak

Todrabum, Phil Hirsch, Paul Handley, Sompop Manarangsan, Sumara Bumpanya, Scott Christensen, Andrew Turton, Angkarb Korsieporn, Apichai Puntasen, Wannida Tantiwitthayapithak, Jaran Jitapichai, Oraphun Metadilogkul, Naryana Supapong, Sakul Zesongdham, Boontien Kamchoo, Katherine Bond, Alex Horstmann, Tanya Hanpol, Chaisiri Kritikorn, Peter Ungpakorn, Chai-Anand Samudavanija, Niyom Rathamarit, Chaichana Ingarata, Tang Choomhiran, Victor Karuman, and Somchai Homlaor.

Special acknowledgement must be made of the invaluable contributions made to the study by the following colleagues, whether in the form of advice, intellectual exchange, research support, or warm hospitality: Suthy Prasartsert, Surichai Wan-Geao, Chantana Banpasirichote, Chokchai Sutta-wet, Oranut Suphapanwadee, Suranuch Thongsila, Naruemon Thaub-chumpon, Somruk Raksasap, Mark Ritchie, Susan George, David Hubbel, Alec Gordon, Amihan Abveva, Victor Karunan, and Aaron Stern.

This book would not have been possible without the moral support as well as intellectual assistance of the following colleagues at Food First and Focus on the Global South: Kamal Malthotra, Peter Rosset, Junya 'Lek' Yimprasert, Nicola Bullard, Marilyn Borchardt, Chanida Chanyapate Bamford, Ehito Kimura, Gina Abesamis, Marjorie Joy Obando, Aileen Kwa, Joy Chavez-Malaluan, Mayuree 'Nok' Reuchakiattikul, Joy Chavez-Malaluan, Marco Mezzera, Chirawattana Charoonpatarapong and Suntaree Nakaviroj. Our crossing the finish was in great part due to Kamal and Peter's constant encouragement and gentle prodding.

The Institute of Asian Studies and the Social Research Institute at Chulalongkorn University provided institutional homes for this research in Thailand, and for facilitating this we would like to especially thank Dr Withaya Sucharitharanugse, Dr Krayudth Dhiratayakinant, Dr Amara Pong-sapich, and Dr Suwattana Thadaniti. Institutional support was also provided by Chulalongkorn University's Asian Center for Migration Studies and the Friends of Women Foundation.

Colleagues at the University of the Philippines Sociology Department, especially Dr Luzviminda Valencia and Dr Clemen Aquino, were very understanding of the demands of the research and were careful not to overload Walden with teaching responsibilities. Solid support for the research also came from Professor Randolf David, Dr Cynthia Bautista, and Dean Connie Paz.

Research on this scale cannot be undertaken without generous financial assistance. Here we would like to thank, especially, Community Aid Abroad, CUSO, Development and Peace, and the CEP Humanity Fund. In the final phases of the write-up of the project, financial support also came from Novib, Hivos, Oxfam Hong Kong, and Oxfam UK.

Translating this work from manuscript to print was no easy feat, and much of the reason for this lay in the skills, support, and patience of

Robert Molteno and his staff at Zed Books. Translating the book into Thai was done with skill and élan by Suranuch Thongsila.

Finally, this book owes so much to the love, inspiration, comradeship, generosity, and support – direct or indirect – of many close and very dear friends, among them Marilen Abesamis-Bello, Greg Young, Annette Ferrer, Ami Ferrer, Li Suan Poh, Angkarb Korsieporn, Benedict and Girlie Ng, Suranuch Thongsila, Anuradha Mittal, Martha Katigbak, Edgardo Rodriguez, Tomoko Sakuma, Zon Moraleda, Evelyn Soriano, Willie Abesamis, Carlos Abesamis, Tonette Garcia, Ria Pugeda, Brid Brennan, Peter Hayes, Lyuba Zarsky, John Cavanagh, and Robin Broad ... and, oh yes, Nadia and Benjamin Zarsky-Hayes and Jesse Broad-Cavanagh.

It must be emphasized, however, that the shortcomings of this book must not be traced to any of the above. For these, the authors alone are responsible.

WB, SC, LKP
Bangkok, 27 July 1998

Foreword

I first read Walden Bello's book *Dragons in Distress: Asia's Miracle Economies in Crisis* six years ago and found it most informative and provocative. It was the first warning to Asian neoclassical economists and planners about the defects of the high-speed growth model. I have read this classic from time to time since then while writing my own book on the impact of three decades of economic growth on Thai labour.

I was given the manuscript of Dr Bello's new book while in the midst of editing my own book, and I initially decided to put it aside and come back to it later. However, after reading the introduction, I changed my mind and kept reading throughout the weekend. I must confess that I have not enjoyed reading a book of this nature for some time. Dr Bello has again demonstrated his superb ability for detailed analyses of realities, and weaves them together to present an accurate interpretation of the Thai situation. Each chapter presents a true, frank, and lucid picture of what happened in the past that led to the current economic crisis. The exposé on labour is superb. No books, even those authored by Thais, have come out with such a clear message. Thus, with this book, Dr Bello has proved beyond a doubt that the high-speed growth model can lead to a country's bankruptcy and to great distress.

The release of this book is very timely since the Thai government and people have been trying to find solutions to the present crisis. Dr Bello has done a great service for Thailand, for which I am personally grateful.

Nikhom Chandravithun

Professor of Labour Law, Thammasat University; Thailand Fellow,
The National Academy for Moral and Political Science;
Member of the State Council

Abbreviations

ADB	Asian Development Bank
AFTA	ASEAN Free Trade Area
AIDS	acquired immune deficiency syndrome
ALRO	Agrarian Land Reform Office
AMC	Asset Management Corporation
APEC	Asia Pacific Economic Cooperation
ASEAN	Association of Southeast Asian Nations
BAAC	Bank of Agriculture and Agricultural Cooperatives
BIBF	Bangkok International Banking Facility
BMA	Bangkok Metropolitan Authority
BMR	Bangkok Metropolitan Region
BMWA	Bankgkok Metropolitan Water Authority
BOD	biological oxygen demand
BOI	Board of Investments (Thailand)
BOT	Bank of Thailand
BTSC	Bangkok Transportation System Corporation
CAP	Common Agricultural Policy (EU)
CBU	completcly built up (automobile)
CBZ	conservation buffer zone
CKD	'completely knocked down' automobile for reassembly
CPT	Communist Party of Thailand
CSW	commercial sex workcr
DIW	Department of Industrial Works
EC	European Community
EGAT	Electricity Generating Authority of Thailand
EIA	environmental impact assessment
EOI	export-oriented industrialization
ETA	Expressway and Rapid Transit Authority
EU	European Union
FFT	Farmers' Federation of Thailand
FIDF	Financial Institutions Development Fund
FLUT	Federation of Labour Unions of Thailand
FRA	Financial Restructuring Authority
FY	financial year
GATT	General Agreement on Tariffs and Trade
GM	General Motors

HIV	human immunodeficiency virus
IC	integrated circuit
IEAT	Industrial Estate Authority of Thailand
IED	Industrial Environment Division (Department of Industrial Works)
ILO	International Labour Organization
IMF	International Monetary Fund
ISI	import substitution industrialization
LCCT	Labour Coordination Centre of Thailand
MITI	Ministry of Trade and Industry (Japan)
MRTA	Metropolitan Rapid Transit Authority
NAIC	newly agro-industrializing country
NESDB	National Economic and Social Development Board
NGO	non-governmental organization
NHA	National Housing Authority
NIC	newly industrializing country
ONEB	Office of the National Environmental Board
OPEC	Organization of Petroleum-Exporting Countries
PAS	protected area system
PCB	polychlorinated biphenyl
PEP	Poverty Eradication Programme
PER	Project for Ecological Recovery
PLMO	Property Loan Management Organization
R&D	research and development
RECP	Rural Employment Creation Programme
RFD	Royal Forestry Department
RID	Royal Irrigation Department
SET	Stock Exchange of Thailand
STD	sexually transmitted disease
STK	National Forest Land Allotment Programme
TDRI	Thailand Development Research Institute
TFSMP	Thai Forestry Sector Master Plan
TNC	transnational corporation
TRIM	trade-related investment measure
UNDP	United Nations Development Programme
UNICEF	United Nations Children's Fund
UNIDO	United Nations Industrial Development Organization
USAID	US Agency for International Development
WHO	World Health Organization
WTO	World Trade Organization

To our very dear colleagues at Focus, Food First, CUSRI, and the Sociology Department and College of Public Administration of the University of the Philippines.

CHAPTER I

Introduction: Survey of an Economic Débâcle

'We have lost our autonomy, our ability to determine our macroeconomic policy. This is unfortunate.'[1] This statement, made by the deputy prime minister of Thailand, Supachai Panitchpakdi, in response to an interviewer's question about the country's relationship to the International Monetary Fund (IMF), was the sort of remark that would have made the great King Chulalongkorn roll in his grave. It was not that Thailand had never been in an essentially colonial situation before – in the nineteenth century, the Bowring Treaty had practically given Great Britain control over the country's foreign trade. The IMF had also been a strong presence in the country before: back in the mid-1980s, together with the World Bank, it had given the government 'structural adjustment' loans with 'conditionalities'. What was new and striking was the degree of submission to an external body and the candour with which a high state official was admitting the condition of subservience.

A second Ayuthaya?

The facts were indisputable. To access a $17.2 billion bail-out or 'rescue' package, the government had agreed to what could only be described as draconian conditions – among them, increasing the level of value-added tax from 7 to 10 per cent, the attainment of a surplus in the government budget, and rises in the prices of public utilities. But what was viewed with most consternation by some was the government's agreeing to open up the country's financial institutions to 100 per cent foreign ownership and its promise to support legislation allowing foreigners to own land, something once regarded as taboo.

Yet it was testimony to the temper of the times that Supachai's remarks were regarded not as controversial but as simply acknowledging the effects of the economic disaster that had befallen the country. Even more remarkable to some outside observers was the fact that it appeared to be only a minority of Thais who exhibited strong negative feelings toward the IMF. Indeed, at the start of the crisis, many Thais saw the Fund in the same way they saw the king: as a possible source of salvation in troubled times. To them, it was not the IMF but the politicians and big business that were the villains.

What hit Thailand in 1997 was no mere recession but, according to some, a historical cataclysm on a par with the Burmese sacking of the ancient Thai capital of Ayuthaya in 1765–67. And it added little to the Thais' self-esteem that Bangkok had served as the 'ground zero' of a financial implosion that went on to engulf the rest of Asia after the 'floating' of the baht on 2 July.

Between 2 July and the end of 1997, the baht fell by over 100 per cent relative to the dollar, and the stock market fell from an already low 800 points to below 400. These were the two prime indicators of a massive flight of foreign capital from the country. Thailand was effectively bankrupt, saddled with a foreign debt of $89 billion, over half of which was due in a few months' time. There was no way Thailand would be able to pay this debt to foreign financial institutions without some external assistance and some relief in the form of debt rescheduling. The country's virtual bankruptcy was underlined in international financial circles by the demotion, by the international credit evaluators Moody's and Standard and Poor's, of the country's government bonds from AA+ rankings to DD-, or junk bond status.

High flyers laid low

To most ordinary Thais at the end of 1997, the full impact of the disaster was still to be felt. But, by any measure, the effects of the economic débâcle were already considerable by then. At the top of the casualty list were the 50,000 employees of the 56 financial firms that had been shut down by the authorities at the urging of the IMF. Once considered the high flyers of the Thai middle class, whose free-spending ways were emblematic of the Thai boom, these aristocrats of the white-collar sector found themselves deprived of use of their credit cards, unable to service their payments on their mortgages, giving up their Mercedes or BMWs (100,000 were repossessed in the second half of 1997[2]), and reduced to looking for alternative employment in the academic and non-governmental sectors that were once disdained for their low salaries.

Television and newspapers featured human interest stories, such as the one about Sirivat Voravetvuthikun, the stockbroker who transformed himself into a sandwich-maker and peddler to survive the slump. Said *Asiaweek*, 'To outsiders, he personifies Thailand's rise and fall – and possible redemption.'[2] Agile operators like Sirivat were, however, exceptional. More common were shock, disbelief, and depression. The shell-shock that accompanied the reversal of fortune of the once privileged was expressed by one former stockbroker who was on the shortlist for a job interview with an NGO: 'We never had any indication we were in trouble, never. I was very busy, being in charge of many of our customers. Then one day the BOT [Bank of Thailand] suddenly tells us we have to shut down because we're bankrupt.'[4]

The finance company employees were joined at the head of the unemployment queue by people who were laid off from the real estate companies whose construction mania had created the massive property oversupply that triggered the crisis, and by workers in sectors that had fed off the real estate boom, like the media, a great deal of whose revenues came from property advertisements. Some 300 employees of one of the country's foremost newspapers, *The Nation*, were laid off and about one half of the country's 5,000 registered journalists faced unemployment.[5]

The effect on the real economy

The fallout from the bursting of the bubble economy appeared to be hitting the real economy faster than people had anticipated. In the second half of 1997, work on most construction projects ground to a halt in Bangkok, leaving the city with ugly half-finished high-rise buildings and disgorging thousands of workers into a contracting economy. Many of the new unemployed were finding their way to the countryside. An average of five migrants had returned to each of the country's 60,000 villages by December, according to NGO estimates.[6] The swarming back into the rural economy was noted by, among others, a social researcher in Pichit, a province three hours from Bangkok by bus, who found that considerable numbers of construction workers appeared to be joining the rural workforce. 'To my surprise, I was talking to field labourers that had been recently laid off from construction jobs in Bangkok. They were dispirited and they were hungry.'[7] In an instant survey of unemployed people in February 1998 in the province of Nan in the far north of the country, the same researcher found that: 'About 80 per cent of those interviewed had returned since December because of the economic crisis.'[8] These findings were in line with data gathered by others. For instance, in the village of Sap Poo Pan in the northeast – the region that produces the greatest number of internal migrants – World Bank researchers found that out of a total village population of 260, 40 out of 110 people working outside the village had already returned by late January 1998.[9]

About one million Thais would lose their jobs in the coming recession, predicted the country's finance minister in September 1997. That was an underestimate, according to other sources, which said that 2.9 million out of the country's workforce of 29 million were expected to be unemployed by the end of 1997.[10] What is certain is that government figures showed that by February 1998, 80,000 workers had been layed off since the middle of 1997. This recorded figure was a gross underestimate, according to labour expert Professor Nikhom Chandravithun, and 'must be added to the 2 million estimated unemployed'.[11]

As in other countries facing economic contraction, clamping down on foreign workers became an easy solution, with the Thai authorities announcing in January 1998 that some 600,000 foreign workers, most of them Burmese and most working in low-paying agricultural, fishing, and construction jobs, would be sent back to their countries to make way for Thai workers displaced from urban industrial jobs. One month later, threat became reality and television sets around the world showed CNN footage of Thai soldiers forcing over one hundred Burmese men, women, and children to walk for three hours from the town of Kanchanaburi to the Burmese border under a glaring sun as their Burmese kin escaping from repression looked on from makeshift refugee camps.

The explosiveness of the economic contraction was underlined for both Thais and the world at large by what amounted to a mini-uprising by workers at the Thai Summit Auto Parts Factory on 21 January 1998. The protestors blocked the busy Bangna-trat Highway in protest against the company's announcement that it would not give them the long-awaited bonuses they had counted on to make ends meet. Then followed several hours of pitched battle that pitted workers againt police and angry motorists and ended with the wholesale arrest of 54 workers and their being herded in prisoner-of-war fashion into police vans. To both the Thais and the international community, the televison images of the event were reminiscent of Korea and came across as a harbinger of things to come.

Twilight zone

To Thais whose jobs were still unaffected by the crisis, the last months of 1997 were experienced as a twilight zone, when one still occupied one's house, drove one's car, and went to work, but with a grim sense that any day now, all that would be gone. 'Nobody, professional or worker, now engages in job-hopping,' said the general manager of a Japanese subsidiary, referring to the practice that became the trademark of the Thai workforce during the boom. 'Everybody's now holding on to whatever job they have and holding very tight.'[12]

Even those with secure jobs could not escape the general depression. 'My job's secure,' said one top-level executive. 'But you end up getting depressed anyway, since every meeting and every time you see friends, discussions always turn to how bad the economy is and how people are hurting. Then relatives call you to ask for help.'[13] With depression blanketing the country, it was not surprising that the suicide rate doubled, with an average of twelve Thais taking their lives each day in January 1998. Even more alarming was the revelation that 17 per cent of over 1,180 Thais polled said they were thinking of killing themselves.[14]

Depression was one of several social consequences of the economic freefall. Another was what a World Bank research team described as 'a breakdown in community trust'.[15] In Teparak, a slum community in Bangkok,

> Increased competition for survival, frustration and psychological stress had led to increased household and community tension. With increased competition for jobs, neighbors who once cooperated are now competing. Stealing, crime, and violence, they stated, was on the rise. People were feeling unsafe and insecure. They expressed great concern for their children's future. Some had been forced by their parents to drop out of school. Surprisingly, this strategy was not to enable the children to go to work but to guard the home as both parents were now working and break-ins had increased. The group added that it was well known that their own neighbors had been the thieves. Within this environment of declining trust and increasing competition, along with decreased time, Teparak was witnessing the weakening of community groups which had evolved over a long period of time.[16]

The sense of foreboding affected not only the employed and the unemployed but also those yet to be employed. 'You will probably wait three years to be employed, instead of the three months that your predecessors enjoyed,' Professor Nikhom Chandravithun, the country's foremost labour economist, warned students at Chulalongkorn University.[17] It was not a pleasant message to the students of Thailand's university for the elite. With their stylishly cut black-and-white uniforms, henna-dyed hair, platform shoes, and Gucci (the real thing!) bags, the Chula co-eds driving a Mercedes or BMW with one hand while holding a fashionably thin cellular phone with the other had been the poster children of the Thai boom. But the message was still not getting through in early 1998: the university probably still had more Mercedes and BMWs per square kilometre than any other campus in the world.

The culture of conspicuous consumption

For their lifestyle of conspicuous consumption, however, the children of the elite had good role models: their parents. The second- or third-generation descendants of Chinese migrants to Thailand who had married into the indigenous Thai elite or middle and lower classes, their parents had lost the thriftiness (some would say stinginess) of the Chinese merchant but inherited his wealth, which they wed to the strong urge to use display of wealth as a means of establishing status characteristic of traditional Thai culture. The offspring of this marriage included Thailand becoming the primary market for Mercedes Benz outside Germany, high-rises and residences in grandiose ersatz classical architectural style, the proliferation of 'fine dining' places where one could spend over a hundred dollars on exquisite continental cuisine and vintage French wine, and the stereotype of Thai travellers being compulsive shoppers who were unfazed by sky-high prices.

Stories of the free-spending ways of the Thai elite and middle class were legion. For example, the management of one of Rome's most exclusive shoe boutiques is said to remember the time, a few years ago, when a well-known politician who was then serving as the deputy minister of agriculture swept into the shop with an entourage of 30 people and told them they could each choose a pair at his expense. 'My husband had to pick a pair,' said the wife of one diplomat in the group. 'It would have been bad form if he didn't.'[18]

But it was not only the upper and middle classes that engaged in conspicuous consumption. Bangkok's awful traffic provided teachers with a good excuse to indulge in a middle-class status symbol, a Toyota Corolla, while in the countryside, farmers who sold their land to developers immediately transformed the proceeds from the sale into a Toyota pickup. So great, in fact, was the demand that rural Thailand became, after the USA, the world's biggest market for pickups.[19]

The increase in tendencies towards conspicuous consumption in the culture cannot be separated from the transformations in the Thai economy in the late 1980s and early 1990s. Indeed, while some visitors and foreign economists bewailed the free-spending ways of the Thai upper and middle classes as the key to Thailand's economic collapse, the reality was much more complex.

The Thai path to development

Some analysts would trace the economic crisis to the late 1950s, when, with strong backing from the World Bank, Thailand embarked on a path of development stressing rapid industrialization. Accompanying this thrust was massive infrastructure spending, particularly for projects supporting urban industry; a strong market orientation; a leading role for the private sector; and a pivotal role for foreign investment.

The first phase of this development process was import substitution industrialization, but with this strategy running into crisis in the early 1980s the technocrat economic leadership, backed strongly by the private sector, launched the country onto the path of export-oriented growth in the mid-1980s. This phase was accompanied by the tremendous infusion of foreign capital, especially from Japanese foreign investors seeking to relocate the more labour-intensive phases of their manufacturing operations away from Japan in an effort to maintain their edge in global competition.

With the rise in income, particularly among the rich and the middle classes, Thailand became an important market in its own right for foreign investors, and, as in many other sectors, the Japanese automobile companies led the way by setting up assembly operations in the country to take advantage of a market still protected by high tariffs. Japanese investment began to taper off in the early 1990s, but Thailand's technocrats and business elite had by then become addicted to foreign capital. Fortunately for them, an alternative source of capital was available, in large volumes, in the form of the huge sums in the control of portfolio investors and big international banks seeking investment opportunities that were more profitable than those in the North.

Globalization of the Thai economy

The effort to attract foreign investment was led by technocrats and bureaucrats who found their views in synch with the free market neoliberal ideology pervading policy, business, and academic circles in the North during the Reagan era. These technocrats believed that Thailand's prosperity lay in minimizing state regulation of the private sector to allow it to play the leading role in economic development, and in a closer integration of the Thai economy with the global economy through accelerated trade, investment, and financial liberalization.

Thus, during the Anand administration in the early 1990s, taxes on completely built up cars (CBUs) were brought down radically in the name of consumer welfare (a move that may have brought down prices for the middle class as consumers but also harmed them by worsening both pollution and traffic). It was, however, not so much in trade – where opposition to full-scale liberalization remained strong – but in the financial sector that the greatest effort to erase the separation between the Thai economy and the global economy was made.

Financial liberalization and the elimination of virtually all significant restrictions on foreign exchange transactions, coupled with the maintenance of high interest rates (to attract investors) and tying the baht at a stable rate to the dollar (to ensure them against foreign currency risk), created a macroeconomic framework friendly to foreign capital. But it was the prosperity triggered by Japanese and other direct investment that acted as the biggest magnet for the tidal wave of portfolio investment that swept the country in the early 1990s, and it was the high growth rates of 7–10 per cent that served as the ultimate collateral for international banks that were eager to lend to Thai financial institutions and enterprises.

Creating the credit economy

This capital went principally not to the productive sectors of the economy but to the highly profitable sectors with a quick turnaround time – which meant the stock market, real estate, and credit creation. Via the finance companies, foreign capital found its way into the hands of real estate developers projecting an immense growth in demand for office space and middle- and upper-class housing. It also was channelled as credit to the people who would buy those houses and condominiums. And much of it went into the creation of credit cards and credit financing that would allow the same social groups to purchase cars, household goods, and the services that came with a Western middle-class lifestyle

Bangkok, in short, became a debtors' instead of a creditors' market, and the easy money, easy credit, and easy terms proved very seductive to the various sectors of Thai society. The proliferation of buildings, cars, and shopping malls created the aura of widespread prosperity that at the same time masked the fact that purchasing power did not have a basis in real wealth but was being artificially created via credit extended from external sources. Consumption and the contraction of credit became the password to the good life, and saving and delayed gratification became not virtues but anachronistic habits that it would be stupid to adhere to in an era of easy money.

The Thai economy was perched precariously on this pyramid of credit when, in 1997, the not unexpected conjunction of massive oversupply of real estate, skyrocketing external debt, and zero growth in exports triggered the flight of foreign capital that lay at its base. The collapse, when it came, was sudden, but it was not totally unexpected.

Royal doubts

The crisis brought not only shock but profound questioning of a model of development based on massive infusions of capital, fast-track export-oriented industrialization, credit creation, minimal regulation of the private sector, and greater integration into the global economy. Surprisingly, the king took the lead, and in a remarkable speech on his birthday in December, he urged going back to a self-sufficient agrarian economy. Summing up the essential points of his speech, *The Nation* pointed out:

> It was not important for Thailand to become an economic tiger ... What mattered was Thais should live a life that would make them have enough to eat and capable of supporting themselves financially.
>
> He said progressive economists might consider his ideal of promoting a self-sufficient economy [an idea that might be considered] obsolete as the country had already been involved largely in the trade economy.
>
> But he contended it was production with the aim of making local communities self-sufficient that would help pull Thailand out of its current crisis.[20]

It was not, of course, a new message, for what the king was saying had been said, much more forcefully and critically, by Sulak Sivaraksa, Prawase Wasi, Nikhom Chandravithun and many in the country's vibrant NGO community for years. What was new was that the king was saying it, and for many Thais, especially those from the rural sector and the middle class, this gave the anti-globalization message a degree of legitimacy it might not have had beforehand.

By the beginning of 1998, disillusionment with the IMF had set in as well, with an institution that had been regarded as a saviour turning more and more, in the eyes of many Thais, into an instrument for the accelerated penetration of the Thai economy – and the other troubled economies of East Asia as well – by US capital.

'The king's right,' said a woman who, like most other small entrepreneurs, had lost up to 30 per cent of her catering business.[21] 'This is a lesson for all of us never to get seduced again by consumerism, by easy money.' Another man said: 'I went to see my friends at Chulalongkorn's Economics Department and told them they need to shut down the department since nobody believes economists any more.'[22]

To an increasing number of Thais, the challenge was no longer just one of reviving their moribund economy but of restructuring it on different principles and priorities. The big questions were where to go and how to get there.

Notes

1. Interview, *McNeil-Lehrer News Hour*, 24 November 1997.
2. CNN, 18 February 1998.
3. 'Surviving the slump', *Asiaweek*, 28 November 1997, p. 52.
4. Interview, anonymity requested, Bangkok, 4 December 1997.
5. Interview, *McNeil-Lehrer News Hour*, 24 November 1997.
6. Figure from Wanida Tantiwitthayaphitak, spokesperson for Forum of the Poor, Bangkok, 21 January 1998.
7. Interview with Angkarb Korsieporn, Bangkok, 12 January 1998.
8. Interview with Angkarb Korsieporn, 20 February 1998.
9. World Bank, 'Social aspects of the crisis: perceptions of poor communities', draft report, February 1998.
10. '2.9 million risk losing jobs by December', *Bangkok Post*, 1 September 1997.
11. Interview, Professor Nikhom Chandravithun, Bangkok, 20 February 1998.
12. Interview, anonymity requested, 15 October 1997.
13. Interview, anonymity requested, 18 October 1997.
14. 'The fall of the spirit', *Newsweek*, 19 January 1998, p. 13.
15. World Bank, 'Social aspects of the crisis', p. 5.
16. Ibid., pp. 5–6.
17. Comments at symposium on 'The Economic Crisis in Thailand', Chulalongkorn University, 14 January 1998.
18. Interview, anonymity requested, Bangkok, 13 December 1997.
19. 'Auctioneers thrive amidst Thai crisis', *International Herald Tribune*, 23 February 1998.
20. 'Nation told it's time to step back before moving forward', *The Nation*, 6 December 1997.
21. Interview, anonymity requested, Bangkok, 19 January 1998.
22. Personal communication, Jaran Ditapichai, Bangkok, 23 January 1998.

CHAPTER 2

Back to the Third World

On 2 July 1997, after fighting off waves of speculative attack against its currency, the Bank of Thailand, the country's central monetary authority, announced that it would no longer intervene in foreign exchange markets and would allow the baht to seek its 'free market equilibrium' relative to the dollar. For over ten years, the baht had been pegged to the dollar at the rate of about $1:B25, and so central to economic policy was this informal but official fixing to the greenback that it had congealed into a doctrine. Indeed, the stable baht/dollar rate became a symbol of both the stability and the dynamism of what had been dubbed Asia's fifth 'tiger'. So, when in a few days the baht floated rapidly downward and lost up to 20 per cent of its value, the shock to the nation's psyche was immense. A world had come to an end.

The political economy of NIChood

That world was born in the late 1950s, but its most spectacular phase – the so-called 'Golden Age' – unfolded in the period 1986–96.

Prior to the recession, Thailand had enjoyed over two decades of rapid development. Its average annual growth came to 8 per cent in the 1960s, 7 per cent in the 1970s, and between 4 and 6 per cent in the first years of the 1980s, when recession hit the country.[1]

Import substitution industrialization

The early phase of Thailand's growth is conventionally attributed to the involvement of the World Bank in drawing up a blueprint for the Thai economy in the late 1950s. Accepted by the government of Field Marshal Sarit Thanarat, the World Bank plan recommended a sharp turn away from strong government control over the economy and proposed that the private sector be encouraged to take the lead in the country's development. It also recommended a strategy of import substitution as a means of industrialization. And it offered the World Bank's resources to set up the infrastructure and other measures necessary to support a programme of industrialization.

Prior to the Sarit reform, Thailand's strongest private actors were a landed class in the countryside and an urban-based commercial bourgeoisie based on banking and trade, especially in agricultural commodities. The state, however, was the dominant actor in the economy, with the Sino-Thai bourgeoisie allowed to make money but clearly at the sufferance of the state bureaucracy and the military. As protection, the emerging capitalist groups incorporated high military and bureaucratic figures into their boards of directors.

With import substitution, manufacturing became a new source of wealth and new capitalist groups emerged with their principal base in industry.[2] But while the local market was reserved primarily for local industrialists, foreign corporations were not excluded. As Kevin Hewison puts it: 'The Sarit government, primed with World Bank and UN advice, saw TNCs as sources of capital which could replace state investment but continue the drive for expanded industrial activity. TNCs were also seen as providing technical and entrepreneurial skills, and the promotion of foreign investment became a pillar of state economic policy.'[3]

The dominant force after the Sarit reforms continued to be the military. However, the reforms promoted the influence of an identifiable new group of influentials connected with the state, the technocracy. Technocrats, who combined expertise in conservative economics with administrative skills, came to dominate the key agencies of macroeconomic management, such as the Ministry of Finance, Bank of Thailand, Budget Bureau, and the National Economic and Social Development Board.[4] The technocrats were clearly subordinate to the military but, as Amar Siamwalla notes, '[t]he relationship between the technocracy and its military members was far from smooth'.[5]

> The latter's need to expand government budgets in general and the military budget in particular was a constant cause of conflict, as were some of their corrupt activities that entered the radar screen of the technocrats (for example, contracts to print banknotes). But by and large, a *modus vivendi* was achieved, because both shared the vision that the economy needed to grow, which for the technocrats was the desired aim and for the military was the means by which they could obtain greater spoils.[6]

The strategy of import substitution industrialization (ISI) began to flag in the late 1970s, with the GNP growth rate tapering down. The analysis of the World Bank was that the slowdown stemmed from the limits of the domestic market as well as from inefficiencies fostered by protectionism. Slowdown turned into crisis in 1983–85, when the domestic slowdown was exacerbated by the conjunction of the effects of the OPEC oil price rise of 1979, the drop in raw material prices, and the debt crisis on the global scene. Bankruptcies increased by almost 27 per cent in the first nine months of 1985, the Board of Trade reported 100,000 layoffs in the first nine months of that year, and Thailand's foreign debt passed the $13 billion mark.[7]

It was in response to these developments that Thailand turned to a strategy of export-oriented industrialization (EOI) around the mid-1980s. As in the 1950s, the World Bank played a very influential role, and its policy by the mid-1970s had shifted from promoting import substitution to supporting export-oriented industrialization. As Robert McNamara, the World Bank president, said in 1975: '[S]pecial efforts must be made in many countries to turn their manufacturing away from the relatively small markets associated with import substitution toward the much larger opportunities flowing from export promotion.'[8] Supporting the shift were young technocrats trained abroad in neoclassical economics. Business associations, such as the Thai Bankers' Association and the Association of Thai Industries, lobbied the government to change course. The textile industry pressed for and got preferential credit as well as refunds of taxes and tariffs imposed on inputs, as did the jewellery industry.[9]

The World Bank threw its weight behind the export lobby in the advice it gave the government as the economy moved into a downturn in the mid-1980s, emphasizing 'the need to open the economy, privatize state enterprises, and perhaps surprisingly, given the debate on foreign debt, reaffirmed the importance of international capital flows in development'.[10] It was a position the Bank was willing to back with deeds: Thailand became the recipient of structural adjustment loans from the IMF and the World Bank, which sought not only to stabilize the economy in the short term but also to orient it in a more open direction by bringing down tariffs, reducing the role of state enterprises, removing price controls, and instituting a more flexible exchange rate.[11]

These trends came to a head in November 1984, when the Prem government devalued the baht by 14.7 per cent, reflecting the government's strategy of 'exporting its way out of crisis'.[12] In addition to the devaluation, the government took other key measures, among which were the reduction of import taxes for materials used in exports, the abolition of several export taxes, the establishment of special credit facilities for exporters, the promulgation of investment incentives favouring enterprises that exported all or most of their output, and the active solicitation of foreign investment by, among other things, allowing 100 per cent foreign ownership in promoted enterprises that exported 100 per cent of their output.[13]

Export-oriented industrialization

With exports serving as the engine of the economy, Thailand grew by 10 per annum in the decade 1985–95 – the fastest in the world, according to the World Bank. By the early 1990s, the country was being touted as

Asia's 'fifth tiger' – an accolade that was formally bestowed by the Bank at the World Bank–IMF Conference held in Bangkok in September 1991. The very upbeat mood at the Bank about the prospects of its Thai pupil was captured in an agency report asserting that the 'only potential macro-economic problem on the horizon is one that many developing countries would wish to have – the problem of managing an economic boom.'[14]

The new globalized context of business provided great opportunities for diversification by the established groups. Foremost among this was the CP (Charoen Pokphand) Group. Starting in agribusiness, textiles, and import trade, CP grew into a giant with high-tech ties to foreign multi-nationals such as Ann Acres, Inc. in chicken breeding, the Mitsubishi Corporation of Japan for breeding the large-sized 'black tiger' shrimp, and the Dekalb Agresearch Company in the USA for developing a hybrid variety of maize.[15] CP became the best-known Thai multinational when it made its decision to base its broiler chicken industry in China.

The new business conditions also created the space for the emergence of new groups, especially in the new growth areas of telecommunications and infrastructure. A notable example was the Shinnawat Group headed by Thaksin Shinnawat, which expanded, through the adroit use of political connections, from computer vendor to telecommunications provider (including control of the popular IBC Network) to 'giant Bangkok mass transit infrastructure developer'.[16]

The private sector and the state

The 1986–96 period also saw the growing autonomy of business from patronage from bureaucratic and military groups – in other words, an end to the 'bureaucratic polity'. Thai business associations emerged as powerful lobbyists; Thai businessmen became active in parliamentary politics and skilfully used it – as in the case of Thaksin Shinnawat, who became a key figure in both the Chuan and Banharn governments – to push their business interests; and the Thai private sector became a haven for talented Thai technocrats who alternated between business and politics, such as Narong-chai Akrasanee, Amnuay Viravan, and Tarrin Nimmanhaeminda. Business, not government, became the favoured avenue for the talented. One result of all this was the shift in the balance of power between the private sector and government, whereby the former became the dominant actor. For all intents and purposes, effective government regulation of business dis-appeared, a point emphasized by the World Bank: 'Economic growth in Thailand over the past few years has been very rapid, but in a private enterprise system where few controls are imposed, increased material standards and private gains have been secured at an observable communal expense.'[17] A similar observation was made by a USAID official: 'Thailand is one place where the pendulum has swung too far in favor of the private sector, and government has to assume a stronger role in the economic decision-making.'[18]

Indeed, one might even say that the state–private sector relationship in Thailand came to resemble that in the Philippines, where government had been turned into colony of an extremely dynamic private sector.[19] Anek Laothamathas has argued that 'only in the areas of financial and monetary policy can one say that the Thai state is highly autonomous in relation to business'.[20] The institutions governing these areas – the Ministry of Finance, the National Economic and Social Development Board (NESDB), and the Bank of Thailand – were described as 'islands of rationality in an ocean of politicized economic management'.[21] (But this characterization probably exaggerated the exceptional character of these agencies; in any event, even these bastions of rationality fell in the mid-1990s and their penetration by business interests was one of the factors behind the collapse of the Thai economy.) Laothamatas has called the Thai system one of 'liberal corporatism', and perhaps this is as good a term as any.

Paralleling the growing autonomy of business from the state was the increased weight of parliament in the balance of power among state institutions. This was especially the case after the events of 1973–76, when the military was first dislodged from its primacy in power. But as with the technocracy–military relationship earlier, a *modus vivendi* was established among the parliamentarians, the technocrats, and the soldiers. The powerful MPs from the rural areas did not dispute the military's supremacy or the technocrats' control of the central economic agencies. What the rural-based MPs in particular were interested in was securing an ever-increasing flow of funds to their local followings. This was facilitated by their gaining control of the key sectoral ministries of agriculture, commerce, industry, and communications. As Amar Siamwalla noted:

> These ministries generated considerable amounts of corruption money. As the economy grew, this corruption money grew in tandem, certainly in absolute terms ...
>
> The key consequence of this development is in the expectations among the constituents, particularly in the rural areas. It is now widely expected that politicians will bring projects into their constituencies.
>
> It is widely expected that such projects will generate side benefits to the rural elite, who are quite active in the construction business. It is therefore widely expected that when the politicians and the rural elites are up for election, money will flow and votes will be bought.

The growth in the influence of parliament reflected in part increasing autonomy of the private sector from the central state bureaucracies, for as the same analyst pointed out:

> political parties have lines of communication with business, and many of the politicians are themselves businessmen ... More importantly, the business in-

fluence sometimes leads to distortions of national policies, distortions which
are not challenged in parliament even if they sometimes blatantly favour particular businesses.[22]

The autonomy of the private sector from the state was propelled even
more by the events of the early 1990s, after the military overthrew the
elected government of Chatichai Choonavan. Careful not to antagonize
the middle-class population that had been alienated by the widespread
corruption of the Chatichai government, the military set up a government
headed by the technocrat-businessman Anand Panyarachun. Anand appeared to personify the type of government desired by the now ascendant
private sector and the urban middle class: relatively independent from the
military, honest, and 'technocratic'. His decision to liberalize the import of
cars and bring down tariffs on other products, while antagonizing some
the beneficiaries of this protected sector, was cheered by capitalist sectors
seeking less government regulation and by the urban middle class, which
saw the measure as 'pro-consumer'.

When coup leader General Suchinda Kraprayoon went for the prime
ministership, the urban economic elites and the middle class were confronted with the spectre of a return to the past, to 'the now familiar
alliance between military officers and provincial politicians to carve up the
national wealth between their respective patronage networks'.[23] The total
takeover of power was stopped in the streets by massive protests of
crowds mainly made up of upper-class and upper-middle-class people.
Prefiguring the base of the new liberal democratic political order that
emerged out of the street clashes were the social characteristics of what
Thais called the 'mobile mob' owing to their ubiquitous cellular telephones:
some two-thirds of the demonstrators had academic degrees, 60 per cent
were working in the private sector, and 60 per cent had incomes in excess
of 5,000 a month.[24]

The Chuan coalition government, which won the elections of September 1992 in an electoral drama that pitted 'angels' against 'devils',
seemed to continue the Anand tradition: honest and technocratic, but also
one that was pro-foreign investment, pro-business, and pro-high-speed
growth. This was clearly seen in the government's failure to take any steps
to lift the ban on unions in state enterprises – a move that had been
promised in the electoral campaign but one which was strongly opposed
by the business sector. It was an orientation that was upheld in the next
few years by the two parliamentary coalitions that succeeded Chuan, the
Banharn and Chaovalit governments. Clearly, what was in place in the
1990s was the consolidation of a formally democratic state, conservative
in its economic orientation and dominated by parties with little ideological
differences whose strength was based on traditional patronage networks
that were greased with money from big businesses.

Despite the shifts in parliamentary politics, at the beginning of 1996 the world press was still full of encomiums for Thailand. Perhaps the most significant from the point of view of the Thai establishment was the World Bank's announcement that the Thai economy, with a 10 per cent per annum growth rate, had been the world's fastest growing economy in the period 1985–95. Later that year, the government's Eighth National Development Plan projected that by the year 2020, the Thai economy 'will be the eighth largest in the world, with an average per capita income of not less than 300,000 baht or about $12,000 at 1993 constant prices. The proportion of people living below the poverty line will be reduced to less than five per cent, resulting in a vastly improved quality of life for the majority of the Thai people.'[25]

By the end of 1996, it was becoming evident that that vision was questionable, and the hammer blows of the first half of 1997 confronted Thais with the unpleasant reality that rather than advancing into the ranks of the developed countries, they faced the prospect of being hurled back to the Third World.

The Japanese Tsunami

Aside from a reorientation toward export promotion, a key reason for Thailand's explosive growth since the mid-1980s was the central role of foreign capital. It was also the factor that would become the country's Achilles' heel. As noted earlier, in 1983–84 Thailand's growth had hit a bump on the road, and like other Southeast Asian countries, it was mired in a recession caused by the conjunction of the rising price of imported oil, plunging prices of its agricultural exports, onerous servicing of a $18 billion foreign debt, and a current account deficit that averaged 5.3 per cent between 1981 and 1985.[26] These difficulties led the government to devalue the baht by 17.3 per cent in 1984. This move was taken in the context of active IMF and Bank involvement in devising and implementing a stabilization and structural adjustment programme, which combined short-term measures designed to stabilize the economy such as cutbacks in government expenditures and currency depreciation, with more strategic measures aimed at transforming it such as deregulation, liberalization, and privatization. This effort was supported by five IMF and Bank stabilization and structural adjustment loans between 1981 and 1990.

By the late 1980s, however, the structural adjustment programme had stalled. While the local business sector was allowed more and more freedom by government, when it came to foreign trade and foreign investment, significant restrictions remained. And although a greater orientation toward export production had been achieved, the impact of the programme was limited in many other ways. Instead of dismantling protectionism, Thailand in fact became in some respects even more protectionist, with Thai technocrats adopting an economic policy of moving the country to a 'second stage of import substitution' aimed at using tariff protection to build capital-intensive intermediate and capital goods industries. The so-called 'Eastern Seaboard Project', which was meant to drive the Thai economy into the twenty-first century, consisted of a petrochemical complex, soda ash plant, fertilizer plant, and steel complex.[27] And like similar capital-intensive, state-led, and protected programmes in South Korea, the Philippines, Malaysia, and Indonesia, the Eastern Seaboard Project evoked scepticism, if not opposition, from the World Bank and the Fund.

The reason adjustment came to a halt is that tremendous amounts of foreign direct investment flowed into the country in the late 1980s, making the World Bank and IMF's seal of approval less important for Thailand as a mechanism for gaining access to world capital markets. This inflow occurred despite continuing restrictions on the freedom of foreign capital in the domestic market. Between 1985 and 1990, foreign direct investment coming into the country rose from a $178 million to $2.5 billion.[28] The bulk of this was Japanese investment, which rose from $124 million in FY 1986 to $1.2 billion in FY 1990.[29] In 1990, total Japanese accumulated investment in Thailand stood at $5.2 billion, of which 85 per cent had come in since 1986.[30]

The main cause for this cornucopia of Japanese direct investment was the Plaza Accord of 1985, which forced the appreciation of the Japanese yen relative to the dollar and other hard currencies in an effort to solve the US trade deficit. What it did was to make production in Japan for the USA and other export markets extremely prohibitive, forcing the Japanese to shift significant sectors of their industrial facilities, particularly the more labour-intensive sectors, outside Japan, especially to Southeast Asia. Indeed, the countries of the Association of Southeast Asian Nations (ASEAN) received close to $15 billion in Japanese direct investments during the period 1986–90.[31]

Japanese investment lifted Thailand out of the recession of the mid-1980s and triggered the wave of prosperity that was to last till 1997. It also brought with it ancillary investment from Hong Kong, Taiwan, and South Korea, the so-called 'first-generation NICs' (newly industrializing countries), as enterprises in these countries sought to relocate their labour-intensive operations elsewhere to escape the rising wages of their work-forces. However, by the early 1990s, foreign direct investment started to level off or decrease. Japanese direct investment, for instance, fell from $1.2 billion in 1990 to $578 million in FY 1993.[32] Total foreign direct investment dropped from $2.4 billion in 1990 to $640 million by 1994.[33] By then, however, a model of economic expansion driven not principally by domestic savings but by foreign capital had taken hold.

Attracting portfolio investment and bank capital

To bridge the projected savings–investment gap of a continuing high-growth stategy, Thai technocrats eyed global capital markets, where trillions of dollars of personal savings, pension funds, government funds, corporate savings, and other funds were deposited in mutual funds and other investment mechanisms that were designed to maximize their value. These portfolio investments were often placed under the management of big international banks or investment houses that were experienced in spotting good investment opportunities that combined high yields with a quick turnaround time. In the early 1990s, noted an Asian Development Bank report, 'the declining returns in the stock markets of industrial countries and the low real interest rates compelled investors to seek higher returns on their capital elsewhere'.[34] Not surprisingly, an increasingly large portion of these speculative funds or portfolio investments was increasingly attracted to Southeast Asian economies that were booming owing to the earlier surge of Japanese investment.

Cornering these funds became a prime object of national economic policymaking among the Southeast Asian governments, although there were voices that warned that these funds could be extremely volatile, coming in one day, leaving the next, as it were, in search of higher returns elsewhere. To attract the funds to Thailand, Thai technocrats evolved a financial strategy with three principal thrusts: the maintenance of high interest rates, the 'pegging' of the baht to the dollar at a fixed rate of exchange, and financial liberalization.

Maintaining high interest rates to suck in foreign capital was a technique the Thais learned quickly from other countries in the early 1990s. Mexico's technocrats discovered the efficacy of this technique fairly early, and US investors responded quite eagerly. As William Greider has noted: 'By borrowing in New York's money market where interest rates were then comparatively low, an investor could buy Mexican stocks or short-term government notes and capture the spread between returns of 5 to 6 per cent in America and 12 to 14 per cent in Mexico.'[35]

Throughout the early 1990s the Bank of Thailand, through various mechanisms, maintained high yields on portfolio investments and loans to Thailand. Lending to Thai banks, finance companies, or corporations at 8 to 12 per cent interest rates allowed creditors to clear a handsome profit, while still permitting the Thai borrowers to rake in the difference between those rates and the 15 to 20 per cent rates at which they re-lent those funds in the local market.

The second ingredient in the Thai formula was keeping the local currency, the baht, pegged at a stable rate to the dollar. The idea was to eliminate or reduce risks for foreign investors stemming from fluctuations in the value of the baht, regarded as a 'soft currency'. This guarantee was needed if investors were to come in, change their money into baht, play the stock market, and move on to more profitable opportunities elsewhere. The peg was not something devised solely by the Thai technocrats. Indeed, as economist Jeffrey Sachs has noted, in both Asia and Mexico, financial authorities 'fell under the influence of money managers who championed the cause of pegged exchange rates', arguing that 'only a stable exchange rate could underpin the confidence needed for large capital inflows'.[36]

A pegged exchange rate was, of course, also needed by local banks and corporations raising money in global capital markets: they needed assurance that they would not be hit by devaluations that would significantly raise the costs of repaying dollar-denominated loans. Fixing the rate directly was avoided; instead this was done through 'market-friendly' means. This was the so-called dirty float: the local currency was allowed to float within a narrow band – say, $1:25.25–25.75 baht – movement outside of which would be countered by the Bank of Thailand selling or buying dollars to keep the exchange rate within the band.

The third ingredient in this formula for attracting foreign portfolio investment and bank capital was the liberalization of the financial sector – the enactment of a transparent set of rules that would assure foreign investors that they were indeed welcome to make profits in an economy previously known for protectionism.

Before the 1990s strong controls on foreign exchange and capital flows in and out of the country insulated the country from the volatility of international currency and capital markets. Relative stability was accompanied by protection of the country's financial institutions from foreign competition. It also meant a rather incestuous arrangement, whereby banks and finance companies that ran into trouble because of wrong decisions could often count on being rescued by the Bank of Thailand, which always feared that letting one key institution lapse into bankruptcy could trigger a domino effect that could radically destabilize the entire financial sector.

By the early 1990s, however, strong pressures for deregulation and liberalization were coming from the World Bank and the IMF, as well as foreign financial institutions, particularly US banks, which were not content with merely lending to Thai banks and financial companies but wanted to engage in retail banking and insurance in what was seen as a domestic market with great potential. Between 1991 and 1994, under the liberal technocrat governments of Anand Panyarachun and Chuan Leekpai, a number of significant moves to open up the system were undertaken, including the removal of ceilings on various kinds of savings and time deposits; fewer constraints on the portfolio management of financial institutions and commercial banks such as replacing the reserve requirement ratio for commercial banks with the liquidity ratio; looser rules on capital adequacy; the expansion of the field of operations of commercial banks and financial institutions; the dismantling of many foreign exchange controls so that the public could freely purchase foreign exchange from the banks without prior approval from the authorities; and the establishment of the Bangkok International Banking Facility (BIBF).

In sum, while Thailand's trade policy and investment policy in the non-financial sector continued to be marked by a significant degree of protectionism, its drive to attract portfolio investment and bank capital led it to engage in a fair degree of liberalization of its capital account and its financial sector. Indeed, one commentator noted that 'in relative terms, Thailand is even more generous than Japan, an economic superpower, in the liberalization of its financial sector'.[37]

The deluge

This approach to attracting foreign capital succeeded beyond expectations, though as one prominent firm saw it, the results were double-edged:

> Since 1987 the Thai authorities have kept their currency locked to the US dollar in a band of B25–26 while maintaining domestic rates 400–500 basis points higher than US rates and keeping their borders open to capital flows. Thai borrowers naturally gravitated towards US dollar borrowings and the commercial banks accommodated them, with the result that the Thai banks now have a net foreign liability position equivalent to 20 per cent of GNP. The borrowers converted to baht with the Bank of Thailand the ultimate purchaser of their foreign currency. Fueled by cheap easy money the Thai economy grew rapidly, inflation rose, and the current account deficit ballooned.[38]

In the early 1990s, however, the negative indicators were simply details in what was, on the whole, a success. Indeed, so impressed were Thailand's neighbours that they basically copied the same three-pronged strategy of financial liberalization, exchange rate stability, and high interest rates that the Thais had copied from the Mexicans.

Net portfolio investment, which averaged only $646 million in 1985–89, came to $927 million in 1992 and skyrocketed to $5.5 billion in 1993 after key reforms were carried out in the Stock Exchange of Thailand (SET).[39] But this was just the beginning. Initially cautious, foreign portfolio investors began to enter in force in 1994, influenced by the continuing high growth rates and the World Bank and Bank of Thailand's optimistic projections that the economy in the coming years would continue along the path of high growth, low inflation, and financial and monetary stability. One couldn't seem to lose with Thai equities. By 1995, foreign investors had become net buyers and Thai investors net sellers of equities at the SET, with the former snapping up 427 billion baht while selling off 379 billion baht.

Issues of stocks and bonds by private entities were, however, not the

Table 2.1 Outstanding lending of Bangkok International Banking Facility[a]

	Amount (in baht)			Share (%)	
	1996	1995	% change	1996	1995
Out–In[a]	807,633.2	680,520.5	18.68	100.00	100.00
Thai banks[b]	330,040.2	254,561.8	29.65	40.86	37.41
Foreign bank branches[c]	222,794.6	152,370.9	46.22	27.59	22.39
New foreign banks[d]	254,798.1	273,587.8	-6.87	31.55	40.20
Out–Out[a]	482,558.5	517,044.5	-6.67	100.00	100.00
Thai banks	16,318.0	10,818.3	50.84	3.38	2.09
Foreign bank branches	9,363.3	4,847.8	93.14	1.94	0.94
New foreign banks	456,877.2	501,378.4	-8.88	94.68	96.97
Total	1,290,191.7	1,197,565.0	7.73	100.00	100.00
(in billion dollars)	*(51.6)*	*(47.9)*			
Thai banks	346,358.2	265,380.1	30.51	26.85	22.16
Foreign bank branches	232,158.2	157,218.7	47.66	17.99	13.13
New foreign banks	711,675.3	774,966.2	-8.17	55.16	64.71

Notes: [a] The Bangkok International Banking Facility (BIBF) has become a controversial institution ever since the Thai financial collapse in July 1997. The BIBF is a system in which local as well as foreign banks were allowed to bring in dollars and other foreign currencies to engage in offshore (out–out) and selected onshore (out–in) financing activities. BIBF out-in became the main conduit for the massive entry of foreign capital in the form of credit that destabilized the country's external accounts. [b] Thai banks in the BIBF included Bangkok Bank, Krung Thai Bank, Siam Commercial Bank, Bank of Ayudhya, First Bangkok City Bank, Thai Farmers Bank, Siam City Bank, Bank of Asia, Thai Military Bank, Thai Danu Bank, Nakornthon Bank, and Bangkok Metropolitan Bank. [c] Established foreign banks in the facility included Bank of Tokyo (Mitsubishi), Sakura Bank, Hong Kong and Shanghai Bank, Chase Manhattan Bank, Bank of America, Deutsche Bank, Citibank, ABN-AMRO Bank, Banque Indosuez, Standard Chartered Bank, Overseas Chinese Banking Corporation. [d] 'New foreign banks' included the Industrial Bank of Japan, Sanwa Bank, Sumitomo Bank, Long-Term Credit Bank of Japan, Dai-Ichi Kangyo Bank, Dredsner Bank, Banque Nationale de Paris, Korea Exchange Bank, Development Bank of Singapore, Société Générale, Internationale Nederlanded Bank, Crédit Lyonnais, Bank of Nova Scotia, American Express Bank, Bank of New York, Bank of China, Bankers Trust Company, United Overseas Bank, Overseas Union Bank.

Source: Bangkok Bank, *Commercial Banks in Thailand* (Bangkok: Bangkok Bank, 1998), p. 36.

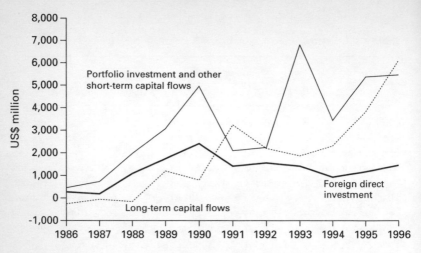

Source: Asian Development Bank, *Key Indicators of Developing Asia and Pacific Countries* (Asian Development Bank/Oxford University Press, 1997), pp. 336–7

Figure 2.1 Foreign capital inflow into Thailand (as estimated by Asian Development Bank in millions of US $), 1986–96

only or even the primary channel of capital flowing into Thailand. Loans to Thai private financial institutions as well as non-financial entities were gladly advanced by international banks. The country's external debt more than doubled, from $21 billion in 1988 to $55 billion in 1994, with private debt climbing from 14 per cent of the total to over 25 per cent.[40]

Overlooked in the borrowing spree were the potentially disastrous consequences of borrowing short-term and at relatively high rates of interest to lend or invest in activities, such as real estate financing, that were long-term in their return.[41]

Indeed, Bangkok became a debtors' market instead of a creditors' market. Thai banks and finance companies became highly prized premium customers who were able to get loans at far better terms than their other Asian counterparts. As one account put it:

> With the country's positive outlook, competition to lend to Thai banks and finance companies has been intense. This had become even more pronounced with the recent migration of banks to the Asian market to chase the relatively few number of good credit risks, thus driving down the cost of funds. Not only are the margins narrowing; to win business, banks are reducing fees and extending their maturity dates.[42]

The inflow of foreign funds escalated with the establishment of the

BIBF in 1993. The BIBF was a system in which local as well as foreign banks were allowed to engage in offshore international banking activities. BIBF licencees were allowed to accept deposits in foreign currencies and to lend in foreign currencies, both to residents and to non-residents and for both domestic and foreign investment. While the main idea was to attract foreign capital to fill the gap between domestic savings and investment needs of Thailand's high-speed development (so-called 'out–in credit'), also important was the ambition of making Bangkok a regional financial centre that would compete with Singapore, wherein banks and other financial insitutitions would bring in capital from abroad to lend to clients using it for investment activities outside Thailand ('out–out loans'). The scheme was linked to facilitating the expansion of Thai business interests in Indochina, which the Bangkok elite saw as a zone of special interest for Thailand owing to its proximity, its numerous resources, its perceived complementarity to the Thai economy, and its potential markets.

The BIBF began operations in 1993, with 47 commercial banks granted licenses – of which 15 were domestic banks, 12 were foreign banks with branches already in Thailand, and 20 were new foreign banks with no branches in the country.[43] Two years after the facility began, BIBF loans came to $41.1 billion in 1995 and reached $49.1 billion by January 1997. In the three years between 1994 and 1997, BIBF loans rose from zero to 26 per cent of commercial bank loans.[44] This popularity undoubtedly stemmed from the fact that the interest on dollar loans was 4–6 per cent lower than domestic rates – a differential that refused to go away even as foreign money flooded the country.[45]

Financiers and realtors: Bonnie and Clyde in Bangkok

Among the prime beneficiaries of the BIBF bonanza were Thailand's finance companies. Previously considered the poor cousins of Thailand's established commercial banks, finance companies have always had a rather controversial profile in the country's financial structure. They were first set up in the late 1960s and licensed to engage in financing housing, real estate development, cars and other consumer items, and exports. Not allowed to engage in retail banking, many finance companies resorted to questionable business practices to raise capital, including widespread speculation and manipulation of stock prices. In the early 1980s, lack of access to capital, fraud and mismanagement, and recession led to the closure of some finance companies. From 127 companies in 1981, the number dropped to 105 by 1987, and further to 92 by the end of 1992.[46]

But to many analysts during the early 1990s, the ranks of finance companies needed to be pruned even further since many were teetering on the edge of insolvency and could remain viable only by merging with banks or other finance companies. The government, however, was spared from making this painful decision by Thailand's achieving A+ sovereign credit ratings in international financial markets in the early 1990s.

To foreign banks and portfolio investors, Thailand's average GDP growth rate of 10 per cent per annum, which appeared to be a long-term trend, served as the collateral for capital they were willing either to loan to Thai companies or to invest in the stock market. As one commentator put it, the building of this 'debt pyramid ... could last as long as the growth rate of the economy and the consequent growth in asset prices were kept up'.[47] This sense of long-term prosperity was perhaps the main factor that prompted influential investment analysts such as Moody's and Standard and Poor's to give Thailand an A+ rating as an investment risk in international capital markets. Indeed, so eager were international banks to lend to Thailand that 'as a result of stiff competition, pricing levels in some cases are not premised entirely on the financial fundamentals of the borrower. Many banks in Asia are anxious to develop good relations with their Thai counterparts, and are increasingly willing to lend to build relationships rather than to make money.'[48] Finance companies, finding raising money at home via promissory notes to the Thai public to be a bit too onerous, went overseas and found to their surprise that they could get lots of money on very good terms.

The finance companies, as well as the banks, made profits basically through arbitrage. Raising dollars in major financial centres where interest rates were at a low 6–8 per cent, they captured the enormous spread between those rates and the 14 to 20 per cent interest rates they charged their clients for real estate and consumer-finance loans in the local market.

The result was a financial *walpurgisnacht*, as finance companies went on a borrowing spree and foreign portfolio investors seeking quick and high returns bought shares in local finance companies, driving the SET index to record highs. In the process, working for a finance company came to be regarded as a fast track to the top that avoided the slow promotions, huge bureaucracies, and stodgy atmosphere of the big established banks (although many of the finance companies were affiliated with powerful banks). Not surprisingly, thousands of the country's best-educated and best-trained professionals – Bangkok's yuppy elite – flocked to the finance companies in the go-go atmosphere of the early 1990s.

Flush with cash, the finance companies and banks channelled their borrowed money to activities that offered the prospect of high profits with a quick turnaround time. Investing in the truly productive sectors of the economy like manufacturing required huge blocks of capital, a strategic commitment to a company, and a willingness to forego high returns in the short term because of the long gestation period of the invested capital. Thus, foreign capital, partly intermediated by Thai finance companies and banks, found its way to the speculative sectors, such as the stock market, real estate, and the creation of consumer credit.

The real estate bust

Of these activities, investment in real estate was by far the favourite of foreign and local capital. In the last few years, construction has been the hottest sector of the economy, 'with property development in all its aspects – construction, building materials, mortgages, loans, legal fees and all manner of other financial services activities – [contributing] 30 to 50 percent of annual GDP growth since 1988', according to one expert.[49] Property-related investment, by one estimate, came to 50 per cent of total investment.[50] Land values were higher than in urban California!

So attractive was investment in real estate that some finance companies not only lent to property developers but, like the high-flying Finance One, diversified into real estate speculation. And here they were joined by many of the country's manufacturers, who, according to one Bangkok Bank analyst, failed to keep their products competitive in work markets because they failed to invest in 'research and development and upgrading workers skills'. Instead, 'they gambled their profits in real estate'.[51]

High-rise after high-rise rose in Bangkok and its environs. Looking down from the top floor of any one of Bangkok's buildings, one could see building cranes alongside rising structures dotting the city for miles around. Accompanying the boom was, in the words of one analyst, a 'style of architectural excess unrivalled in Asia'.[52] 'Bangkok's fantasies in three dimensions are notorious: office towers which mimic gothic cathedrals or Roman temples; gargantuan corinthian columns clinging to the sides of glass-sheathed skyscrapers; condominium developments stuffed with miniature tudor mansions and rococo villas.'[53]

Several things came together for property development to become a hot sector. One was the supply of money seeking profitable investment as Bangkok became known as Asia's prime growth area in the late 1980s. As noted earlier, for speculative capital, manufacturing and agriculture were dismissed as low-yield sectors, where decent rates of return could be achieved only with significant amounts of investment over the long term.

On the demand side were the new rich and, equally important, the new middle class that was spinning off from the prosperity of the late 1980s and early 1990s. For real estate developers, the middle class were those people who were making between 15,000 and 30,000 baht a month.[54] The middle class, according to one prominent economist, probably made up some 17 to 18 per cent of the population.[55] In Bangkok alone, there were over 1,783,000 people who were estimated to be in the middle class, and 57 per cent of these in 1993 were house owners.[56] The economics of targeting this class as opposed to the lower class was frankly acknowledged by a top executive of Land and Houses, a well-known developer:

The biggest market is the low end, but to make money from the low end is difficult. If you cater to the low end your margin is small, so that means you cannot give them good service, unlike the middle market, which may be smaller. But you can sell at a higher margin and provide the company with a better image in the long run.[57]

For the real estate developers, the especially important part of the middle class were the so-called 'baby boomers,' or people born in the 1960s. The mentality of catering to what Bangkokians labelled the 'yuppies', after the latters' counterparts in the North, was articulated by another top executive of Land and Houses, which shifted most of its housing activity to target them: 'In the past, people older than thirty thought about buying a house. At present, a salaried man over 25 is spending more and houses prove a popular commodity as they signify stability of life. The group of such people is large and incessantly expanding as their earnings keep rising.'[58]

For the new Thai middle class, a large and expensive residence and other accoutrements were not simply a luxury: they were a social necessity. As one account put it:

Thai society is highly stratified; people are treated according to their perceived status and wealth. Thais who expect deference from clerks, policemen and their peers must drive a fancy car and carry the latest, smallest mobile phone. For women, carrying a $1,000 imported handbag means respect.[59]

Not only was spending on up-market housing and cars a social necessity – it was good business. 'You're seen as a more reliable business partner or client if you're seen with a late-model car and have a house instead of an apartment,' asserted the Thai manager of a Japanese-owned factory.[60]

But whether motivated by conspicuous consumption, social necessity, or sound business sense, personal spending by the Thai middle and upper classes registered explosive growth. In 1995, Thais spent 80 billion baht on foreign travel, 10 billion baht on foreign education, and 7 billion baht on watches and jewellery.[61]

To support such high levels of spending, credit had to be created. And it was created through various mechanisms, including the massive dissemination of credit cards. The number of credit cards increased sixfold between 1983 and 1988.[62] Outstanding credit cards at the end of September 1996 stood at 1.9 million. This worked out to nearly 7 per cent of the population having credit cards – a rather high figure even when compared to some advanced industrial countries. The creation of such credit was, in turn, made possible by foreign loans contracted by local banks, which accounted for 70 per cent of all credit cards issued.[63]

In short, the purchasing power of the middle class was being created by credit, and the projections of the expansion of demand by property developers were ultimately based on the expansion of credit via foreign capital. It was this illusion of an ever-expanding purchasing power that caused them to throw caution to the winds and to build on projections of demand rather than on more cautious, traditional methods of pre-selling residential and commercial units before building them.

Other factors contributed to the making of the massive glut. One was the relatively low price of land acquisition, which came to only 10 per cent of total development costs.[64] Another was the loose accounting practices of the banks and finance companies: for instance, even if buyers had put down only a minimal amount of money, say 10 per cent, developers could book the projected profits as current income as though the bank had processed the entire mortgage.[65] A third factor was the lax government regulation of this sector, which was manifested in the Bank of Thailand's adopting a hands-off stance, at least until the end of 1994; the absence of zoning laws; the lack of effective implementation of building codes; and the absence of government-imposed limitations on the number of real estate projects per area.

The property sector appeared so promising in the go-go atmosphere of the early 1990s that some developers sometimes dispensed with the mediation of banks and went directly to foreign creditors, or raised cash by floating bonds or offering convertible securities in the Stock Exchange. For instance, during 1992–94, ten Thai developers floated twelve convertible issues worth US $1.098 billion, or Bt 27.45 billion, and attracted 'a large number of fans at the time due mainly to the bullishness of the stock market, which increased the attractiveness of convertibles'.[66]

With the property sector being so hot, everybody knew that it would sooner or later be hit with a glut. But everybody also felt confident that they would be able to sell, make a profit, and clear out before the glut developed. It was a classic bubble. Not surprisingly, by late 1994 the signs of a runaway market, marked by continuing huge capital flows coming to the property sector coexisting with a building glut, were becoming obvious, with disturbing monuments like Bangkok Land's massive but virtually deserted residential complex near the airport and the near empty 30-storey towers in Bangna-Trat. Early the following year, the government's Housing Development Board came out with a study warning that massive oversupply was about to overtake the real estate market.

In the early 1990s the cranes dotting the Bangkok landscape were a sign of the boom. In the late 1990s, they were a sign of doom, serving as memorials to the property glut that was destroying the Thai economy. Yet even when the property market downturn came in 1995, an amazing 172,400 new homes were built in Bangkok.[67] And as the property sector lurched deeper into crisis in 1996, buildings continued to rise inexorably, as if construction was on an automatic pilot mode that could not be switched off. By early 1997, housing units totalling about $20 billion were unsold in Bangkok alone, and more residential and office units continued to be added.[68]

The government began to move to place curbs on lending to the real estate sector. However, these moves were a little too late and were contradicted by macro-policy moves. Afraid that foreign capital might move out in response to the emerging crisis, the Bank of Thailand raised the already relatively high interest rates to keep Thailand as an attractive investment area. This same policy, however, contributed to the woes of developers – already saddled with properties they could not move – by discouraging home buyers. Payments to financial institutions dwindled or stopped, and by the beginning of 1997, half of the loans made to property developers were 'non-performing'. A frequently quoted figure was that non-performing loans came to about $3.1 billion, although some analysts felt that the figure could come to as high as $3.8 billion.[69]

Playing pretend

It was, however, impossible for the banks and finance companies to declare so many of their borrowers as problem debtors without calling into question their own financial status. It was in the interest of both creditors and borrowers to sit tight, keep the real state of things under wraps, and resort to 'creative accounting' to maintain the aura of financial stability. Indeed, the chairman of Bangkok Bank advised against publicly disclosing the extent of non-performing loans since this would result in a situation where 'many will be unable to continue their operations'.[70] The creditors also knew that moves to seize the assets of their clients would mean taking over properties whose actual market value was far below their declared value when they were attached as collateral to loans. The financiers' dilemma was underlined by one analyst:

> A disturbing element of Thailand's falling property market involves valuations for huge property developments … [S]ome financial institutions are still valuing the hard-to-assemble land at peak topped prices for collateral … [B]ecause the project's concept has not been reevaluated for a down market, some investors question whether 'real' collateral values may not require a massive asset write-down – resulting in collateral below outstanding loan balances.[71]

The reluctance of the financiers to press property developers for scheduled payments and the hope that both groups placed on a government bailout created what many regarded as the strange dynamic in Bangkok's property market: the coexistence of a glut with continuing high property prices. As one commentator noted caustically:

> The commercial banks are willing to discuss loan rescheduling and debt restructuring for major debtors who, in turn, do not want to reduce the prices of their unsold housing units and condos to reduce their debt loads and reinvigorate their cash-flow positions.
>
> Yet they together expect gullible consumers to borrow at 15.5 per cent [a rate much higher than rates offered to US homebuyers] – not fixed rate, of

course – to buy housing units which are haunted by heavy debts. Even for properties that are sold the risk remains as there is no assurance that the developers will be around to provide due maintenance and services.[72]

But it was more than just real estate developers and the finance companies that were engaged in a game of pretend in 1995 and 1996. The international creditors of the Thai private sector preferred to ignore the emerging problem, dismiss it as a temporary problem of liquidity for real estate borrowers, or simply allow their doubts to be wiped away by the continuing, mesmerizing 7 per cent plus GDP growth rate.

Important in assuring foreign portfolio investors and banks were fund managers and investment advisers, whose interests were served by continuing to pretend that, in spite of some 'kinks' in the property sector, the economy was basically sound. One of the most authoritative of these experts, who was converted by business publications such as the *Asian Wall Street Journal* into the guru of the Thai and Asian investment scene, was Neil Saker, head of the Regional Economic Research of Crosby Securities in Singapore. In a December 1996 assessment, Saker wrote:

> We believe that current pessimism about the Thai economy is based on a number of key misconceptions. We do not believe any of the following:
>
> *Thailand is entering a recession.*
> *Investment is collapsing.*
> *Export growth is collapsing.*
> *The Bank of Thailand has lost control.*
> *Current account deficit is unsustainable.*
> *Thailand faces a debt crisis.*
> *There is a chance the Baht will devalue ...*
> *Economic prospects for 1997: expect a rebound.*[73]

Such illusions promoted by Saker and other investment gurus were, however, rudely banished at the beginning of 1997 – a point this narrative will return to after looking at how one Thai finance company's history illustrated the manic dynamics of the Thai financial sector.

Finance One: the crisis in microcosm

The crisis of Thailand's financial sector is captured in microcosm by the saga of Finance One, which was, at the beginning of 1996, the premier finance company in the country. Finance One was a company whose methods thrived in what one Bangkok news commentator described as a 'bull market rewarding high revenue generators and disregarding risk in pursuing business'.[74] The company not only engaged in traditional activities like financing real estate development and sales on instalment of pickups and other vehicles, but also invested large amounts of funds in stock market speculation, buying up real estate, also for speculative purposes, and snapping up troubled or smaller finance companies and securities firms.

This was classical empire-building, and indeed, Finance One's chief, Pin Chakkapak, was given the sobriquet 'merger king' by Thailand's business community, which both admired and feared his ambition to become the country's prime financial power. The fortysomething Pin, in fact, became a hero and role model for Bangkok's financial yuppies, who saw boldness where more cautious observers saw recklessness.

Finance One, in fact, appeared to be simply taking to the extreme what many finance company entrepreneurs engaged in. They contributed little of their own personal money in their ventures and financed their activities mainly from capital from investors, depositors, and creditors, local and international. The operation was virtually riskless, since it would be others' money that would be lost if a venture collapsed and the financial operator could walk away from the wreck without fear of being stripped of his or her personal assets owing to the country's weak bankruptcy accountability laws.[75]

To finance its imperial acquisitions and operations, Finance One borrowed heavily from foreign financial institutions, with its borrowings coming to $622 million by the end of 1996.[76] Another key source was stock market offerings, which local and foreign investors snapped up. Finance One shares traded at a high of 177 baht, or $7, apiece, in January 1996.

Most of the capital raised from foreign and local sources found its way to real estate financing, which accounted for about 30 per cent of Finance One's total loans and investments of 65 billion baht or $2.5 billion. Another 17 billion baht was sunk in hire-purchase lending, with a focus on financing vehicles like pickup trucks – a growth area in the early 1990s, when Thailand assumed the reputation of being the world's second biggest market for pickups. Some 5.5 billion baht was tied up as speculative capital in the stock market.

Most of these loans and investments began to go sour, very quickly, in 1996, as the extent of the glut in housing began to hit home. With word that many of its loans to developers were lapsing into the 'non-performing' category, Finance One's share price plunged by some 80 per cent, from a high of 177 baht in January 1996 to 34 baht at the end of January 1997. Alarmed, local depositors demanded repayment of promissory notes they had made out to Finance One and its subsidiaries. In the first quarter of 1996, Finance One could still report a net profit of $6 million. By the first quarter of 1997, it admitted a loss of $15 million.

Suddenly in need of cash, the company 'found its borrowing costs surging', especially in the interbank market, where the company was a heavy borrower.[77] By late 1996, Finance One was lucky to be able to find anybody who would lend it significant amounts of cash. A government-sponsored attempt to force a marriage between Finance One and Thai Danu Bank (an institution that, ironically, Finance One had tried to gobble up earlier) ended in failure, when the latter assessed Finance One's stocks as virtually worthless. Unable to convert its assets into cash in order to service its debts to its various creditors, the company rapidly lurched towards bankruptcy. For the financial world, confirmation of Finance One's parlous state came in March 1997, when one of its subsidiaries defaulted on a $13.5 million debt payment on a foreign borrowing.

Botched rescue

As more and more finance companies tottered on the brink of collapse, the Bank of Thailand set up the Financial Institutions Development Fund (FIDF) to 'inject liquidity' into the cash-strapped finance companies to assist them in restructuring their portfolios along more healthy lines. This was followed by the creation of the Property Loan Management Organ- ization (PLMO), which would issue bonds to raise about $3.85 billion to buy collateralized property loans from the finance companies at 'fair market value'. The PLMO would then ease the terms of the loan for the real estate borrowers, allowing them, for example, a five-year grace period before they had to start paying interest on the loans.

Many saw these institutions as serving no other purpose than to bail out the finance companies, the finance companies' foreign creditors, and property developers. As one analyst pointed out in the case of the PLMO: 'Purely from the point of view of financial institutions, any sort of freebie subsidy isn't something you turn away ... [a]nd the 100 billion baht [$4 billion], is a meaningful amount of money.'[78] Somebody, of course, had to pay for the bailout, and the rescue fund simply shifted 'the cost of bad investment decisions to Thailand's taxpayers, who will guarantee the bonds, and to government and state enterprise employees, who will be forced to buy them through their pension funds'.[79] In the meantime, until they were really guaranteed a bailout, the property developers were going to work together to hold the line against any drop in real estate prices – which explains why the massive glut was not accompanied by any significant price decline in 1997.

Equally dismaying was the experience of the FIDF. The Fund was established to provide some liquidity assistance to finance companies that were in trouble. But on the lookout as usual for opportunities to turn a profit, stable firms joined troubled ones in knocking on the door of the FIDF for help. And many got what they wanted from a government that had very fuzzy criteria to distinguish viable from ailing firms.[80]

When they did get assistance, a number of companies did not apply the funds to restructuring their portfolios on a sounder basis, as they were obligated to, but used them to try to turn a quick profit. As one observer told *The Nation*: 'Back in March and April, when the financial crisis was taking shape, it was considered fun to make a profit this way ... and it looked exactly like a *"Chamoy"* pyramid game, because those who borrowed at 20 per cent then loaned it out at 22 per cent ... Those who borrowed at 22 per cent then loaned it out at 24 or 25 per cent.'[81] One executive, Jirachai Nugoon, president of Teerachai Trust Co., admitted: 'It's true that some of us borrowed money from FIDF and relent it because interest rates were lower than elsewhere ... [F]or that we were partly wrong.'[82]

All in all, as of December 1997, when the 58 financial firms were finally closed down, the Bank of Thailand had pumped in an astounding 430 billion baht (over $17 billion at the exchange rate prior to 2 July) to try to save them.[83] It was a blunder that was worse than the FIDF's wasting of $7 million that was pumped in to try to save the Bangkok Bank of Commerce (BBC), a small bank that had run into trouble two years earlier for channelling massive amounts of foreign borrowings into politically motivated loans.

The blame for these developments must not be solely assigned to the machinations of the finance companies or the BBC. What one analyst has described as the 'collective incompetence' of the technocracy in the face of the financial crisis had been developing for some time.[84] Factional competition for top positions, the brain drain to the private sector, corruption by powerful business groups – all this had eroded the judgement, morale, and competence of agencies that were once regarded as 'islands of nationality'. By mid-1997, Thailand had, as one prominent economist described it, 'a non-functioning technocracy'.[85]

The panic

By that time, panic had begun to gather in Bangkok's financial markets. The national accounts for 1996 that came out in early 1997 confirmed the foreign investors' worst fears.

The foreign debt stood at $89 billion, of which almost 80 per cent was private debt and slightly under half was short-term debt. The net foreign liabilities of Thailand's banks now came to 20 per cent of GNP.

The current account deficit had reached alarming proportions. The current account, which sums up a country's external trade in goods and services, is a very sensitive measure to creditors since it indicates whether a country will be able to earn the foreign exchange that will enable it to service its debt over the long term. Thailand's traditionally high current account deficit now looked worrying in the wake of the developing crisis in the domestic economy, and many investment analysts reminded their clients that its ratio to GDP was the same as Mexico's when the latter experienced economic meltdown in December 1994.

The current account deficit was especially a cause for alarm if one took into account the fact that the vaunted Thai export machine came to a standstill, registering zero growth in 1996, compared to 21 per cent and 24 per cent respectively in 1994 and 1995. This was not unrelated to the subversive effects of the speculative sector on the productive areas of the economy. As one of the few reliable investment analysts put it, 'in the normal course of events' manufacturers would have:

> gradually moved upmarket to more sophisticated products. In Thailand for the last several years many of them have put their manufacturing businesses on the backburner and devoted all the money into property instead. Now they are starting to come back to manufacturing but the pots and pans shop is still a pots and pans shop and the money it needs has vanished into property.[86]

But there was an even more fundamental reason that the export slowdown occurred, and this stemmed from the contradiction between encouraging foreign capital inflows and keeping an exchange rate that would make one's exports competitive in world markets. The former demanded a currency pegged to the dollar at a stable rate in order to draw in foreign investors. With the dollar appreciating in 1996 and 1997, so did the baht, and so did the international prices of Thai exports. This process cut deeply into the competitiveness of an economy that had originally staked its growth on ever-increasing exports.[87]

It was, for many investors, time to go, and potentially there was, at the end of 1996, around $24 billion of 'hot' money in portfolio inflows and non-resident deposits that might try to move out. And move it did. Stocks plunged to record lows as foreign portfolio investors stampeded to sell off their investments, with share prices plunging in late May 1997 by 65 per cent of their value during the balmy days of early 1994. And with hundreds of billions of baht chasing too few dollars, tremendous pressure for devaluation developed. This placed the Bank of Thailand, the country's central economic manager, in an unenviable position that was aptly captured by the following report:

> The central bank has little latitude in these uncomfortable circumstances ... The baht is under pressure, and the Bank of Thailand legally has to keep it in a narrow band. The central bank can't raise interest rates to support the currency without triggering further damage to its wounded property and finance firms. And, if it cut interest rates to ease the burden of repayment, it would trigger even worse capital flight.[88]

Sensing a grand opportunity to make profit from this outward movement of capital, speculators – led by George Soros and his infamous Quantum Fund – moved in, betting on the eventual devaluation, intent on making a killing on well-timed purchases and sales of the dollar and baht.

With some $39 billion in reserves at the beginning of 1997, the Bank

Table 2.2 Indicators of Thailand's move from boom to bust

Economic indicators	1995	1996	1997[a]	1998[b]
GDP (current prices, billion baht)	4,188.9	4,598.3	4,870.0	5,230.0
Real GDP growth (%)	8.8	5.5	0.0	-2.0 (-5.5[c])
Agriculture	2.5	3.8	3.0	2.8
Manufacturing	11.2	6.9	-0.7	-1.4
Construction	7.4	6.1	-12.7	-23.9
Investment growth (%)				
Private sector	10.9	2.0	-13.2	-4.7
Public sector	12.3	20.8	6.4	-30.3
Exchange rate (baht:$, average)	25.0	25.4	31.4	45.0
International trade				
Exports (billion baht)	1,381.7	1,387.9	1,790.1	2,649.5
(% growth in US$)	(24.7)	(-1.9)	(3.8)	(3.1)
Imports (billion baht)	1,755.5	1,796.5	1,874.5	2,605.5
(% growth in US$)	(31.8)	(0.6)	(13.4)	(-3.1)
Trade balance (billion baht)	-374.0	-417.6	-84.4	44.0
Trade balance as % of GDP	(-8.9)	(-9.1)	(-1.7)	(0.8)
Current account balance (billion baht)	-37.6	-372.2	-37.1	65.2
Current account balance as % of GDP	(-8.0)	(-8.1)	(-0.8)	(1.3)
International reserves (billion $)	7.0	38.7	27.0[d]	

Notes: [a] Estimate.   [b] Forecast.   [c] Estimate of IMF and government as of 27 May 1998. 'No recovery in sight, says Tarrin', *The Nation*, 27 May 1998.   [d] This estimate must be taken with caution. In the first quarter of 1997, the Bank of Thailand had about $37.9 billion in reserves. It spent some $9 billion in the futile defence of the baht on the spot market, and committed another $23.4 billion in forward swap obligations over the next 12 months to August 1998. Actual usable reserves were thus likely to be much lower. See, among other accounts, Soonruth Nunyamanee and Chiratas Nivatpumin, 'Counting the cost of defending the baht', *Bangkok Post*, 1 September 1997, p. 5.

Source: Bangkok Bank, 'The economy in 1997 and trends for 1998', *Bangkok Bank Annual Report* (Bangkok: Bangkok Bank, 1998), pp. 14–15.

of Thailand tried to defend the value of the baht. The Bank's sale of massive quantities of dollars stabilized the baht in two spectacular battles with speculators in November 1996 and late January and early May 1997, when other Southeast Asian banks came to its rescue. However, the cost was high, with the Bank's reserves dropping from $37.9 billion in January to $27.9 billion in August. When one included in this figure the $23.4 billion in 'forward swap obligations' made by the Bank – that is, agreements to honour currency exchange agreements maturing in the near future at a rate of exchange higher than the current rate – then net reserves actually

Table 2.3 Critical economic indicators for Thailand and its Southeast Asian neighbours on the eve of the outbreak of the Asian financial crisis, mid-1997

	Thailand	Malaysia	Indonesia	Philippines
Current account deficit as % of GDP	8.2	7.0	3.5	4.3
Export growth rate in 1996	0.8	-0.2	7.0	24.0
External debt (in billion US$)	89.0	36.0	109.0	42.0
Private sector debt as % of external debt	80.0	33.0[a]	50.0	35.0
Short-term debt as % of external debt	50.0	21.0[a]	29.0	17.0
Real estate and real estate-related loans as % of commercial banks' exposure[b]	15–20	20.0	20–25	15–20

Notes: [a] 1995. [b] These figures are generally regarded as underestimates since many loans taken out for non-real-estate-related categories, like manufacturing, were actually used for real estate and real-estate-related activities.

Sources: Asian Development Bank, International Monetary Fund, Goldman Sachs, Moody's International Investor Service, Bangko Sentral ng Pilipinas, Bank of Thailand, Bangkok Bank, and others.

probably totalled only $7 billion.[89] Thus, by the time of a renewed attack in late June, the Bank threw in the towel and allowed the baht to 'float' beyond the margins of the narrow band in which it had tried to restrict its fluctuations in value relative to the dollar. It went on to lose close to 20 per cent of its value in just a few days.

Foreign capital, regarded as the strategic factor in Thailand's model of development, had turned its back on the country, and with devastating effect. The same global financial markets that had rewarded Thailand with billions of dollars worth of capital when the mood about the country's prospects was upbeat now reacted in herdlike fashion to negative assessments, behaving in a manner that radically worsened the situation, as the baht went on a freefall and the stock market plunged to record lows. As Stanley Fischer, a deputy director of the IMF, was to put it later, after the Thai devaluation triggered the wider Asian financial crisis: '[M]arkets are not always right. Sometimes inflows are excessive, and sometimes they may be sustained too long. Markets tend to react fast, sometimes excessively.'[90]

The financial crisis and the structural crisis

The crisis of Thailand's real estate and financial sectors unfolded within an economy whose pillars were fragile in the first place. The crisis intersected with, and was amplified by, what can be most appropriately described as the maturing of the structural defects of the Thai economy.

The first key flaw of the Thai development model that was exacerbated by the crisis was, of course, its tremendous dependence on foreign capital.

The second key defect of the Thai economic structure that contributed to and was aggravated by the financial crisis was its heavy dependence on a fragile export sector. Continually rising exports were supposed to produce the foreign exchange that would be used to pay off the private sector's massive foreign debt. This is why the zero growth in exports in 1996 was so shocking. And when people looked at the reasons for the failure of the country's vaunted export machine, they realized that it could only be partly attributed to slowdowns in some of Thailand's major export markets, like ASEAN and the European Union. As noted above, a strategy of relying on foreign capital inflows in the form of portfolio investment and short-term loans contradicted an exprt-oriented strategy in a fundamental way. The former demanded a 'strong' currency stably pegged to the dollar to attract foreign investors; the latter a 'competitive currency' subject to managed depreciation. As the dollar appreciated, so did the baht, and so did the international policies of Thai exports, leading inexorably to a decline in competitiveness. Unfortunately, the rise in prices was not neutralized by improvements in quality of exports resulting from investments directed at making the country's workforce more skilled and its production processes more skill-intensive and technology-intensive. Instead, many

Table 2.4 Income share by quintile groups, 1975/76–1992

Quintile	1975[a]	1981[a]	1990[a]	1992[b]
Lowest 10%	–	–	–	2.5
Lowest 20%	6.1	5.4	4.1	5.6
Second 20%	9.7	9.1	7.4	8.7
Third 20%	13.9	13.4	11.6	13.0
Fourth 20%	21.0	20.6	19.7	20.0
Top 20%	49.3	51.5	57.3	52.7
Top 10%	–	–	–	37.1

Notes: [a] Mehdi Krongkaew, cited in Nikhom Chandravithun, *Thailand: The Social Costs of Becoming the Fifth Tiger*, Woodrow Wilson Asia Program Occasional Paper, no. 68 (Washington, DC: Woodrow Wilson Center, 1995), Table 13.   [b] World Bank, *World Development Indicators 1998* (Washington, DC: Washington, DC, 1998), p. 70.

Table 2.5 Thailand's level of inequality compared with selected countries

Country	Gini coefficient[a]
Sierra Leone	62.9
Brazil	60.1
South Africa	58.4
Mexico	50.3
Malaysia	48.4
Venezuela	46.8
Ecuador	46.6
Thailand	*46.2*
Philippines	42.9
Indonesia	34.2
Egypt	32.0
Vietnam	35.7
Pakistan	31.2
India	29.7

Note: [a] The Gini coefficient or index measures the extent to which the distribution of income among individuals or households within an economy deviates from a perfectly equal distribution. A Gini index of zero would represent perfect equality while an index of 100 would indicate perfect inequality.

Source: World Bank, *World Development Indicators 1988* (World Bank: Washington, DC, 1998), Table 2.8, p. 70.

manufacturers redirected their profits from research and development and workers' retraining to real estate or stock market speculation. Speculative fever subverted everything.

A third key problem that could only be exacerbated by the financial crisis was the tendency of high growth to go hand in hand with an increasing deterioration in income distribution. While Thailand's decade of growth had probably resulted in rising absolute incomes for significant sections of the population, it was also accompanied by the emergence of Latin American levels of inequality, with the portion of household income going to the top 20 per cent of households rising from 54 per cent in 1988 to 57.5 per cent in 1994, and that going to the bottom 20 per cent declining from 4.6 to 4 per cent.[91] With recession and stagnation now overtaking the economy, income inequality will now be compounded by a decline in real income, resulting in a likely expansion of the number of people living in poverty, bringing down a significant number of the six million – about 10 per cent of the population – that now hover just above the poverty line.[92]

A fourth major structural flaw that is now likely to be deepened is the erosion of the position of agriculture within the national economy. In the past, urban industrial development was pursued at the expense of agriculture and the rural population, with a massive net transfer of resources from agriculture to industry achieved by a number of mechanisms to keep down the price of rice and agricultural commodities. As a result, between 1976 and 1988, the income of urban people rose from 2.4 times that of rural people to three times. This trend is likely to be exacerbated, as the government is likely to follow price policies aimed at keeping down food prices in order to pacify an urban population that is experiencing mass unemployment.

A fifth structural weakness of the economy that has been exacerbated by the financial crisis has been the overwhelming priority given to market forces and the private sector in development. In fact, this tremendous bias toward the market might be said to be one of the factors that brought on the financial crisis. Although government did play an activist role in some sectors of the economy, like manipulating trade policy to promote the development of the heavy industrial sector, in most other sectors, the tendency was for government to abdicate its planning, monitoring, and guiding role. This was certainly the case in the financial and real estate sectors.

But, also not surprisingly, infrastructure development lagged behind market decisions, resulting in the creation of tremendous traffic jams in Bangkok and chaotic land-use patterns, with factories and commercial establishments rising alongside residences in helter-skelter fashion. Virtual non-regulation of business was also the rule when it came to the environment, resulting in a truly monumental environmental débâcle. Bangkok has achieved the distinction of having one of the highest levels of air pollution of all capitals in the world; key sections of the mighty Chao Phraya river are biologically dead, partly because of uncontrolled waste dumping; and millions of tons of hazardous waste constitute a veritable public health time-bomb, having been dumped illegally, often beside aquifers that served as the sources of drinking water for communities.

Ironically, the absence of a proactive stance on the part of government resulted in one positive development: reactive government spending meant to catch up with the unplanned explosion of private sector activity served as the lifeline of the economy in 1996 and early 1997, as the private sector entered into crisis. As one report put it: 'The major factor stimulating growth this year was public sector investment in infrastructure projects, with investment by state enterprises recording growth of 19.4 per cent and government investment soaring by 28.9 per cent.'[93] Looking for a lifeboat, the private sector realized that its profits depended on government spending and that the cut in government expenditures that accompanied a stabilization programme would hurt it. With the IMF's demand for cutting back government expenditures, however, this source of stimulation for economic activity disappeared in the second half of 1997.

The IMF austerity programme, which is discussed in Chapter 3, would do more than reduce government spending, however. For the IMF was not simply to impose a stabilization programme but to accelerate the free market reform of the economy. The ultimate result of this process was likely to be a state sector that would be even less capable of serving as a check on the market and a regulator of the private sector.

Finally, the financial crisis was likely to accelerate one of the most serious flaws of the Thai development model: the rapid deterioration of the environment and the rundown of the country's natural capital. While, at first glance, the deceleration of the growth rate expected in the next few years might seem positive from an environmental point of view, in fact, under the current economic and social regime, it is likely to have a net effect that is negative for two reasons. First, it was unlikely that agriculture would be able to absorb the hundreds of thousands who were flocking back to the countryside as they lost their jobs in the cities – resulting in greater stresses on Thailand's remaining forested area, to which many of the displaced were likely to flee to earn a living. Second, in the competition to attract increasingly scarce foreign investment, it was likely that the already lax enforcement of air and water pollution regulations would be loosened still further.

In sum, Thailand's downward economic spiral was likely to turn into a process wherein the negative structural aspects of the development model of fast-track capitalism would lend positive reinforcement to one another.

Notes

1. Kevin Hewison, *Power and Politics in Thailand* (Manila: Journal of Contemporary Asia, 1989), p. 54.

2. Akira Suehiro, 'Capitalist development in postwar Thailand: commercial bankers, industrial elite, and agribusiness groups', in Ruth McVey, ed., *Southeast Asian Capitalists* (Ithaca, NY: Southeast Asia Program, Cornell University, 1992), p. 53.

3. Hewison, p. 59.

4. Amar Siamwalla, 'Why are we in this mess?', *Business in Thailand* (undated), p. 49.

5. Ibid.

6. Ibid.

7. Hewison, p. 63.

8. Robert McNamara, *1975 Address to Board of Governors* (Washington, DC: World Bank, 1975), pp. 28–9.

9. Pasuk Phongphaichit and Chris Baker, *Thailand: Economy and Politics* (Oxford: Oxford University Press, 1995), p. 149.

10. Hewison, p. 73.

11. Ibid.

12. Pasuk and Baker, p. 151.

13. Ibid.

14. William Easterly and Patrick Honohan, *Financial Sector Policy in Thailand: A Macroeconomic Perspective* (Washington, DC: World Bank, 1990), p. 16.

15. Suehiro, pp. 59–60.

16. Ukrist Pathamanand, 'An observation of Thai capitalist groups: growth and change', unpublished paper, Institute of Asian Studies, Chulalongkorn University, 1997.

17. World Bank, *Thailand: Country Economic Memorandum* (Washington: World Bank, 10 October, 1991), p. 6.

18. Interview, Julie Otterbein, USAID, Bangkok, July 1993.

19. Paul Hutchcroft, 'Booty capitalism: business–government relations in the Philippines', in Andrew MacIntyre, ed., *Business and Government in Industrializing Asia* (London: Allen and Unwin, 1994), pp. 195–215.

20. Anek Laothamathas, 'From clientilism to partnership: business–government relations in Thailand', in Andrew MacIntyre, ed., p. 207.

21. Ibid., p. 210.

22. Amar Siamwalla, p. 52.

23. David Peters, 'Balance of power', *Manager*, November 1996, p. 27.

24. Kevin Hewison, 'Emerging social forces in Thailand: new political and economic roles', in Richard Robison and David Goodman, eds, *The New Rich in Asia* (London: Routledge, 1996), p. 138.

25. NESDB, *The Eighth National Economic and Social Development Plan (1997–2001)* (Bangkok: NESDB, 1996), p. ii.

26. World Bank, *Thailand: Country Economic Memorandum: Building on Recent Success – A Policy Framework*, vol. 1 (Washington, DC: World Bank, 1989), p. 2.

27. K. S. Jomo et al., *Southeast Asia's Misunderstood Miracle: Industrial Policy and Economic Development in Thailand, Malaysia, and Indonesia* (Boulder, CO: Westview Press, 1997), p. 76.

28. Ibid., p. 71.

29. Figures from Ministry of Finance, Japan.

30. Figures from Ministry of Finance, Japan.

31. Figures from Ministry of Finance, Japan.

32. Figures from Ministry of Finance, Japan.

33. Jayati Ghosh, Abhijit Sen, and C. P. Chandrasekhar, 'Southeast Asian economies: miracle or meltdown?', *Economic and Political Weekly*, 12–19 October 1996, p. 2779.

34. Min Tang and James Villafuerte, *Capital Flows to Asian and Pacific Developing Countries: Recent Trends and Future Prospects* (Manila: Asian Development Bank, 1995), p. 10.

35. William Greider, *One World, Ready or Not: The Manic Logic of Global Capitalism* (New York: Simon and Schuster, 1997), p. 260.

36. Jeffrey Sachs, 'Personal view', *Financial Times*, 30 July 1997.

37. Thanong Khantong and Vatchara Charoonsantikul, 'BIBF's map unchartered territory,' *The Nation*, February 1997, p. B10.

38. HG Asia, *Communiqué Philippines* ('Philippine figures hide a thing or two') (Hong Kong: HG Asia, December 1996.

39. Tang and Villafuerte, p. 11.

40. Ibid., pp. 3, 22.

41. Amar Siamwalla, p. 49.

42. 'Thais' market triumph', *Asiamoney*, May 1995, p. 16.

43. Ibid., p. 78.

44. Thanong Khantong and Vatchara Charoonsantikul, 'BIBFs map unchartered territory', *The Nation*, February 1997, p. B10.

45. Amar Siamwalla, p. 49.

46. Pakorn Vichyanond, *Thailand's Financial System: Structure and Liberalization* (Bangkok: TDRI, 1994), p. 3.

47. Amar Siamwalla, p. 49.

48. Pakorn Vichyanond, p. 3.

49. Ed Paisley, 'Asia's property perils', *Institutional Investor*, January 1996, p. 61.

50. Ibid.

51. Interview, anonymity requested, 29 April 1997.

52. Scott, quoted in Hewison, 'Emerging social forces', p. 151.

53. Ibid.

54. Peter Janssen, 'Homes for the tiger generation', *Asian Business*, July 1996, p. 57.

55. 'Who they are and how they came about', *The Nation Yearbook 1994* (Bangkok: The Nation, 1994), p. 7.

56. Ibid.

57. Janssen, p. 57

58. 'Home is where the credit is', *The Nation Yearbook*, p. 70.

59. Paul Sherer, 'Shopaholic Thais shatter stereotype of Asian savers', *Asian Wall Street Journal*, 13 June 1996, p. 1.

60. Interview, anonymity requested, 7 May 1995.

61. 'Academics, chief execs raise alarm over national debt', *The Nation*, 21 December 1996.

62. Hewison, 'Emerging social forces', p. 152.

63. Ibid.

64. Paisley, p. 64.

65. Ibid.

66. Ibid.

67. Janssen, p. 57.

68. 'Property firms in Thailand get rescue fund', *Asian Wall Street Journal*, 12 March 1997, p. 1.

69. 'Funds rushed to help developers', *The Nation*, 14 May 1997, p. B1.

70. 'Nightmare', *The Economist*, 21 June 1997, p. 45; cited in Arthur Alexander, 'Asia's financial crisis: linked to its economic miracle', *IEI Report*, no. 19A, 15 May 1998, p. 45.

71. K. I. Woo, 'Somprasong fuels realty fears', *The Nation*, 4 November 1996, p. E1.

72. Sophon Onkgara, 'Bankers and developers can't have it both ways', *The Nation*, 20 April 1997.

73. Neil Saker, 'Guest viewpoint: Thailand update: market pessimism is overblown', *BOI Investment Review 2*, 31 December 1996. Saker was quick to reinvent himself, and after the crisis broke out the *Wall Street Journal* converted him into an authority on the Asian financial crisis. The market, with its short memory, seldom punishes charlatans.

74. K. I. Woo, 'Policy makers rethinking merger plans', *The Nation*, 9 May 1997, p. B10.

75. Interview, Ukrist Pathamanand, Bangkok, 23 October, 1997.

76. Jiwamol Kanoksilp and Sirriporn Chanjindamanee, 'Fin-One on "Defensive"', *The Nation*, 5 February 1997, p. E2.

77. 'Finance One's problems illustrate frailty in Thai financial system', *Asian Wall Street Journal*, 12 March 1997.

78. 'Property firms in Thailand get rescue fund', *Asian Wall Street Journal*, 12 March 1997.

79. Ibid.

80. *The Nation*, August 1997.

81. Ibid.

82. 'Finance firms in Thailand express regret', *Asian Wall Street Journal*, 5–6 December 1997.

83. Ibid.

84. Amar Siamwalla, pp. 51–2.

85. Ibid., p. 52.

86. HG Asia, *Communiqué: Thailand* ('Thailand worth a nibble perhaps but not a bite') (Hong Kong: HG Asia, 1996).

87. Jayati Ghosh and C. P. Chandrasekhar, Speech at School of Public Administration, University of the Philippines, Manila, 3 July 1998.

88. Vatchara Charoonsantikul and Thanong Khantong, 'Devaluation seen as no quick fix for economy', *The Nation*, 6 May 1997, p. 1.

89. 'Counting the cost of defending the Baht', *Bangkok Post*, 1 September 1997.

90. Stanley Fischer, 'Capital account liberalization and the role of the IMF', paper presented at seminar on Asia and the IMF, Hong Kong, 19 September 1997, p. 4.

91. Nanak Kakwani and Medhi Krongkaew, 'Big reduction in poverty', *Bangkok Post Yearend Economic Review 1996*, p. 23.

92. Estimate provided in James Wolfensohn, 'Asia: The Long View', *Financial Times*, 29 January 1998.

93. 'The economy in 1996 and trends in 1997', *Annual Report 1996* (Bangkok: Bangkok Bank, 1997), p. 42.

CHAPTER 3

Thailand under the IMF

Thailand's financial crisis was at least three years old before it dramatically attracted global attention with the *de facto* devaluation of the baht on 2 July 1997. It cannot be said, however, that the IMF had been particularly worried during that period. Indeed, as late as the latter half of 1996, while expressing some concern about the huge capital inflows, the Fund was still praising Thai authorities for their 'consistent record of sound macroeconomic management policies'.[1]

A cosy relationship

The complacency of the Fund and its sister institution, the World Bank, when it came to Thailand – indeed, their failure to appreciate fully the danger signals – is traceable to several factors. One is that both the Fund and the World Bank had been instrumental in promoting Thailand, with its openness to capital flows and its high growth rate (the highest in the world in the period 1985–95, according to the Bank), as a model of development for the rest of the Third World. It was after all during the IMF–World Bank annual conference in Bangkok in September 1991 that Thailand was officially canonized as Asia's 'Fifth Tiger'.

But probably more important is that the massive capital inflows into Thailand in the form of portfolio investments and loans had not been incurred by government to finance deficit spending. Indeed, the high current account deficits of the early 1990s coincided with the government running budget surpluses. As a group of perceptive Indian analysts from New Delhi's Jawaharlal Nehru University School of Economic Studies and Planning noted: 'Part of the reason for this silence was the perception that an external account deficit is acceptable so long as it does not reflect a deficit on the government's budget but "merely" an excess of private investment over private domestic savings.' In this view, countries with significant budget deficits, such as India in 1991, were regarded as profligate even when their foreign debt was much lower than Thailand's. The latter's debt, because it was incurred not by government but by the private sector, was simply reflecting what the Bretton Woods institutions regarded as 'the appropriate environment for foreign private investment rather than public or private profligacy'.[2] In other words, the market would ensure that equilibrium would be achieved in the capital transactions between private international creditors and investors and private domestic banks and enterprises. So not to worry.

Thailand was, in fact, well on the road to the full financial liberalization that had been urged on it by the Fund and the World Bank throughout the late 1980s and early 1990s. As noted in Chapter 2, between 1990 and 1994, under the liberal technocrat government of Anand Panyarachun and its successor, the first government of Chuan Leekpai, a number of significant moves to deregulate and open up the financial system were undertaken, including the removal of ceilings on various kinds of savings and time deposits; fewer constraints on the portfolio management of financial institutions and commercial banks by replacing the reserve requirement ratio for commercial banks with the liquidity ratio; looser rules on capital adequacy; expansion of the field of operations of commercial banks and financial institutions; dismantling of all significant foreign exchange controls; and the establishment of the Bangkok International Banking Facility (BIBF).[3]

The BIBF was perhaps the most significant step taken by the Thais in the direction of financial liberalization. As noted in the previous chapter, this was a system in which local and foreign banks were allowed to engage in both offshore and onshore lending activities. BIBF licensees were allowed to accept deposits in foreign currencies and to lend in foreign currencies, to both residents and non-residents, for both domestic and foreign investments. BIBF dollar loans soon became the conduit for most foreign capital flowing into Bangkok, coming to about $50 billion in three years' time.

Thailand's liberalization was, of course, incomplete, but the IMF did not raise a word of protest against the two other key elements of Thailand's macroeconomic financial strategy. The maintenance of high interest rates – about 400–500 basis points above US rates – was most likely seen as a necessary inducement for foreign capital to come into Thailand. Besides, in the context of rapid growth, it was the usual IMF formula to contain overheating and inflation. As for the fixing of the exchange rate at a steady $1:baht 25 through Bank of Thailand intervention in the foreign exchange market, this was most likely seen to be a necessary condition for investors to exchange their dollars for baht without fear that they would be hit by devaluations that would drastically reduce their value. Moreover, the Fund did not have a reputation of being a partisan of floating exchange rates for developing countries, which could plague them with volatile external accounts that could be quite destabilizing.

Thus, when the IMF was requested by the Thai authorities to come in to rescue the economy in mid-July 1997, it was to fix a crisis that had as one of its root causes a Fund prescription (the rapid liberalization of the capital account) that had led to a problem that the Fund had not foreseen and worried about (private sector overborrowing). The attitude of the Thai financial technocrats was not unlike that of a player approaching the coach with a quizzical look that said: 'What happened? But I was just following your instructions.' By that time, however, the Fund was apparently beginning to rewrite history, saying that it had strongly warned the Thai authorities all along about a developing crisis – prompting economist Jeffrey Sachs to write wryly that 'the IMF arrived in Thailand in July with ostentatious declarations that all was wrong and that fundamental surgery was needed' when, in fact, 'the ink was not even dry on the IMF's 1997 annual report, which gave Thailand and its neighbours high marks on economic management!'[4]

It took almost a month for the IMF and the government to negotiate an agreement, which was announced on 20 August. In return for access to $16.7 billion – later $17.2 billion – in commitments gathered from bilateral and multilateral donors, the Thai authorities agreed to a stabilization and structural adjustment programme with two principal components.

First, a stabilization programme would cut the current account deficit through the maintenance of high interest rates and the achievement of a 'small overall surplus in the public sector by 1998' via an increase in the rate of value-added tax (VAT) to 10 per cent, expenditure cuts in a number of areas, increases in the prices of some utilities and petroleum products, and greater efficiency in state enterprises via privatization.[5]

The second component was structural reform of the financial sector. 'At the heart of the strategy', noted the Fund in its statement, 'has been the up-front separation, suspension, and restructuring of unviable institutions, immediate steps to instil to confidence in the rest of the financial system, strict conditionality on the extension of FIDF resources, and the phased implementation of broader structural reforms to restore a healthy financial sector.'[6] Part of the financial reform would also 'require all remaining financial institutions to strengthen their capital base expeditiously. This will include a policy of encouraging mergers, as well as foreign capital injection.'[7]

Even before the baht devaluation, the Chaovalit government had suspended 16 finance companies, including Finance One, once the country's premier finance company. At the time of the announcement of the agreement, the government declared that another 42 would be suspended, bringing the total to 58 of the country's 92 finance companies. This was not an unpopular move, since the finance companies were widely known to be bankrupt and had absorbed some hundred billion baht in subsidies from the FIDF, which many of them had spent not to restructure their loan portfolios but to re-lend, thus expanding, instead of reducing, their exposure.[8] What the IMF was interested in was a quick government decision to shut down those firms that could not be salvaged.

The IMF's key question when it came to the stabilization part of the package was: would the government go through with the agreement to raises taxes, particularly on petroleum?

The Chaovalit government hesitates

It took another two months before the government could come up with the full details of the stabilization programme. On 14 October, the Thai authorities publicly underlined their commitment to the IMF to generate a budget surplus equivalent to one per cent of GDP by decreeing a series of taxes, including increases on duties on luxury imports, surcharges on imports not used by the export sector, and, most controversial, an oil tax of one baht per litre of gasoline. On the expenditure side, the fiscal budget of 923 billion baht was cut by 100 billion baht, bringing it down to 823 billion baht.

On the financial sector reform, the authorities announced the creation of the Financial Restructuring Authority (FRA) to oversee the screening of the rehabilitation plans submitted by the 58 suspended companies, which would be the yardstick used to determine whether or not they would be allowed to reopen. Also to be established was an Asset Management Corporation (AMC), with seed money totalling one billion baht from the government, which would oversee the disposal of the assets of the finance companies ordered closed.

The government also promised to allow foreigners to own up to 100 per cent of financial institutions, to tighten rules for classifying loans as non-performing, to provide full government guarantees for depositors and creditors, and to improve the bankruptcy laws to allow creditors to collect their collateral faster.

At this point, the IMF's main concern was to immediately translate promise into reality. But because of popular opposition the Chaovalit government rescinded the petroleum tax three days after announcing it. Having presided over the unravelling of the economy, the government simply did not have the legitimacy to make its decision stick. The cabinet also failed to approve the emergency measures that were necessary to put the financial restructuring plans in motion. And it procrastinated on identifying the finance companies that would be closed.

When Finance Minister Thanong Bidaya resigned over the rescinding of the oil tax, the Chaovalit government's credibility hit rock bottom. The rising tension and confusion was captured in the following account:

> In late October and early November, rumours swept regional markets that the IMF might hold back the second phase of stand-by credits due in December. IMF officials reportedly were frustrated by the glacial pace of reforms and the indecisiveness by the government in acknowledging the seriousness of the

problems. Foreign creditors began to slash their credit lines and call back outstanding loans to Thai institutions. As the baht slid toward 42 to the dollar, fears emerged that Thailand might declare a debt moratorium.[9]

On the other side of the barricades, street demonstrations called for the resignation of the government, with many of them beginning to take on an anti-IMF colour. Critics began to be more vocal about their opinions that the tight-money, tight-fiscal-policy austerity package was a misguided cure that would only worsen the disease. As two influential analysts put it: 'IMF officials ... believe that once its prescription of an austere economic programme is followed strictly, confidence would return and capital would flow back into Thailand to improve liquidity and stabilize the baht. But this wishful thinking has not happened, with the country still paralysed by capital continuously flowing out of the system.'[10] In the meantime, 'without capital, Thai business in general is heading for a breakdown'.[11]

Chuan in the breach

With its credibility with both the public and the IMF hitting rock bottom, the Chaovalit government finally announced on 3 November – just a few hours before the arrival of an IMF team that would review government compliance with the agreement – that it would step down and allow a new parliamentary coalition to take power.

IMF pressure was instrumental in getting the National Assembly, in the interim between the Chaovalit government's announcement that it was stepping down and the formation of the second Chuan government, to pass four emergency decrees that were necessary to get the financial restructuring going. And when the new government was constituted the Fund did not relax its timetable, demanding that it immediately decide which finance companies to shut down permanently and which to rehabilitate. Indeed, it timed its decision on whether or not the next tranche of $800 million would be released on the government's announcement. Thai compliance, said Karin Lissakers, US delegate to the IMF, 'would be an important political signal that we had overcome political resistance to action'.[12]

On 7 December 1997, the Chuan government announced that all but two of the 58 finance companies would be closed. The IMF money was released. But talk about how the Thai authorities had exercised admirable political will was tempered by the government's admission that the financial crisis and the IMF stabilization programme would bring about a worse than expected contraction in 1998, with the Fund and government bringing down their estimate of economic growth from the 2.5 per cent projected at the time of the August agreement to 0.6 per cent.

At the time of the next IMF review, in mid-February 1998, the contraction was projected to be even worse, with the figure of 0.6 per cent growth revised downward to an average of -3.5 per cent for the year, but greater than -6 per cent for the first two quarters! This dismal projection, which held out the possibility of an even greater freefall, prompted the Fund to yield to the government's request that it be allowed to run a budget deficit of 1 to 2 per cent of GDP rather than be forced to turn up a surplus of 1 per cent. Explaining the Fund's concession, Hubert Neiss, the IMF's Asia–Pacific director, admitted that 'the economy had slowed down to such an extent that a continued stringent austerity regime may prompt a new economic crisis.' However, the government was not able to shift the Fund from its insistence on maintaining high interest rates, which were running at 20 per cent and above.

The Fund's new understanding with the Chuan administration committed the latter to push a revision of the Alien Business Law to allow foreigners more liberal investment privileges in the non-financial sectors of the economy; to prepare legislation to tighten up the country's bankruptcy laws; and to speed up the privatization or substantial privatization of key state enterprises such as the Telephone Organization of Thailand, Thai Airways, and the Communications Authority of Thailand. Finally, the revised agreement committed the government to announce stricter rules on classifying loans as 'non-performing' by the end of March 1998 and to force the banks to recapitalize on that basis.

Indeed, since it came into office in mid-November, the new government had, in fact, been hustling the banks to recapitalize along the lines demanded by the Fund to counter the savaging of their assets by the currency plunge – that is, by allowing foreign partners to take a big, if not majority, stake in the corporation, a step that had been made possible by emergency legislation approved by the National Assembly in October.

For some institutions, the choice was between receiving an infusion of foreign money or being brought more directly under the control of the government. Indeed, the government nationalised four near-bankrupt banks in order to restructure, sell, or dismantle them.

With the legal ground being secured, foreign banks began to work out deals with cash-short Thai banks. The Japanese Sanwa Bank announced that it would take a 10 per cent stake in one of the country's biggest banks, Siam Commercial Bank – a move that would bring total foreign shareholding in that bank to 35 per cent. Citibank declared that it would move to gain a 50.1 per cent ownership share in First Bangkok City Bank. But while this deal remained suspended as of February 1998, ABN-AMRO, a Dutch financial group, said that it had arrived at an agreement to get majority ownership in the Bank of Asia.

By February 1998, after over three months in office, the Chuan government had gained the reputation of being very compliant with the IMF, definitely much more so than the preceding Chaovalit government and the Suharto government in Indonesia. It would be accurate to say that, while there were differences on interest rate policy and government spending, both the government and the IMF had achieved a meeting of minds. The key to recovery was winning back the confidence of foreign capital, and the key to winning that confidence was to adhere to the IMF austerity programme.

Critique of the stabilization programme

When the IMF came to Thailand in mid-July, many sectors of Thai society had welcomed it as a force that could discipline what was perceived as an irresponsible and profligate gang of politicians, businessmen, and technocrats whose irresponsibility, profligacy, and ineptitude had brought the country to its knees. However, once the agreement with the IMF was announced in mid-August, doubts began to arise about the wisdom of the programme.

Why engineer a recession?

The stabilization part of the programme, many critics began to assert, was inappropriate. The Fund prescription basically demanded the maintenance of high interest rates to keep foreign capital from exiting the country and a sharp reduction in government expenditures in order for the government to achieve a budget surplus. Both were expected to combine with the financial crisis not only to slow down the GDP growth rate but to make it negative in 1998.

The issue raised by both foreign and domestic critics was: this was a crisis not of the public sector but of the private sector, which had gone on a borrowing binge. In fact, the Thai government had been consistently running a government surplus until 1996. So why squeeze the public sector, which had become the main element of a counter-cyclical process to prevent a deepening of recession as private investment slowed down?

Wasn't the avowed aim of both Thai and IMF authorities – the return of foreign capital – in fact likely to be thwarted by a deep recession? As Harvard's Jeffrey Sachs, the main proponent of this view, put it: '[T]he region does not need wanton budget cutting, credit tightening and emergency bank closures. It needs stable or even slightly expansionary monetary and fiscal policies to counterbalance the decline in foreign loans.'[13] Sachs went on to claim that the Fund's behaviour in fact worsened what was already a delicate situation in the autumn of 1997:

[T]he IMF deepened the sense of panic not only because of its dire pronouncements but also because its proposed medicine – high interest rates, budget cuts, and immediate bank closures – convinced the markets that Asia indeed was about to enter a severe contraction ... Instead of dousing the fire, the IMF in effect screamed fire in the theatre. The scene was repeated in Indonesia and Korea in December. By then panic had spread to virtually all of East Asia.[14]

There was no clear answer to these concerns except that foreign capital would somehow be assured by Thailand's willingness to undertake an austerity programme.

The 'moral hazard' issue

Another concern that emerged had to do with the actual use of the $17.2 billion rescue fund. The 20 August agreement stated that this sum would be devoted 'solely to help finance the balance of payments deficit and rebuild the official reserves of the Bank of Thailand'.[15] What this meant was that the funds could not be used to bail out local institutions. 'Financing the balance of payments deficit' was, however, a broad canopy that covered servicing the huge foreign debt of the Thai private sector, which in mid-1997 came to $72 billion. Over half of this was short-term debt. The IMF-assembled funds provided a guarantee that the government would be able to immediately address the immediate debt service commitments of the private sector, as the government and the IMF sought to get the creditors to roll over or restructure their loans. The rescue agreement thus fell right into the pattern of the IMF–US Mexican bailout in 1994 and the IMF structural agreements with indebted countries during the Third World debt crisis of the 1980s, in which public money from Northern taxpayers was formally handed over to indebted governments only to be recycled as debt service payments to commercial bank creditors. Thus, the Fund, critics charged, was encouraging 'moral hazard' or irresponsible lending because it assured lenders of a bailout if their decisions led to market penalities.

To many, furthermore, there was something fundamentally wrong about a process that imposed full market penalties for Thailand while exempting international private actors from them – indeed, *socializing* their losses. As *The Nation* put it: 'The penalties imposed on foreign creditor banks which have lent to the Thai private sector must be precise and applied equally ... Thailand and Thai companies may bear the brunt of the financial crisis but foreign banks must also share part of the cost because of some imprudent lending. It would be irresponsible to lay the blame entirely on Thailand.'[16]

Advancing the US agenda

A third set of concerns had to do with the opening up of the economy to foreign economic interests. Particularly worrying to many Thais was the IMF's insistence that the country's financial institutions, which had suffered big losses from the combination of non-performing loans and escalating foreign debt burdens owing to the precipitous drop of the baht, be recapitalized. Mergers among Thai banks and financial institutions were one alternative, but one that was frowned on by the Fund. Infusing the banks with state resources in return for greater state ownership was, of course, a non-starter, given the Fund's own anti-statist leanings.

This left the Fund's preferred option, which was to recapitalize mainly through capital infusions from foreign partners in return for granting the latter greater ownership rights. As noted above, the legal ground for this was prepared by the National Assembly's passing of a decree allowing foreign entities to own up to 100 per cent of equity in Thai financial institutions. This led to Japan's Sanwa Bank purchasing a 10 per cent share in one of the country's biggest banks, Siam Commercial Bank; negotiations by Citibank to acquire a 50.1 per cent ownership share in the First Bangkok City Bank; and the Dutch-owned ABN-AMRO Bank's acquisition of a majority stake in the Bank of Asia.

The Fund also stepped up the pressure on the Chuan government to liberalize the Alien Business Law to allow foreigners more liberal investment privileges in the non-financial sectors of the economy and to revise landownership laws in order to allow foreigners to own land.

Of particular concern was what many saw as the one-to-one correspondence between the IMF approach and the US agenda not only in Thailand but in East Asia as a whole. It was no secret that US officials had long considered the complex of protectionism, mercantilism, industrial policy, and activist state intervention in the economy that envelops most East and Southeast Asian economies as a system that handicapped US economic interests exporting or investing in Asia while unfairly assisting Asian firms in penetrating the US market. In the case of Thailand and Southeast Asia, the assessment in Washington was that while they might have liberalized their capital accounts and financial sectors, they remained highly protected when it came to trade and were flirting dangerously with 'trade distorting' exercises in industrial policy like Malaysia's national car project, the Proton Saga, or Indonesia's drive to set up a passenger aircraft industry.

Prior to the crisis, however, US efforts to move the Asian economies significantly in the free-market direction desired by US corporations had brought meagre results. Thus, a golden opportunity to push the decade-long US agenda in its foreign economic policy for East Asia opened up with the financial crisis, and Washington was exploiting it to the hilt, in the view of many Asians. US officials and former officials were not ones to conceal their designs. As the *Financial Times* noted in February 1998: '[I]ntriguingly, in recent weeks, US officials hinted to their domestic audience that they will use the opportunity provided by the crisis to force radical structural reform on other countries that would amount to what some critics see as an "Americanization" of the world economy.[17] Summing up Washington's strategic goal without having to use the euphemisms of his colleagues in the administration, Jeff Garten, under-secretary of commerce during President Bill Clinton's first term, said: 'Most of these countries are going to go through a deep and dark tunnel ... But on the other end there is going to be a significantly different Asia in which Americans have achieved much deeper market penetration, much greater access.'[18]

With respect to Thailand, US Trade Representative Charlene Barshefsky told the US Congress that the Thai IMF programme's 'commitments to restructure public enterprises and accelerate privatization of certain key sectors – including energy, transportation, utilities, and communications – which will enhance market-driven competition and deregulation [are expected] to create new business opportunities for US firms.'[19]

Reform or collapse?

By the first quarter of 1998, Thailand had gained the reputation of being quite compliant with IMF directives. As IMF representative Hubert Neiss put it: 'Thailand has turned the corner, along with Korea ... [Thailand has] won a battle or two but not the war yet ... Indonesia is still in the intensive-care unit.'[20] As a reward for delivering on the essentials of the IMF programme, the Fund allowed the Thais to run a government deficit of 1–2 per cent of GDP instead of forcing them to stick to the original commitment of turning a surplus. And after a visit to Washington in March, Prime Minister Chuan brought home additional assorted carrots, including $1 billion in Export–Import Bank credits, a release from an obligation to buy F-18A planes from the Pentagon, a $3.5 million investment in a minimill from George Soros, and a message from Bill Clinton urging investors to return to Thailand.[21]

With Chuan gracing the covers of *Business Week* and *Time*, it was evident that Washington and the Western business community were lining up behind the prime minister to carry through the reforms that would 'dismantle crony capitalism'. To many Thais, however, crony capitalism might be a problem, but dismantling it did not necessarily have to take the route of the extremely costly, dangerous, and wrongheaded IMF programme.

A key concern was that by early 1998 the programme had provoked a much deeper recession than either the government or the Fund were willing to officially acknowledge, with all the devastating social consequences of such a development. Indeed, Fund staffer Neiss seemed to indicate this possibility when he admitted that the reason the Fund had allowed Thailand to run a deficit in 1998 was that 'the economy had slowed down to such an extent that a continued austerity regime might prompt a new crisis'.[22] A key economic adviser to Chuan also noted in late March that the economy would contract in the coming months at an annual rate of 6.5 per cent – 'a recession much deeper than the one predicted by the IMF'.[23] By July, the economy was expected to contract by 8 per cent. If this turned out to be the case, then estimates of a 2 to 3 million unemployment rate by the end of 1998 were conservative and the pain for the whole nation would be much, much deeper.

As the year wore on, it became clear that the patient was being killed by the IMF medicine. Except for two major banks, no other banks could attract significant foreign investment for recapitalization owing precisely to investors' fears of throwing money into a dead economy. The reality of a massive collapse that some private analysts projected as a 20 per cent contraction of the economy over two years' time[24] finally pushed the country's technocrats to adopt a tougher stand in their negotiations with the Fund.

They were successful, during the negotiations in August 1998, in getting the Fund to agree to a government deficit of 3 per cent of GDP in the coming year. This would reportedly translate into 250 baht that would be injected 'directly into the system and address the social safety net problem'.[25]

At the same time, Finance Minister Tarrin unveiled a comprehensive reform package to jumpstart a 'non-functioning financial system' 30 to 35 per cent of whose total exposure consisted of non-performing loans. The main thrust of the package was to pump in 300 billion baht or $7.2 billion of government money into the banks to recapitalize them, in return for equity and a say in management. With the government directly controlling six banks and twelve finance companies, this latest move amounted to a 'creeping' nationalization of the whole banking system. Faced with no other choice but to beg for government help, bankers labelled the reforms 'innovative'. Yet the reality was closer to what one newspaper described as 'do or die financial restructuring'.[26]

But foreign investment was still seen as the strategic variable in resuscitating the economy. So coupled with the government spending increase and the virtual nationalization of banking came a very significant move towards investment liberalization as the government scrapped a 26-year-old executive decree that restricted foreign investments and opened up 33 new businesses to 100 per cent or majority foreign ownership. Foreign investors were also allowed to participate in 'reserved businesses' as majority shareholders.

With Panglossian panache, an IMF senior official asserted that the package brought Thailand to the 'threshold of recovery'. Yet the challenge from the Thais to his agency's blundering programme had probably come too late to prevent the recession from becoming a depression. As one observer put it, the financial sector might have been temporarily bailed out, but 'the real sector, that part of the economy which most of us live in, continues its downward spiral with no light at the end of the tunnel – except that of the oncoming train'.[27]

Notes

1. Quoted in Robert Chote, 'Thai crisis highlights lessons of Mexico', survey, *Financial Times*, 19 September 1997, p. 16.

2. Quoted in Jayati Ghosh, Abhijit Sen, and C. P. Chandrasekhar, 'Southeast Asian economies: miracle or meltdown?', *Economic and Political Weekly*, 12–19 October 1996, p. 2779.

3. See Pakorn Vichyanond, *Thailand's Financial System: Structure and Liberalization* (Bangkok: TDRI, 1994), p. 3.

4. Jeffrey Sachs, 'The IMF and the Asian flu', *The American Prospect*, March–April 1998, p. 17.

5. IMF, 'IMF approves stand-by credit for Thailand', press release no. 97/37, 20 August 1997.

6. Ibid.

7. Ibid.

8. 'Finance firms in Thailand express regret', *Asian Wall Street Journal*, 5–6 December 1997.

9. Soonyuth Nunyamanee and Chiratas Nivatpumin, 'The year they sank the baht', *Bangkok Post Economic Review Yearend 1997*, p. 19.

10. Vatchara Charoonsantikul and Thanong Khantong, 'Is the IMF doctor mistreating its Thai patient?', *The Nation*, 11 November 1997.

11. Ibid.

12. Bob Davis, 'Thailand tests IMF's resolve on reform', *Asian Wall Street Journal*, 8 December 1997.

13. Sachs, quoted in Vatchara Charoonsantikul and Thanong Khantong.

14. Sachs, 'The IMF and the Asian flu'.

15. IMF, 'IMF approves stand-by credits for Thailand'.

16. 'IMF package no free lunch for Thailand', *The Nation*, 9 August 1997.

17. 'US looks to G7 backing on Asia crisis', *Financial Times*, 20 February 1998.

18. Quoted in 'Worsening Asian flu lowers immunity to US business', *New York Times*, 1 February 1998.

19. Testimony of Ambassador Charlene Barshefsky, USTR, before the House Ways and Means Subcommittee, US House of Representatives, 24 Feburary 1998.

20. Quoted in 'Discipline must be maintained despite breathing space: Supachai', *Bangkok Post*, 14 February 1998.

21. 'Can Thailand turn around?', *Business Week*, 6 April 1998, pp. 14–18.

22. 'IMF agrees to relax condition', *Bangkok Post*, 13 February 1998.

23. Quoted in 'Can Thailand turn around?'.

24. Russel Kopp, quoted in 'Thailand: banking chaos', *Business Week*, 17 August 1998, p. 26.

25. Russell Kopp, quoted in 'Thailand: banking chaos', *Business Week*, 17 August 1998, p. 26.

26. Thanong Khantong and Vatchara Charoonsantikul, 'Leading up to Tarrin's banking reform package', Section B, *The Nation*, 17 August 1998.

27. Kanjana Spindler, 'Vested interests still in control', *Bangkok Post*, 19 August 1998.

CHAPTER 4

The Failure of Industrial Deepening

Thailand had the the world's fastest growing economy between 1985 and 1995, with the World Bank calculating the growth at an average of 10 per cent a year. This growth was, however, basically unplanned. Its impact on the rural areas and on urban infrastructure will be discussed in other chapters. Another dimension of this lack of planning has been in the area of technology. Economic growth has not been accompanied by industrial and technological deepening. Part of the problem has been lack of government and private sector initiatives to implement strategic planning in the area of technology. But a great part of the problem has resided in the practices of multinational corporations, which have spearheaded the industrialization drive in Thailand.

Thailand's technological problem is essentially a problem of human resources. As a World Bank report on the poor state of human resource development in Thailand puts it: 'Technological capability is essentially embodied in people, not in machinery. In the process of acquiring, using and diffusing, adapting and developing technology, the most important input is a technical human capital base able to assess and decide on technology matters.'[1]

Prior to the onset of the financial crisis, HRD (human resources development) had become the new buzzword, particularly for the Eighth Plan. As the country's deputy permanent secretary for labour and social welfare told a key APEC meeting in January 1996:

> It is evident that human resources management will be the most important element in the strategies for maintaining the competitive strength of the economy in the next century. Education, skill development, wages and incentives structures, workplace environment, technology upgrading, and management efficiency, will require close attention of the government, business leaders, and individual citizens.[2]

Most critical, in the view of the minister, was that:

As we approach the year 2000, it is clear that Thailand will need to develop a highly educated workforce to produce higher technological products. Thailand will have to rely much more on productivity improvements for which continuous upgrading of skills and constant attention to management efficiency will be essential ... It is a continuous and ongoing process dictated by the demands of the market place.[3]

Between aspiration and reality, however, lay a grand canyon.

The education bottleneck

Perhaps the most glaring human capital problem faced by the country is the bottleneck at the secondary school level. The share of the employed population with a secondary or vocational school education is just 9 per cent, which is not surprising given the fact that the enrolment rate at secondary school is only 30 per cent.[4] In fact, a comparison reveals that Thailand's secondary enrolment rate is the lowest of the major countries of ASEAN, with the Philippines reporting 68 per cent, Malaysia 53 per cent, and Indonesia 39 per cent.[5] 'Cultural factors', it is said, are primarily responsible for this low rate of attendance, but lack of official compulsion (until recently) and other forms of government intervention such as subsidies and incentives are also said to be critical. In any event, given its decisive importance in providing the human resource infrastructure for techno-industrial deepening, the lack of official attention to secondary schooling may prove to be one of the key obstacles to Thailand's effort to get out of the Third World. Looking ahead to the year 2000, one study projects that for countries at Thailand's level of expected GDP then, the average secondary enrolment ratio will be about 63 per cent – a figure that underlines the size of the task of streamlining and upgrading secondary education.[6]

The university situation is only marginally better from a techno-economic point of view. The share of the employed population with a university degree was less than 3 per cent.[7] Between the early and late 1980s, some improvement was registered in the production of science and technology (S&T) graduates: at the bachelor's degree level, the figure for S&T graduates rose from 17.4 per cent to 18.4 per cent; at the postgraduate level, from 33.9 per cent to 39.7 per cent; and at the below bachelor level, from 39.5 to 45.2 per cent.[8]

However, in terms of the projection of demand brought about by the foreign investment-driven industrialization strategy, the gap between the relatively snail-paced growth in S&T education and personnel supply was stark. In both a base scenario (5 per cent growth rate or slightly higher in GDP) and a high scenario (7.5 to 8 per cent growth rate), there would develop 'serious shortages of bachelor degree manpower in all areas', indicating 'the need for an urgent quantum leap in the output levels, especially in the engineering and basic science disciplines'.[9] There would also be a 'crucial shortage of postgraduate S&T manpower in virtually all areas of specialization'.[10] In the cutting-edge electronics industry, the high-scenario case projected the gap at the postgraduate and bachelor's degree level to worsen significantly, reaching 344 and 3,001 persons respectively by the year 2001.[11]

Surveys of key industries carried out in the late 1980s and early 1990s confirmed the growing gap between the need for trained personnel and the actual supply. In the computer industry, for instance, subsidiaries of multinational corporations surveyed had to import about a third of their engineers owing to the shortage of locally available engineers.[12] In the machine tool industry, there was a 'severe shortage of technical manpower in the metallurgical field', which was not surprising, given the fact that Thai universities produced fewer than twenty metallurgy graduates a year.[13] In the mould and die industry, which provides critical components for the automobile, machine parts, metal products, and plastic products industries, there was 'a serious shortage of engineers, experienced technicians, and skilled labor', resulting in only 25 per cent of the surveyed firms employing engineers, and only 45 per cent employing draftsmen.[14] In the ceramics industry, laboratory staff were in short supply in all firms, a not unexpected condition given that there was only one university with a training pro-gramme in ceramics, producing only about 17 graduates in the late 1980s.[15] In the textile industry, competitiveness has become greatly dependent on the presence of skilled personnel, and the 'shortage of these skills is already apparent and creates serious problems for small and medium firms which cannot compete with large firms in paying high wages'.[16]

Given these conditions, industry lobbies began to raise the demand for relaxed immigration rules to allow a more liberal entry of trained per-sonnel. Moreover, foreign investors began to raise the possibility of moving to other investment locations if the technical personnel block was left unresolved. For instance, the director of the Industrial Promotions Department of the Japan External Trade Organization (JETRO) noted that if Thailand could not solve its skilled labour bottleneck, 'Japanese firms will increasingly look to places like Vietnam, where you have a better-educated labour force.'[17]

Even if the financial crisis had not erupted, Thailand would have run up against structural obstacles such as the education bottleneck.

The R&D fiasco

In the early 1990s, Thailand increasingly found itself less competitive with many of its neighbours when it came to wages – hence the preoccupation of officials not only with the educational levels of the workforce but also with research and development (R&D). Yet total R&D expenditures in

Thailand came to only 0.22 per cent of GDP in 1987, which was rather low compared to those of the most dynamic Asian NICs.[18] In the mid-1980s, the rate was 1.8 per cent of GNP for Korea and 1.04 per cent for Taiwan.[19]

Government R&D in support of economic activities came to only 0.17 per cent of GNP. While the mid and late 1980s saw the founding of a number of government R&D institutes or government-linked university-based research centres, in fact public R&D was in a rather embryonic state. As one analyst saw it:

> In fact, it is true to say that government has not yet had a comprehensive technology policy for the economy. Technology promotion has hitherto been peripheral and rather disjointed. Although R&D activities in the government sector are larger in terms of the number of R&D personnel and expenditure compared with the private sector, R&D activities in universities are to serve teaching purposes and fulfil academic interests. R&D activities in other government institutions, which possess some advanced equipment and tools, have played a minor role in supporting private R&D activities.[20]

The problem was also, according to some analysts, one of ideology. As they saw it, the Thai government limited its role in developing industry to providing what it considered the appropriate broad incentive structure for development, first through protectionism from the 1960s up to the late 1980s, then via a strategy of trade and investment liberalization in the 1990s. Other key functions that were central to industrial advance, such as sponsorship of basic R&D, active provision of technical services to industry, and a targeted effort to improve technological levels, were basically ignored by government. Yet, as one study argued:

> developing technical human capital and strengthening the basic technological infrastructure should not be seen as a form of government intervention. In fact, we feel that these roles are part of the obligations that a government should provide to society in order to facilitate the development of a country. Due to their characteristics of long lead time, large investment and low initial return, market force alone is ... insufficient to adequately ensure viability.[21]

As for industrial targeting and other direct ways of encouraging investment by manipulating the incentive structure, the study argued that the experience with cutting-edge industries like electronics in other NICs showed the critical importance of activist government policies. Thus, 'interventions are sometimes necessary and justifiable for specific purposes.'

The importance of government intervention in R&D was especially critical given the fact that, as one report underlined: 'Technology acquisition through in-house development is barely practised in small and medium industries.'[22] Thai firms contributed only 5.5 per cent of total R&D expenditures, a pathetic figure compared to Japan and Korea, where private-sector R&D constituted more than 80 per cent of total R&D.[23] Again, by another comparative measure, ratio of R&D to total sales, Thai firms performed poorly, spending only 0.1 per cent on R&D, whereas expendtitures of Japanese and Korean firms came to 3.3 per cent and 2.1 per cent of total sales.[24]

Surveys of the status of R&D in various industries confirm this. In the mould and die industry, for instance, R&D is relatively rare, owing to 'the scarcity of qualified manpower, the lack of facilities and supporting institutions, and the lagging stage of technological development'.[25] Indeed, given the lack of a viable technological infrastructure, it has become more practical for firms to acquire technology from the outside rather than via innovation.[26] This holds true even for leading firms.[27]

Weakness in R&D in the mould and die industry, and in the area of metal parts production generally, has had critical consequences in terms of deepening the industrial structure of Thai industry. As a UNIDO study pointed out: 'The weakness of Thai supporting industries often compels foreign investors to either source from abroad (sophisticated moulds, e.g., are a significant import item) or to encourage their traditional suppliers to move to Thailand as happened for instance in the case of Mitsubishi car manufacturing.'[28]

Electronics has been Thailand's cutting-edge industry, but the majority of local firms have remained 'stagnant in technology as reflected in the low intensity of skilled manpower, the lack of R&D activities, and the high cost of production'.[29] Over 25 years of protection, tax and tariff policies 'have been used to protect the assembly of licensed products rather than accumulate the capability to produce them'.[30] Instead, whatever research capability and facilities are available in electronics in Thailand come almost entirely from a number of electronics laboratories in government universities.[31]

For the most part, says one analyst who has focused on electronics firms, very few Thai firms have been able to develop products mainly by themselves. A few companies, certainly, have been able to develop some innovative R&D capabilities, such as some Thai firms specializing in the PABX (private automatic branch exchange) telecommunications device and computer cards, but these are relatively few and their impact on the whole industry is quite 'marginal'.[32] Indeed, even among these 'advanced' firms, there appears to be no budget devoted strictly to R&D, nor does it go beyond an 'ad hoc' basis.[33] For the most part, Thai-owned firms 'have no technical people, no R&D, and prefer to buy technology from foreign firms. There is nothing wrong with this, but the question is: is it adequate?'[34]

The reluctance of Thai firms to invest in R&D and real estate became even greater during the real estate and financial boom of the early 1990s. Instead of pouring resources into R&D, they reinvested their profits – or the loans they incurred – into real estate and the stock market, thus contributing to the loss of competitiveness of Thai exports. As one Bank of Bangkok analyst asserted: 'The manufacturers failed to keep their products competitive in world markets by investing in research and development and upgrading workers' skills. Instead, they gambled their profits in real estate.'[35]

Foreign investment and technology transfer: electronics

What about the foreign electronics firms, which have, after all, spearheaded the growth of the industry in Thailand? Many of these companies were invited in under the rationale that they would be transferring technology or spurring technological innovation. Yet the findings of a very intensive study of 50 local and foreign firms conducted by the Thailand Development Research Institute (TDRI) showed that in terms of three critical dimensions of technological innovation – 'acquisitive', 'operative', and 'innovative' capabilities – the ratings registered by wholly foreign-owned firms and joint ventures were lower than those for Thai firms.[36] The low level of technological innovation reflects the fact that in foreign-owned firms and joint ventures 'almost all product development in the industries, particularly products manufactured for export, has so far taken place overseas, with export products being manufactured according to the specifications required by and submitted from parent firms or buyers overseas'.[37] In other words, the foreign subsidiaries or joint ventures are meant to be centres not of technological innovation but of cheap labour using sophisticated equipment. As another TDRI study puts it, 'the main reason that the industry is in Thailand at all is because of the country's favorable labor costs and efficiency'.[38]

The integrated circuit industry is perhaps typical of the technological operations of foreign electronics companies in Thailand. There are at present more than ten multinational producers of integrated circuit (IC) producers in Thailand, but most of their operations consist of low-value added, low-skilled chip-assembly work.[39] Perhaps an indication of the absence of significant technological spinoffs from the industry is that more than twenty years after the first assembly factory was set up in Thailand, there are hardly any supporting industries for IC fabrication.[40] Such supporting industries for the multinationals are in their other subsidiaries abroad, but the problem here is that an expected spinoff in terms of backward and forward linkages to support the development of a local electronics industry has not materialized.

Without facilities for technological innovation, multinational IC subsidiaries can hardly be expected to diffuse technology to their country of location. For instance, the first IC manufacturer in Thailand, which is now the country's biggest manufacturer of memory chips, began chip production 19 years ago. However, the basic technological design for production in Thailand continues to be done out at the multinational's headquarters in Silicon Valley, California, and transferred to Thailand via its subsidiary in Singapore.

The company began rudimentary R&D activities only eleven years ago, but these were directed not at innovation but at 'troubleshooting' and 'improvement', which are relatively minor activities in the overall technological process of turning out the memory chip. The Thai subsidiary's key activity has remained that of labour-intensive assembly of the chip.[41] The situation with this particular firm, already probably the most advanced in terms of in-house R&D capability, is shared by the other IC firms.

In other areas of electronics, a similar situation prevails. A study of Japanese and Thai joint ventures in consumer electronics notes: 'The introduced technologies were characteristically labor-intensive, stagnant, fragmented and dependent.'[42]

> The labor intensiveness of introduced technologies was due mainly to the massive cheap labor forces available in the country. In addition, the attitude on the part of the Japanese joint-venture partners, who looked at investment in Thailand merely as a mechanism for penetration into the protected market, made their marketing strategy passive. Most of these firms restricted their production activities to the minimum necessary level of product assembly, relying solely on imported parts and components from the mother companies. As a result, the learning process was concentrated mainly on assembly and related technologies, thereby fragmenting the transferred technology. On top of that, technological development was stagnant as a result of low competition due to the protected market. Because the learning process had been limited, dependency on imported technologies was unnecessarily prolonged.
>
> The learning process in Japanese joint ventures was concentrated on assembly technology, production, and quality controls. It barely widened to other related areas, except for one Japanese joint venture. Most of the electronic and other mechanical parts still had to be imported. For most firms, even after two decades localization of parts had been achieved only in such items as carton boxes, packaging materials, wooden television cabinets, packaging foams, and so on.

Foreign investment and technology transfer: the car industry

In both electronics and automobile manufacture, the Thai government adopted policies aimed at getting the production of components and parts localized, in the hope that this would result in the creation of a local network of support industries that would eventually support the final assembly stage of the production process. In both areas, the policy has had mixed success.

In 1961, the government embarked on what one account describes as 'a resolute policy of promoting local capability in the automobile industry'[43] via the setting up of local assembly plants and the mandatory sourcing of components and parts from local suppliers. The milestones of the process were the decreeing of compulsory local content to be no less than 25 per cent in 1972, the total banning of CBU (completely built up) units, and the raising of the local content cutoff to 50 per cent within five years in 1978.

In terms of localization, it cannot be disputed that the policy has had some success, at least in terms of broad quantitative indicators. Local content rose from 20 per cent in 1980 to 45 per cent in 1983 to 54 per cent in 1989.[44] For locally assembled pickup trucks, the localization rate reached almost 80 per cent.[45] As analyst Richard Doner notes, there were some efforts to skirt local content requirements through various kinds of cheating, such as adding all sorts of non-essential gadgets and accessories to meet the required percentage while having to avoid sourcing key components locally. Nevertheless, around 1981, 'assemblers ran out of accessories and non-essentials and were forced to consider local purchase of major functional components whose cost and quality problems were quite significant. This was especially the case for commercial vehicles which begin with relatively few luxuries. Consequently, the 1979–81 increases in localization, however modest, engendered serious assembler opposition to further, more expensive, increases.'[46] Moreover, the rate of localization compared favourably to Malaysia in the early 1990s, when the local content of the Proton Saga, the so-called Malaysian national car, reached only 36 to 40 per cent.[47]

By the early 1990s, some 200 auto parts producers, most of them Thai, were engaged in the manufacture of an impressive range of commodities, including mufflers, radiators, side frame chassis, wire and harness of the auto electrical system, electroplating, automotive lights, shock absorbers, wheel discs, and air filters.[48] The problem, however, was the parts manufactured were largely the less sophisticated parts of the automobile, and while the range of products was diverse, they were still a small part of the 5,000 components that go into the making of an automobile. As one study points out, the Thai automotive components industry still lacks the capability to manufacture the really critical parts like the transmission gear, camshaft, and crankshaft.[49] In a rather scathing description of the capacities of Thai component makers, the report says that:

> [T]hey largely produce fake and imitative spare parts for the spare part [sic] market. They just can copy the outlook of the products without knowledge of product specification and underlying technology. Besides, they do not use proper and appropriate process [sic]. For instance, they tend to use casting instead of forging process for connecting rods.[50]

In sum, in terms of the 'overall technology status of Thai firms [it] can be said that they almost have no design capability. Furthermore, only a few firms have only some manufacturing capability ... [T]hey have no design, product-specific, and production-management technologies.'[51]

Why technology transfer has been so limited has been a source of conflicting interpretations from both the Japanese end and the Thai end. While Japanese analysts boast about the automobile industry achieving a 60 per cent localization ratio for automobiles and 75 per cent for motor-cycles,[52] Thai commentators have blamed the Japanese side. For instance, only about three firms engaged in subcontract work for the Japanese replied in a survey that they expected to benefit from technology transfer.[53] A frequent complaint of Thai firms with technological assistance contracts with Japanese firms is that 'Japanese experts who came to assist Thai counterparts ... are ... non-qualified technicians, and sometimes they seem not to fully transfer their know-how to the Thai side.'[54]

On the part of the Japanese, they grudgingly conceded that, as one of them put it, 'strict regulation by the Thai government has succeeded in promoting the industrialization of Thailand', but asserted that it was 'a tough job for Japanese firms to follow the frequent changes in policy'.[55]

Thailand as Japan's technological dependency

So, overall, what can be said to have been the effects of the Thai government's localization and related policies in the automobile industry? A dispassionate analysis would have to conclude that the process benefited Japan more than Thailand. Pushed by government, the car assemblers became more than simple 'screwdriver' factories. However, rather than the creation of a Thai auto industry, what happened was the consolidation of operations in Thailand by the large multinational assemblers, most of whom were Japanese firms like Toyota, Mitsubishi, and Nissan. In terms of the auto parts industry, the real beneficiaries were not the mainly Thai small and medium-sized firms. The 20 firms that developed into large-scale operations during the 1980s were mainly Japanese joint ventures.[56] And it was from these subsidiaries that the Japanese giants procured about 70 per cent of their parts.[57]

What occurred was the consolidation of Japanese control of the domestic market – in the early 1990s, the second largest national market for commercial cars in the world, second only to the United States[58] – while also allowing them to establish a base to export cars to the United States and elsewhere when the continued appreciation of the yen made production in Japan more and more expensive in the late 1980s. Despite almost two decades of a determined government effort to build up a domestic industry, the future of the Thai automobile industry was overwhelmingly decided in Tokyo, rather than Bangkok, according to the large multinationals' specification of the role of Thailand in the corporations' global production and marketing plans.

This became very clear in the late 1980s. Previously the Japanese saw Thailand's value as principally a protected market where they reigned supreme. Following the drastic rise in the value of the yen relative to the dollar forced by the Plaza Accord of 1985, however, labour-intensive manufacturing in Japan was no longer viable because of its high comparative cost. Thailand and Southeast Asia now became important mainly as a low-cost, low-wage region that could serve as the relocation area for the manufacturing operations of Japanese industry. Eliminating protective trade barriers thus became a key interest of the Japanese conglomerates, which now sought to locate different parts of their manufacturing operations in different Southeast Asian countries, thus making the region an integrated production base.

In the period 1988 to 1993, some $40 billion worth of Japanese investment swirled through the Asia–Pacific region in one of the most rapid and massive outflows of direct investment towards the developing world in recent history.[59] Over half of this – $22 billion – went to the ASEAN countries.[60] To show how massive this was, one can compare it to US investment in the region: for the same period, this came to $21 billion for the whole of Asia, $11 billion of which went to ASEAN.[61] By the end of the period, much of the region had, for all intents and purposes, been integrated into the Japanese economy.

Certainly, it is not only Japanese billions that have flowed to different points of East Asia in the past decade. Investment from Korea, Taiwan, and Hong Kong have also been prominent, indeed in many countries outstripping the volume of Japanese investment. Such investments are, however, not usually strategically planned, being undertaken, for the most part, by small and medium-sized establishments with short-term perspectives. Japan's investment drive, in contrast, has been promoted by the Japanese government and planned by corporate giants operating with global and regional perspectives.

One dimension of this integration was horizontal – that is, splitting up the production of different goods or components of one product among different countries. In Matsushita's strategy, for instance, each country is assigned specific items to produce for export: colour televisions and electric irons in Malaysia, semiconductors in Singapore, and dry-cell batteries, floppy disk drives, and electronic capacitors in the Philippines.[62]

In addition to integration along lines of product specialization, a process of backward integration was tightening the links of the region to the core economy before the eruption of the financial crisis. In the first phase of this process, which began in the mid-1980s, Japanese automobile and consumer electronic firms relocated their plants to the region. This was followed by the outmigration of smaller Japanese companies that supply parts and components for the assemblers. A third phase of backward integration was about to begin before the crisis, with relocation of heavy

Table 4.1 Japanese direct investment in Thailand and in ASEAN, FY 1986–96 (in millions of US$)

	1986	1987	1988	1989	1990	1991	1992	1993	1994	1995	1996	Total
Thailand	124	250	859	1,276	1,154	807	657	578	719	1,240	1,453	9,117
ASEAN	856	1,525	2,713	4,684	4,082	3,696	3,867	3,042	4,942	5,323	6,279	41,009

Source: Japan Ministry of Finance.

and chemical industries that provide basic inputs to both the big manufacturers and their suppliers.

Japan's long recession in the early 1990s hardly blunted this process.
While investments in Europe and the US have slowed considerably, the
movement of capital to the Asia–Pacific region continued at a brisk pace:
Japan's investment in the region rose from $5.9 billion in FY 1991 to $9.6
billion in FY 1994, while investment in Europe fell from $9.3 billion to
$6.2 billion, and its investment in North America dropped from $18.8
billion to $17.8 billion.[63] Moreover, in 1993, profits from Japan's operations
in Asia exceeded those from the USA for the first time, an astonishing
development when considered against the fact that as recently as 1980,
only 2 per cent of Japan's corporate profits originated in Asia.[64]

Interestingly enough, then, Japan's recession accelerated the regional-
ization of the Japanese economy, as pressures built up on more firms to
save on labour costs by moving their operations to China and Southeast
Asia. This paradoxical phenomenon was captured by one commentary
which asserted that 'the hollowing out' [of Japanese industry] is tantamount
to an increased ' "interdependence" [with Asia]'.[65] It also appears that
rather than following an internationalist investment strategy in the late
1980s and early 1990s, the Japanese government and Japanese corporations
have moved toward a more Asia-focused investment strategy. Japanese
investment in Asia as a proportion of total Japanese foreign investment
rose from 12 per cent in 1990 to 23 per cent in 1994.[66]

Thailand was a centrepoint of the Japanese move into Southeast Asia.
In 1987, according to one report, Japanese investment approvals by Thailand's Board of Investments exceeded the cumulative Japanese investment
for the preceding 20 years.[67] Between 1988 and 1993, Thailand received
$5.3 billion in Japanese investments, or almost five times more than it had
received in the previous 37 years.[68] More established in Thailand than in
other countries, the Japanese automobile giants sought to make the country
the hub of their Southeast Asian production diversification programme.
Toyota, for instance, brought out a master-plan to assemble vehicles from
diesel engines and electrical equipment manufactured in Thailand, while
transmissions would be made in the Philippines, steering links in Malaysia,
and gasoline engines in Indonesia.[69] Nissan and Mitsubishi unveiled similar
plans.

Seeing the countries of the region no longer only as protected markets
but as complementary sites of an integrated production base for vehicles
destined for both regional and international markets, the Japanese became
supporters of ASEAN tariff-reduction schemes such as the Industrial
Complementation/'Brand-to-Brand' Complementation' programme, which
promoted linkages in manufacturing operations across borders by offering
a 50 per cent margin of preference to products manufactured under this
programme.[70] The Japanese car giants also threw their weight behind the

ASEAN Free Trade Area (AFTA), realizing that, if implemented, this would lead to the eventual elimination to significant obstacles to the flow of car components across ASEAN borders. As one Australian government report noted:

> Japanese firms, such as automotive and motorcycle companies, have worked longer and harder at making ASEAN integration work than most other companies ... [For instance] ... one Japanese motorcycle maker reported that an arrangement to ship components between its plants in Malaysia and Thailand had required years of patient work with government officials in each country.[71]

The same report quoted an official of Siam Nissan Automobile, Nissan's Thai subsidiary, as saying: 'Taking advantage of AFTA, we want to concentrate production of specific auto parts in specific countries, and thus promote a horizontal division of labor.'[72]

At the same time that the Japanese car and other conglomerates moved to a position of favouring fewer trade barriers between Thailand and other ASEAN countries, free traders began to gain significant influence at the expense of protectionists in the higher circles of the economic planning agencies of the Thai government. The second-stage import substitution policy designed to deepen the industrialization process that reigned in the 1980s, of which a relatively effective local content policy was one manifestation, slowly gave way to a wide-ranging programme of liberalization.

Among the most significant policy moves to issue from the confluence of these events was the decision by the caretaker government of Prime Minister Anand Panyarachun in 1991 to drastically slash tariffs on cars from 300 to 100 per cent for CBUs and from 112 to 20 per cent of imported components of CKD units.[73] This translated into a significant reduction of the total tax from 616.8 per cent to 210.8 per cent for CBUs and from 125.3 per cent to 106 per cent for CKDs.[74] But perhaps more important was the decision, under severe pressure from the Japanese assemblers, to freeze local content at 54 per cent, instead of incrementally increasing it according to previous policy.

The local content policy was, in fact, earmarked for extinction under the Uruguay Round of the General Agreement on Tariffs and Trade (GATT), which came into effect in 1995. Following strong pressure from the United States and the European Union, and with the acquiescence of Japan, local content policies were declared as 'trade-related investment measures' (TRIMs) that obstructed the free flow of goods across borders and were thus illegal under GATT. This was not surprising, for it had been not only Thailand but also Malaysia and Korea that utilized local content policies to set up domestic auto industries that the USA, European, and Japanese transnationals viewed as strategic threats to their global market dominance. Local content regulations had also severely interfered with the inter-subsidiary trade of the multinationals, where via transfer pricing and other mechanisms to reduce tariffs, they were able to reduce costs and prices in a hotly competitive market.

The final laying to rest of the local content policy – and thus of Thailand's ambition to build a national, integrated auto industry – was instigated not by the Japanese but by General Motors. In negotiation with the World Trade Organization created by the GATT Uruguay Round, Thailand agreed to lift its local content regulations by the year 2000. By threatening to sink $750 million into establishing a manufacturing facility in the Philippines instead of Thailand in a move to break into the Japanese-dominated Southeast Asian car market, GM forced the Thai government to advance its scrapping of local content rules to July 1998 – 18 months ahead of schedule.[75]

What this meant, among other things, was bankruptcy for many of the mainly Thai-owned component and spare-parts manufacturers that had grown up under the 25-year-old local content policy that had been applied with 'strict regulation' by the Thai government.[76] This does not mean that there will be no survivors among the parts manufacturers, but these are likely to come from the ranks of the twenty or so manufacturers that function as joint venture subsidiaries of the big Japanese car giants.

Moving to the bigger picture, the conversion of Thailand in the Japanese multinationals' plans from being only a market to be protected to a key component of regional production base has had severe consequences for the country. Aside from becoming an appendage of a regionalized Japanese economy, Thailand became a massive deficit economy in its trade with Japan. The deficit climbed from $5 billion in 1990 to $6.5 billion in 1994.[77] This situation was not, of course, unique to Thailand: China, the Southeast Asian countries, and the Northeast Asian NICs currently had a combined trade deficit of $50 billion with Japan, even as they boasted of a combined trade surplus of more than $60 billion with the United States.[78] This was basically a reflection of Japan's virtual monopoly of advanced technology, which allowed it to add more value to its products relative to the low-tech manufactured products, processed agricultural goods, and raw materials that it imported from the dependent East Asian economies. Indeed, much of the deficit was accounted for by the trading relatonship between the Japanese mother companies in Japan and their subsidiaries in the Asian countries, which Hisahiko Okazaki, the former ambassador to Thailand, described as one of trading 'captive imports, such as products from plants in which the Japanese have invested', in return for 'captive exports, such as necessary equipment and materials'.[79]

The other consequence of Thailand's reorientation from being a market to being a production base is that, in the absence of industrial depth, its competitive advantage began to revolve mainly around two factors: its ability to offer a looser environmental regime than other governments in the region, and its ability to offer lower labour costs.

On the first item, the Japanese for the most part had their way, since, although Thailand has some good environmental laws, they are scarcely implemented, as will be documented in later chapters. A foreign adviser to a key environmental agency asserted that Japanese firms were just as eager to circumvent the installation of adequate environmental controls as were Taiwanese, Thai, and Korean firms. The clout of the Japanese car companies in this area was, in fact, displayed in 1996, when they were able to resist the move for car engines to graduate to much tougher Euro-standards.[80]

On the second item, Thailand was in trouble, indeed, as the increasing tightness of the labour market brought about by the combination of an overvalued currency and massive overinvestment raised wages in Thailand to two and even three times higher than in neighbouring countries. By the mid-1990s, the Japanese were grumbling about high wages and threatening to move elsewhere. A key official of the MITI office in Bangkok said that with higher wages, Vietnam was increasingly an attractive destination, and its workforce allegedly had the advantage of being more highly educated, on average, than the Thais.[81] Another Japanese, this time the director of a Japanese clothing subsidiary at the Lat Krabang industrial zone, said that with increasing labour costs and infrastructure bottlenecks in Bangkok, a 'herd mentality' was developing among Japanese, and that Jakarta was beginning to be seen as the ideal location.[82]

The financial crisis and foreign investment trends

This was, of course, the situation prior to the Thai and Asian financial implosion that began in July 1997. It is not at all clear how the financial crisis will affect the trends outlined above. Will foreign direct investors follow the lead of the banks and portfolio investors and pull their capital out of the region? In particular, how will Japanese investors react?

On the one hand, nearly all the key Japanese manufacturers – Toyota, Mitsubishi, Isuzu, and Hino – have either shut down or reduced operations in Thailand. However, some analysts say that new investment flows from Japan are not likely to be reduced that much, since the Japanese are continuing to pursue a strategic plan of making Southeast Asia an integrated production base. In Thailand alone, it is pointed out, more than 1,100 Japanese companies are established and only a massive economic downturn can reverse the momentum that has built up. As one Japanese executive asserted: 'It [Japanese investment] is a long-term strategy where investments are increased on a year-to-year basis, so I don't think a 10 to 20 per cent devaluation will force Japanese investors to change their investment strategies for Thailand.'[83]

However, there are new conditions that make the situation different from that of the early 1990s. First of all, Japanese investment strategies in the last few years have targeted Southeast Asia both as export platforms for third-country markets and as prosperous middle-class markets to be themselves exploited. These markets will contract severely over the next few years as depressive IMF programmes take hold. In Thailand, for instance, a negative 8 per cent growth rate is expected for 1998 and it will be a long time before decent growth rates are again recorded.

Second, diverting production from Southeast Asian markets to Japan will be difficult since Japan's recession, instead of giving way to recovery, is expected to deepen, with a contraction of GDP expected in 1998, following an average growth of only 1.3 per cent a year since 1992.

Third, redirecting production to the USA is going to be very difficult, unless the Japanese want to provoke the wrath of Washington, which is already warning Japan not to 'export its way out of recession'.

Fourth, using the IMF as a battering ram, the USA is pushing for the liberalization of trade and investment regimes in the region. What this means is that increasingly, US corporations will have an easier time establishing a competitive presence in the region – a future prefigured by Ford and GM's decision to locate assembly plants in Thailand.

The upshot of all this is that Japan could be burdened with significant overcapacity in its Southeast Asian manufacturing network, which could trigger a significant plunge in the level of fresh commitments of capital. Whatever the case, it is unlikely to affect the technological equation: as in the past, foreign investment inflows are unlikely to result in greater technological acquisition by Thailand.

Conclusion

In sum, despite high growth rates, Thailand was unable to develop the technological infrastructure needed to bring its industrial development to a newer stage. This was, of course, the same problem that the earlier NICs had experienced, although in Thailand's case the situation was worse. The failure to develop technological capability coincided with a weaker commitment to the program of industrialization via import substitution, and gradually the 1980s policy of 'second stage import substitution' was shelved. The rise of free marketeers in the the higher reaches of government coincided with a transformation of Thailand in the eyes of multinationals – especially the dominant Japanese multinationals – from being only a market to be penetrated to becoming a part of a larger regional production base. In this scheme, tariff barriers and local content policies designed for national industrialization increasingly had no place, and by the mid-1990s Thailand had given up its three-decade-long policy of national industrialization amidst the tremendous pressures for globalization.

Notes

1. Carl Dahlman and Peter Brimble, *Technology Strategy and Policy for Industrial Competitiveness: A Case Study of Thailand* (Washington, DC: World Bank, 1990), p. vii.

2. Ministerial Statement of Thailand at the APEC Ministerial Meeting on Human Resource Development, Manila, 8–11 January 1996.

3. Ibid.

4. Ibid.

5. CUSRI, *The Survey on Industrial Human Resource Development in the Kingdom of Thailand* (Bangkok: CUSRI, 1991), p. 61.

6. World Bank, *Decision and Change in Thailand: Three Studies in Support of the Seventh Plan* (Washington, DC: World Bank, 1991), p. 171.

7. World Bank, *Technology Strategy and Competitiveness* (Washington, DC: World Bank, 1990), p. vii.

8. Ibid., p. 64.

9. TDRI, *The S&T Manpower Situation in Thailand: An Analysis of Supply and Demand Issues* (Bangkok: TDRI, 1988), p. 85.

10. Ibid.

11. Ibid., p. 79.

12. TDRI, *Development of Machinery and the Equipment for Information Industries in Thailand* (Bangkok: TDRI, 1992), p. 133.

13. Ibid.

14. Ibid.

15. CUSRI, *Survey on Industrial Human Resource Development*, pp. 129–30.

16. United Nations Industrial Development Organization (UNIDO), *Changing Techno-Economic Environment in the Textile and Clothing Industry: Implications for the Role of Women in Asian Development Countries* (Bangkok: UNIDO, 1993), p. 28.

17. Interview, official of JETRO, anonymity requested, Bangkok, June 1993.

18. World Bank, *Technology Strategy and Competitiveness*, p. 27.

19. Ibid., p. 28.

20. Anupap Tiralap, unpublished thesis on electronics industry, Chapter 5, p. 10.

21. TDRI, *Development of Machinery*, p. 147.

22. TDRI, *The Barriers to and Strategies for Technology Acquisition* (Bangkok: TDRI, 1991), p. 173.

23. TDRI, *Private Sector R&D: 'Lessons from the Success'* (Bangkok: TDRI, 1993), p. 120.

24. Ibid.

25. TDRI, *Development of Machinery*, p. 98.

26. Ibid., p. 98.

27. Ibid.

28. UNIDO, *Industrial Development in Thailand in the 1990s: Prospects, Constraints, and Priority Areas for Technical Assistance* (Bangkok: UNIDO, 1990), p. 31.

29. Tiralap, pp. 5–23.

30. Ibid., pp. 5–9.

31. TDRI, *Future Potential of Electronics in Thailand* (Bangkok: TDRI, 1992), p. 47.

32. Anupap Tiralap, interview, Bangkok, 1 September 1993; see also TDRI, *Private Sector R&D*, pp. 92–108.

33. TDRI, *Private Sector R&D*, pp. 93, 95.

34. Tiralap.

35. Interview, anonymity requested, Bangkok, 29 April 1997. Unfortunately, the

one electronics enterprise, Alphatec Corporation, that took seriously the task of developing an R&D capacity in order to move from low-end assembly of computer chips to high-end innovation, collapsed in 1997 owing to bad financial management. See Peter Waldman and Paul Sherer, 'Alphatec's dubious actions foreshadowed Thai woes', *Asian Wall Street Journal*, 9 September 1997.

36. TDRI, *The Development of Thailand's Technological Capability in Industry* (Bangkok: TDRI, 1992), pp. 63–70.

37. Ibid., p. 69.

38. TDRI, *Case Studies of R&D Performance in Electronics* (Bangkok: TDRI, 1992), p. 126.

39. Ibid., p. 130.

40. Ibid., p. 109.

41. TDRI, *Private Sector R&D*, pp. 96–101.

42. Prayoon Showattana, 'Technology transfer in Thailand's electronic industry', in Shoichi Yamashita, ed., *Transfer of Japanese Technology and Management to the ASEAN Countries* (Tokyo: University of Tokyo Press, 1991), pp. 179–80.

43. Kovit Satavuthi, 'Industrial structure: the automobile industry', in Samart Chaisakul and Mikimasa Yoshida, eds, *The Thai Economy in the Changing Decade and Industrial Promotion Policy* (Tokyo: Institute of Developing Economies, 1990), p. 65.

44. Ibid.

45. Mingsarn Santikarn Kaosa-ard, 'TNC involvement in the Thai auto industry', *TDRI Quarterly Review*, March 1993, p. 13.

46. Richard Doner, 'Domestic coalitions and Japanese auto firms in Southeast Asia: a comparative bargaining study', Ph.D. dissertation, University of California at Berkeley, 1987, p. 456.

47. Mingsarn Santikarn Kaosa-ard.

48. Kovit Satavuthi, p. 69; Samart Chiasakul and Prasert Silalipat, 'The role of Japanese direct investment in developing countries: the case of Thailand', in *The Role of Japanese Direct Investment in Developing Countries* (Tokyo: Institute of Developing Economies, 1992), p. 188.

49. TDRI, *The Barriers to and Strategies for Technology Acquisition*, p. 61.

50. Ibid., p. 60.

51. Ibid.

52. Ichiro Sato, 'Comment' in Shoichi Yamashita, ed., *Transfer of Japanese Technology and Management to ASEAN Countries* (Tokyo: University of Tokyo Press, 1991), p. 196.

53. Chiasakul and Silalipat, p. 223.

54. Ibid., p. 248.

55. Johzen Takeuchi, '"Technology transfer" and Japan–Thai relations', in Yamashita, ed., *Transfer of Japanese Technology*, p. 215.

56. Ibid., p. 211.

57. Mingsarn Santikarn Kaosa-ard, p. 13.

58. Ibid., p. 9.

59. Japan Ministry of Finance figures.

60. Japan Ministry of Finance figures.

61. Richard Cronin, *Japanese and US Economic Involvement in Asia and the Pacific: Comparative Data and Analysis*, CRS Report for Congress (Washington: Congressional Research Service, 1994), p. 13.

62. Rob Steven, *Japan's New Imperialism* (Armonk, NY: ME Sharpe, 1990), p. 116.

63. Japan Ministry of Finance figures.

64. 'Deregulation the key to trade with Japan', *The Age* (Melbourne), 12 November 1994.

65. 'Japan's survival depends on ties of interdependence', *Asahi Evening News*, 4 December 1994, p. 3.

66. Japan Ministry of Finance figures.

67. TDRI, *Thailand's Economic Structure: Summary Report* (Bangkok: TDRI, 1992), pp. 2, 26.

68. Cronin, p. 12.

69. Toyota Motor Corporation.

70. East Asia Analytical Unit, Department of Foreign Affairs, Australia, *ASEAN Free Trade Area: Trading Bloc or Building Block?* (Canberra: East Asia Analytic Unit, 1994), p. 29.

71. Ibid., p. 8.

72. Quoted in ibid., p. 97.

73. Mingsarn Santikarn Kaosa-ard, p. 15.

74. Ibid.

75. 'Thailand gets nod as GM plant host', *Bangkok Post*, 31 May 1996, p. 15.

76. Quoted in Johzen, p. 214.

77. Japanese Ministry of Finance figures.

78. 'Japan's survival depends on ties of interdependence', *Asahi Evenine News*, 4 December 1994, p. 3.

79. Quoted in 'New Strategies toward Super-Asian Bloc', *This Is* (Tokyo), August 1992; reproduced in *FBIS Environment Report*, October 1992, p. 18.

80. Interview, foreign environmental specialist, anonymity requested, Bangkok, 24 March 1994; interview, environmental official, anonymity requested, Bangkok, 15 March 1996.

81. Interview, JETRO official, anonymity requested, June 1993.

82. Interview, managing director, Japanese firm, anonymity requested, Lad Krabang, January 1994.

83. Quoted in K. I. Woo, 'Doyen of Yamaichi Securities stays bullish on Thailand', *The Nation*, 18 July 1997.

CHAPTER 5

Labour and Capital

As in other countries in Southeast Asia, Thailand's industrialization has been largely propelled in recent times by two key incentives for foreign and domestic investors. One has been the assurance of what one foreign adviser called zero-investment in pollution control[1] – a policy that has made Bangkok one of the world's leading cities in terms of industrial pollution. The other has been cheap labour.

Emergence of the industrial working class

Thailand's industrialization began in earnest in the late 1950s. Nevertheless, the growing predominance of industry in the nation's economy was not paralleled by a proportional expansion of the industrial labour force. From 34 per cent of GDP in 1995, agriculture contributed only 12.4 per cent in 1985. Manufacturing's share shot up from 15.5 per cent to 26.1 per cent.[2] However, the proportion of the workforce engaged in agriculture fell only slightly, from 72.2 per cent in 1972 to 66.4 per cent in 1988. Even more slight was the rise in the manufacturing workforce during the same period – from 7.7 per cent to 8.4 per cent.[3] By 1988, there were only 2.4 million workers in the manufacturing sector, up from 500,000 in 1961.[4]

Most of the emerging industrial working class was concentrated in Bangkok. This concentration, its relatively small size, and the strategic weight of industry were factors that should have facilitated union organizing. However, fragmentation and dispersal of the labour force made this difficult. It was estimated that in 1980, 96 per cent of fifteen thousand manufacturing firms employed fewer than fifty workers and two-thirds employed fewer than ten.[5] Not surprisingly, state enterprises, which tended to concentrate larger numbers of workers than private factories, became the cutting edge of the drive to organize labour in the 1960s and 1970s.

Organizing labour

Even as a numerically limited force, however, organized labour was seen as a threat to elite interests in the 1970s. The cause for elite concern was the militant turn in labour organizing during the period 1973–76, when a parliamentary government reigned briefly in Thailand. The overthrow of the Thanom-Praphat military regime was accomplished by a diverse coalition of forces that included workers in an atmosphere of growing economic hardship provoked by the 1973 oil price rise and the government's identification with a failed US military adventure in Vietnam. The mood of the period is captured in the following account:

> The uprising ushered in a new era for workers, and the alliance and intellectual input from the students contributed significantly to the frequent success of the method of collective bargaining. During the last few months of 1973, 501 strikes took place involving 177,807 workers – the highest number of work stoppages in a year, ever. The strikes were spearheaded by state enterprise employees, who were generally better-organized than workers in the private sector.
>
> But the private sector employees followed suit. Soon workers from such diverse businesses as banks, hospitals, and taxi companies were making demands for better pay, benefits and working conditions to be on a par with the state enterprise employees.
>
> As demands were met, a wave of euphoria spread through the country's major industrial areas. Political awareness was at an unprecented high as workers nationwide rose to claim what they considered their rightful share of wages.[6]

Key strikes during this period included a five-day strike by 50,000 textile workers, most of them women, at Sanam Luang, in October 1993, and a massive street protest by over 80,000 workers at the Rama V Monument outside the Government House, which successfully pressured the government to postpone raising the price of rice.[7] Over a thousand strikes were registered in Thailand in that period, and by late 1976, some 185 unions had been formed.[8]

As it turned out, these were the best years of the labour movement in the postwar period, where it achieved some degree of unity, in two formations: the left-leaning Labour Coordination Centre of Thailand (LCCT) and the more moderate 'labourist-oriented' Federation of Labour Unions of Thailand (FLUT), which included mainly state enterprise unions. At this time, what would serve as Thailand's basic labour law was also passed: the Labour Relations Act of 1975. This milestone law, according to Professor Nikhom Chandravithun, transformed what were then regarded in law only as 'workers' associations' into full-fledged labour unions that could represent workers in the collective bargaining process.[9] It required that all undertakings having twenty or more workers have agreements on conditions of employment that would cover hours and time of work, wages, welfare benefits, procedure for the submission of grievances, and termination of employment.[10] It also allowed unions to be recognized along enterprise lines or industrial lines and permitted them to be amalgamated into new unions or formed into federations for collective bargaining. Moreover, that they could form a national organization was now recognized.[11]

There was, however, another view of the 1975 Labour Law, and this saw it as a response by government and management to the upsurge of workers' strikes in the 1973–76 period. As one account put it, the act 'was a result of the government and company management deciding to go to Parliament together ... to "put the lid on labour unrest ... . Management ... was given new and absolute powers to lay off and dismiss their workers, even for "not being able to get along with the employee" till today workers, particularly trade unionists, are dismissed in this manner, making it a convenient way ... to destroy unions.'[12] The law, among other things, forbade state enterprise workers from striking – a precedent that would be later expanded to ban state enterprise unions altogether under succeeding authoritarian regimes.

As it was, the labour union movement would never again reach the level of prominence that it achieved in the period 1973–76. When the military returned to power in the October 1976 coup that overthrew the democratic government of Seni Pramoj, organized labour was a special target. And like the peasant and student movements, the workers' movement was forced underground by the repression, with violent methods used to disperse strikes and even several union leaders murdered.[13] Strikes and assemblies were banned. Employees of state enterprises, which had been the leading edge of the workers' movement, were removed from coverage under the labour relations law by being classified as 'civil servants'.

Nevertheless, as Mabry and Kundhol point out, the military recognized that 'attempts to suppress worker organizations would merely drive them underground, politicize them, and perhaps radicalize them'.[14] Thus more pragmatic elements in successive military-dominated regimes began to relax controls, and among the measures taken were restoring enterprise workers to coverage under the labour relations law, eliminating restrictions on the rights of unions to assemble, and a more relaxed policy toward protest demonstrations and strikes, which were still formally banned under martial law. Cautious liberalization was the order of the day under the regimes of General Kriangsak Chamanan and General Prem Tinsulanonda.

But probably the key effort under the succeeding regimes was, as two analysts put it, 'to reinforce the conservative force within the labour movement'.[15] Part of the strategy involved eroding the unity of the Labour Congress of Thailand (formerly the FLUT), which survived the 1976 coup, by supporting a rival leadership within it and sponsoring a rival federation, the National Free Labour Union Congress. This strategy of splitting and manipulating the labour movement to clip its power reached its height when a labour rally to protest against rising prices was instrumental in forcing Kriangsak to step down from power in favour of Prem in 1980. The assembly, which ended up calling for the resignation of

Kriangsak, 'was attributed to an arrangement between the chief of ISOC [the military intelligence agency] and one of the leaders of its surrogate labor federation, the NFLUC'.[16]

Union and federation leaders were manipulated by different factions of the elite to achieve particularistic interests, to the detriment of class solidarity. This politics of co-optation was, of course, not new, being a tradition that extended back to the late 1940s, one that resulted partly from what Pasuk and Baker describe as 'the military's internal power game to found bases of support'.[17] Many labour leaders began to form informal or, in some cases, formal links to key political personalities and political parties. In many sectors of the union movement, it was difficult to apply what three labour researchers said of the Thai union movement, even when they wrote in the early 1980s: 'Unlike the bureaucracy, parts of the business sector, the court-political groups, the unions are not built primarily on patron–client or "classmate" connections. Unions represent a new social entity, a group yet to be honored with invitation to Court and yet to link with political parties.'[18] Indeed, by the early 1990s, there were no fewer than three national labour leaders who were serving as senators in parliament, having been invited to take up these positions largely by conservative political forces.[19]

Despite intensified efforts to co-opt the labour movement, however, labour continued to be a force whose demands for better pay, freer conditions for organizing, and safer working conditions were a stimulus for democratization. True, intramural conflicts among top labour leaders as well as the aggressive push by state employees to increase their salaries, which were already considerably higher than those of private sector workers, led to some public disenchantment with unions.[20] But the campaign to push through the long-awaited Social Security Act in 1990 saw the unions being supported by students and non-governmental organizations.[21]

Not surprisingly, when the National Peacekeeping Council led by General Suchinda Kraprayoon overthrew the elected Chatichai government in 1991, one of its first acts was to dissolve unions in state enterprises. The significance of this move is underlined by Teena Gill:

> Before the coup nearly 60 per cent of the estimated 7 million workers in 69 state enterprises were organized under 123 unions. Being the single biggest organized section of the country's industrial workforce, they had played an important role in supporting struggles in the private sector where only 5.6 per cent of the more than 4.5 million workers are organized. In addition, the 'advisors' to private sector unions hailed from these larger state enterprises.[22]

The unions were replaced by emasculated bodies called 'employee associations', and even the formation of these bodies was made especially difficult by the fact that to be certified, at least 30 per cent of the workforce had to indicate their willingness to be part of it. Draconian penalties were levied against striking workers, including one year's imprisonment and a 20,000 baht fine. Moreover, the government's registrar of unions was granted what one foreign investigative body characterized as 'overly broad authority ... to oversee the internal affairs of state enterprise workers associations'.[23]

In classic fashion, the military regime also tried to pit one labour group against others. An instance of this occurred during the critical May 1992 events when one of the newly established national trade union centres organized a concert to fight drought on 17 May to draw the attention of workers planning to join a pro-democracy rally.[24] But while it cultivated some labour leaders, the Suchinda government was aggressively anti-labour. This thrust was best underlined by the disappearance of a well-known militant labour leader, Thanong Pho-An, head of the Labour Council of Thailand. It was strongly suspected that Thanong was murdered by forces close to the regime.

Though not in an organized fashion, workers participated in the May events that led to the ouster of the Suchinda dictatorship in May 1992. However, the new democratic government of Chuan Leekpai did not move to revoke the ban on unions in state enterprises, nor did it pursue a serious investigation of Thanong's disappearance. Despite the creation of a more liberal atmosphere, labour did not gain more clout during the democratic governments of Chuan Leekpai, Banharn Silapa-Archa, and Chaovalit Yongchaiyudh, all of which were much, much more responsive to the needs of foreign investors owing to their sense than only the massive inflow of foreign capital could maintain the momentum of rapid growth in Thailand.

Labour in the boom years

Labour's political clout did not match its growth in numbers. Owing largely to the inflow of foreign capital and the boom this triggered in the domestic economy, between 1985 and 1994, the number of workers and employees rose by 113 per cent, from 3.2 million to 6.8 million people. In percentage terms, workers and employees rose from 13.9 per cent to 20.6 per cent of the total workforce.[25] Within this sector, however, it is said that the workforce in the core manufacturing sector constituted only 2.5 million in the early 1990s – probably partly a reflection of the fact that the new wave of foreign investment tended to employ capital-intensive methods of production.[26]

In Thailand, the expanding working class continued to be concentrated mainly in Bangkok, which became overwhelmingly the centre of foreign investment-driven industrialization. The most significant source of the new workers was Isan or the northeast, the poorest region of Thailand. A very familiar sight during this period was trains coming into Bangkok's

Hualumpong train station disgorging hundreds of people fresh from Isan, who were met by labour recruiters or found themselves looking at railway station advertisements promising attractive job placements that, more often than not, did not live up to the conditions or salary levels promised.[27] It was also during this period that many villages in the northeast were depopulated of the middle generation, who went to work in Bangkok, leaving grandparents to look after the children. Indeed, many villages survived mainly on remittances from young workers in Bangkok.[28]

The conditions of this new class were far from ideal. Arunee Srito, deputy chairperson of the Labour Congress of Thailand, claimed that 60 per cent of more than 250,000 factories around the country paid their workers less than the minimum wage specified by law, which in 1996 was 157 baht ($6.20).[29] In Bangkok alone, complaints about not paying the minimum wage against over two thousand establishments were received by the Labour Protection and Welfare Division of the Labour and Social Welfare Ministry.[30]

However, with the rapid entry of foreign investors, conditions of labour tended to vary more. According to one national labour leader, Taiwanese and Koreans were the least preferred employers, given their hardline opposition to union organizing, dismal salaries, and poor working conditions. Thai employers were only slightly better. The Japanese were higher on the preference ladder, credited with providing generally better wages and working conditions. They were also more open to unions, though they made sure these were company unions. American and European firms were generally at the top of the list.[31]

Organizing the expanding working class did not become any easier in the early 1990s. As labour organizers have discovered in other countries, organizing recent migrants from the rural areas is an extremely challenging task. Indeed, analysts Pasuk and Baker see 'the gradual release of surplus labor from the countryside' as one of the two principal causes of the erosion of labour bargaining position, the other being the Thai authorities' conscious attempt to suppress independent labour organizing.[32] Also, dispersal continued to be the norm. Only 4.9 million out of the 11.7 million people in non-agricultural occupations were working in the 65,000 establishments with ten or more workers in 1990. Two-thirds of these establishments employed fewer than 50 workers. Indeed, there were only 725 establishments with more than 1,000 workers.[33] As Andrew Brown and Stephen Frenkel have underlined, 'the effects of rapid economic change have contributed to the fragmentation of the workforce. About a quarter of the workforce are self-employed, and a further 14 per cent are employed as household labor. Those who are employed as wage labor work in a diverse range of industries and occupations, many in small workplaces.'[34] In any event, unionization was appallingly low, with only 2 per cent of the private sector workforce organized into unions in 1990.[35]

Out of Thailand's 300,000 registered factories in 1996 there were only 900 unions, constituting only a 0.3 per cent unionization of factories.[36]

Nor were intra-labour rivalries less acute. As of 1996, there were eight national trade union centres, the biggest of which was the Labour Congress of Thailand, with 123,000 members in 139 trade unions and five federations. Also, there were 18 trade union federations that were registered.

As the parliamentary regimes of the 1990s kept their distance from labour because of their concern about maintaining the image of Thailand's workforce as a docile one in order to attract foreign investment, big business and the bureaucracy continued to pursue policies aimed at neutralizing labour. While most employers continued to maintain hardline policies against labour organizing, some business representatives and businessmen-politicians began to espouse a more liberal policy that would 'allow labor politics at the workplace' in order to take it away from the street. This section of the business elite worked with the bureaucracy to evolve a corporatist tripartite structure 'for setting the minimum wage, arbitrating disputes, and discussing government labor policy', and to push social security legislation.[37]

Businessmen and technocrats also evolved a mechanism that was successful in containing union organizing, especially in export-oriented industries: the industrial estate. By 1995, there were some 56 industrial estates throughout Thailand. Twenty-five of these were run either wholly by the Industrial Estate Authority of Thailand (IEAT) or jointly by the IEAT and the private sector. These estates, among them the huge Lat Krabang industrial estate on the outskirts of Bangkok and the Northern Region industrial estate in Lamphun, were patterned after those established in Taiwan and Singapore: they offered tax breaks, subsidized infrastucture, exemption or reduction in import and export taxes, and a variety of other incentives to foreign and local investors. But the main function of the industrial estates was to provide a site where foreign investment could be efficiently wedded to cheap labour. And one of the most important incentives was not written down in the promotional materials handed out to foreign investors: that the government would try its very best to maintain a union-free environment in the industrial estate. 'One of the reasons we set up shop here', said one personnel manager of a Japanese firm at the huge Lat Krabang industrial site, 'is that we won't have to deal with unions. Now, there are unions around, but by and large we've been successful in keeping out undesirable unions.'[38] Their efforts were not totally successful, however: especially among Taiwanese and Korean firms, efforts to organize independent unions in Lat Krabang were making some headway in the early 1990s.

Working women

One of the most notable features of the last decade has been the rapid incorporation of women into the industrial labour force, a development that has had significant implications for the status and role of women. The proportion of adult women joining the industrial labour force has risen markedly. With a more than 76.3 per cent female labour force participation rate, it is one of the highest in the world – higher than, for instance, Hong Kong (48.6 per cent), Japan (48.6 per cent), and South Korea (44.9 per cent).

In particular, there has been a rapid increase in women working in the export-oriented manufacturing sector, where Thailand's rate of growth of total industrial output and employment has been the fastest. The exports of manufactures are made up primarily of the kinds of goods produced by female labour, so that, as one analyst puts it, in the South, 'industrialization in the postwar period has been as much female led as export led'. The rapid growth of manufactured exports has therefore led to a specific demand for easily exploitable low-wage female labour and a fast growth of female employment in industry.[39] Depending on the sector, women make up between 50 per cent and 95 per cent of factory workers. They are concentrated in industrial lines that produce Thailand's key exports: garments and footwear, where 78.8 per cent of the workforce are women, textiles (95 per cent), leather goods (100 per cent), precious stones (52.2 per cent), and food processing (51.1 per cent).[40]

If one includes the tourist, entertainment, and sex industries that play such a key role in Thailand's present economy, then the role of women is even more pronounced. In what Mathana Phrananiramai classifies as the 'amusement industry' 45.5 per cent of the workforce are women, as are 66.3 per cent of those in 'personal services'.[41] Accurate figures on women working in the sex industry are, of course, difficult to pin down, and they range from the Ministry of Labour's estimate of 500,000 to some NGOs' figures of 800,000 to one million.[42] In any event, in 1989, female-dominated labour-intensive industries were said to have generated nearly 50 per cent of Thailand's GDP.[43]

When asked why there are mostly female employees in their factories, the common reply of managers is that women's fingers are more nimble and suitable for tedious work. Indeed, one personnel manager at a Taiwanese firm at Lat Krabang stated, with no indication that he was being ironic, that 'Thai women, because of their long fingers, are particularly adept at assembly work'.[44] However, one can guess their reasoning goes beyond this. Factory owners and management are well aware that the majority of the workers are young, poor, uneducated women from the rural areas of Thailand. They exploit the fact that due to cultural and economic circumstances these young women are more submissive and compliant than men. Studies show that because of their obligations to their families and lack of economic alternatives, poor, uneducated women are more willing to endure poor working conditions, and to do tedious work for lower wages.[45] Furthermore, working environments are even set up to discourage married women with young children – for instance, it is common for large factories to provide dormitories for single, female workers exclusively. Many employers practise employment discrimination against married women because of the belief that married women are absent from work more frequently than single women and less devoted to work due to other household responsibilities.[46] Furthermore, the new pregnancy and maternity leave law has been strengthened and is seen as a drain on company finances.

Across the globe there are marked gender differences in the sectoral distribution of labour, employment status, average earnings, and promotional prospects.[47] Following the global trend, there is a substantial wage gap between the sexes in Thailand. In 1989, for instance, it was estimated that women's wages were, on average, 20 per cent lower than those of men.[48] Most of this difference in earnings is attributable to the unequal distribution of male and female workers in different types of jobs according to their wage level.[49] Even in heavily feminized industries, such as manufacturing, men form the majority of those occupying supervisory positions. According to Kate Young, 'a task is first defined as women's work, then the wage rate for unskilled work is set for it'.[50] The majority of Thailand's female workers are economically trapped in jobs with no promotion opportunities; women are concentrated at the lower-end of the job scale, without formal responsibility for production and decision-making rights within their place of work; and most women are denied jobs that entail training for higher levels of complexity, which are accordingly better paid.

Unfortunately, the gender divide also manifests itself in the ranks of the trade union movement. One of the country's most prominent labour leaders, Arunee Srito, has been active in the labour movement for many years. Over twenty years ago Srito began working as a factory worker in the Thai Krieng (Thai Durable) Textile Company and soon after became active in labour organizing. Today she is one of the strongest women leaders in the country. Srito was formerly president of the Thai Krieng Labour Union and president of the Federation of Textile Union (mother organization of 26 textile labour unions with a membership of 20,000, of whom 88 per cent are women), chairperson of the Campaign Committee on Health and Safety of Workers, and chief of the Thai Trade Union Congress, Women's Affairs Section.

However, Arunee stands out in a sea of men. Among 839 labour unions in 1993, men accounted for 60 per cent of total membership, while women accounted for 31 per cent of the total. In the mixed unions, there were only nine female chairpersons.[51] And even though women outnumber men in textile union membership, men dominate the decision-making positions.

Hazards at work

A great many of Thailand's working men and women labour under hazardous working conditions. Indeed, the statistics are rather disturbing. The numbers of occupation-related deaths increased from 282 in 1988 to 927 in 1996. The injury rate per 1,000 workers rose from 32 in 1988 to 44.4 in 1995. And when compared to Korea – widely known for its poor record when it comes to occupational safety – Thailand has a worse record: an injury rate of 43 per 1,000 employees in 1992, compared to Korea's 15 per 1,000.[52] An excerpt from *Thailand's Report on The Status of Women and Platform for Action for the Fourth World Conference on Women, Beijing, China, 1995* describes the kinds of acute health hazards affecting women in Thailand's factories:

> A study of the health status of female industrial workers in Thailand found that during a ten-year period female workers in textile factories had been sick at the average occurrence rate of 30 per cent. Women workers in the electronic industries had been suffering from exposure to lead, aluminum, trichloroethylene and often hundreds of other chemicals at work. The prevalence of abnormal lead levels of those women workers in the large electronic industries was 36 per cent, 24 per cent higher than that of traffic police in Bangkok exposed to lead oxide from vehicle exhausts. The women workers affected by lead poisoning in Thailand became ill with encephaloneuropathy, hematopathy, nephropathy and disorders of the gastro-intestinal tract and reproductive function. Such poisoning and consequent diseases also caused spontaneous abortion among women workers, abnormal birth outcomes and in their children delayed growth and mental development.[53]

Mysterious deaths in Lamphun   In the mid-1990s two tragedies underlined the poor state of occupational safety in Thailand. The first was the case of eleven young workers at the Lamphun industrial estate who died suddenly and mysteriously in 1993 and 1994, along with two child dependants. The official government report claimed that the most of the workers had tested positive for HIV and had died of AIDS-related diseases. However, the fact that the workers who died were in their prime, in their early twenties, and were reported by workers to be in fairly healthy condition caused scepticism about the diagnosis. As one respondent said, 'People develop AIDS several years after they become HIV-positive. They do not suddenly die.'[54] Moreover, the same report admitted that two of the remaining workers had died from encephalitis, a brain disease 'with a suspected occupational etiology', and the other two had worked with substances such as toluene.[55]

With no independent commission allowed to investigate the deaths, their link to the workplace remains undetermined. However, interviews carried out in Lamphun underlined the belief of many residents and co-workers that exposure to substances used in electronics production was the cause of death. Mayuli Tewiya, a young woman who worked at the Electro-Ceramics Co. Ltd of Japan, was stricken by many of the same symptoms that struck other workers who died: severe headaches and pains which made it impossible to work. Mayuli, whose work was punching substrate boards from alumina, was diagnosed as probably suffering from metallic, specifically aluminum, poisoning, by doctors at a private hospital, but this was not confirmed by doctors at the industrial estate clinic. Tested for HIV, she turned out negative.[56] Mayuli was later examined by one of the country's leading occupational health specialists, Dr Oraphan Meta-dilogkul, who asserted that aluminum poisoning was the culprit: 'The amount of alumina in her body finally accumulated to the point that it started to harm her brain and nervous system.'[57]

Two months after Mayuli was stricken, a co-worker doing the same work at the same company, Wongdeuan Nochote, died suddenly. Wong-deuan was described by a friend interviewed as very healthy and very industrious at the time she collapsed at her work and died. She tested negative for HIV, and her co-workers strongly suspected metallic poison-ing.[58] A confidential medical report, obtained by one newspaper, later confirmed this: cranial tomography indicates that the most likely cause of Wongdeuan's death was encephalitis or inflammation of the brain caused by overexposure to chemicals in the workplace:

> To make ceramic circuit boards, the factory required 750 kg of alumina and trichloroethane every other day. Both chemicals can be dangerous at high levels. Other poisonous chemicals were used such as MBK, glycerine, acetone. 'DOP' and 'D-160' were chemicals not identified on containers. Wongdeuan and her fellow workers never received clear information about chemicals they were in contact with, and in what ways they could be dangerous.
>
> In the substrate printing department there was a lot of dust, an odorous smell and loud noises. Nose masks and ear plugs had to be used. Dust was clearly falling to the floor. Ventilation systems in the work area were not sufficient, and chemical dust and smells were not adequately dispersed. The work area was not very big, with over a hundred workers in the department.
>
> Wongdeuan's duties were to control the punch machine printing around 10,000 substrate boards a day.
>
> She never took holidays, working night shifts and overtime; her salary before death was 5,320 baht.
>
> While at work, she often had tolerable symptoms of headaches, for which she used local medicines, just as a great many fellow workers with headaches.
>
> Fellow workers showed high levels of alumina: One case had 560 micrograms of aluminium in lymph, 116 micrograms per cent in urine. A control group in the same age group showed aluminium levels of 7 micrograms in urine ...

Many of Wongdeuan's fellow workers had had headaches, and quit. One worker was 3 months pregnant and had a miscarriage. Another missed her periods, becoming pale and drawn. Other people suffering the same kind of violent head-aches were diagnosed by doctors ... as being poisoned by alumina at work ... The report thus reached this somber conclusion: that Wongdeuan had died from encephalitis, suspected to be from poisonous chemicals in her workplace.[59]

However, in spite of strong evidence that toxic poisoning in the workplace was the cause of the death of the workers, no serious official medical investigation has yet been conducted of the Lamphun tragedy – which testifies, according to some, to the extent to which the government will go to protect the interests of foreign investors.

The Kader fire   The other major incident that drew attention to the dismal state of working conditions was the fire on 10 May 1993 in an export processing zone 20 km from Bangkok. At the Kader Industrial (Thailand) Toy Co., a joint venture of Taiwanese, Hong Kong, and Thai business interests, 189 factory workers were killed, 17 were reported missing and 444 were injured. It was the world's worst ever factory fire.

Even before the fire, authorities already knew of Kader's appalling safety conditions. In fact, the industrial safety department of the Thai Labour Ministry had issued several warnings to Kader, which was partly owned by the powerful Thai CP (Charoen Phokphand) Group. The building's fire prevention system was poorly constructed and illegally modified; there were no fire alarms or extinguishing equipment. Fire exits were blocked and all exits, except for the main entrance, were sealed shut. Not surprisingly, when the fire broke out, the factory became a death-trap. As one account put it:

high casualties from the incident were not caused by the outbreak of fire itself. Poor construction resulted in the factory building collapsing less than half an hour after it caught fire. Many workers were crushed to death by the tumbling building. Others had to jump from upper floors because there were no fire exits.[60]

Soon afterwards, one factory worker was scapegoated for starting the fire with a cigarette. However, after much pressure was applied by Thai NGOs, with help from the media, a local outcry and threats of an international product boycott led to government action. After lengthy negotiations, the company ended up paying 100,000 baht ($4,000) to the relatives of each dead worker – far less than the demand for 300,000 advanced by a workers' support group. As for government promises to help the victims and penalize Kader, nothing developed. Two executives of the company were arrested but were later released on bail. No civil proceedings were brought against the company. As in many other cases, the Kader fire incident simply wound down, with no sanctions imposed on the offending corporation. In the eyes of many, Kader was one more instance of the government dragging its feet in protecting its citizens in the interest of not endangering a pro-foreign investment economic policy.

Squeezing labour for international competitiveness

In the late 1980s, it became increasingly clear that with the rise in wages accompanying rapid economic development, Thailand might soon price itself out of the competition for labour-intensive production and faced being upstaged by lower-wage countries like Vietnam and China. The preferred option of many analysts was upgrading the skills of the labour force via reforms in the educational system. Thailand's secondary school enrolment ratio, 30 per cent, was lower than that in Malaysia, Indonesia, and the Philippines.[61] This translated into some 20 million of the workforce of 30 million being essentially unskilled.[62] There was no sign, however, that either the government or the private sector planned to do anything about this, with few vocational or retraining programmes in sight in the mid-1990s.

Companies talked about moving into more technology-intensive production, that is bringing in more sophisticated machinery, shedding labour, and making the smaller workforce more efficient. Labour was, however, sceptical about this rationale, and the conflict came to a head in the struggle at the Thai Durable Textile Company in 1993. All sides felt that the stakes were high. As one account put it: 'On one side are the 800,000 textile workers whose jobs are threatened by new technology; on the other, the textile companies whose very survival in a global market depends on shedding workers and converting to high-tech production.'[63]

To the company, it was a question of meeting the competition from low wage countries like China, Vietnam, Pakistan, and India by replacing 545 old looms with 200 'high tech air jet looms'.[64] This move would entail sacking 376 workers. From the perspective of the workers, however, there was a great deal of questioning whether the company was really planning to go high-tech or was simply planning to find ways of utilizing cheaper, non-unionized labour. One of the workers sacked, Arunee Srito, the president of the union, said that the question from the workers' perspective was not just the level of severance pay, the company's failure to offer retraining, or its inhumane laying off of workers with long-time service like her, who had been working in the company for some 20 years. It was, from her perspective, part of a strategy that would ultimately rely once more on cheap labour: 'the company is gradually replacing older workers with younger ones ... Old workers are more efficient, because they have more experience, but the company prefers young workers – they are cheaper. They're also docile, afraid, and know nothing about strikes.'[65]

In a massive show of force, the 10,000 workers, most from Thai Durable and other textile companies threatened by massive layoffs, staged a march in front of the government house, an act which pressured the government to order the company to reinstate workers pending negotiations. The conflict eventually settled down to a stalemate, with the government offering the remaining workers better pay but still refusing to push the company into taking most of the laid-off workers back.

As it was, the suspicions of Thai workers about the motivations of employers were not unfounded. True, some firms did adopt new labour-saving machinery, and it is estimated that between 1993 to 1995 roughly 10,000 women labourers in Thailand were replaced by machines.[66] But for the most part, the Thai textile and garments industry remained, as did many sectors of industry, tremendously backward in terms of basic machinery throughout the 1990s. The reason was not, however, mainly workers' resistance but the preference of many manufacturers to invest their capital in speculative investment, either in the stock market or in real estate. As one Bangkok Bank specialist asserted, 'the manufacturers failed to keep their products competitive in world markets by investing in research and development and upgrading workers' skills. Instead, they gambled their profits in real estate.'[67] Or, in the pithy words of a prominent investment firm, in the normal course of events, manufacturers would have 'gradually moved upmarket to more sophisticated products. In Thailand for the last several years many of them have put their manufacturing businesses on the backburner and devoted all the money to property instead. Now they are starting to come back to manufacturing but the pots and pans shop is still a pots and pans shop and the money it needs has vanished into property.'[68]

Instead of shifting to high-tech production with a more skilled workforce, Thailand's manufacturers took the easy way out: relying on ever cheaper labour. Some companies behaved in a draconian manner. For instance, Suzuki Thai Motorcycle Company laid off hundreds, then replaced them with new workers.[69] But there were methods less draconian in implementation but equally drastic in their results, such as reducing the size of factories to contain production costs and inhibit unionizing, and farming out more and more production to temporary workers, contract workers, and migrant workers.[70] All this came under the operative slogan of 'flexibility to meet the competition'. Summing up the results of various studies of trends in the late 1980s, one analyst reported that:

> there are indications that both casualization and subcontracting have increased throughout Thai industry in recent years. Survey data collected for the Thai Development Research Institute show that the ratio of temporary and contract workers outside the Bangkok area has increased significantly over the 1980s. A 1988 labour survey in the Bangkok area found that about 19 per cent of factory workers were employed on a temporary basis ... A more focused survey of

four industrial areas near Bangkok showed a rapid increase in the number of firms employing at least 20 per cent of their workforce on a temporary basis between 1983 and 1988. In one industrial area, over 60 per cent of all workers were employed on a temporary basis in 31 surveyed factories.[71]

The author emphasized that 'in many cases, the decision to make increased use of temporary workers has followed labour disputes or worker efforts to establish labour unions'.[72]

The Eden Company, maker of Mickey Mouse and Bugs Bunny wear for Walt Disney Corporation, became the key symbol of how the new strategy of flexibility was impacting on workers. Through various means – including, some critics say, the use of child labour – Eden managed to reduce its workforce from 4,000 workers in 1991 to 1,000 by 1996. Other companies took more drastic action: an artificial flowers company in a Bangkok suburb first farmed out the more labour-intensive parts of the flower-making process to subcontractors, paid 50 baht, compared to 157 for a factory worker, then went on to dispense with factory workers altogether, retaining only an office to 'receive orders and send jobs to subcontractors'.[73]

Child labour and migrant labour

Two means of cost reduction have received much attention in recent years: child labour and migrant labour. While employers' groups vehemently deny that using children has become a means of remaining competitive, the fact is that child labour is prevalent in manufacturing work in Bangkok. NGOs estimate that there are about 500,000 children below the age of twelve employed in commerce and industry throughout Thailand.[74] In 1993, the Department of Social Welfare and Labour Protection inspected about 30,000 companies and found 21,648 children in 5,400 of them. However, the department admits to only 95,000 to 120,000 child workers in the industrial sector.[75]

The other controversial cost-cutting measure has been the reliance on migrant, mainly undocumented, workers. Owing to unattractive economic conditions in their home countries or to political repression or to both, hundreds of thousands of people from neighbouring countries have flocked to Thailand in search of jobs. According to the Immigration Department, Thailand in 1994 sheltered 525,480 undocumented migrant workers. An astounding 334,123 were found to be Burmese, and about 100,000 each of Chinese and Indochinese nationalities were detailed. Pakistani, Bangladeshi, Nepalese, and Sri Lankans totalled 81,357.[76] To many NGOs, however, the official figures were underestimates, and that a more realistic estimate was that there were about one million undocumented workers.[77]

Migrant workers do not have an easy time in Thailand, especially the

Burmese, who have in recent years become subject to physical attacks from Thais for a variety of reasons, including resentment stemming from the perception that they are taking away jobs from Thais. At the same time, Burmese workers have been tagged as potential or actual spies by the Thai government, with one Thai legislator claiming that 'many Burmese are sent to work as assistants or maids in the houses of prominent public figures, where they try to gather information or steal state secrets'.[78] As in other countries, migrant workers have, in other words, become a political football, a convenient scapegoat for different interests.

For employers, however, they have become a convenient source of cheap labour that keeps down wage levels. A study by Voravidh Chareoanlert and Bandit Tanachaisettawut has esitmated that Thai employers have been able to save about Bt.12.94 billion ($516 million) a year owing mainly to the lower wages they give to undocumented workers.[79] Not surprisingly, employers formed one of the pressure groups behind the government's 1996 decision to legalize some 742,000 undocumented workers and allow them to work in fisheries, agriculture, mining, construction, salt-farming, and brick and jar making. While government and business claimed that this move was necessary owing to a shortage of Thai workers, labour, academics, and NGOs claim that the real aim was to create a force that would dampen wages and make the formation of unions more difficult. Critics claimed here was no real shortage of workers, or that Thais were unwilling to take on certain jobs, like those that would involve work in the fields. The problem was not the work but the wages, and instead of paying decent wages, employers preferred to squeeze more profits by relying on a 'second-class tier of workers who are allowed to work only in the "most dirty, difficult, and dangerous" fields'.[80]

But the opposition to legalizing undocumented workers went beyond the question of job displacement for many Thais. The workers and their families made use of public services, such as medical care, which meant that the public, rather than the employers, had to shoulder part of the burden for their being in the country. It was also argued that Thailand would 'become both a refugee state and a safe haven for continuous flows of illegal workers from other countries and a transit center for the trafficking of human beings, particularly children and women'.[81]

The debate on the status of undocumented workers continues and has, in fact, intensified with Thailand's recent economic collapse. Often, however, the arguments obscure the real-life tragedies that the workers suffer, be they legal or illegal. A particularly poignant story was told by one Burmese worker, whose experience parallels in many ways those of many other people from Thailand's neighbouring state, where the political situation cannot be divorced from their reasons for escaping into Thailand. He was hospitalized after the truck he was transported in, with other undocumented workers, caught fire.

'I had a rubber plantation back home, but I didn't have much time to look after it,' said U Hla, pointing out that the forced labor system in Burma prevented him from earning his income at home.

'Once in a while, men in our village would be summoned as porters for the Burmese army. At other times, we had to serve as laborers for the government's construction project. It was very tough and laborious work. If we dont want to do the job, we have to pay money as a substitute, or we may be put in jail,' he said.

After five months working as a construction worker in Thailand, U Hla returned to his family in Burma with about Bt 15,000. Less than a month had passed before he decided to come back, this time with his 27-year-old brother.

'If you went around several Burmese villages, you would see that there are hardly any people [of working age] left. Getting across the border into Thailand is not too difficult. There are people who would arrange things for you at the border and there are others who travel around rural Burmese villages acting as a broker, asking villagers to come to work in Thailand,' explained U Hla.

'Burma is a nation with plenty of natural resources. We have gold, silver, and gemstones. If we had a good government, our people would be able to make a fair enough living. In that case we would not have to participate in slave labor in another country,' said U Hla.[82]

Losing strategy

As many academics had warned, squeezing labour to regain a competitive edge was the wrong strategy for Thailand. For as Chulalongkorn University economist Lae Dilokvidhyarat noted, wages take up only 10 per cent of overall production cost, so that gains from getting even cheaper labour are quite marginal. What is key is how the other 90 per cent of investment is deployed, and it was in this area – which included investment in human resource development and sophisticated machinery – that Thai manufacturers were severely deficient. As observers noted, the zero growth in exports in 1996 was not just a conjunctural trade crisis but a structural crisis that represented the failure of a strategy that went for the easy way of squeezing labour rather than the more strategic route of investing in human resource development, sophisticated machinery, and research and development.

While the high growth rate had managed to stave off massive labour discontent for most of the previous decade, 1996, with its zero export growth, was another story – one of reduced industrial output, lower profits, fewer wage increases, and reduction or elimination of bonuses. It was not surprising that worker discontent reached higher levels. What was surprising was that the most dramatic manifestation of this discontent would surface at a Japanese company, given the fact that even among workers, the Japanese were known to be more more accommodating to workers than Thai, Taiwanese, or Korean entrepreneurs. Angry that management had decided to reduce drastically their year-end bonuses from 1995 levels, workers burned down the Sanyo Universal Electric Companys factory in Bangkok.

Economic collapse and class conflict

But even labour was stunned by the speed with which the Thai economy unravelled in the first half of 1997. While the layoffs hit the financial sector first – some 50,000 workers, by some estimates – there was no doubt that the impact on the real economy would come soon. With the finance minister predicting that 10 per cent of the workforce, or 2.9 million people, would be out of work by December 1997, labour was understandably agitated enough to contribute contingents to the rallies supporting the country's new draft constitution and workers' rights in September, under banners that read: 'Poor people pay off the debt while evil capitalists sell off the country'.[83]

But organized action continued to be hindered by the fragmentation and rivalries in the labour force, and it was likely that the response to the deepening economic crisis would be more like the torching of Sanyo, angry but spontaneous. These fears came true on 21 January 1998. When the management of the Thai Summit Auto Parts Factory announced that it would not give workers the year-end bonuses they had been expecting, the workers, many of them chanting 'Sanyo, Sanyo' – referring to the torching of the Sanyo plant over a year earlier – staged what amounted to a mini-uprising. When they blocked the busy Bangna–Trat Highway, a veritable pitched battle ensued for several hours, which saw workers pitted against motorists and the police. The episode ended with the wholesale arrest of workers and their being herded prisoner-of-war fashion into police vans.

Said labour expert Professor Nikhom Chandravithun: 'This is what happens when you don't provide people with avenues to express their grievances. Because management has opposed the formation of effective unions, it is provoking anarchic expressions of this kind simply because people find they just don't have another channel to voice their demands.'[84]

Unfortunately this was unlikely to be an opinion that management and government would take seriously into account.

Notes

1. Interview, anonymity requested, 24 March 1994.
2. Figure from Nikhom Chandravithun, *Thailand: the Social Costs of Becoming the Fifth Tiger* (Washington, DC: Woodrow Wilson International Center, February 1995), Table 2.
3. Figure from ibid., Table 10.

4. Ibid., Table 10.

5. Andrew Brown and Stephen Frenkel, 'Union unevenness and insecurity in Thailand', in Stephen Frenkel, ed., *Organized Labor in the Asia–Pacific Region* (New York: ILR Press, 1993), p. 90.

6. Thana Poopat, 'Can unions rebound from the doldrums?', *The Nation*, 21 January 1996.

7. Chintana Ratanarak, 'Finding a life's work in labor', *Bangkok Post Sunday Magazine*, 13–19 August 1995, p. 11.

8. D. Morrell and S. Chaianan, quoted in Andrew Brown and Stephen Frenkel, p. 86.

9. Nikhom Chandravithun, *Thai Labor: A Long Journey* (Bangkok: Thai Watana Panich, 1982), p. 97.

10. Ibid., p. 98.

11. Ibid., p. 97.

12. Teena Gill, 'Thai labor: calm before the storm?', *The Nation*, 23 September, 1993.

13. Poopat.

14. Bevars Mabry and Kundhol Srisermbhok, 'Labor relations under martial law', *Asian Survey*, vol. XXV, no. 6, June 1985, p. 618.

15. Ibid.

16. Ibid.

17. Pasuk Phongphaichit and Chris Baker, *Thailand: Economy and Politics* (London: Oxford University Press, 1997), p. 185.

18. Jan Odhnoff, Bruce McFarlane, and Peter Limqueco, *Industrialization and the Labor Process in Thailand: The Bangkok Area* (Göteborg: ILO, 1983), p. 23.

19. Stefan Chrobot, *Trade Unions in Transition: Present Situation and Structure of the Thai Labor Movement* (Bangkok: Friedrich Ebert Stiftung, 1996), pp. 35–7.

20. Poopat.

21. Ibid.

22. Teena Gill, 'Thai labor: calm before the storm?', *The Nation*, 30 September 1993.

23. Trade Policy Staff Committee, United States Trade Representatives Office, 'Worker rights review summary: Thailand', Washington, DC, July 1993.

24. Sakool Zuesongham and Voravidh Charoenlet, 'Fragmentation of the trade unions: inevitable or not?', undated manuscript, p. 19.

25. Figure from Stefan Chrobot, p. 32.

26. Sakool Zuesongham and Voravidh Charoenlet.

27. See, among other accounts, 'The easiest of targets', *Bangkok Post*, 8 April 1996, p. 25.

28. Nikhom Chandravithun, *Thailand: The Social Costs*, p. 9.

29. 'Bittersweet problem worries labor officials', *The Nation*, 9 December 1996, p. C12.

30. 'Overworked, underpaid', *The Nation*, 9 December 1996.

31. Interview with labour leader, anonymity requested, Bangkok, April 1994.

32. Pasuk and Baker, p. 173.

33. Chandravithun, *Thailand: The Social Costs*, p. 4.

34. Brown and Frenkel, p. 90.

35. Fred Deyo, 'State, industrial restructuring, and human resource strategies: Thailand and East Asia', unpublished manuscript.

36. Interview, Somyot Pruksakasemsuk, director of the Center for Labor Information Service and Training (CLIST), Bangkok, June 1996.

37. Pasuk and Baker, p. 203.

38. Interview, personnel manager of Japanese company, anonymity requested, Lat Krabang Industrial Estate, 6 April 1994.

39. Susan Joekes, *Women in the World Economy* (New York: Oxford University Press), 1987, pp. 81–2.

40. Chandravithun, *Thailand: The Social Costs*, p. 6; also interview with Somyot Pruksakasemsuk, director of the Center for Labor Information Service and Training (CLIST), Bangkok, June 1996.

41. Cited in Chandravithun, *Thailand: The Social Costs*, p. 6.

42. Ibid.

43. Mathana Phananiramai, 'Women's economic roles in Thailand', paper presented by TDRI for Conference on Women and Industrialization, Seoul National University, September 1993, p. 9.

44. Interview, personnel manager of Taiwanese firm, anonymity requested, Lat Krabang Industrial Estate, September 1993.

45. *Young Women Workers in Manufacturing: A Case Study of Rapidly Industrializing Economies of the ESCAP Region*, United Nations study (Bangkok: Economic and Social Commission for Asia and the Pacific), 1987, pp. 3, 35.

46. Phananiramai, p. 22.

47. Kate Young, *Planning Development with Women: Making a World of Difference* (New York: St. Martin's Press), 1993, p. 71.

48. Chandravithun, *Thailand: The Social Costs*, p. 6.

49. Joekes, p. 18.

50. Young, p. 78.

51. *Thailand's Report on The Status of Women and Platform for Action for the Fourth World Conference on Women, Beijing, China, 1995* (Bangkok, Thailand: National Commission on Women's Affairs Office of the Prime Minister), p. 33.

52. Bundit Thanachaisathavit, 'Situation of victims of occupational diseases/harm in Thailand', unpublished factsheet, Labour NGOs Network, undated.

53. *Thailand's Report on The Status of Women and Platform for Action for the Fourth World Conference on Women, Beijing, China, 1995*, p. 27.

54. Kanlaya Todrabum, interview, 26 March 1994.

55. 'Life and death in Lamphun', *The Nation*, 28 October 1994, p. C1.

56. Mayuli Tewiya, interview, Lamphun, 27 March 1994.

57. Quoted in 'Industrial estates expansion pushed all over Thailand', *Thai Development Newsletter*, no. 31, 1996, p. 73.

58. Interviews, anonymity requested, Lamphun, 26 and 28 March 1994.

59. 'A painful way to go', *Thailand Times*, 12 December 1994, p. C1.

60. 'Fire kills at Thai toy factory', *Asian Labor Update*, no. 12, July 1993, p. 4.

61. CUSRI, *Survey on Industrial Human Resource Development in the Kingdom of Thailand* (Bangkok: CUSRI, 1991), p. 62.

62. Chitraporn Vanaspong, 'Lay-off crisis', *Bangkok Post*, 17 November 1996.

63. James Eckardt, 'High-tech shake-out', *Manager*, October 1993, p. 44.

64. Ibid.

65. Quoted in Ibid.

66. Supawadee Petrat and Jaded Chaowilai, 'How to support the rights of women workers in the context of trade liberalization: a perspective from Thailand', paper presented to Women Working Worldwide conference.

67. Interview, anonymity requested, Bangkok, 29 April 1997.

68. HG Asia, *Communiqué: Thailand* ('Thailand worth a nibble perhaps but not a bite') (Hong Kong: HG Asia, 1996). (Internet version.)

69. 'Workers issue strike threat', *Bangkok Post*, 8 July 1996, p. 1.

70. Somyot Pruksakasemsuk, *Globalization and the Situation of Thai Workers* (Bangkok: Center for Labor Information Service and Training, 1997).

71. Fred Deyo, 'State, industrial restructuring, and human resource strategies: Thailand and East Asia', unpublished manuscript.

72. Ibid.

73. Chitraporn Vanaspong, 'Lay-off crisis'.

74. Chandravithun, *Thailand: The Social Costs*, p. 7.

75. Ibid.

76. Chitraporn Vanaspong, 'Discovering the right path for human labor', *Bangkok Post*, 12 May 1996, p. 21.

77. Prangtip Daorueng, 'Workers flex muscles as business frets', *Interpress Service*, 6 January 1997.

78. 'Most illegal alien workers called spies', *The Nation*, 22 March 1996, p. 1.

79. Cited in 'An illegal population take root', *The Nation*, 2 June 1997.

80. Yindee Lertcharoenchok, 'Industrialists' cries of labor shortage prove to be a myth', *The Nation*, 2 June 1997.

81. Ibid.

82. Varaporn Chamsanit, 'Slaves to labor', *The Nation*, 31 January 1996.

83. Seth Mydans, 'In Thailand, once Asia's tiger, anger boils', *New York Times*, 17 September 1997.

84. Interview, Professor Nikhom Chandravithun, Bangkok, 20 February 1998.

CHAPTER 6

Bangkok: Vicissitudes of
a Megalopolis

To many people, Thailand is synonymous with Bangkok. This is not surprising, not only because the city is home to a significant portion of the country's population, but also because it concentrates so much of the nation's production and wealth and the needs of its elite dominate national decision-making. Bangkok, to the distress of many Thais, has also become a household word internationally, not only for its free-wheeling commercial sex but as an exemplar of the ecological crisis of urban-industrial society.

Three decades indeed make a difference. As recently as the late 1960s, one could refer with some approximation to reality to the 'placid canals and the pleasant, quiet, tree-lined streets of old Krung Thep'.[1] But beginning in the late 1950s, the opting for a strategy of rapid industrialization and modernization by the Sarit regime unleashed a burst of entrepreneurial energy that has transformed Bangkok from the 'Venice of the East' to a veritable Leviathan. Indeed, government has long since ceased to be able to control the forces of private capital that it let loose. In fact, from being the director of change, government has become the directed, and a great many of the city's problems stem from the dramatic failure of government to discipline and channel the energies of the private sector.

Prime among primates

Bangkok, it has long been noted, has occupied a position of primacy over its surroundings that has not been enjoyed by any other capital city in Southeast Asia. Bangkok's size, population-wise, rose from 43 times the size of the next biggest city (then Chiang Mai) to 51 times in 1980.[2] By 1988, Bangkok's primacy appeared to have declined, with Bangkok being only 27 times the size of the next largest city, then Nakhon Ratchasima.[3] But Bangkok's declining primacy could be an illusion, since the various indices of primacy used in urban measurements refer strictly to the area covered by the Bangkok Metropolitan Authority (BMA) and exclude the surrounding cities that now form the BMR (Bangkok Metropolitan Region). If the latter is used, say Peter Rimmer and Mehdi Krongkaew, 'the primacy index could be higher and counter any suggestions of polarization reversal'.[4] Currently, the BMR has nine million inhabitants, or 11 per cent of the total population of Thailand in 1990 – up from 8.1 per cent in 1990.[5]

Bangkok's supremacy over Thailand is, of course, nothing new. After the old royal capital of Ayuthaya was captured and sacked by the Burmese in 1765–67, the political and administrative centre of the kingdom was transferred first to Thonburi on the east side of the Chao Phraya River, then to Krung Thep – or what Westerners came to call Bangkok – in 1782. Since then, Bangkok has been synonymous with the rule of the reigning Chakri dynasty, inaugurated by King Rama I and continued today by King Bhumibol or Rama IX. In the last 215 years, integration into the national community has meant political and cultural subordination to the Bangkok-based rule and Central Thai culture for the formerly autonomous Lanna kingdom in the north, the Lao peoples on the eastern bank of the Mekong river in the northeast, and the heterogeneous communities of the south, which had a strong Muslim and Malay component.

Alongside Bangkok's administrative supremacy developed a commercial dominance, the spearheads of which were the Chinese and Europeans. Encouraged by Thai royal policies, peasants from what are now the Fujian and Guangdong provinces in China migrated to Thailand, where they were reincarnated over time as workers and merchants. They were valued by the Thai aristocracy for their ability to procure and move desired commodities and their serving as a tax base to sustain the aristocracy and the bureaucracy. Chinese merchants based in the traditional Chinese district of Sampeng soon came to dominate trade in a whole host of agricultural commodities, including rice.

The Europeans were a different story. They established their banks and commercial houses in Bangkok from a position of strength, as the Thai monarchs granted significant commercial concessions in order to prevent the country from being formally colonized. European, particularly British, merchant houses sought, in particular, to control two things: the extraction and export of natural resources useful for Western industries, like timber, and the import of manufactured goods, from textiles to cars, into the country. Bangkok thus became the centre for the economic colonization of Thailand and the springboard for the commercialization of economic relations in the rest of the country.

The Second World War not only ended the dominance of the European trading houses and banks, paving the way for the postwar dominance of the big Thai–Chinese commercial families. It also ended the Euro-oriented modernization carried out by the Thai government, which was especially pronounced under King Chulalongkorn or Rama V (1853–1910) and began

the strong influence of the USA and US-controlled agencies like the World
Bank on Thai development.

Los Angelizing the 'city of the angels'

Among the areas of strong US influence was urban planning, and here
one cannot overstress the critical importance of the Greater Bangkok
Plan 2533, produced by the American team Lichtfield and Associates in
1960. The Lichtfield team sought to restructure Bangkok around the
automobile, undoubtedly inspired by the concept of the automobile city
à la Los Angeles that was popular at the time in US urban planning. The
Lichtfield plan proposed the construction of over thirty highways to form
a 'ring road' and a star-shaped network of roads overlaying the existing
canal system. As Manop Bongsadadt has noted, although the Lichtfield
master-plan was never formally adopted, 'most of the proposals were
carried out through American funding. Many klongs were filled in, and
many roads were constructed. The Ring Road and Corridor Road system
of connecting regional cities were implemented, and Bangkok has been
an automobile city ever since.'[6]

What was problematic, of course, was that having committed themselves
strategically to the automobile, city planning authorities failed to follow
through on the infrastructure requirements following the initial construction of the basic road network. Until the first Bangkok Expressway
opened in the early 1980s, there had been very little public investment in
road construction.[7] By the late 1980s, the total length of roads – major,
minor, and access roads – came to only 2,800 kilometres, or a total of
only 38.44 square kilometres.[8] This figure comes to only about 2.5 per
cent of the total area of Bangkok, a figure that was 'far too low when
compared with the recognized standard in other cities of about 20–25 per
cent'.[9]

A crisis of major proportions ensued when this inertia in infrastructure
construction combined with a tremendous growth in the numbers of
motor vehicles. In the 1980s, the number of motor vehicles rose by 25
per cent a year, with the number of registered vehicles hitting two million
– of which a million were private cars – by 1990.[10] The situation worsened
in the early 1990s, with motor vehicle registrations growing by 450 automobiles and trucks per day, and motorcycle registrations by 410 per day.[11]
By the mid-1990s, Bangkok led all other big Asian cities when it came to
vehicles per kilometre: the Thai capital had 502 vehicles, while Kaoshiung
in Taiwan had 450 and Jakarta had 446.[12] At the rate cars were hitting
Bangkoks streets, noted a traffic management team from the Massachusetts
Institute of Technology (MIT), traffic flow management schemes 'will be
negated within a very short period of time'.[13]

Some transportation experts deride the surface public transportation

Table 6.1 Increase in registered vehicles, Bangkok, 1990–96

Type of vehicle	1990	1993	1996
Cars	598,223	727,054	1,026,233
Microbus and passenger pickup trucks	300,938	364,782	316,580
Vans and pickup trucks	268,598	272,190	462,803
Motorcycles	728,679	1,105,084	1,527,834

Source: Alpha Research Co., *Thailand in Figures*, 4th edn (Bangkok: Alpha Research, 1998), p. 167.

system, saying that buses are relatively scarce and old and most of them are not equipped with air conditioning.[14] On the other hand, with its mix of buses, boats, taxis, taxi-scooters (*tuktuk*), and 'taxi-motorcycles', Bangkok's public transportation system is a very flexible surface system, especially when one compares it to the systems in other Third World countries. It seems then that it is not the public transportation system that constituted the problem, but the inexorably worsening ratio of motor vehicles to road surface.

What seemed to be happening was that people were buying cars not only because they were a status symbol that could be indulged in owing to the rise in income brought about by the rapid economic growth. Cars, which were at least five times the average annual income of Bangkok residents, were also seen as a necessity simply because the public transportation system was not an attractive alternative for the emerging middle class. And, of course, more cars hitting the road made the situation even worse.

By the early 1990s, the MIT team concluded that Bangkok had 'possibly the worst traffic congestion of any city of similar size in the world'.[15] Average travel speed in the middle ring-road zone was measured at 7.7 kilometres per hour by a Japan International Cooperation Agency (JICA) study, with the rate as low as three to five kilometres in the most seriously congested places.[16] This situation had indelible impacts on personal and social behaviour, as Helen Ross's study, based on her interviews with urban residents, describes well:

> The impacts of the traffic, air pollution, and noise are unevenly distributed between locations and income groups. The different groups have different opportunities to adapt to the problem, and thus suffer different impacts from the traffic.
>
> The overwhelming impact of the transportation system is on people's time, which in turn has impacts on family life and health. People have little time at home to rest, spend time with their families and friends, or carry out their household responsibilities or recreational activities.

Car and bus commuters alike make astonishing arrangements to cope, at great expense to their well-being. Individuals and families go to some bizarre lengths to adapt. Whether or not the distance to be travelled is far, people will leave home early (5 or 6 am) to ensure a faster run through the traffic, even if this means commencing work one to two hours before they are required. Leaving early helps secure space on a bus, or a parking spot for middle-class owners.

The middle-class strive to own cars, often more than one per family, at extraordinary expense and sometimes hardship, to avoid uncomfortable and even slower bus travel.

The sense of control over one's route, timing, and personal environment seems particularly important. Air conditioning cocoons people away from the worst of the air pollution, and it is possible to conduct more essential domestic activities in a car than on the bus. Poorer people just suffer the delays and discomfort, and try not to think about it.

Middle-income families try to spend time and conduct essential domestic activities together in the car. Meals and preparation for the day are rushed, or carried out on the way to work. Travelling can account for a large proportion of the time couples and children spend together, and it is not unusual for children to be dressed, fed or do homework in the car.[17]

The response to the intense traffic congestion was a further Los Angelization of Bangkok, with the emphasis being put on the building of expressways. Following the completion of the 27.1-kilometre First Stage Expressway in 1987, three projects became operational by the end of 1996: part of the Second Stage Expressway (29.8 kilometres), the At Narong-Ramintra Expressway (18.7 kilometres), and the Don Muang Tollway (15.4 kilometres).[18] This was, however, a mere 91 kilometres opened up over a 13-year period, and people wondered how long the Expressway and Rapid Transit Authority (ETA) would be able to deliver the other 951 kilometres it promised to construct.

Ideology worsened the situation. In 1991, the technocrat government of Prime Minister Anand Panyarachun, believing in the efficacy of free markets, decreed sharp cuts in the import duties on completely built-up-units (CBUs) entering the country, resulting in a flood of imported cars in the early 1990s. Interestingly enough, the economic crash of 1997, brought about by the same free market forces that significantly worsened the traffic, had as one of its few positive side effects a significant easing of the situation, as 100,000 cars were repossessed from bankrupt owners in the last six months of that year.

Disneyland east: the mass transit chaos

To some other government authorities, the solution lay mainly not in more expressways but in building up mass transit systems. Indeed, plans for a more modern mass transit system began in the early 1970s, when a German team made studies over a four-year period and came up with a proposal to build a three-line electric system. About six mega-projects have been proposed since then, but decision-making has been paralysed by a number of factors. Perhaps most critical among these was the severe competition among different private contractors, who lined up different agencies in the bureaucracy behind their proposals, sometimes employing massive kickbacks to secure official approval. In the case of the Hopewell Network, for instance, the transport and communications minister was reported to have been given a substantial kickback to award the project to a Hong Kong-based mega-project construction group.[19] Another key project, the so-called Skytrain Network, was awarded to SNC-Lavalin of Canada in 1988 by the Interior Ministry, cancelled by a succeeding government under pressure from competing agencies and contractors, then resurrected again, this time as an underground system. Again, bureaucratic competition appeared to be greatly influenced by moneyed interests.

The bitter conflict among private interests and their allies in competing government ministries was inevitable in Bangkok's corrupt urban politics, since big money in government contracts was at stake: $2.4 billion in the case of the aborted Skytrain project, $3.2 billion in the case of the long-delayed Hopewell Network.[20]

The paralysis of decisionmaking on a mass transit system is a sign not only of the deterioration of the ability of government to engage in rational and forward planning, but also of the shift in the balance of power between the public and the private sector in favour of the latter. Much the same point is made by Helen Ross, who says that 'informal mechanisms, in which powerful interests move where they wish ... have a strong influence over the development of the landscape', with the result that '[c]entral administrations are unable to dictate what development is appropriate where, and master plans and zoning are largely a hollow exercise.'[21]

This is not, of course, to underplay the real problem of bureaucratic conflicts and inertia. There are, for instance, over fifty government agencies responsible for planning and decisionmaking on fiscal matters and investment projects.[22] In the area of transportation alone, four agencies have jurisdiction over road construction, five over transportation regulation, and three over transportation management.[23] No coordinating body exists to resolve conflicts among these agencies, since the Bangkok Metropolitan Administration has no control over roads and railways, buses, and traffic management.[24]

The result of this combination of money politics and bureaucratic competition was that planning or implementation of the rapid mass transit mega-projects proceeded without coordination, creating the possibility that more choke-points than now exist can emerge in the future. Lack of coordination posed problems at different intersections and elevations.[25] This was not an abstract fear, for even with the two ongoing or planned

projects (the 60-km Hopewell elevated road and train system, and the
BTSC's 23.7-km BMA Electric Train) and a third (the 21-km state-run
MRTA's underground system) likely to go forward, there are 30 locations
where the networks either crisscross each other or existing expressway
systems.[26] Not only are there no plans for crossing and interchange points,
but other fundamentals in transit construction have not been addressed,
including the integration of stations, the coordination of rolling stock
and operating practices, coordination of ticketing systems, and the integration of the networks with the existing bus system.[27] The absurdity of
the situation is underlined by Kraiyudth Dhiratayakinant:

> [I]f nothing is done, one of the mass transit systems would be travelling in the
> air about seven storeys off the ground at certain interchanges. The construction
> cost would be skyrocketing due to height alone ... It has been commented that
> if all three projects have been completed along with existing and planned
> expressways, the Bangkok Metropolis would look like a real world counterpart
> of Disneyland.[28]

Citizens versus mass transit

Out of frustration and anger with this chaotic situation a citizens' movement arose that was critical of the mass transit strategies. Leading this was
Khunying Chodchoy Sophonpanich of the civic organization Thai Environmental and Community Development ('Magic Eyes'), which had earlier led
a relatively successful effort to get Bangkokians to stop littering. Motivated
by environmental and safety concerns, physical space restrictions of the
inner city, and the desire to look out for the well-being of Bangkokians,
Chodchoy and her allies pushed for the right to information, and for a say
in how the mass transit projects were being built. It is useful to look
briefly at this struggle, for it exposed the flaws of technocratic decision-
making in Bangkok.

Up to March 1995, when a civil suit was filed by Chodchoy for the
right to information, there was little public information about three
ongoing and planned projects: the Hopewell-State Railway of Thailand
(SRT); the Bangkok Transportation System Corporation (BTSC), run by
the Tanayong Company and Bangkok Metropolitan Administration (BMA);
and the up-and-coming state-run Metropolitan Rapid Transit Authority
(MRTA) elevated railways.[29] Planning, design, construction, and financing
details were largely kept secret. Chodchoy[30] and her team of environmental
lawyers and activists made a critical contribution to the way Bangkokians
viewed the evolving fiasco of mass transit projects.

Beginning in July 1993 by taking out full-page advertisements in the
major English and Thai newspapers, Chodchoy and her group urged
Bangkokians to voice their opinions on the various mass transit projects.
From this juncture, things snowballed into a huge controversy. The

advertisements solicited a total of two thousand letters from the public. As the public became more and more aware of the real costs of the construction of the mass transit systems, the government had no choice but to hold a series of public hearings in 1995 to listen to concerns raised by various concerned groups and individuals. As a result, Chodchoy's group was able to gather critical data and research contributed by professionals, engineers, architects, and doctors on the socio-economic, environmental, and human health impacts of the planning, design, construction, and physical placements of the various mass transit projects.

The BTSC project, for example, would reduce the volume of traffic by only 6 per cent – making very little difference to the stated purpose of traffic reduction – and in fact would most likely encourage ownership of cars because people could be spurred on by the prospect of less traffic to drive. A 200-km mass rail network would be needed instead of the 23.7 km being built for a substantial impact on the reduction of traffic volume, according to authorities consulted by the the civic opposition.[31]

The planned BTSC structures would also contribute to severe air and noise pollution during and after construction. In many roads, the above-ground structures supporting the mass transit rail would be higher than the buildings, creating a tunnel effect where roads and sidewalks become air pollution traps. This air pollution can be prevented only if traffic decreases by 50 per cent after the sky train is completed.[32] The structures would also obliterate the sky, blocking sunlight from the inner city, which is polluted enough as it is.

Some parts of the train structure would be only one metre away from adjacent buildings. The Central Station would be 30 metres or 10 floors above ground, causing operating fans to blow polluted air against existing buildings. The tunnel effect is especially dangerous here because the dust particles, carbon dioxide, hydrocarbons, sulphides and nitrogen oxides would have no room for escape, exacerbating the dangers to the health of pedestrians and occupants of buildings adjacent to the station.[33] Another manifestation of the tunnel effect is the heightened noise pollution level, which is estimated by experts to be, at 86 decibels, higher than the 70 that is permissible.[34] The noise would not only affect pedestrians and occupants of buildings adjacent to the rail tracks, but would also reach commuters inside the trains due to its high volume.

Other significant issues are the loss of space taken by the BTSC structures, and safety concerns. Given the restrictions of small confines of space in inner parts of Bangkok, siting of rail structures in certain areas was almost physically impossible without severely cramping alternative uses of that space. In some roads, supporting rail structures take up as much as one-third of existing roads, or eat away up to two metres of sidewalks.[35] Chodchoy has argued that the road space could be allocated to public buses instead of increasing traffic congestion by the construction of rail structures. Not only would businesses along these narrowed sidewalks be affected, but the lives of pedestrians would be endangered by having to walk on roads during and possibly after construction.

Another safety issue is that of fire hazards. Due to the close proximity of buildings to the rail and station structures, there would not be space for the hoses and ladders of fire-engines to be manipulated into high-rise buildings. In January 1996, the Police Department assistant chief confirmed this for a fact, and also unsuccessfully called on the Bank of Thailand to reconsider lending to the project.[36]

Following public pressure, the Ministry of Science, Technology, and the Environment held a series of public hearings for which Chodchoy's group furnished data and figures on the social, environmental, health and economic costs of the various mass transit projects – especially the planned MRTA elevated train system – that had been obtained through painstaking empirical investigations done at the citizens' initiative. These hearings led to three positive gains. First, the government made a ruling that there would not be any elevated train structures permitted within 25 square km of inner Bangkok. Second, the government agreed with the protesters to site the state-run MRTA project underground instead of above ground. Third, a master-plan was drafted to tackle the mass transit problems in Bangkok.

But there was a hitch in the 25 square km ruling because the contract between BTSC and the BMA permitted elevated structures within this area, and so did the contract between Hopewell Thailand and the State Railway of Thailand. The government requested changes in the BTSC contract in compliance with the new ruling but were threatened with a lawsuit, and the BTSC elevated rail project proceeded as originally planned.

However, the fight was not over. Chodchoy was adamant that the public had a right to know of details of the BTSC project despite the absence of any changes in the original design and planning. With the backing of 77 individuals, Chodchoy sued the BMA and the governor of Bangkok – a first in the history of Thailand – for the release of information on the project. Chodchoy won. With the information obtained, she pointed out areas that required changing, and was successful in getting concessions from the BTSC project in three problematic areas.

The first was in the Supan Kwai area, where entire sidewalks would be taken up by structures supporting the railtracks. These structures are U-shaped, straddling roads and resting on sidewalks. Shopkeepers were angry at the prospects of losing customers, not to mention the air and noise pollution they would be subjected to during construction. Pedestrians would also be forced to walk on the roads, endangering their lives. It was finally conceded by BTSC that they would change the supporting structures to ones that were T-shaped.

The second concession concerned a station to be situated in front of an all-girls convent called Mater Dei. Parents and school authorities were worried about the impact of heightened air and noise pollution on the health of the students since the station would be situated adjacent to a fenced field where sports activities are carried out. There were also worries about the dangers to the students from mingling with the commuters. They demanded that the station be moved 80–100 metres further up the road. After much negotiation, BTSC agreed to halt further construction outside the school until a similar station being built on Silom Road is completed. The air and noise pollution resulting from the construction of the Silom station will be observed and studied, before a decision is made whether to proceed with construction at Mater Dei.

The third concession was the design of the railtracks coming down Pahonyothin Road towards Victory Monument. The original design curved so sharply that the trains would need to brake considerably, and could possibly topple over if the tracks were slippery after a heavy downpour. The original design truly stretched the limits of skytrain engineering, exhibiting the carelessness with which the project was designed.[37]

These were small concessions, and in order to get the project to be substantially revised, if not cancelled, Chodchoy and her group appealed to the World Bank, which held 20 per cent of the equity in BTSC via its private investment arm, the International Finance Corporation. The basis of Chodchoy's appeal was the Bank's own guidelines for lending, which compelled it to take environmental impact as a key consideration and committed it to hold public consultations on any project.

In a meeting in Washingon DC with World Bank officials, Chodchoy discovered that a BTSC-organized meeting, defined as a public consultation exercise, had actually taken place – attended by invited guests! When she protested that a public consultation must necessarily involve as much publicity as possible with open invitations to the public, she was told that it was not the position of the World Bank to question the authenticity of its clients' reports.

In the case of Hopewell, a citizens' movement was not needed to stop or modify it. Although the contract was signed in 1990, the project was late in meeting all its promised deadlines on key parts of the routes. It had the signs of a project that would go horribly wrong. Gordon Wu, the Hong Kong owner of Hopewell, had difficulty finding backers for his complicated multi-deck road and rail system. Besides financial viability, conflicts with other megaprojects, environmental problems, and land expropriation issues could not be resolved. Also known as BERTS (Bangkok Elevated Road and Train System), the original contract with the State Railway of Thailand cost a total of 80 billion baht (slightly over $3 billion).[38] However, by 1997, BERTS had skyrocketed to US$6 billion.[39] The baht devaluation July 1997 finally brought the grand scheme to an end. Construction stopped and it was reported that Gordon Wu wrote off HK$5 billion investment in Hopewell Thailand on 28 October 1997.[40]

Land management: unleashing the private sector

The situation in the transportation sector is really part of a much bigger problem, which is the near absence of effective planning in all dimensions of urban existence. Much the same situation exists in land use. That is, land use management by the authorities or zoning is nonexistent. Thus expansion has been largely spontaneous, determined almost solely by market forces. Bangkok has spread, as one description has it, 'horizontally and haphazardly'.[41] This must be qualified: government has played a role through its road construction programme, but this has been unplanned.[42] The process has usually been that major highways built on the urban frontier, which was then dominated by ricefields and other land devoted to agricultural uses, endowed land along the road with rising market value, bringing about what has been called 'ribbon development' or the unregulated expansion of both residential and commercial housing on both sides of the highway.

Housing developers then moved in, buying farm lots further from the highway on which they built housing estates, largely ignoring land subdivision regulations as well as building codes. While electricity and water were usually provided by developers, sewage disposal was not, and government was slow in picking up this function. Initially set up randomly on former paddies, the various developments were soon linked by a minor network of roads built up by developers over the rest of the agricultural land that was acquired. The provision of roads, however, was inadequate and without reference to a broader plan, so that it exacerbated congestion along the main public roads, as travellers had no access to secondary roads to get to their destination.[43] Later, one saw the emergence of shopping centres or malls, indeed, 'megamalls' to service the middle and lower middle classes in the housing estates, but with this process largely unregulated, this new building activity worsened an already chaotic situation. A good description of what is fast becoming a typical Bangkok neighbourhood is provided by the MIT team:

> Currently, massive development is occurring along already congested arterial streets, adding friction to the traffic and confounding the possibility of reserving transit lanes and managing traffic flows. In the centers of superblocks, large developments have occurred in locations with inadequate and tortured access, and without adding public open space or facilities. Pedestrians must navigate across broken sidewalks that are usually too narrow, through areas of uncontrolled street vending, across poorly drained areas, and in many cases are forced into dangerous roadways. Despite the quality of new buildings, which

Table 6.2 Informal settlements, dwellings, and households in Bangkok and vicinity

	Settlements	Dwellings	Households	Population
Bangkok (BMA)	1,032	129,033	177,593	852,500
Nonthaburi	88	6,929	9,941	48,000
Samut Prakan	278	28,849	36,063	173,000
Pathum Thani	44	3,818	5,167	25,000
Total	1,442	168,629	228,764	1,098,500[a]

Note: [a] In 1990, the population of the Bangkok metropolitan area was 6,396,000, which meant that some 17 per cent of the city's population lived in shantytowns.

Source: Yap Kioe Sheng, 'The slums of Bangkok', in Yap Kioe Sheng, ed., *Low-income Housing: A Review of Some Housing Submarkets*, HSD Monograph 25 (Bangkok: Asian Institute of Technology, 1992), p. 31.

are often of world-class standards, the public environment leaves little to be proud of, even in the most prestigious districts.[44]

Perhaps even more harsh is the conclusion of a Chulalongkorn University interdisciplinary team, which found that urban development spearheaded by private developers led to 'an extremely chaotic suburban pattern with defective morphological structure, irregular subdivision of plots and inefficient public utilities'.[45] While one may deride these comments as springing from a bias for Western-style urban order on the part of Western or Western-influenced urban planners, it must be noted that this bias is shared widely among the population, which realizes that something has gone drastically amiss in the development of Bangkok.

There are three other consequences of unplanned development that are of great distress to the population. One is that there is absolutely no real control on the conversion of agricultural land surrounding Bangkok – the so-called Green Belt – into urban land uses. This has a negative impact on farmers, who have no choice but to sell their lands; on consumers, who may face higher prices for produce that has to be obtained from much more distant sites as the Green Belt shrinks; and on the environment, as so-called sink capabilities of green areas are significantly reduced. Second, the provision of necessary public social infrastructure, like parks, schools, and recreational areas – spaces that make up what is called the 'urban commons' – lags severely behind private development and is often ignored altogether. Bangkok's concrete jungle is rarely broken by public spaces.

Private land development agencies have become the main providers of both residential housing and commercial establishments. Indeed, according to the Chulalongkorn University team, 'the private land and housing developers exclusively controlled the development of new urbanized areas with only minor intervention from the public sector'.[46] This is hardly a case of benign neglect, however, for the pre-eminence of the private sector in the provision of mass housing has been achieved not in spite of government but, in many instances, because of government decisions. The first housing development boom, for instance, began in the late 1950s, after the government passed Revolutionary Proclamation 49, which introduced an era of unrestricted land transaction, subdivision, and speculation, because it 'removed legislative constraints on landholding'.[47] An attempt to impose some controls via Revolutionary Proclamation 286, passed in 1972, which tried to get developers to install minimum facilities in land subdivisions, may have had the intention of imposing some public controls, but it actually had the unintended effect of concentrating control over the market in a fewer hands, since the financial requirements it imposed drove many small developers out of business, leaving only the financially stronger developers who shifted their activity from simple land subdivisions into the development of housing estates (*Mubaan Jyadsan* or MJDs) for the elite and middle classes seeking to escape from the increasingly crowded city centre. From then on, MJDs became the 'main driving force for the physical urbanization of Bangkok'.[48] Attesting to the ascendancy of developers was their ability to twist the arm of the BMA to reject, in the early 1970s, all efforts by public planners to rationalize the development of Bangkok.

External events in the 1970s and 1980s, particularly the oil price shocks of 1973 and 1979, conspired to create even greater activity in land, as bank capital that would have been originally earmarked for manufacturing became speculative capital flowing into the real estate market. Another massive inflow of funds occurred as Hong Kong capital sought newer, secure havens as the reintegration of the crown colony back into China became a proximate reality.

The late 1980s saw another real estate boom, this time focused not only on MJD development but also on the construction of condominiums, for which the property rules were loosened in order to allow members of the growing Bangkok expatriate community to own their units, something which was not possible when it came to land. Again, private developers received a boon from government policies that permitted insurance companies to invest in the land and housing market and promoted financial liberalization that brought foreign capital flooding into the real estate sector.[49]

With the *laisser-faire* policy prevailing in the housing sector, those with little purchasing power, meaning the poor, were marginalized from decent and adequate housing. This was not an insignificant number of people, since with the increasing economic disparity between Bangkok and the countryside, migrants were streaming into Bangkok. The city's population grew by 4.3 per cent between 1960 and 1970, and by 4.8 per cent between 1970 and 1978, compared to 3.3 per cent and 2.7 per cent respectively for the whole of Thailand. Most of the increase during this period of rapid growth was likely to be accounted for by internal migration rather than natural increase, although the latter was probably a stronger factor from the mid-1970s on.[50] Most of these migrants were poor, and found their way to slums such as the one that mushroomed in the port area of Klong Toey.

Klong Toey may have been one of the most massive slums, but there were many like it. There were some 1,100 slums and 200 squatter settlements in Bangkok in 1988, up from 632 slums and 108 squatter settlements in 1974.[51] These settlements encompassed some 1.1 million of Bangkok's population of about 7.7 million, or around 14 per cent. Though successful cases of slumdweller or squatter resistance, as in Klong Toey, made the news, most slums had a very fragile existence. Of 1,020 Bangkok slums identified in 1984, about 117 had disappeared by 1988, most probably via eviction of the residents.[52]

Market forces, or the rise in land values, was most likely the trigger for these evictions. Certainly, rising land value was the main cause of eviction from private lands at the city centre, where in just four years, 1984 to 1988, slum housing declined by some 11,376 units within a radius of 10 kilometres from the centre.[53] This was simply a result of the combination of the lack of any sort of land use regulation and the absence of effective demand from the lower-income sections of Bangkok's population.

While surveys indicate that only 3.4 per cent of Bangkok's population live under the poverty line – compared to 14.6 per cent for the total urban population and 31 per cent for the northeast's urban population – a number of urban experts have treated this figure with caution. First of all, the largest absolute numbers of the poor are in the 1,000 slums located within Bangkok's inner ring.[54] Second, more focused studies of the Bangkok population reveal, in fact, a higher degree of actual poor than the national statistics. For instance, Somsul Bunyabancha estimated that on the basis of a minimum of 3,000 baht a month to pay for bare nececessities such as food and energy, some 1.2 to 1.5 million people in Bangkok should be considered as poor, a figure that comes to 22 to 27 per cent of the city's population.[55]

Third, the distribution of income in Bangkok has worsened recently, with the poorest 60 per cent of the population suffering a drop in their real income from 31.6 per cent in 1986 to 26.8 per cent in 1990 – a figure that implies that 'although the poor fared better in absolute terms on the average, the nonpoor fared even better as a consequence of social and economic changes'.[56]

That low incomes were marginalizing large numbers of Bangkokians out of the market emerges in a number of studies. Based on the typical cost of a low-cost housing unit offered on the market, it has been estimated that the percentage of Bangkok residents who could not afford low-cost housing was 80 per cent in 1980, 64 per cent in 1986, 50 per cent in 1991, and 60 per cent in 1993.[57] Although demand was obviously great, effective demand was extremely limited, especially in terms of developers' perception of alternative uses of their capital. Not surprisingly, developers put on the market low-cost housing that could accommodate only 70 per cent of people's demand in 1988, which led analyst Fook Tuan Seik to remark that although some private developers were beginning to service low-income groups, the role of the private sector was still rather 'insignificant'.[58] What passed for low-cost housing appeared to benefit, in fact, primarily middle-income groups or the upper end of the low-income population.

Being evicted from the central part of Bangkok, yet with no access to affordable housing, the urban poor concentrated in slums or squatter areas on the fringes or periphery of the city, with the continuing streams of rural migrants adding to their numbers, resulting in even denser slum areas mushrooming 11 to 20 kilometres from the centre of the city. Here, living conditions were in fact often much less desirable than in their former homes in the city centre. For one, with no direct connections to the water supply, shantytown residents had to buy low-quality water in quantities enough only for drinking and cooking at 27 times higher than the price charged by the Metropolitan Water Authority. And because most of them had to draw electricity illegally from better-off neighbours, they ended up paying seven times more than the price charged by the Metropolitan Electricity Authority while facing greater risk of short-circuiting and fire.[59]

The following description probably holds for most of the slums found in the fringes of the city, given Bangkok's particular ecology of being located on a flood plain:

> To reduce flooding of their plots and houses, landowners raise the level of the land with earth. However, the cost of land fill is quite high and unused land usually remains unfilled. Such parcels of unfilled land are the prime sites for informal settlements. Because the land on which the slums are being built is low, most slum houses are built on posts. In some slums there is stagnant water under the houses throughout the year, creating very unsanitary conditions.
>
> Sometimes the landowner provides wooden walkways, electricity and water supply as well as the house, but usually the slum dweller has to build his own house of wood, corrugated iron sheets and waste materials. Human waste disposal systems are rudimentary. Most slum dwellers use concrete rings to build a cesspool under their toilet. If the tank was sealed, it could not pollute soil, but as a sealed tank fills up quickly and has to be emptied after some time,

most households use a tank without a bottom. The sewage soaks into the subsoil and pollutes the land and the water under the houses.

The stagnant water, the inadequate infrastructure and the lack of ventilation create poor living conditions in the slums. Children suffer from respiratory problems, heart and kidney diseases and malnutrition. Some slums have a very high rate of drug addiction which is nowadays often accompanied by a high incidence of AIDS due to the sharing of contaminated needles. Because slum houses are built of wood and because slums have, almost by definition, poor access to the public road, slum dwellers tend to be very concerned about the risk of fires, as these can spread quickly and often block the only exit from the settlement.[60]

Fire indeed became a critical problem once land values escalated and residents were slow or reluctant to move. Although the landowner has traditionally been vested with absolute rights over his land, the emergence of a new generation of slum and shantytown residents conscious of their rights as traditional users of land and fired up by the successful resistance to eviction by the people in Klong Toey and other large settlements has made fires the best way of freeing up the land for commercial uses or upmarket private housing. As Yap Khioe Sheng has noted:

> The standard contract between the slum dwellers and the land owner stipulates that the lease is automatically terminated if a fire destroys the houses. Moreover, the regulations of the Bangkok Metropolitan Administration state that structures destroyed by fire cannot be rebuilt within 45 days, to allow officials to look into the cause of the fire. A fire is, therefore, a blessing for a land owner who wants to evict slum dwellers from his property. Slum dwellers who return to the site to rebuild their houses become virtual squatters on the land they rented and occupied for years.[61]

Klong Toey: rallying point for the urban poor

The big exception, of course, to the omnipotence of landowners in the land market was the slum of Klong Toey, which managed to face down the powerful Port Authority of Thailand when the latter sought to evict residents in the 1970s. But Klong Toey was not alone in successful resistance to developers. The residents of the large shantytown at Rachadapisek faced down a commercial developer to whom the landowner, State Railways of Thailand, leased the land encompassing the settlement. The developer had recourse to thugs, but the residents, as one account put it, chose to meet 'force with force, prompting the developer to call off the thugs belonging to a so-called "influential person." '[62] The developer than called on the police, but the residents countered with well-publicized demonstrations outside the home of the chief of police. Eventually the stalemate was resolved only when the developer and the Metropolitan Waterworks Authority agreed to contribute the relatively large amount of

4.9 million baht to purchase a relocation site identified by the residents as the place on which to build their community.[63]

As for the Klong Toey community, which was able to stay in place in spite of what can only be described as a determined effort to evict them by the Port Authority of Thailand, there were several conditions that led to success. First, compared to other slum communities, Klong Toey was a massive slum of several thousand families, and, when organized, as they were in Klong Toey, this mass proved very difficult to evict.

Second was the excellent leadership forged by community activists, headed by schoolteacher Prateep Ungsongtham, around whose community school the first meetings of the slumdwellers' organization took place. A key characteristic of the local organizing, which probably accounted for its strength, was its democratic character, with positions of leadership achieved in the struggle against evictions legitimized through elections.[64] The Duang Prateep Foundation, which was formed from the prize money that Prateep Unsongtham was given when she won the Magsaysay Award, pioneered, in fact, a new type of community organization in Thailand: '[P]eople-based, institutionalized, and well accepted by the public ... [t]his organization acts as intermediary between people organization and the government or public at large on various aspects and circumstances.'[65]

Third, the leadership was able to form an alliance with external groups, making their cause a well-publicized city-wide and national issue. Both concerned academics and NGOs from the outside became part of an effective alliance that brought publicity to the anti-eviction struggles, translated the community's demands into pressure on city and national politicians, and garnered external financial assistance for community struggles.

Fourth, good leadership and numbers helped transform the community into a political force that national and urban politicians found necessary to cultivate, especially when the governments in power were relatively democratic and depended on electoral support to remain in power.

Fifth, the leadership was able to employ very flexible tactics, which combined pressure on the authorities with working at creative solutions with other government agencies. The National Housing Authority (NHA), for instance, which was established in 1973 partly as a response to the Klong Toey struggle for land, quickly became more of an ally than an antagonist of the Klong Toey community. It was the NHA that developed a new approach to slum housing that won the cooperation not only of the Klong Toey residents but also of slumdwellers in other communities. While not without its problems, slum upgrading, when it was being implemented, reached quite an impressive number of urban families. Aside from Klong Toey, some 132 slums are reported to have been upgraded by the NHA.[66] It was also close cooperation between the NHA and the Klong Toey residents that delivered the final solution to the Klong Toey stalemate: land-sharing. The NHA directly leased 61 per cent of former squatter land after it upgraded the area and built low-cost housing. In turn, the residents vacated the remaining 39 per cent for use by the Port Authority.[67] The residents then built their own housing with loans from two NGOs and with technical assistance from the Royal Thai Army.

But the NHA record must not be overrated, and Klong Toey was probably its one great shining moment. For the NHA's original mandate of providing public low-cost housing has been undermined since Klong Toey, and it has been subverted by pressure from developers, who saw the venture in public enterprise housing as representing a strategic threat to their interests, and their allies in the government bureaucracy.

The original NHA mandate of providing public housing on a massive scale was seen as too expensive by the authorities, forcing it to shift to the slum-upgrading approach. Under this concept, slum families would receive subsidies for infrastructure but not for housing plots or for their initial shelter. But the move to slum upgrading was not motivated only by economy. It was also an approach that was seen as not competing with the private developers.[68]

And yet this innovative approach has been undermined since the early 1980s by a new approach that would make NHA projects self-financing. What this did was to push the NHA to begin building middle- and upper-income housing in order to make a profit to finance its housing activities aimed at the lower-income groups. But this turned out to be a failure, since the NHA is not well equipped to compete with the private sector. As a result, as Yap Khioe Sheng puts it, 'the NHA now appears to supply housing to all income groups except the urban poor'.[69]

The free market, noted one experienced urban poor advocate, was simply 'out of control', pushing people ever more swiftly from the core to the fringes of the city, unchecked by a government that had abdicated from its role of protecting those with little market power. Even Klong Toey, he predicted gloomily, 'will sooner or later disappear because market forces have made the land too valuable to have only single-storey structures above it'.[70]

In sum, from infrastructure to housing, the problems of Bangkok from the 1970s to the 1990s were caused largely by the absence of planning on the part of government and by an increasingly uncontrolled private sector. Instead of acting as a check on the market and the private sector, in fact, government increasingly took a pro-active role in stripping away legal and regulatory blocks to the dominance of the market and the private sector.

In the housing sector, this resulted in the increasing marginalization of the poor in a market that increasingly responded only to the needs of the middle class and the rich.

Notes

1. Marc Askew, *The Making of Modern Bangkok: State, Market, and People in the Shaping of the Thai Metropolis* (Bangkok: TDRI, 1993), p. 46.

2. Kraiyudht Dhiratayakinant, 'Urbanization, inefficient urban management, and income inequality', paper presented to Fifth International Conference on Thai Studies, London, 6–9 July 1993, p. 4.

3. Peter Rimmer and Mehdi Krongkaew, 'Urbanization problems in Thailand's rapidly industrializing economy', paper presented to conference 'The Making of a Fifth Tiger? Thailand's Industrialization and its Consequences', Canberra, Australian National University, 7–9 December 1992, p. 5.

4. Ibid.

5. Paritta Chalermpow Koanantakool, *Urban Life and Urban People in Transition* (Bangkok: TDRI, 10–11 December 1993), p. 25.

6. Manop Bongsadadt, 'Bangkok: the primate city of Thailand. The past, the present, and the possible future', in *Proceedings of the Fourth International Conference on Thai Studies, Kunming, May 11–13*, vol. 4 (Bangkok: 1990), p. 334.

7. Medhi Krongkaew and Pawadee Tongudai, 'The growth of Bangkok: the economics of unbalanced urbanization and development', Discussion Paper Series, no. 90, Faculty of Economics, Thammasat University, May 1984, p. 39.

8. Anuchat Poungsomlee and Helen Ross, *Impacts of Modernization and Urbanization in Bangkok: An Integrative Ecological and Biosocial Study* (Bangkok: Institute for Population and Social Research, Mahidol University, August 1992), p. 19.

9. Ibid.

10. Ibid., p. 19; Rimmer and Mehdi, p. 14.

11. Ralph Gakenheimer et al., *Concept Plan for Bangkok: Metropolitan Development* (Cambridge, MA: Massachusetts Institute of Technology, July 1993), p. 6.

12. 'The Asiaweek quality of life index', *Asiaweek*, 5 December 1997, p. 53.

13. Ibid.

14. Anuchat and Ross, p. 19; see also Gakenheimer et al., p. 4.

15. Gakenheimer et al., p. 1.

16. Anuchat and Ross, p. 19.

17. Helen Ross, 'Environmental and social impacts of urbanization in Bangkok', paper presented to Fifth International Conference on Thai Studies, School of Oriental and African Studies, London, 1993, pp. 13–14.

18. 'Development of Bangkok's infrastructure: gathering momentum', in Bangkok Bank, *Annual Report 1996* (Bangkok: Bangkok Bank, 1996), p. 22.

19. Kraiyudht, p. 14.

20. Rimmer and Krongkaew, p. 19.

21. Ross, p. 5.

22. Kraiyudht, p. 13.

23. Rimmer and Krongkaew, p. 18

24. Ibid.

25. Ibid.

26. Prinya Muangarkas and Supoj Wancharoen, 'Mass transit: moving in stops and starts', *Bangkok Post*, 2 July 1996, pp. 16, 19.

27. Ralph Gakenheimer et al., 'Concept plan for Bangkok metropolitan development: inception report', (Cambridge, MA: Massachusetts Institute of Technology, January 1993, p. 12.

28. Kraiyudht, p. 15.

29. Craig Stuart and Kesrin Wangwongwiroj, 'Sky train', *Manager*, March 1994, pp. 26–9.

30. Chodchoy is a wealthy socialite and daughter of the founder of Thailand's biggest bank, the Bangkok Bank.

31. 'A ride on the skytrain: not for the squeamish while below a sick city chokes itself to death', *Thailand Times*, 21 August 1995.

32. Ibid.

33. Ibid.

34. Ibid.

35. Interview with Khunying Chodchoy, Bangkok, 21 November 1997.

36. Prinya Muangkas and Supoj Wancharoen, pp. 16, 19.

37. 'A ride on the skytrain'.

38. Prinya Muangkas and Supoj Wancharoen, pp. 16–19.

39. 'Client perspectives: the word from Wu', *Impact*, vol. 1, no. 2, Fall 1997.

40. Simon Fluendy and Joanna Slater, 'Pity the poor tycoons', *Far Eastern Economic Review*, 6 November 1997, p. 80.

41. Rimmer and Kongkraew, p. 13.

42. Roy Archer, *The Possible Use of Urban Land Pooling/Readjustment for the Planned Development in Bangkok*, HSD Working Paper no. 17 (Bangkok: Human Settlements Division, Asian Institute of Technology, 1985), p. 8.

43. Askew, *The Making*, p. 45.

44. Ralph Gakenheimer et al., 'Concept Plan ... Inception Report', p. 10.

45. Institute of Environmental Research, *Changes in Suburban Area North of Bangkok Metropolis* (Bangkok: Institute of Environmental Research, Chulalongkorn University, 1986), p. 36.

46. Ibid.

47. Seisuke Watanabe, 'Who benefits from the urbanization of Thailand in the late 1980s?', paper presented at Fifth International Conference on Thai Studies, School of Oriental and African Studies, London, 1993, p. 12.

48. Ibid., p. 13.

49. See, among others, Watanabe, p. 13.

50. Mehdi Krongkaew and Pawadi Tongudai, p. 13.

51. Yap Kioe Sheng, 'Low-income housing sub-markets', in Yap Kioe Sheng, ed., *Low-income Housing in Bangkok: A Review of Some Housing Sub-markets* (Bangkok: Asian Institute of Technology, 1992), p. 9.

52. Yap Kioe Sheng, 'The slums of Bangkok', in Yap, ed., *Low-income Housing*, pp. 44–8.

53. Ibid., p. 42.

54. Rimmer and Krongkaew, p. 10.

55. Paritta, p. 59.

56. Somchai Ratanakomut, Charuma Ashakul, and Thienchay Kirananda, 'Urban poverty in Thailand: critical issues and policy measures', *Asian Development Review*, vol. 12, no. 1, 1994, p. 217.

57. Pronchokchai, in Yap, *Low-Income Housing*, pp. 48–9.

58. Fook Tuan Seik, 'Private sector low-cost housing', in Yap, ed., *Low-income Housing*, p. 105.

59. Somchai Ratanakomut et al., p.219.

60. Yap, 'The slums', p. 36.

61. Ibid., p. 39.

62. Yap, 'Housing sub-markets', p. 26.

63. Ibid.

64. S. Boonyabancha et al., *Struggle to Stay: A Case Study of People in Slum Klong Toey Fighting for their Homes* (Bangkok: Duang Prateep Foundation, 1988), p. 17.

65. Ibid., p. 22.

66. Yap, 'Housing sub-markets', p. 16.

67. S Boonyabancha et al., p. 13.

68. Foo Tuan Seik, p. 100.

69. Yap, 'Housing sub-markets', p. 13.

70. Joseph Maier, interview, Bangkok, 18 March 1994.

CHAPTER 7

Pollution Haven

Upon hearing of the government's plan to decentralize industry to the rest of the country, a friend joked that one might take a leaf from Paul Theroux's futuristic novel *O-Zone*, declare Bangkok a region to which pollution would be confined, and save the rest of the country from industrial hell. The idea was ghoulish, but it underlined the reality that industrial concentration is present in Bangkok in its 'extreme form'.[1]

The BMR and the adjoining Central Region accounted for close to 75 per cent of value-added in manufacturing and 52 per cent of industries (27,000 out of 50,000).[2] This statistic does not, however, adequately capture the environmental consequences of rapid and concentrated industrial-ization. For the total number of factories in Thailand grew from 600 for the whole kingdom in 1969 to 20,000 by 1979 to 50,000 by 1989.[3] This exponential growth was occasioned by a shift from import-substitution manufacturing to export-oriented industrialization in the 1970s, followed by the great migration of Japanese manufacturers into the country in the 1980s following the appreciation of the yen after the Plaza Accord of 1985.

Foreign investment and pollution

Thailand was quite unprepared for the massive surge of foreign investment in the late 1980s, particularly from Japan. Between FY 1985 and FY 1990, some $3.7 billion in Japanese direct investment came into Thailand.[4] In 1987 alone, Japanese investment approvals by Thailand's Board of Invest-ments (BOI) exceeded the cumulative Japanese investment for the preceding 20 years.[5] Thailand drew not only Japanese corporations seeking to escape high labour costs but also significant investment from Taiwanese-, Hong Kong-, and South Korean-owned firms. Nevertheless, the Japanese were dominant, accounting for over half of total foreign investment inflow by the end of the 1980s.[6]

The Thais probably did not expect that the BOI's efforts to attract invesment would elicit such a response. In any event, they were unprepared, particularly in terms of planning the infrastructure that would accommodate the massively stepped up investment. Location of investment was left up to the foreign investors, which meant they set up shop in the Bangkok Metropolitan Region in large numbers. Indeed, 70 per cent of all foreign investment was in the 'inner ring' of the BMR.[7] As one report noted:

> The most compelling reason for the greater concentration of foreign investment in the inner ring relates to the greater reliance on imported inputs of foreign investors as well as the importance of port access for export-oriented companies. Furthermore, foreign investors are less familiar with Thai geography and less able, therefore, to perceive the advantages of locating outside the BMR and the outer ring ... The lack of social infrastructure, such as schools and hospitals, outside of the extended metropolitan area also discourages foreign managers from investing in other parts of Thailand. In brief, it appears that industrial-ization based of encouraging foreign investment contributes to the concentration of industrial and manufacturing investments in the BMR.[8]

Concentration within the BMR did not mean, however, that industries were confined to specific areas. Concentration was accompanied by a dispersal of industries within the area, leading to 'both the unsystematic growth and congestion of Bangkok and ... a heavy burden on the government which is faced with the problem of providing public infrastructure over a spread-out area, at substantial loss of economies of scale and concentration. While there are also economic benefits to the decentral-ization of industry, the pattern observed in and around BMR is one of a scattered but not decentralized distribution of industries.'[9]

What efforts to guide the industrialization process have taken place have been minuscule and rather ineffective. A system of government-run industrial estates was set up in 1972, and today there are some 21 public and private industrial estates in operation. Most of the estates, however, are within a 150-kilometre radius of Bangkok, reflecting the failure of the system to act as a decongesting mechanism. Narrow economic criteria responsive principally to private sector production needs dominated the selection of sites for industrial estates.[10] In fact, only one public industrial estate, Lamphun, was located outside the BMR, but it has had a mixed record and a very slight impact in terms of relieving industrial congestion.

Another effort has been the so-called Eastern Seaboard Project, which was launched in 1983 to create an alternative port and industrial site to Bangkok. But low investment levels and slow implementation of planned infrastructural projects have made its immediate future questionable. More-over, being but 80 to 150 kilometres away from Bangkok, the Eastern Seaboard project 'is likely [to] contribute to the process of urbanization in the extended Bangkok metropolitan region by creating a large BMR–ESB conurbation area'.[11]

One of the results has been a massive addition of freight traffic to Bangkok's already unbearable car traffic, with some 200,000 trucks and pickup trucks. This is partly a result of the fact – again a product of lack of planning – that the bulk of all goods hauled throughout the country passes through the BMR even though Bangkok is not their ultimate destination.[12] And where road development does take place to ease the traffic, the lack of accompanying land-use policies makes it worse by promoting ribbon development of private estates along the major highways, where unintegrated secondary road networks built by private developers lead to traffic clogging up the main arteries.[13]

Water shortage is another aspect of the problem. The failure to anticipate the water needs of rapid industrialization in the Bangkok area has led to industries relying excessively on pumping up groundwater to make up for their lack of access to piped water. In Samut Prakan, for example, of the 52,895 cubic metres of water used daily by a sample of 59 factories, only one-half of one per cent came from piped water, with most of the rest – 95 per cent – coming from groundwater pumping.[14] A classic case of a private solution without private regulation, groundwater pumping has contributed to a situation whereby the average water withdrawal of 1.4 million M3/day was double the city's underground water basin's recharge capacity of 0.6 to 0.8 million M3/day.[15] This led to a drastic lowering of the artesian water table. In 1959, the deepest level recorded was 12 metres below ground surface in central Bangkok; by 1981, the lowest level was about 52 metres below ground surface. One of the consequences has been Bangkok's famous problem of land subsidence, which ranged from 5 centimetres to 10 centimetres, the most critical area being eastern Bangkok, parts of which are now below sea level.[16] As one report notes:

> Land subsidence is evidenced by sinking of walkways, building floors, and streets some of which become flooded during heavy rain. Social costs are quite substantial. Sinking structures need repair and maintenance or even reconstruction. Flooded streets also cost society in terms of clean-up time and time wasted in immobile traffic. Damage caused by the 1983 flood was estimated at 66 billion baht.[17]

Industrial location and water management problems underline the claim by one key NESDB report that 'Infrastructure provision in the region has lacked the institutional setup to adequately coordinate and implement infrastructure projects.'[18] It is, however, in the area of environmental controls that the public planning fiasco is most evident.

Forms of pollution

This pace of industrialization would strain the capacity of any country, and any city, to deal with it environmentally. The number of waste-producing industries increased from 211 in 1969 to 7,030 in 1979 to 26,235 by the end of the 1980s.[19] The production of polluting industries accounted for more than half of GDP in the 1970s and 1980s.[20] Most of these industries were located in the BMA and its adjacent provinces. The BMR was especially prominent when it came to the generation of hazardous wastes, with factories in the region producing 71 per cent of serious waste hazards including oils, halogenated organic sludges, still bottoms, heavy metal sludges, halogenated solvents, acid waste, and alkaline waste.[21] This is not surprising given the fact that the BMR has, among all regions, the highest share of industries that are the major sources of toxic and hazardous waste: metal products and machinery, textiles and clothing, plastic products, transport equipment, and printing.[22]

The Chao Phraya river running through Bangkok, together with the nearby Bang Pakong, Thachin, and Mae Klong rivers, all of which drain into the East Coast Gulf Area, accounted for some 53 per cent of the biological oxygen demand (BOD) load (a measure of the depletion of oxygen content in the river created by the dumping of biodegradable waste) in Thailand's major rivers and waterways in 1986.[23] While industrial waste accounts for only about 25 to 30 per cent of the BOD load released into the lower section of Chao Phraya River – the other 75 per cent being residential in origin – this is still very significant, coming to about 20,000 tons a year.[24]

In terms of air pollution, the BMR, in one study conducted by Japanese scientists, now ranks as the worst in terms of air pollution of 70 capital cities studied. The transportation sector has been a leading cause of emissions of sulphur dioxide, nitrogen oxide, carbon monoxide, and carbon dioxide. This is not surprising, for there are now, by some estimates, 2.4 million cars, 2 million motorcycles, and 200,000 trucks and pickup trucks – with another 400 to 500 new vehicles hitting the road every day.[25] Industry, however, is fast rivalling the transportation sector as a key source of air pollution, accounting for over 40 per cent of sulphur dioxide emissions, over 23 per cent of carbon dioxide emissions, and 35 per cent of suspended particulate matter or dust.[26] The proportion is expected to increase as industrialization in Bangkok intensifies in the coming years. Reflecting the concentration of industry in Bangkok, the BMR accounts for 46 per cent of industrial nitrogen oxide emissions, 56 per cent of industrial carbon dioxide emissions, and 58 per cent of industrial sulphur dioxide emissions.[27] The consequences for human health of the crisis of air pollution are quite grave. The Ministry of Public Health has estimated that some 900,000 Bangkok residents per year suffer from environmentally induced respiratory illnesses: 40 per cent from vehicle exhaust, 40 per cent from construction dust, and 20 per cent from industrial emissions.[28]

With the massive construction boom that marked Bangkok over the last decade, dust has become a major source of air pollution. In September 1996 Bangkok registered its highest ever dust levels in the area of Sathupradit Road, where massive construction is taking place for the Expressway and Rapid Transit Authority of Thailand. The 4,840 ug/cm air dust level recorded was eight times higher than the standard, set at 330 ug/cm.[29]

Lead poisoning is caused by gasoline emissions, and lead intake from inhalation has become a particularly grave problem, with a 1990 USAID survey discovering that 100,000 men a year suffered from a range of ailments related to large lead intakes. Lead intake was also discovered to have been the cause of the deaths of 400 people a year in Bangkok, and a contributor to heart disease suffered by another 800.[30] The impact of lead on children is creating grave concern. Lead levels in the blood of children living in Bangkok are now said to be 16 to 18 micrograms per 100 millilitres, compared to 14 micrograms for children living in rural Kanchanaburi, a difference considered significant.[31] The level of lead in Thai children's blood (20 to 40 micrograms per decilitre) is now 20 times that of American children.[32] While the level of lead was still below the officially acceptable level of 40 micrograms per 100 millilitres and 50 micrograms for adults, the latter is now considered to be a dangerously anachronistic guideline. As Dr Aphichet Nakieka, an environmental health specialist, has underlined: 'A lead level in children in excess of 20 micrograms per deciliter poses a great threat to their physical and mental health. This level is unacceptable to U.S. doctors ... If the level exceeds 25 micrograms per deciliter the child should be taken to a hospital in order to remove the lead from his blood.'[33] Indeed, using more modern standards as a yardstick, blood tests conducted on the umbilical cords of 100 newborn infants at Sirirat Hospital 'found a level of lead so high that it could affect the bodily and mental development of the infants. Among these infants was one in which the level was high enough to affect the brain.'[34] Indeed, a loss of IQ points for 700,000 children up to the age of seven for each cohort was asserted by a USAID study.[35]

There is now also a growing fear that Bangkok's rising accident rate might in large part be attributable to the inhalation of gaseous fumes. According to Dr Thephanom Muangman, dean of the Faculty and Environment Studies at Mahidol University, most public bus drivers spend twelve hours a day on the road and are particularly susceptible to accidents after inhaling gaseous fumes:

> Accidents in the afternoon are mainly caused by public buses or *khor sor mor kor* (Bangkok Mass Transit Authority buses). The survey found that these drivers suffered mental disorders after breathing in a certain amount of exhaust gas over long periods of time. It has been proven that gases are powerful enough to devastate the central nervous system, brain functions, and consciousness ...[36]

The disposal of hazardous waste typifies the way in which the situation has gone out of control. In 1986, Thailand produced some 1,149,324 metric tons of hazardous waste, and over 70 per cent of this was accounted for by the BMR, where a total of 10,152 factories were the key polluters.[37] At that time, there was no systematic plan for the disposal of toxic waste, with companies left to their own devices, which meant that a large part of it was deposited with ordinary garbage or dumped with little care for both site and manner of disposal. A favourite means of disposal was simply dumping it in waterways. A 1991 study showed that 25 of Thailand's 43 rivers were contaminated with heavy metal.[38] In the Gulf of Thailand, for instance, into which the Chao Phraya and three other major polluted rivers flow, dissolved mercury content ranges from 0.7 to 4.0 ppb (parts per billion), compared to 0.1 ppb found in non-polluted waters. Also reported was 'a biomagnification of mercury in the food chains, as evident from the samples of shell-fish, fish, and fish-eating birds collected from the [Chao Phraya] river and the Gulf of Thailand'.[39]

By 1991, according to one authoritative study, solid waste output had increased to almost 2 million metric tons and by 1996, it was expected to reach 3.5 million tons.[40] Yet efforts to deal with this problem have remained minuscule. In the late 1980s, a small pilot-scale hazardous waste treatment centre was set up at the Bang Khun Tian district of Bangkok, but only a very small proportion, about 50,000 out of almost 2 million metric tons, of the country's hazardous waste output was being processed for disposal there in the early 1990s.[41] By the mid-1990s, the situation had improved somewhat, but only one-tenth to one-fifth of the country's hazardous waste was being processed.[42] Three other treatment centres were expected to be on stream by 1996, but by that time, their modest additions in terms of capacity – another 200,000 tons – would have been far outstripped by the exponential growth of toxic waste to 3.5 million tons. Moreover, popular opposition, for instance in Chon Buri, had stymied the construction of at least one of these proposed plants, and made the outlook uncertain for future plants. Not surprisingly, a very significant part of the wastes ended up 'dumped in uncontrolled sites, illegal landfills, canals, rivers and even farmland'.[43]

A case that highlighted the dangers of hazardous waste occurred in the northeast, where a foreign paper company was accused of having dumped waste containing dioxin into the Phong river near Khon Kaen over a number of years. The Phoenix Paper Company denied this, but as one specialist explained, the company's production process consisted of producing white paper via chlorine bleaching, which produced dioxin, a particularly harmful carcinogenic substance.[44] A sample of Phong river water sent to the Louis Pasteur Institute in Paris by Khon Kaen University specialists was judged to have a level of dioxin content higher than World Health Organization standards of safety. But the company countered by sending a sample to a Finnish insitute, which found that the dioxin content was much lower. 'The problem here', noted the expert, 'is that whatever the amount of dioxin the company dumped into the river it is perfectly

Table 7.1 Estimates of volume of hazardous wastes generated in Thailand, by type of waste (tons per year)

Waste type	1986	1991	1996[a]	2001[a]
Oils	106,372	188,254	332,779	589,508
Organic sludge and sewage	187	311	522	876
Inorganic sludge and solids	3,737	6,674	11,951	21,533
Heavy metal sludge and solids	302,316	536,322	946,565	1,658,192
Solvents	19,760	36,163	66,532	214,306
Acid wastes	18,505	31,432	53,973	46,105
Alkaline wastes	5,679	9,839	16,846	29,909
Off spec. products	12	25	52	107
PCB	0	0	0	0
Aqueous organic residues	116	242	499	1,037
Photo wastes	8,820	16,348	30,398	57,809
Municipal wastes	7,231	11,787	19,090	31,093
Infectious wastes	46,674	76,078	123,219	200,699
Total	531,154	932,68	1,634,104	2,813,980

Note: a = projected.
Source: Department of Pollution Control, Ministry of Science, Technology, and Environment, cited in Pitsamai Eamsakulrat, Direk Patmasiriwat, and Pablo Huidobro, 'Hazardous waste management in Thailand', *TDRI Quarterly Review*, vol. 9, no. 3 (September 1994), p. 9.

legal because Thailand has no standards for dioxin!'[45] In the meantime, in a move that some observers interpreted as an admision that it had indeed been employing a dangerous technology, the company shifted from using chlorine for bleaching to using oxygen, a process that produced no dioxin.[46]

A major concern has been the disposal of extremely dangerous PCBs, exposure to which entails high risk of incurring cancer. None of the waste-treatment plants, either active or planned, is designed to treat PCBs. In previous years, Thailand shipped its PCBs to France for disposal at the Tredi Plant.[47] In the early 1990s, for instance, it sent some 90 tons to France. However, in April 1994 the Basle Convention on the Control of Transboundary Movement and Disposal of Hazardous Wastes outlawed all shipment of hazardous wastes across national boundaries. This meant that PCBs now had to remain in Thailand, with no permanent means of disposal. What was worse was that a very significant part of the PCB wasteload, which was estimated at thousands of tons, could not be located, with much of it suspected of being placed in simple landfills, dumped into the sea, or stored haphazardly. PCBs are very stable and not bio-degradable, and upon release into the environment they find their way into the food chain.

But hazardous waste in Thailand is not produced only by local industries.

A not insignificant amount is shipped to Thailand from the rest of the world. In 1989, for instance, some 161,937 kilograms of toxic wastes were estimated to be housed at the port of Klong Toey, either unclaimed by local consignees or sent to consignees who did not even exist.[48] In 3,000 tons of waste imported from the United States for storage in the Mab Ta Phut industrial estate, there were 4.5 kg of thalium and 2 kg of uranium, which were not disclosed to the Department of Industrial Works when it approved the shipment.[49] Thailand also accepts industrial waste from around the region, from countries such as Malaysia and Singapore.

Related to this shipping of hazardous waste to Thailand is the transport of extremely dangerous chemicals within Thailand, from industrial areas to be dumped in national parks, non-hazardous landfills, and open spaces or incinerated openly in provincial areas. Residents near Huay Kha Khaeng National Wildlife Sanctuary openly burn printed circuit-boards to recover the copper. The presence of the circuit-boards in a municipal waste site was traced to an electronics firm near Bangkok, which admitted to mixing them with solid waste.[50]

The chemicals stored at Klong Toey were regarded as a menace by an environmental consulting firm, Engineering Science, which recommended a number of measures to dispose of the waste.[51] The government did not act on the recommendations, and in March 1991 a major explosion rocked the port and the surrounding Klong Toey slum, Bangkok's biggest, killing ten people. But that was not the end of it: over the following few years, stillbirths, miscarriages, birth defects, skin diseases, and other chemical-related illnesses marked the lives of those exposed to the fumes.[52] Indeed, according to a leading chemical hazards expert in the country, Dr Oraphan Metadilogkul, some 10,000 people among the 100,000 residents of Klong Toey slum were exposed, but there was no system to identify, much less monitor, most of the people affected by the accident.[53] And despite a ban on the storage of the types of hazardous chemicals that caused this explosion, the same chemicals were found poorly stored in a depot in the heart of Klong Toey port as late as April 1997. The chemicals included inflammable oxidizing agents, nitric acid, and organic peroxide.[54] To pacify the public after the explosion, the military regime then ruling the country transported the toxic wastes to the town of Kanchanaburi in western Thailand to bury them in a landfill in a military reservation. The problem was that, despite government assurances, the landfill was in fact in a sensitive location, being only six kilometres away from two villages and located in the watershed area of a tributary of the Mae Klong river, described by one report as 'a main lifeline of the western part of the country'.[55] Residents protested, and over the next few years, their fears were confirmed. Investigation of the site in 1993 revealed that the cement containers filled with formaldehyde and heavy metals had cracked and the wastes had leaked into the soil, possibly into underground streams.[56]

The Klong Toey explosion and the dramatic deaths at Lamphun discussed in Chapter 5 are two manifestations of the toxics problem in Thailand. There have been other cases of mass poisoning, such as the one that hit more than 1,200 villagers from the Rhon Pibul district in Nakhon Si Thammarat Province in 1987. They reportedly suffered 'symptoms of poisoning by arsenic leaching from piles of tin mining tailings and ore dressing that contaminated their water wells'.[57] But equally grave is the not-so-dramatic rise in cancer cases and deaths due to cancer. Deaths due to malignant neoplasm rose from 9.06 per 100,000 people in 1961 to 40.96 in 1991. Also, the average incidence of malignant neoplasm and the rate of perinatal morbidity and mortality were significantly higher in the three heavily industrialized provinces in the Eastern Seaboard than the average for the remaining 24 provinces.[58] Mercury poisoning is also a big concern, given that Thailand produces and uses about 320 million batteries a year, with the disposal of used batteries being an uncontrolled and haphazard process. With battery waste dumped into rivers, mercury is ingested by aquatic animals and enters human beings via the food chain. Blood samples of women who had recently given birth to babies at Sirirat hospital revealed a level of mercury in their blood of 2 micrograms per decilitre – quite a dangerous level.[59]

The hazardous waste problem is only one of the dimensions of the environmental crisis produced by high-speed industrialization. Another is the dumping of largely biodegradable waste in the country's waterways. There is no better example of the crisis of industrial waste dumping than the fate of the Chao Phraya river and the great body to which it flows, the Gulf of Thailand. Chao Phraya, or the 'Lord of Rivers', while probably not yet biologically dead, is close to it, according to some reports. The situation is most critical at the lower stretches of the river as it slices across Bangkok; here some 2,300 industrial sites border on the river.[60] The biological oxygen demand (BOD), a measure of the presence of decaying organic matter that competes with life forms natural to the habitat for oxygen, has long exceeded the standard of 4 milligrams per litre in the lower part of the river. Some 25 per cent of the BOD load – measured at 183,634 kilograms in the late 1980s – is said to originate from industry, the rest being produced by residential organic waste.[61] In any event, in many parts of the lower stretch, the water is fast approaching an anaerobic state, that is, a state of being biologically dead. The oxygen content south of the Memorial Bridge and especially near the Klong Toey Port Area has been at the zero or near zero mark.[62]

The consequences for human health are grave. Uncontrolled human waste dumping from residences along the river has raised the coliform bacteria (human waste) count to extraordinary levels. At the entrance to Klong Phra Khanong, for instance, the count is over 1.3 million MPN (most probable number) per 100 millilitres, compared to a standard of

50,000 per millilitre.[63] Also alarming is the fact that at Sam Lae, where the Metropolitan Water Authority draws its water for use in Bangkok, the water has reached critical pollution levels. As of 1991, the BOD level, which by the official standard should not have exceeded 2 milligrams per litre had shot up to 4.6 mg/l. Moreover, the volume of bacteria in 100 millilitres of water stood at 700,000 colonies – way past the standard of 20,000 set for the river at the Sam Lae area.[64] It is not surprising that one of Bangkok's booming industries is the bottled water business, which peddles at least the illusion of clean drinking water.

In recent years, it has been periodically stated that industry accounts for only 25 per cent of the BOD load in the Chao Phraya.[65] It is important to note, however, that this figure has been disputed, with some specialists claiming that factories contribute 30 per cent of the load.[66] Moreover, as one report notes, 'because one factory may discharge large quantities of wastewater containing several times the BOD content of domestic waste-water, the highly concentrated wastewater will immediately affect down-stream water quality'.[67] The impact on animal life in the river has been drastic, with the fish species in the Chao Phraya dropping from 121 in 1967 to 31 in recent times.[68]

Industrial wastewater as a critical source of pollution is a problem not only for the Chao Phraya river. Effluent from sugar mills located along the Mae Klong river has 'transformed it from one of Thailand's clearest rivers into a highly polluted one'.[69] The Phong river near Khon Kaen in the northeast has also been severely polluted by factories on its banks, which have at various times released molasses, dioxin-contaminated waste, and waste from flour production, all in a three-year period.[70] The first of these incidents was devastating, causing 'the Nam Phong river and the Chi river to be putrid to such an extent that it would be difficult to estimate the damage'.[71] In the last of these incidents, according to one account, 'the small fish died before the others but the catfish and carp are floating as if drugged. So many fish are dying that the villagers are tired of taking them.'[72] Said one villager: 'The government has said that factories should be built to give villagers work. We only request that no more factories be brought in. Three factories [meaning the paper mill, the sugar refinery and the liquor distillery] are bad enough. Take them somewhere else.'[73]

Eventually, effluents and hazardous wastes flow into the Gulf of Thailand. The water flow in the inner part of the Gulf requires as long as 50 days for waste water from the rivers to disperse in the outer part of the Gulf. As a consequence, the confined waste leads to an increase in plankton in the inner part of the Gulf, and the increase in plankton kills fish because of heightened competition for dissolved oxygen.[74] Mean-time, hazardous wastes like mercury are absorbed by crabs, clams, lobsters, and fish, thus entering the food chain and eventually the bodies of human beings.[75]

Another argument that is often repeated is that big manufacturers are less likely to pollute the river than smaller industries because of better monitoring of the former than the latter, which are far greater in number and are likely not to have wastewater treatment facilities.[76] However, a survey conducted by the National Environment Board of factories operating in Samut Prakarn province found that only 60 per cent of those with wastewater treatment systems actually ran them.[77] Moreover, the efficiency of those systems in operation was rated at only 68 per cent.[78] Inspection was key in making the factories operate their plants, but, according to the top environment official monitoring the Chao Phraya river, 'some factories may have stopped their engines, especially at night when there is no danger of being inspected'.[79]

Related to this argument was the notion that foreign investors were more likely than local firms to comply with wastewater treatment and other environmental regulations. This has been disputed by a number of experts. As one foreign expert with a great deal of experience with government environmental monitoring agencies said: 'They're all the same, whether Australian, Japanese, Chinese, American. If they can do it, they would make zero investment in environmental controls.'[80] He gave the example of a German firm making refrigerators, saying that they used a lower-grade, more environmentally harmful technology than the mother firm used in Europe. 'They can do it in a much better fashion, but they choose not to.'[81] As for Japanese firms, another expert claims that 'Japan has managed to clean up its environment to a great extent by exporting pollution via the export of dirty industry ... Textile factories which discharge harmful acetate dyes have been moved to Thailand.' The same expert stated that: 'Asahi's mercury-discharging soda plants have been relocated on the Chao Phraya River.'[82] The Japanese food-processing industry, which has taken the form of joint ventures in Thailand, has substandard waste-treatment facilities, according to a Japanese firm specializing in wastewater equipment.[83] As for Taiwanese firms, they are 'among the worst violators' of environmental regulations.[84]

Crisis of regulation

The current crisis of the urban environment in Bangkok is clearly a case of industrialization outrunning the environmental regulatory framework. There are several indicators of this.

First of all, standards: Thailand's effluent standards for wastewater pollution are dangerously outmoded, according to some experts. They were copied, it is claimed by some sources, from Texas environmental standards in 1982, and they have not been updated since then to take into account new technical data on water pollution and Thailand's accelerated industrialization. As mentioned earlier, for instance, the country still has no standards on dioxin levels.[85] Nor are there standards for soil pollution.[86] Air pollution standards are also dangerously outmoded. For instance, Thailand's standard for atmospheric lead is six times that of the United States, having been set several years back when the harmful effects of lead had not yet become apparent.[87]

Second, there is a separation between policy formulation and policy implementation, leading to weak enforcement. For instance, the National Environmental Quality Act, considered to be the 'most important legislation for providing mechanisms for comprehensive, integrated environmental management' mandates the Office of the National Environment Board (ONEB) with the authority to formulate environmental standards but not enforcement capacity, quite unlike other countries where the central environmental agency also monitors compliance and imposes sanctions.[88] In the case of Thailand, enforcement of industrial pollution regulation is with another agency, the Industrial Environment Division (IED) of the Department of Industrial Works (DIW).

Third, enforcement capability is currently weak. For industrial pollution enforcement, for instance, the ONEB cannot directly monitor and enforce the findings and recommendations of an environmental impact assessment (EIA) that an industry must submit with its licence application, nor does this power fall clearly to the IED. If the industry does not enforce the recommendations of the ONEB and the IED, the only way that the former may be brought to account is by ONEB disapproval of the next EIA submitted with a licence renewal application; this does not, however, prevent the damage caused by earlier noncompliance.[89] According to one study:

> Certain categories of industries which produce significant volumes of waste-waters are not even required to submit EIAs. For those which are, land is often preselected, Board of Investment (BOI) privileges are granted, and in many instances work on the project begins before an EIA is prepared and submitted to ONEB. The prevailing attitude among project planning and executing agencies is 'to develop first and minimize adverse environmental impact later.'[90]

The study concludes that: 'In theory, the EIA is a powerful tool for environmental protection; in practice, it has little impact.'[91]

Moreover, while the IED can, theoretically, make periodic inspections to monitor compliance with pollution standards, inspection of firms is in fact done only when a licence is granted or renewed or when a complaint is made by the public.[92] This is related to the severe understaffing of the IED: it has only 143 officials to monitor 50,000 factories in the BMR, which means one official for every 350 factories.[93] It is also connected to financial niggardliness on the part of higer levels of government in allocating funds for the enforcement of standards,· despite the vastly increased environmental problems. As one report noted, 'the budget of

1,900 baht per factory seems too small an amount to allow effective monitoring and enforcement. Realistically, monitoring of industrial waste emission should be carried out on a monthly basis but with the available budget and workforce, the task of environmental monitoring and enforcement is undoubtedly inadequate for the enforcement of standards and other pollution control regulations.'[94]

A fourth problem has to do with the quality of the bureaucracy. With salaries rising in the dynamic private sector, most of the best talent has migrated there, and this has affected environmental enforcement bureaucracy as it has the larger bureaucracy. As one expert noted, when he came to Thailand in the mid-1970s, government officials had once enjoyed a great deal of respect from the public, but this had shifted 180 degrees. His office, an environmental office, was now staffed with many people who were there because they could not make it in the private sector. Moreover, corruption in the inspection division was one of the biggest problems in enforcement, such that high officials in it were seen as both 'very, very rich and very, very corrupt'.[95]

For instance, a sugar mill accused of polluting the Phong River in 1992 with discharges of pollution had agreed to contribute 6 million baht to the study of the impact of molasses on the river. 'But not a single baht has been turned over, and this is probably because one of the directors [of the regulatory agency] is a shareholder of the sugar mill.'[96] He continued: 'The willingness to compromise is very, very high, and the willingness of government to confront business is very, very low. Government officials basically are afraid to confront industry.'[97]

A fifth problem has been a contradiction between the policy thrusts of the different government agencies. The environmental agencies' effort to control pollution was contradicted by the desire of other agencies to attract investment at all costs. Thus the Board of Investments has the authority to accept the applications for firms it is promoting. Permit processing includes coordination among the DIW, ONEB, and the BOI (Board of Investments), but 'much of the actual authority is left with the BOI'.[98] Now this is a problematic arrangement in light of the fact that the BOI has recently given promotion privileges to industries classified as potential hazardous waste generators, including chemical products, electronics, textiles, and metal fabrication. Indeed, an analysis of BOI-promoted industries showed that the proportion of approved investment for toxic waste-generating industries increased from 25 per cent in 1987 to 55 per cent in 1989.[99] This is hardly surprising, since the frame of mind of many of the technocrats who head the agencies charged with attracting foreign investment is that, as one account puts it, 'Thailand must compete with lots of neighbors and with other regions, and there will be environmental and cultural "trade-offs" in the course of economic development.'[100]

Still another case of the contradiction between economic growth and environmental enforcement resulting in opposing bureaucratic moves was the sharp reduction in the tariffs on imported cars by the Anand Panyarachun government in 1991. Guided by neoclassical doctrine about consumer sovereignty, it did bring down the price of cars – but sharply increased the cost to the environment and public health as it contributed to significantly more cars hitting an already crowded city.

In sum, Bangkok may be truly said to be a city that is out of control. The transportation crisis, the housing crisis, and the environmental crisis all show how an extremely dynamic private sector has subverted government regulation and leadership, leading to a situation very different from the classical 'bureaucratic polity' model, where business was thoroughly under the thumb of the state. Today, as one USAID official told us, 'Thailand is one place where the pendulum has swung too far in favor of the private sector, and government has to assume a stronger role in the economic decisionmaking.'[101] Or as the NESDB report puts it:

> [T]he underlying cause of most urban fringe development problems confronting Thailand today is not urban land development *per se*, but failure to achieve adequate coordination between private development and investment in infrastructure, particularly environmentally-related infrastructure. Land speculation and loss of agricultural land appear to be symptoms of the problem rather than true causes. When landowners and the beneficiaries of land development are not held responsible for protecting the environment and paying for the necessary infrastructure, sprawling, environmentally unsound development is a predictable consequence.[102]

Interestingly, also in agreement was the World Bank, which over the past 15 years had been one of the main advocates of less government regulation:

> Economic growth in Thailand over the past few years has been very rapid, but in a private enterprise system where few controls are imposed, increased material standards and private gains have been secured at an observable communal expense. This is especially evident in the Bangkok Metropolitan Region where a promotional 'laissez-faire' policy of industrial location and development has been associated with a relatively uncontrolled proliferation of factories in and around the capital.[103]

Even more weakening of state regulatory mechanisms is likely to be one the consequences of the financial crisis that hit Thailand in the middle of 1997. Almost certainly, one of the first casualties will be pollution controls, which will be loosened to cut costs. Further deregulation as required by the IMF rescue package would see a worsening of the transportation, housing, and environmental crises in the city. Among other things required by the IMFs structural adjustment measures are the privatization of state enterprises and a reduction in government spending.

This is bad news for government agencies, which need resources – both human and material – more urgently now than ever, as the urban population faces unemployment. The possibility of implementing an activist urban and environmental policy may be remote at the moment, but a future of even greater government deregulation and freer play for the private sector is no future at all.

Notes

1. NESDB, *National Urban Development Policy Framework*, ch.3, Area 7, vol. 2 (Bangkok: NESDB, 1992), p. 18.

2. Ibid.

3. Phanu Kritiporn, Theodore Panayatou, and Krerkpong Charnprateep, *The Greening of Thai Industry* (Bangkok: TDRI, 1990), pp. 8–11.

4. Figures from Japan Ministry of Finance.

5. TDRI, *Thailand's Economic Structure: Summary Report* (Bangkok: TDRI, 1992), pp. 2, 26.

6. NESDB, Area 1, ch. 1, vol. 1, p. 72.

7. NESDB, Area 1, ch. 1, vol. 1, p. 22.

8. Ibid, p. 21–3.

9. Phanu Kritiporn et al., p. 53.

10. NESDB, Area 1, ch. 1, vol. 1, p. 26.

11. Ibid.

12. NESDB, Area 1, ch. 1, vol. 1, p. 15.

13. See, among others, ibid., p. 39.

14. NESDB, Area 1, ch. 2, , vol. 1, p. 32.

15. Ruangdej Srivardhana, 'Water resources management and issues', paper presented at the Ninth Biennial Conference of the Agricultural Economics Society of Southeast Asia, Asia Hotel, Bangkok, 21–24 June 1993, p. 11.

16. Ibid., p. 12.

17. Ibid.

18. NESDB, Area 1, ch. 1, vol. 1, p. 11.

19. Phanu Kritiporn et al., p. 12

20. NESDB, Area 7, vol. 2, Introduction, p. 9.

21. Phanu Kritiporn et al., p. 34.

22. Ibid., p. 48.

23. Ibid., p. 10.

24. Ibid., p. 11.

25. 'Exhaust, dust pollution at "dangerous levels",' *Naeo Na*, 29 July 1993, p. 2; reproduced in *JPRS*, 25 October 1993, p. 14; 'Poor Bangkok air quality discussed', *The Nation*, 9 September 1993; reproduced in *JPRS*, 24 November 1993, p. 16.

26. Phanu Kritiporn et al., pp. 161–4.

27. Ibid. p. 56.

28. 'Exhaust, dust pollution at "dangerous levels"'.

29. 'Dust pollution hits record level', *The Nation*, 5 September 1996.

30. 'Poor Bangkok air quality'.

31. 'Incidence of environmentally induced illnesses', *The Nation*, reproduced in *JPRS*, undated.

32. 'Doctor comments on lead levels, standards', *Siam Rat*, 17 June 1991; reproduced in *JPRS*, 17 June 1991, p. 17.

33. Ibid.

34. 'Study on Bangkok children's lead levels', *Dao Siam*, 26 February 1991; reproduced in *JPRS*, 31 May 1991, pp. 21–3.

35. Pitsamai Eamsakulrat, Direk Patmasiriwat, and Pablo Huidobro, 'Hazardous waste management in Thailand', *TDRI Quarterly Review*, September 1994, p. 9.

36. 'Poor Bangkok air quality', p. 17.

37. Phanu Kritiporn, pp. 61–3.

38. *TDRI Quarterly, Review*, September 1994, p. 10.

39. Ibid.

40. Ibid., p. 8.

41. Ibid., p. 13.

42. *The Management and Control of Hazardous Waste: Hazardous Waste Management in Thailand* (Bangkok: Thailand Environmental Research Institute, February 1995, p. v.

43. *The Nation*, reproduced in *Foreign Broadcast Information Service* (FBIS), 3 March 1992.

44. Interview with foreign water pollution specialist, anonymity requested, Bangkok, 24 March 1994.

45. Ibid.

46. Ibid.

47. *The Nation*, reproduced in *FBIS*, 12 February 1992, p. 19.

48. Ibid., p. 35.

49. *The Monitoring*, p. 9.

50. Ibid., p. 16.

51. Pitsamai Eamsakulrat et al., p. 8.

52. Oraphun Metadilogkul, interview, Bangkok, 23 March 1994.

53. Ibid.

54. 'Hazardous organic chemicals found poorly stored in depot', *Thai Development Newsletter*, no. 3 (January–June 1997), p. 18.

55. *The Nation*, reproduced in *FBIS*, 31 May 1991.

56. 'Kanchanaburi dumping', *Sunday Post*, 28 November 1993.

57. Pitsamai Eamsakulrat et al., p. 10.

58. Ibid.

59. 'Lead, Mercury levels concern experts', *Matichon*, 14 April 1993; reproduced in *FBIS*, 28 May 1993.

60. Boonyuk Vadhanaphuti, Thanom Klaikayal, Suwit Thanopanuwat, and Natha Hungspreug, 'Water resources planning and management of Thailand's Chao Phraya river Basin', in Guy Le Moigne et al., *Country Experiences With Water Resources Management* (Washington, DC: World Bank, 1992), p. 201.

61. Phanu Kritiporn et al., pp. 29–30.

62. 'Growing pollution problems in Chao Phya river surveyed', *Bangkok Post*, reproduced in *FBIS*, 26 June 1991.

63. *Bangkok Post*, reproduced in *FBIS*, 29 March, p. 10.

64. 'Growing pollution problems in Chao Phya river surveyed'.

65. Ruangdej, p. 13.

66. *Matichon*, reproduced in *FBIS*, 24 November 1993, p. 18.

67. Phanu Kritiporn et al., p. 31.

68. *Daily News* (in Thai), reproduced in *FBIS*, 28 September, 1994.

69. Phanu Kritiporn, p. 10.

70. *Bangkok Post*, reproduced in *FBIS*, 15 September 1993.

71. *Athit*, reproduced in *FBIS*, 28 September 1994, p. 16.

72. Ibid.

73. Ibid.

74. 'Gulf of Thailand crisis examined', *Bangkok Post*, 8 March 1993, p. 15; reproduced in *FBIS*, 8 March 1993, p. 15.

75. Pitsamai Eamsakulrat, p. 10.

76. *FBIS*, 26 June 1991, p. 24.

77. Ibid.

78. Ibid.

79. Ibid.

80. Interview, wastewater pollution specialist, anonymity requested, Bangkok, 24 March 1994.

81. Ibid.

82. Mark McDowell, 'The development of the environment in ASEAN', in *Pacific Affairs*, vol. 6, no. 2 (1990), p. 327.

83. According to interview, wastewater pollution specialist, anonymity requested, Bangkok, 24 March 1994.

84. Ibid.

85. Ibid.

86. Ibid.

87. Suwanna Ruangkanchanasetr and Chamaiphan Santikarn, 'Lead poisoning a severe threat to the nation's health', *TDRI Quarterly Review*, March 1994, p. 25.

88. Phanu Kritiporn et al., p. 86.

89. Ibid.

90. Manida Unkulvasapul and Harris Seidel, *Thailand: Urban Sewage and Wastewater Management in Sector Development.* Vol. 1: Summary and Main Report (UNDP/World Bank: Bangkok, 1991), p. 86.

91. Ibid.

92. Interview, wastewater pollution specialist, anonymity requested, Bangkok, 24 March 1994.

93. 'Where the pollution comes from', *Bangkok Post*, reproduced in *FBIS*, 26 June 1991, p. 25.

94. Phanu Kritiporn et al., p. 94.

95. Interview, foreign water pollution specialist, anonymity requested, Bangkok, 24 March 1994.

96. Ibid.

97. Ibid.

98. Phanu Kritiporn et al., p. 88.

99. Ibid., p. 94.

100. Thomas Fox, 'Life and death in Lamphun', *The Nation*, 28 October 1994, p. C1.

101. Interview with USAID official, anonymity requested, September 1993.

102. NESDB, vol. 1, p. 40.

103. World Bank, *Thailand: Country Economic Memorandum* (Washington, DC: World Bank, 10 October 1991), p. 6.

CHAPTER 8

The Erosion of Agriculture

In his message to the country on his seventieth birthday on 5 December 1997, King Bhumibol urged his subjects to leave behind the seductions of the city and return to agriculture in response to the economic crisis engulfing Thailand. Not only was agriculture the source of real and lasting economic worth, the king said, but agricultural enterprise was also the source of the best of Thai values.

It was a very attractive message to a people in the grip of a depression provoked by the cataclysm that indiscriminate globalization had wrought on their economy. But some asked whether there really was an agricultural economy that Thailand's millions could return to. Or did the king have a romanticized view of a countryside that had been irrevocably transformed by the very forces that had driven the urban-industrial economy off the cliff?

The two faces of the Thai countryside

Thailand's agriculture evokes contrasting images. One is that of a rich, well-watered, inexhaustible land, an image captured in King Ramkhamhaeng's saying: "This land of Sukhothai is thriving. There is fish in the water and rice in the fields. Whoever wants to trade in elephants, does so. Whoever wants to trade in horses, does so."[1] Ramkhamhaeng's observation seems as applicable to the twentieth century as it was to the thirteenth. Currently, Thailand is Asia's only net food exporter. And Thai rice has become the symbol of the bounteousness of the Thai countryside: in the early 1990s, Thailand's rice exports accounted for 35 per cent of the world's rice exports and came to almost twice the volume of US rice exports.

Thailand, moreover, is not simply portrayed as a monocrop success story. It is also pictured as a land of entrepreneurial farmers who have created a diversified agriculture by taking advantage of world demand for a wide range of commodities, starting with cassava, kenaf (a jute substitute), maize, and sugarcane in the 1960s and 1970s, moving on to soybeans, oil palm, and coffee in the 1980s, and, in the 1990s, pioneering in the production and export of prawns, frozen fowl, fruits, and flowers.

Table 8.1 GDP and workforce shares of major economic sectors (%)

	Agriculture			Industry			Services		
	1975	1985	1995	1975	1985	1995	1975	1985	1995
GDP	26.9	15.8	10.4	25.8	31.8	40.0	47.3	52.3	49.6
Work force	M W	M W	M W	M W	M W	M W	M W	M W	M W
	76 71	64 63	40 43	7 10	11 15	20 27	17 19	25 22	50 38

Source: Asian Development Bank, *Key Indicators of Developing Asian and Pacific Countries* (Manila: Asian Development Bank, 1997), pp. 20, 8.

But there is another face to Thai agriculture, and this is that of a sector that was already in the grip of a profound crisis before the financial débâcle. This crisis has many dimensions, but a central one is the contradiction between Thailand's status as an agricultural superpower and the continuing low living standards of the bulk of the agricultural population. In the early 1990s, over 40 per cent of the rural population, by some estimates, continued to live below the poverty line, underlining the persistence of highly inequitable access to the income from agricultural growth.

The pervasiveness of rural poverty reflects a broader phenomenon, which is the fact that the countryside has been left behind, far behind, by the city. The contribution of agriculture to GDP fell from around 40 per cent in 1960 to slightly over 10.4 per cent in 1995, while that of industry rose from 18 per cent to close to 40 per cent.[2] Reflecting this trend, the gap in income between rural people and urban dwellers has widened precipitously: whereas the average income of a worker in agriculture was one-sixth of that of workers in other sectors in the early 1960s, by the early 1990s, it had gone down to one-twelfth.[3] With more than three-quarters of those defined as poor living in the countryside, poverty has become, according to economist Amar Siamwalla, 'almost entirely a rural phenomenon'.[4]

The statistical trends shown in Table 8.1 reflect the underlying structural dynamics that have changed the face of the Thai countryside. Thailand's agrarian condition today is a result of government policy, the commercialization of agricultural production, and social struggle. The central policy factor has been the subordination of agriculture to the interests of the urban-industrial sector. The main structural condition has been the advanced integration of Thai agriculture to the world market, resulting in the intense commercialization of production relations. And the decisive social and political event was the political defeat of the Thai peasantry in the 1970s.

Subordinating the countryside to the city

Bangkok today dominates Thailand in a way that no other capital city lords it over any other large East Asian country. It is home to almost 15 per cent of the population and accounts for over 42 per cent of the gross domestic product. This position of dominance did not arise solely from natural market forces: the city had a lot of help from Bangkok-based policymakers.

This assistance took the form of a string of post-Second World War policies that consistently sacrificed the interests of the rural sector, made up largely of numerous but politically powerless smallholders, to the interests of an urban coalition dominated by extremely powerful commercial, bureaucratic, and military elites.

The most prominent instrument for the subordination of the country-side was the rice premium or an *ad valorem* tax on rice exports.[5] The tax, which was changed at irregular intervals, could sometimes reach 30 per cent of the world market price.[6] By tightly controlling the flow of the marketable surplus to the world market, the premium had the effect of insulating the domestic market from international rice price movements and consistently depressing the domestic price of rice, which was Thailand's staple food. The result was that rice producers were deprived of substantial income, this being transferred instead in the form of lower food costs to 'urban employers, workers, and, perhaps most importantly, civil servants, the bureaucratic elite's key constituency'.[7]

In imposing and maintaining the rice premium, the government was not pursuing an anti-export policy. Indeed, the consistent policy of most of the regimes since the mid-nineteenth century was to play on Thailand's 'comparative advantage' as an agro-exporting country in the world market to gain the foreign exchange necessary to finance the government's strategic objectives, including industrialization. But this general pro-export thrust was modified by the government's pursuit of other objectives. In establishing and maintaining the rice premium, the government acted from a variety of motives. With the rice premium providing some 20 per cent of all government revenues in the 1960s, the tax was central to financing an expanding government bureaucracy. Also important was the influence of a few well-connected trading firms that were skilled at spreading around key sectors of the bureaucracy part of the huge profits they made by controlling the bulk of the country's rice exports. But probably the most important consideration was the need to maintain political stability.[8]

Since inflation was usually a trigger for political unrest in Bangkok, the rice premium was seen as an important political mechanism which assured an adequate domestic supply of rice and low rice prices. Control of rice prices was strategic in the politics of containing unrest, since a low rice price had a depressing effect on the prices of most other agricultural activities.[9] The importance of the premium for urban stability is underlined by estimates showing that without the export tax, the increase in the wholesale price of rice could have reached as high as 90 per cent and the rise in the cost of living could have been close to 25 per cent.[10]

The idea that the rice premium would be used as an instrument of industrialization was probably not central in the government's initial calculations. Yet its subsidization of industrial development was probably the rice premium's most important effect. And as succeeding Thai regimes realized the value of the rice premium in promoting a pro-industrialization policy, this became an added incentive to maintain it. As Mehdi Krongkaew put it, via the rice premium, 'the government (unknowingly, perhaps) helped reduce wage costs to non-agricultural employers, which further helped to stimulate the import substituting industrialization, and an overall transfer of agricultural surplus to non-agricultural development purposes'.[11]

A now classic study by Amar Siamwalla and Suthad Setboonsarng has, in fact, found that, except for 1970, there was a net transfer of real wealth from agriculture for all years between 1962 and 1981.[12] The resource outflow was particularly heavy between 1973 and 1976, when agriculture was squeezed of over 40,000 billion baht, most likely to make up for industry's much higher import bill following the Arab oil embargo of 1973 and to pacify a restive urban population during this inflationary and politically volatile period.

The problem does not lie in the fact that agriculture was taxed to promote industry. All societies seeking to industrialize with minimal dependence on foreign capital find that they have few options but to promote a net flow of real resources from agriculture in the early stages of development. Rather it was the highly unbalanced character of the process that was problematic. What should have been a transitory policy to get industry on its feet became a permanent policy of squeezing agriculture.

Moreover, a substantial part of government revenues should have been recycled back to the agricultural sector to counter the rice premium's negative impact on income by subsidizing production inputs and extension, upgrading farmers' technology, and supporting land reform and other social reforms designed to help the lower strata in the countryside. However, only a small part of the national budget – 7–13 per cent – in the period 1961–81 was devoted to expenditures in agriculture, despite the fact that agriculture accounted for 25-40 per cent of gross domestic product, 50–90 per cent of exports, and 60–82 per cent of the workforce.[13] Moreover, the bulk of expenditures on agriculture focused on activities, like dam construction and roadbuilding, that were designed to promote commercialization and greater production for export, rather than on those that would directly uplift rural incomes, like subsidies for small producers, land reform, and support for smallholder technological innovation.

In short, government strategy has been consistently a lopsided, short-sighted one of milking and permanently subordinating agriculture to urban commercial-industrial interests, with little concern for the future of agriculture, rather than a balanced one aimed at gradually reducing the agricultural sector's subsidization of industrialization and making agricultural prosperity instead one of the engines of subsequent industrial growth.

As Kosit Pampriemras, a respected former minister of agriculture and cooperatives, put it, government policy has been generally to ignore the farm sector in favour of manufacturing, investing surplus funds generated by farm exports into non-agro industry. 'Thailand has a huge comparative advantage in agriculture. But you cannot reinvigorate your agriculture without ploughing back a huge amount of capital.' Instead, says Kosit, current policy 'has made agriculture weaker and weaker. The result is you lose competitiveness, and you leave farmers eternally poorer.'[14]

In this sense, one speaks not about a calculated and careful use of agricultural resources to subsidize the creation of a manufacturing sector, but about squeezing the agrarian sector to serve urban-industrial interests allied to key sectors of the bureaucracy.

This distortion or abuse of the industrialization rationale to favour urban elite interests is evident not only in the rice premium but in import-substitution policy. While import substitution is generally a sound path for a country seeking to industrialize, it is often abused to favour selected interests with special ties to the bureaucracy so that its balance of social costs and benefits is lopsidedly skewed toward them.

The development of a fertilizer industry is one example, where both motives apparently operated, with drastic consequences for agriculture. To begin with, as Scott Christensen notes, the development of the industry was treated solely as an industrial concern, with little consideration of its impact on agriculture.[15] Restrictions were placed on imports of urea, the cheapest available source of nitrogen nutrient, while a monopoly was granted in the 1970s to Thai Central Chemical, a client firm of Bangkok Bank, to build a plant to produce ammonium phosphate, a lower-grade fertilizer. The upshot of these arrangements was that Thailand had 'one of the highest fertilizer price-to-paddy ratios in all of Asia.'[16] This abuse of industrial policy undoubtedly contributed to a disincentive to fertilizer use, a trend that also emerges clearly in the comparative figures: among twelve Asian and Pacific countries, Thailand had the lowest average nutrient (fertilizer) consumption in the mid-1980s.[17]

The inequitable burden imposed on agriculture by these tax and industrial policy mechanisms not only had immiserizing effects on small farmers, but acted, along with the lack of secure title to land for most farmers, as a disincentive to technological innovation in agriculture during an era that was marked elsewhere by what the World Bank characterized as 'extraordinary technical advance'.[18] While the high cost of fertilizer probably saved Thailand from the less desirable aspects of the Green Revolution package, like the massive use of pesticide and fragile high-yielding seed varieties, it also made for a relatively inefficient agriculture. Yields for major crops in Thailand were lower than in most other Asian countries. For instance, while yield in Thailand was only 330 kilograms per rai (equivalent to two-fifths of one acre) of riceland in Thailand, it was 648 kg per rai in Korea.[19] A contrast with Japan shows up the relative inefficiency of Thai riziculture: Thailand used 60 million rai of land to produce 12 million tons of rice, while Japan employed 13 million rai to produce 10 million tons.[20]

Moreover, the disincentives for intensive farming at a time of growing domestic and foreign demand for Thai agricultural products constituted one of the key factors leading Thai farmers to prefer extensive cultivation, or bringing in new land, most of it carved out of the forest, as a means to expand production – a topic to be covered more fully in Chapter 9.

Commercialization and agrarian crisis up to the 1970s

The subordination of agriculture to urban-industrial interests occurred within a context where agriculture, in particular rice, had already been significantly commercialized and oriented toward supplying both the city and the world market. Commercialization or the commodification of agricultural production accelerated following the Bowring Treaty of 1855, when Britain, in search for cheap rice for its colonies and raw materials like timber for its industries, dragged Thailand into the world market. This orientation of agriculture to urban and international markets became a consistent element of Thailand's economic policy. The strategy of squeezing agriculture to serve industry simply accentuated this process, which made Thailand a key exporting country but, as in other cases of the rapid spread of capitalist production relations, also promoted social differentiation and triggered social stress.

Tenancy and landlessness in central Thailand The trend of social differentiation and economic deterioration were most advanced in the central region. This area comprises the vast Chao Phraya river basin, extending from the low lands around the Mae Klong and Tha rivers in the west to the Bang Pakong river in the east. With its six million hectares of cultivated or potentially cultivable land ranging from moderately to extremely fertile and particularly suitable for rice cultivation,[21] it is not surprising that this is the part of Thailand that was integrated earliest into the capitalist world economy.

With commercial rice production becoming a profitable activity, many aristocratic families of the old *sakdina* system of sociopolitical stratification took advantage of peasant ignorance of the landmark Land Law of 1901, which institutionalized private landownership as a category distinct from usufruct, to transform their rights over labour to rights over land farmed by subsistence rice producers. While small independent farms were the rule in the rest of the country, the nobility accumulated large holdings along the newly constructed canals immediately to the north and west of Bangkok.[22] For instance, when the Rangsit Canal project was undertaken, the Svitongse family, who operated the Siam Canal Company, was able to acquire 800,000 rai of land in Pathum Thani, Ayuthaya, and Saraburi provinces.[23]

Peasant dispossession was accelerated by the dynamics of the international market. The central region was particularly vulnerable, notes one analyst, '[to] a succession of booms and busts and thus, wherever commercialized economy developed, peasants became extensively dependent upon conditions external to the local economy, conditions over which they had no control'.[24] This led to more and more farmers falling from independent farming status to the status of tenant or that of landless worker, as aristocrats took advantage of busts to gain possession of lands from subsistence farmers.

By the early 1970s, a study of eleven provinces in the central region found that 39 per cent of farmers were full tenants and another 30 per cent were part tenants.[25] By 1981, over 36 per cent of all landholdings were rented.[26] Conditions were not easy for these tenants, with rents rising from about a quarter of the crop in prewar days to half or more of the crop in the postwar period.[27]

Landless workers were also an increasing proportion of the population, reaching up to 14 or 15 per cent of rural families in the central region by the mid-1970s.[28] Landlessness was especially marked in the provinces of Pathumthani (26 per cent of all rural households), Samut Prakan (31 per cent), and Ayuthaya (38 per cent). Landless workers were the 'lowest of the low', with one survey showing that their income came to 8,046 baht a year, compared to 20,712 baht for tenant farmers, and 28,786 for full owners.[29]

While some farmers lost their lands to Bangkok-based elites, others lost it to Chinese moneylenders to whom they had pledged their land as collateral, as the commercialization of more and more of their production increased their vulnerability to lost incomes from the wide price swings of the market.

But other factors served to accelerate the deterioration of the conditions of the peasantry. One was, paradoxically enough, government investment in rural development projects designed to upgrade agricultural productivity. Central Thailand received the lion's share of funds for irrigation from the government, so that by the late 1970s it accounted for 68 per cent of all irrigated land in comparison to the country's other regions.[30] So well irrigated was the central plain that by the early 1960s, the government was encouraging farmers to plant a second crop during the dry season. But this increase in productive capacity was not matched by reforms in the system of land tenure, so that benefits from irrigation did not flow equitably to all farmers, but went primarily to the 'wealthier farmers in the Central Plain'.[31]

Immiserizing effects were also associated with another object of rural development policy, which was to upgrade productivity via the adoption of more chemical-intensive agricultural technology. Although Thailand as a whole has been slower than some other East Asian countries in adopting fertilizer- and pesticide-dependent technology, the process in the central region was faster than in other parts of the country. But, as in rice-growing areas of India, Bangladesh, and the Philippines, the purchase of modern inputs and machinery put small farmers in a quandary. The high cost of the inputs forced many to mortgage their lands to merchants and moneylenders. And when they could no longer bear the cost of servicing the loans, they either yielded the land to their creditors or sold it to get the money to repay the loans.

At this point, central Thai farmers were confronted with four choices: continue in rice farming as low-income tenants, become wage labourers either by migrating to Bangkok or engaging in non-farm rural livelihoods, shift over to upland farming on encroached forest land, or organize to gain secure control of their land. The last option was not out of the question, and when a series of urban political events exposed the fragility of the system of elite rule, farmers in the central plain took the lead in what would become a massive effort to organize the Thai peasantry as a social and political force – a subject that will be taken up later.

Commercialization and social relations in northern Thailand Perhaps next to the central region, the commercialization of agriculture has been most advanced in the north, which covers a 17 million hectare area from Changwat Nakhon Sawan in the south to the border with Burma and Laos in the north. Only about a third of the land area, however, is suitable for cultivation, with most of this being in the lower northern plain and in the valleys of the upper north traversed by the Ping, Yom, and Nan rivers.[32]

With land relatively scarce, especially in the mountainous upper north, cultivation is done in relatively small plots that are either rainfed or serviced by traditional indigenous irrigation systems. While the average farm size for Thailand is 28.28 rai, in the upper north it is only 12.29 rai. But because of the rich alluvial soils in the valley bottoms, the land is more productive, with yields in 1987 coming to 476 kg per rai, compared to only 292 kg per rai for the country as a whole.[33]

The rapid spread of market relations in the north came a few decades later than in the extremely fertile central valley, partly because of a belated interest in the resources of the area by the colonial powers, particularly Britain, and partly because of the late political and administrative integration into the central government structure managed from Bangkok. But from the 1920s the commercialization of rice production accelerated, and social relations in the countryside evolved from the pre-capitalist system of power and privilege to one based on private ownership, commodity production, and tenancy and labour relations.[34]

Commodification of production, as in the central plain, was accompanied by the displacement of many independent smallholders and the accumulation of control over land by village-based wealthy peasants and town-based Chinese commercial interests, both of which developed close ties to the government apparatus. By the 1930s, in fact, tenancy had become a common practice among peasants in the north, with sharecroppers furnishing nearly all the cultivation inputs, except for the land tax, which was paid by the landlords, who in return retained one-half of the crop after harvest.[35]

In the 1960s and 1970s, the combination of the continuing low price of rice and the fuller integration of the region's agriculture into the national and international economy pushed many owner-cultivators into growing non-rice cash crops like tobacco, soybeans, garlic, and temperate vegetables. But shifting to these crops also meant increased dependence on the market, since peasants not only had to rely on the sale of crops that, unlike in the case of rice, they could not store and consume, but also had to purchase capital inputs, like fertilizer and pesticides, which greatly determined productivity in these crops.[36] In the early 1970s, for instance, it was reported that in the Chiang Mai area almost 90 per cent of all households used chemical fertilizers for tobacco production and 83 per cent used them for producing garlic.[37]

As in central Thailand, the combination of market forces and an increasingly inequitable tenure system ensured that the greater productivity made possible by the Green Revolution would be cornered by the richer strata and create difficulties for the poorer strata. Anan Ganjanapan describes this paradoxical process of increased productivity-cum-immiserization:

> [P]oor peasants had to pay higher costs of production than did the rich, for both hired labor and new inputs, while they could not afford to invest as heavily as could the rich. This was clear in the case of fertilizer applications: as poor peasants were forced to buy fertilizer on credit, they received less for their money; with small amounts of fertilizer, poor peasants could not get returns high enough to cover the actual cost of their labor, as could the rich. In other words, by becoming involved in cashcrop production, the poor peasants actually grew poorer.[38]

By the 1970s conditions had clearly worsened. Tenancy in the north became more widespread: in one survey, the percentage of tenant households rose from 18.3 per cent of all households in 1967–68 to 27 per cent by 1976.[39] Landlessness had also shot up, with the figure of landless households in one district in the province of Chiang Mai coming to 36 per cent in 1974.[40] Landlords had also become more aggressive, taking in many cases two-thirds of the harvest as rent.[41]

The micro-dynamics of peasant distress under conditions of commodity production, spreading tenancy, and high rents are captured by Anan in his classic study of the northern village of Bang San Pong, where some tenant farmers came to the conclusion that they would probably be better off being simply labourers:

> Under these conditions, many tenants thought that the rice they produced from their rented land was more expensive than rice currently available in the market. Although no tenants yet wanted to leave the land they rented, they voiced their frustration, expressing the opinion that they might be better off working as wage laborers, buying their rice from the market. This is an indication that because of the increased rents tenants' labor is actually paid less than its market value. Consequently, several tenants believe that they have become poorer producing intensively for the market. In this sense, tenants receive less return for their labor in intensive commercial production than they did when they worked to grow mainly for subsistence. Most of their surplus labor is now captured by landlords through high rents.[42]

Faced with these worsening conditions, peasants had several options. As in other parts of Thailand, some went to farm in encroached forest lands in the upland areas, hoping that the poorer quality of the soil and scarcity of irrigation would be offset by their specialization in non-rice commercial crops that were more appropriate for such conditions. This brought them into competition with tribal peoples who already lived in upland areas or considered them their areas of expansion, often, as in the case of the Hmong, with the same idea of growing commercial crops.[43] In the last few decades, the half-million or so minority peoples in the uplands have been forced into competition for scarce land and resources, with perhaps three million Thai moving up from the lowlands.[44]

But there was another option, and in the 1970s many tenants and landless labourers in the north rallied around the flag of land-tenure reform. As was the case in the central plain, the most fertile soil for the seeds of political protest was found in those areas where tenancy was most common and dispossession most prevalent.

From subsistence to commodity production in the northeast The northeast was paradoxical. On the one hand, it was the poorest region of the country, where 74 per cent of people lived below the poverty line in 1963, compared to 40 per cent in the central plain, 65 per cent in the

north, and 57 per cent in the nation as a whole.[45] On the other hand, tenant-farming families formed a much lower proportion of rural households in the northeast than in the central plains and north: in 1971, only 3.9 per cent of farm households in the northeast rented their land, compared to 18.9 per cent in the north and 34.8 per cent in the central plain.[46]

This phenomenon of great poverty-cum-relative equality seemed to be rooted in the very poor soils and lack of moisture in what is called the Korat Plateau, which covers an area of some 17 million hectares from the Petchabun-Bangrek range to the Laotian and Cambodian borders.[47] The area has little potential for irrigation, forcing farmers to remain dependent on monsoon rains, which are unreliable. Rice can be grown on some of these sandy, quickly drained, and infertile soils, but with much lower yields than in other parts of the country.

In fact, only 21 per cent of the plateau is said to be suitable for rice cultivation, although 34 per cent of the region is in paddy-fields.[48] Although the northeast accounted for some 46 per cent of Thailand's rice-fields, it was responsible for only slightly over one-third of its production. And the productivity gap has worsened over time: while yields in the northeast were on par with those in the central plain at the turn of the century, they had fallen to 70 per cent of the latter by 1950–52 and 61 per cent by the late 1970s.[49]

Yet the very poverty rooted in poor soil also prevented the growth of severe class differentiation. Rice produced was mainly consumed by households, and since production conditions permitted only a small margin of surplus that could be collected as rent, it must have been difficult, notes one analyst, "for any political leaders to obtain sufficient wealth from the cultivators to sustain higher living standards than the rest of the population".[50] Thus, while class differences did and do exist, a relative egalitarianism compared to the north and the central plain prevailed in the northeast, and peasant communities were able to achieve a relative autonomy *vis-à-vis* town-based elites.

The strategy of survival evolved by these communities in the midst of a harsh environment consisted of the organization of nucleated settlements at slightly elevated sites, cultivation of glutinous rice under wet-field conditions to meet basic food needs, and the preservation of common fields and forests where sufficient fish could be grown during the rainy season and later preserved in order to meet villagers' protein requirements during the rest of the year.[51] Cooperation within the whole settlement or among groups of kindred was a central principle of social organization which 'helped to compensate for the unpredictability of the water regime and remoteness from other communities'.[52]

Although the market economy had spread to most of the northeast by the mid-twentieth century, the conditions of production and consumption in Nakhon Ratchasima (Korat) described by Charles Mehl were probably typical for the whole region:

> [A]griculture remained only marginally commercialized for most households. Families still produced virtually all the food they consumed and many household items. Each family also provided almost all the labor for its agricultural activities: only a few farmers hired outside laborers to help plough and harvest their rice fields. The 1950 agricultural census showed only four per cent of all agricultural activities on all farms in the province being carried out by full and part-time wage labor.[53]

But since the 1960s this rough equality amidst poverty has increasingly come under stress from increased commercialization, the social consequences of agricultural diversification, and more active interest in the area from the central government.

Commercialization accelerated as Thailand's rice economy was integrated more fully into the world economy. Rice production rose, and while most of the rice was consumed to support the region's growing population, some of it was exported. From barely one per cent of Thailand's rice exports in 1905, the northeast's contribution rose to one-tenth two decades later and one-quarter in the early postwar era.[54]

By and large, however, the scarcity of water and other harsh conditions of production permitted relatively little rice surplus for export, and farmers seeking to supplement subsistence needs were attracted by world demand to go into the production of less water-intensive commercial crops like kenaf, maize, and cassava.[55]

Exports of Thai kenaf (a substitute for jute in the manufacture of burlap bags) have, for the most part, come from the northeast, where production shot up from 10,000 metric tons in 1955 to 520,000 metric tons in 1965.[56] Similarly, demand for cassava from Europe to feed to livestock triggered a 'boom' in the northeast, leading to the quadrupling of land devoted to cassava in just four years in the mid-1970s and to the northeast becoming the top producer of the crop among all regions.[57]

A not unimportant reason for the rise of commercial agricultural production in the 1950s to 1970s was government investment in rural infrastructure. The growing government interest in the rural areas was a result of (1) the natural extension of the effective authority of the Thai central state, which had been going on since the late nineteenth century; (2) a conscious effort to create the infrastructure for the integration of the rural areas into the market economy under the influence of the World Bank–USAID ideology of developmentalism; and (3) an effort to preempt or defuse insurgency in sensitive rural areas. The part of the national budget devoted to agriculture rose from 7.3 per cent in 1961–66 to 15.1 per cent in 1972–76, with close to half of the agricultural budget going to irrigation.[58]

The northeast was a favoured recipient of rural development assistance, partly because of central government fears that the combination of poverty and the cultural proximity of northeasterners to people in Laos, across the Mekong, would be fertile soil for insurgency. Bilateral aid from the United States, in particular, was directed at the region – perhaps not surprisingly in light of the proximity of Laos, Cambodia, and Vietnam, where the USA was directly engaged in a major war. Building up a road network became a priority in the northeast, with close to two-thirds of the 17,000 kilometres of road built under the American-funded Accelerated Rural Development Program located in the northeast.[59]

But the rice and commercial crop boom promoted by these efforts had its costs. First, increases in production were achieved not through intensive cultivation but through the extension of production to upland and lowland forested areas. With the northeast's forest area being drastically reduced from 46 per cent in 1961 to 27 per cent by 1978, one analyst contends that the 'commodity crop boom has ... been a powerful new engine of destruction of the Korat Plateau woodlands'.[60]

Another key consequence was increasing social conflict over land and scarce water resources, as individuals sought to maximize their interests by privatizing what were formerly regarded as communal property, like ponds, pasture land, and forests, leading to violent confrontations and to the erosion of community solidarity and values.

A third result was increasing social differentiation. With more people exposed to the vagaries of the market, it was not surprising that increasing numbers of villagers fell into debt and eventually lost their lands, forcing them to become either tenant farmers or landless workers. While the northeast still has a lower percentage of rented land than either the central plain or the north, the figure nevertheless went up from 0.3 per cent in 1962/63 to 2.7 per cent in 1975/76 to 5 per cent by 1991.[61] In fact, while tenanted land in the central plain fell by 3 per cent between 1980 and 1991, it rose by an astounding 56 per cent in the northeast.[62]

The micro-dynamics of these macro-trends are brought to sharp relief in Charles Mehl's summary of a study conducted by the National Economic and Social Development Board (NESDB) of the interaction of local land tenure and world market-induced commercialization in the Khong district in Nakhon Ratchasima:

> 21 of 90 families surveyed by the NESDB researchers were full tenants. Around 1960, the price of kenaf was high, about 4 to 5 baht per kilogram, so farmers borrowed money to purchase seed and to hire labor to plant the crop over much of their holdings. By the time they harvested the crop, the market for kenaf collapsed and they received only 0.50 to 0.75 baht per kilogram, not enough to cover their investment costs. Prices did not improve and people abandoned kenaf as a crop. They were able to earn enough money from rice sales and other sources of cash income to cover the annual interest payments,

but few could repay their entire debts. Almost all had borrowed from a local merchant at interest rates of 50 to 75 per cent per year.[63]

In the early and mid-1970s, after several years of severe drought destroyed most agricultural production in the community:

> Those who had more land to mortgage went further into debt, and those who defaulted on their loans lost their land to that same merchant. He now rents their lands to the former owners at substantial rates. Those who remain in debt struggle to keep their lands. The NESDB survey found 29 of the 90 households had their land either mortgaged to the merchant or under a contractual relationship with him called *khai faak*, in which the borrower has a stipulated number of years to redeem the land, else it becomes the property of the moneylender … If they are faced with two or three more years of drought, they are likely to default on their loans, lose their land to the merchant, and join the ranks of tenant farmers in the village.

But the winners from the cash crop roulette often found themselves in just as precarious a situation as the losers, leading to what might be described as scorched-earth or strip-mine-style farming. In his study of the village of Nong Kok in Nakhon Ratchasima, Mehl discovered that the basis of much of the new wealth, which was the acquisition of reserve forest land and the cultivation there of maize and cassava, was 'extremely precarious':

> The markets are unstable: severe European Economic Community quotas on cassava products have led to plummeting prices in the past two years, while maize prices fluctuate according to United States production and grain prices. Just as critical is the instability of land possession. The government does not recognize possession and utilization of official forest area (except for land tax collection), even when the 'forest' no longer has trees.[64]

Not surprisingly, some of the farmers of Nong Kok 'exploit the land in the hills as much as they can, as quickly as they can. At the same time, they use their new wealth to create opportunities for their children, mainly through formal education, to move out of agriculture into other activities and, for many, out of the village.'[65]

Though not as pronounced as in the north and the central region, then, increased social differentiation and more unequal income distribution also accompanied the more intensive commodification of agricultural production in the northeast. If poverty could be tolerated because of its 'relatively democratic distribution' before the 1960s, its being accompanied by increasing inequality, triggered by the opening up of forest lands and upland areas to commercial crop cultivation, in the succeeding decades increasingly fuelled social antagonisms.

Social struggle, reform, and peasant defeat

These trends brought the rural sector to what Andrew Turton describes as a 'state of unparalleled crisis' by the 1970s.[66] This brings us to the third key determinant of the conditions of the countryside today: the development of the social struggle. Specifically, the defeat of the peasantry's attempts to organize for fundamental economic and social reform in the 1970s had major consequences on the evolution of the agricultural economy in the 1980s and 1990s.

The overthrow of the Thanom-Praphat regime in 1973 by a coalition of students and other urban-based social sectors exposed a degree of fragility and vulnerability in the ruling system that was not lost on peasants. While peasant revolts against the state took place in the late nineteenth and early twentieth centuries these were localized, spontaneous, and sometimes millenarian in character, like the 'Holy Men Rebellions' in the northeast.[67] The peasant organizing that unfolded in the democratic interlude between 1973 and 1976 was different, being the first time the peasantry had sought to organize itself autonomously as a class on a national scale and on the basis of a secular programme.

While communist cadres probably played some role in the formation of the key peasant organization, the Farmers' Federation of Thailand (FFT), the central role was filled by peasant grassroots leaders, and the success of the FFT was due precisely to its non-ideological style of organizing. The Federation served to bring together issues, concerns, and demands from different regions and different sectors of the Thai peasantry, not all of whom experienced the same problems to the same degree:

> Some were demands for immediate action, such as grants of land for the coming planting season, price regulation, reduction of farm rents, suspension of court cases involving farmers, release of those arrested for trespass, and help for flood victims. Others were longer term demands, such as those for land reform and permanent provision of land to the landless, and a solution to the problems of indebtedness and high interest rates. Some demands were more immediately political, such as the lifting of martial law in the outlying provinces, which prevented farmers from demonstrating. Over time, the demands escalated which seems to indicate a growing political consciousness and perhaps confidence.[68]

The peasant support for the Federation apparently came principally from the north and the central plain, where rates of tenancy and landlessness were highest. With an estimated membership of 1.5 million farmers nationwide,[69] the geographical scope of the Federation's organizing was unprecedented. So was the breadth of the programme, which sought to speak 'for the rural poor, the landless, those with smallholdings, tenants, and in a wider sense for all those who experienced injustice and denial of democratic freedoms'.[70] Most significantly, notes another observer, the

FFT represented a historical juncture: the peasants of Thailand 'had set up their own organization and drawn up a program of struggle to help solve the basic problems of Thai farmers.'[71]

Peasant organization was accompanied by direct action, with peasants in some provinces, supported by students, retaking land from landlords and moneylenders who had confiscated the land upon the peasants' defaulting on their debts.[72] Local and national mobilizations by peasants demanding higher rice prices and land reform hit provincial capitals as well as Bangkok.

Pressure from the peasantry was instrumental in wringing concessions from the elite reformist governments that reigned, in unstable fashion, between 1973 and 1976. These concessions included a half-hearted effort on the part of the government to reverse the past policy of keeping rice prices low to benefit urban groups. While keeping urban consumers happy remained a prime objective of the government, it also committed itself to raise or stabilize the income of paddy farmers. The formula chosen to maintain this delicate political balancing act consisted of setting minimum prices for rice on the open market, government purchase of rice at guaranteed prices, and the sale of subsidized rice to low-income groups, particularly those in Bangkok.[73]

But more important than the reform in rice policy was the attempt of the government of Prime Minister Kukrit Pramoj to deliver to the country-side a rural reform package consisting of the following measures: requiring commercial banks to transfer 5 per cent of their deposits as loans to farmers; the creation of a special fund for development projects in the countryside, the so-called Tambon Fund; the implementation of land rent controls; and land reform and redistribution.

In hindsight, the Tambon Fund was the Kukrit Pramoj government's most successful rural programme. One might describe it as a massive New Deal-type public works programme that sought to accelerate the disbursement of government resources to the countryside and to create jobs by putting people to work on infrastructure projects. Some 20 per cent of government capital expenditure was devoted to the programme in 1975 and 1976, and this infusion of cash went to provide an estimated three months' employment for 700,000 people each year.[74]

But the reformist character of the Tambon Development Programme must not be exaggerated. It was, in great part, a conventional 'counter-cyclical', Keynesian effort to arrest the impact of the decline of investment in agriculture during the troubled recessionary times of the early 1970s. Public investment in agriculture had, in fact, dropped from 1.2 per cent of GNP in 1970 to 0.4 per cent of GNP in 1974, with serious effects on the incomes of the thousands of rural people who had come to rely on casual and semipermanent work in government construction projects. Tambon spending had the impact of restoring the real volume of government construction activity in the rural areas in 1975 to 1970 levels, although it considerably exceeded the latter the following year.[75]

There were, certainly, innovative aspects to the Tambon programme, including its focus on small infrastructural projects that did not take too long to complete, high wage levels relative to prevailing rates, and the selection of projects by the Tambon (subdistrict) Council. But again, the actual impact of these innovations on the grassroots must not be exaggerated. Selection of projects by the Tambon Council, for instance, did not necessarily mean that the process was under popular control since the Council was made up of appointed *Phu Yai Ban* or village headmen. Indeed, in many cases, the biggest beneficiaries of the Tambon Programme were local authorities and local business elites, who put together construction deals to corner the massive inflow of funds being pushed by Bangkok and became rich in the process.[76] Perhaps the most important aspect of the decentralization promoted by the programme was the democratization of corruption.

While the elite reformist governments of 1973 to 1976 might be said to have tried hard to introduce a more equitable rice price policy and achieved some success with the Tambon Development Programme, they failed to translate the centrepiece of their agricultural programme – land tenure reform – from parliamentary act to agrarian reality. In comparison with land reform experiences such as those in Taiwan and Korea, the land tenure reforms in Thailand were very limited. The Land Rent Control Act of 1974 and the Land Control Act guaranteed tenancy contracts for six years and fixed the landlord's share at a maximum of half the crop, after deducting one-third for whoever shouldered production costs other than labour.[77] The Land Reform Act stipulated a rather generous maximum holding of 50 rai of land, with surplus land liable to expropriation and distribution to peasants, after compensation at market value. Moreover, land up to 1,000 rai could be retained if landowners could convince the local land reform committee that their land was being farmed 'productively'.[78]

This legislation ran up against the realities of Thailand's power structure. Indeed, land reform served as the cement for the counterrevolutionary unification of powerful fractions of the elite, which had been temporarily in disarray during the reformist period. Although these measures were clearly cautious in character and quite limited in their likely impact, they were perceived as threatening the very foundations of elite rule in Thailand, with significant negative impact not only on landowners but on the urban and bureaucratic elites as well. As one analyst pointed out:

[A]grarian reform would have threatened a large number of rural landowners and absentee landlords, large numbers of whom were businessmen, high-ranking military and bureaucratic elites, noble families and the royal family itself. Large tracts of the best land of the country were owned by this powerful group of elites. They were so thoroughly integrated into the commercial, industrial, and banking sectors that any attempt to expropriate their holdings, or to challenge their position was likely to bring on an economic and political crisis. The Crown Property Bureau and the royal family together, for example, were reported to have had the largest landholdings in the country while many of the largest holdings in the fertile areas of the Central region were owned by noble families. Added to this was high-level military and bureaucratic officials who, in collaboration with some businessmen, had invested heavily in land speculation in the 1960s.[79]

Not surprisingly a counterrevolutionary movement began, with the landed elites forming paramilitary goups to initiate a wave of terror against the FFT and its student supporters. These formations included the Red Gaurs, Nawaphon, and the Village Scouts, who counted among their supporters the military, the police, and key business elites.[80] Confronted with this rightist reaction, the parliamentary regime put the land reform on hold and sided with landed interests in specific struggles with peasants. This retreat did not, however, prevent its authority from being eroded, as the military and key sections of the bureaucracy began to work with the economic elites to regain control of the political process via extra-parliamentary means. In a situation reminiscent of the Allende period in Chile, the authority of the legal powerholders evaporated, and the question of power came increasingly to be determined by the battles on the streets, with the advantage gained by those who could deploy superior resources in organization, firepower, and ideological combat.

The right combined terror tactics with ideological appeals designed to win the hearts and minds of the rural population in the battle with the left and the organized peasant movement.[81] The centrepiece of the right-wing ideological offensive was the slogan 'Nation–Religion–King'. In the case of the Village Scouts, one of the central organizations of the counterrevolution,[82] there was a sophisticated effort to fuse this hegemonic ideology with traditional rural Thai culture to create a more secure village basis for the existing order. This effort included indoctrination programmes that were clearly fascist-modernist in inspiration. Indoctrination, noted one observer, was 'emotionally stretching, from the lightheartedness of child's play to the seriousness of patriotism, humiliation to happiness, and competition to cooperation'.[83] The purpose of the exercise was 'to make the participants feel important, and identify themselves closely with the nation, the religion, and the king'.[84]

Despite the importance of ideology in the social struggle, force and repression were the principal means by which the threatened elites sought to protect their privileges. Peasant leaders were murdered systematically, with 18 FFT leaders assassinated between February and August 1975 alone.[85] The assassination wave reached its climax with the murder of

Intha Sribanruan, vice-president of the FFT, on 31 July 1975. This bloody suppression of the peasantry preceded and prefigured the massive 6 October 1976 massacre at Thammasatt University, when scores of students were killed, hundreds wounded, and thousands arrested in a coordinated assault by police and paramilitary groups including Nawaphon, Red Gaurs, and Village Scouts.

Containing the countryside after 1976

The bloody events of 1975–76 put an end to what had been a historic development in Thai history: the first effort of the peasantry to self-organize as a class. While there have been many instances of peasant protest since then, these were, most often, local in both scope and demands. Certainly the peasantry is, politically, much weaker today than it was in the 1970s. The dimensions of the defeat of 1975–76 are succinctly captured by Victor Karunan:

> In Thai society today, farmers are the weakest in terms of their organization and strength. They also suffer from the lack of a unified direction for the future of Thai society and how that future can be realized. Today, the FFT is no longer in their midst to provide the necessary organization and leadership to express their sentiments and grievances. They must evolve their own organization and means of expression. Ideologically too, farmers in Thailand are weak. The interruption in their past history of struggle and a certain 'loss of memory' are also affecting them adversely.[86]

The defeat of the peasantry in 1975–76, although it might be temporary, nevertheless had strategic consequences for the pattern of countryside development in the 1980s and 1990s. With the breaking of the back of the peasant movement, the opportunity for an alternative pattern of development was narrowed considerably. While they did not have an explicit alternative to the prevailing economic strategy, implicit in what the peasant movement and its allies were proposing was a vision in which agriculture would either be the pivot of the economy or at least maintain a healthy balance with the urban economy.

Borrowing from the Keynesian paradigm, one might say that the key to the realization of this vision was a reinvigorated rural smallholder economy, whose prosperity would increasingly serve as a an engine of urban-industrial development, not so much as a source of capital extracted by various mechanisms but as a source of demand. This would, in turn, have facilitated the emergence of an economy with more diverse sources of dynamism: export markets, the domestic urban market, and an expansive rural market. Indeed, with the higher incomes created by the combination of growth and a more equitable distribution of land and income, the rural areas and provincial cities, where 85 per cent of the population lives, would themselves become a key market for agricultural production. With prosperity coming to the rural areas, the growing income and social gap between the countryside and the city could be removed; and, with concomitant political reform, a significant amount of political power could be devolved to the countryside, thus arresting the continued concentration of power in Bangkok.

Instead of the unfolding of this alternative pattern of growth or something roughly similar to it, the 1980s and 1990s have seen an even greater domination of economic direction by urban-industrial priorities. After the October 1976 coup, rice policy reverted to its traditional emphasis of keeping domestic rice prices low to serve urban-industrial interests and contain urban unrest.[87] More important, the land-tenure reforms came to a screeching halt. The Land Rent Control Act was practically forgotten, as tenancy arrangements once again became common giving landlords rights to one-half to two-thirds of the harvest. The Land Reform Act as a means of expropriating and substituting private land was abandoned.

The collapse of land reform   The Land Reform Act of 1975 was originally meant to be implemented through the expropriation of private land in excess of 50 rai. But at the time of writing, the Agrarian Land Reform Office (ALRO) has not yet expropriated any private land for redistribution to peasants. Instead, what private land was redistributed was done through commercial deals with landlords, most of whom were unwilling to sell their land cheap given the inflation of land value that had accompanied Thailand's economic boom since the mid-1980s. To be sure, bureaucratic rules and rivalries have been part of the problem, since 16 agencies have some say on different dimensions of land reform and 16 different types of title deeds are involved.[88] Landlord craftiness was also part of the problem: as a preemptive measure, many landlords seeking to avoid any challenge to the 50-rai upper limit on landholdings divided up their land among family members instead of turning it over to tenant farmers or landless peasants.[89]

Nevertheless, it was not bureaucratic conflicts or landlord deviousness that were mainly responsible for the snail's pace of land reform. As Suthep Thaugsuban, land reform chief under the first Chuan Leekpai administration (1993–95), asserted, the reason was a lack of political will: 'I cannot say whether this is fair or unfair to previous administrations, but they failed to assign importance to the land reform project because it would affect the landlords, who felt that land reform was a communist idea.'[90]

Not surprisingly, then, of over 17 million rai of rented farmland in the country, only 0.3 million rai were redistributed to tenants.[91] As of late 1993, only 383,760 rai of farmland had been purchased from private landowners. And contrary to the impression given by Thaugsuban, the progress of agrarian reform in private land under Chuan was not measurably different from that of previous administrations: only 5,384 rai of private land had been purchased for distribution in the first eight months of the first Chuan administration, compared to an average of 22,250 rai in the previous 17 years.[92] Perhaps the sorry state of land reform is captured in one set of statistics: in over 17 years, only 43 families have received full landownership rights as a result of the reform, and the area covered amounts only to 795 rai![93]

With the suspension of land reform activity in private land, tenancy and labour conditions have worsened. As a key study of land conditions in the 1980s by the Chulalongkorn University Social Research Institute (CUSRI) pointed out:[94]

> Owner cultivators became part tenants, sharecroppers, and finally through lack of institutional control over tenancy arrangements, they became landless farmers and wage laborers, constituting a pool of unemployed labor with no viable alternative of seeking gainful employment on the land.

By the late 1980s, there were about one million tenant households cultivating an area of 6 million rai.[95] In the northeast, where tenancy had previously not been as great a problem as in the north and central region, land under tenancy increased from one million rai in 1975 to three million in the late 1980s.[96]

As for the landless, it was estimated in 1984 that they made up 10 per cent of the nation's agricultural population. This was, however, an underestimate, according to CUSRI, which claimed that if the Food and Agriculture Organization (FAO) definition of functional landlessness were to be applied to the Thai case, this would cover not only people with no land but those with up to five rai of land. In this case, the percentage share of the landless would shoot up to 33 per cent of the agricultural population.[97]

Ersatz reform The crisis of landownership in the traditional rice-growing areas translated into a crisis of the forests, as land-hungry peasants streamed in ever greater numbers into the land frontier. Even as tenancy and landlessness in the main agricultural areas were at an all-time high, there were an estimated 10 million people occupying, without secure property rights, over 30 million rai of public land. This migration had, in the process, reduced forest cover to 20 per cent of Thailand's land surface.[98] Unwilling or unable to carry out its original mission of expropriating private land for redistribution, ALRO gained a new *raison d'être*, which was to preside over the regularization of land tenure in encroached public lands and forest reserves. In fact, about 95 per cent of the 7,567,389 rai that have been distributed by ALRO under 'land reform' has been public land.

This process of tenure regularization, however, has had its own problems. It is, for one, a fallback from the optimal solution, which would be to reduce the flow of the landless to forest areas by redistributing land in the traditional farm areas. Second, as Anan has pointed out, land reform here is really giving farmers ownership of very poor-quality land, compared to the prime land they would have had in the traditional farming areas.[99]

Third, 'land reform' in encroached forest areas has served not only the purpose of giving marginalized peasants control over the basic means of production, but also that of facilitating the government's gaining or regaining 'institutional control over land of indeterminate status', since with the granting of land to the beneficiaries came a set of strict ALRO regulations over land alienation, sale, and rental.[100] In this regard, land reform, some analysts have asserted, benefited not so much the peasantry but the state because it enabled the latter to establish a stronger institutional presence in the countryside, especially in frontier areas. It thus became a key weapon in the government's arsenal of rural development initiatives, which became more important as the state tried to prevent disenchanted peasants from going over to radical solutions, like joining the Communist Party, after the violent destruction of the open peasant mass movement. It was not surprising that land reform as conservative state-managed rural development was first targeted at Lamphun, in the north, which was an area of severe repression of peasant leaders in 1974 and 1975, and at three key central region provinces – Pathum Thani, Nakorn Nayok, and Ayuthaya – which had likewise experienced a great degree of peasant agitation stemming partly from the fact that, in the early 1970s, they had the highest shares of rented to total cultivated land in the country, ranging from 56 to 74 per cent.[101]

Fourth, ALRO, while reinforcing the institutional presence of the state, has been unable effectively to regularize tenure over land for small cultivators, especially in encroached frontier areas. For despite legal prohibitions on the non-sale or non-alienation of land in land reform areas, according to one authoritative observer: 'In point of fact, ALRO land titles are being sold, that is, the right to use land is being sold, and you have a process whereby much land comes under the control of a few influential people, so that the infrastructural development that occurs in land reform areas is really infrastructural development for privately controlled land.'[102] Indeed, some experienced NGO workers in rural areas would go further and say that, in many areas, ALRO not only has been unable to stop land concentration but has itself facilitated it, with the land reform office serving as the 'middleman' bringing together buyers and sellers in these illegal deals where formal ownership remains with some people but actual control passes on to others via a cash transaction.[103] In short, the extension of central state authority via 'land reform' is a process that has accommodated itself to the realities of local power, creating an informal system of land control greased by corruption that has managed to marginalize smallholders even further.

Land reform for the rich under Chuan When the coalition government headed by Chuan Leekpai came to power in 1993, hopes were high that it would push forward the long-stalled land reform process. Instead, redistribution of private land proceeded at the usual snail's pace, while the redistribution of deforested public land was used blatantly to reward the rich and influential allies of the government in southern Thailand.

The Sor Por Kor 4-01 programme was one of the key mechanisms for redistributing forest land brought under cultivation. From 1975 to 1992, however, only 3.3 millio rai of reformed land had been distributed under Sor Por Kor 4-01 to 181,270 families.[105]

The Chuan government came to power in 1993 with a promise to energize the programme. Land distribution under the Sor Por Kor was intended to give land rights to over 1.5 million landless villagers through the entire term of the government. The government started off by adopting, on 4 May 1993, a 'special clause' that allowed for the application of land title deeds after receipt of Sor Por Kor documents if it could be proved (by showing land tax receipts) that the land in question was settled before being declared a forest reserve. The commonly accepted evidence was payment of a land tax or fees. Before the measure, the Land Reform Act of 1954 had allowed application for full title deeds only if occupancy occurred before 1954 or if the land in question was declared as part of the government's land reform programme.

The Chuan government claimed that the special clause passed by the cabinet aimed to plug holes in the weaker 1954 Land Reform Act, which had promoted cheating and corruption, rife in the history of land distribution in Thailand. Opposition parties and other legal experts claimed otherwise, saying that the rich would be among the beneficiaries. They claimed that the clause was very much against the purpose of the 1954 Act, which intended to provide land for farming and not for sale even though there existed provisions for full title deeds and their sale.[106]

Supporters of the cabinet resolution have claimed that it prevents forest encroachment by quickly distributing land through the issue of Sor Por Kor 4-01 documents, with the possibility of application for land ownership.[107] It if difficult to understand how the government could have expected this to work, given the volume of misappropriation of land after the clause came into effect. Besides the clause, land distribution procedures under the Sor Por Kor scheme were relaxed by the Chuan government to include degraded land, the issuance of Sor Por Kor documents was speeded up, and bigger budgets were allocated. In light of the relaxed procedures, it was alleged that some people who occupied land one day before it was earmarked to be declared as reform land miraculously became eligible for land title deeds.[108]

Sor Por Kor 4-01 became symptomatic of the problem afflicting all Thai land reform attempts: cronyism almost completely overwhelmed good intentions, and the process ended up benefiting mainly the rich and middle class. Sor Por Kor 4-01 documents were handed to financiers and supporters of the coalition government, especially those associated with Chuan Leekpai's Democrat Party. The difference in this scandal was that it took place within the new framework of democracy and freedom for political opposition, under a reformist government from whom many Thais had expected cleaner behaviour.

Suthep Thaugsuban, the deputy agriculture minister and head of the Agriculture Land Reform Office, who directly oversaw Sor Por Kor land distribution, had no choice but to resign to maintain the credibility of the Chuan government as the heat intensified in the last months of 1994. Thaugsuban's resignation removed a major block to the revocation of the ownership documents of six well-off allies of the land reform chief in February 1995.[109] This was a humiliating blow to the Democrat Party, which had already lost the confidence of the people as the saga unfolded in late 1994 and the months leading to the no-confidence motion tabled by the opposition on 17–18 May 1995.

The most sensational cases were those involving the relatives of the Democrat member of parliament for Phuket, Anchalee Thepabutr. She was secretary to Suthep Thaugsuban, and also sat on the provincial-level committee responsible for recommending land distribution in Phuket. Her husband and Phuket provincial councillor, Thosaporn Thapabutr, was given 98 rai of land, out of which 73 rai had to be returned because they were rich forest land. Her father was given 37 rai of land but was forced to return 33 rai, which were either rich forest land or unused agricultural land.[110]

The other rich businessmen who obtained Phuket land and were later forced to return partial or whole plots were Banlue Tantivit, Thanes Ekvanich, Charoen Thavornvongwong, Suthin Thepabutr and Boonkeng Drisaengsuchart. Banlue Tantivit, owner of the Patong Resort Hotel, had to return all of the 69 rai of rich forest land he had obtained. Charoen Thavornvongwong of the Dilok Group, which owned hotel, mining and automobile businesses, had to return 1.7 rai of land not exploited for agricultural purposes. Mr Boonkeng, who owned a transport company, had to return 2.7 rai of rich forest land out of 68 rai received.[111]

The investigations into these and other related cases are not over, and may become a point of contention again given that Chuan Leekpai recently returned to power in November 1997. In July 1997, it was reported that new evidence in at least three Phuket land reform cases might result in the reopening of the cases. They involved charges of malfeasance on the part of the Chuan Leekpai cabinet, dereliction of duty by three land officials, and accusations against 15 wealthy recipients of Sor Por Kor documents providing false information.[112] Questions that remain unsettled include the thorny ones of who should be the new owners of land returned by its rich recipients, and how to bring justice to those less wealthy people who may have to return land received between 1993 and 1995. Suthep, in defence of his government's Sor Por Kor distribution procedures, had claimed that following the strict 1989 Council of State's ruling, which permitted only poor, landless peasants to receive land, this would affect over 700,000 people who have received land since 1989.[113] After the land scandal broke, some Phuket land, and land in other parts of Thailand distributed to wealthy people was returned. Close to 400 people lost their land rights in Nakhon Ratchasima.[114] However, whether as large a number as 700,000 stand to lose their land remains to be seen.

The land reform process sank even deeper into the mire. The investigation into the scandal was led by a group of 16 MPs made up of both opposition and coalition members. At the helm was Newin Chidchob of the opposition party, Chart Thai, but most of the 16 were from Chart Pattana, a party of the coalition government led by Chuan. To counter allegations of cronyism, the Chuan government pointed to the fact that families of Chart Pattana politicians also received land under the Sor Por Kor scheme.[115]

Sor Por Kor 4-01 had, in effect, become a tool for politicians to hurl attacks at each other in the struggle for leadership in the Thai government. Evidence of the misappropriation of land was overwhelming and undeniable, and the opposition, led by Banharn Silapa-Archa, defeated Chuan's government in the no-confidence motion in May 1995. After the general election of 2 July 1995 the cabinet of the new prime minister, Banharn Silapa-Archa, finally scrapped the 4 May 1993 resolution.[116]

Land law experts Wanich Chutiwong of Chulalongkorn University and Tongroj Onchan of Kasetsart University both believe that scrapping the resolution was appropriate, since other more effective means should be found to prevent cheating in applications for land entitlement.[117] The Chuan cabinet resolution basically accommodated people who lacked the necessary evidence to apply for land title deeds. Wanich believed that a long-term solution that addressed the problems inherent in the original Land Act itself would be the effective solution. However, it would be very difficult to amend the Land Act itself, since the Interior Ministry's Land Department would not willingly tolerate interference in its legal powers and benefits.

Land reform quickly diminished in importance for the different Thai governments that came to power since each pursued the same development model, which favoured urbanization by squeezing agriculture. The land scandal of the Chuan government in 1995 only served to emphasize this trend because despite all its good intentions its land distribution scheme became a means of enriching the coffers of the rich. Instead of purchasing private land for distribution, the scheme reclassified forest reserves as degraded, and in some cases rich forest land was distributed. A lot of space existed for corruption and the abuse of power. Land reform is a volatile and urgent issue, but as of 1998 there was little chance that the new Chuan government would seek new ways of addressing it since that the focus of the entire nation was on how to pull Thailand out of its financial crisis.

Rural development The practical shelving of land reform did not, however, mean an end to the state's active involvement in rural areas. While it lost interest in redistributive reform after the breakup of the peasant movement in the mid-1970s and the self-destruction of the communist insurgency in the late 1970s it had to pay attention to the heavily populated countryside, if only to prevent it from again emerging as a source of instability.[118] 'Rural development' shorn of substantive redistributive aspects thus became an even greater activity in the 1980s. As Philip Hirsch observed, the 1980s brought about 'a machinery of development activities at the local level, and, with them ... a plethora of developers.'[119]

Among the key rural development measures were expanded access to credit for farmers and enhanced public works programmes in the countryside. Credit for farming enterprises did increase, most of it via the Bank of Agriculture and Agricultural Cooperatives (BAAC), which was used by commercial banks to fulfil the legal requirement of channelling at least 13 per cent of their investments into the agricultural sector that had been adopted during the reformist interlude of 1973–76. However, most studies of the BAAC loan programme reveal that it has been biased toward larger farmers rather than smallholders. Moreover, the stipulations that have accompanied loans as to the types and qualities of production inputs have been strongly biased against smallholder subsistence agriculture and designed to speed up the spread of commercial capitalist agriculture. As one analyst has noted, these BAAC loan biases have resulted in 'loss of control over production, and thus represented a contradiction in terms of survival of the small independent producer'.[120]

The two rural public works programmes of the 1980s were the Poverty Eradication Programme (PEP) and the Rural Employment Creation Programme (RECP). These were thinly veiled attempts to reproduce the investment and job-creation scheme of the Kukrit Pramoj government, the Tambon Fund Programme. But the PEP and RECP were also influenced in their approach by the World Bank anti-poverty approach that Robert McNamara had forged in the late 1970s, which sought to avoid land reform and other redistributive measures and focused on upgrading the 'productivity of the poor' by delivering rural development packages integrating credit, agricultural technology, extension, and infra-structure projects. In a Thailand that was still nursing the wounds of the 1973–76 period of intense conflict, the idea that poverty could be alleviated by a strategy of distributing credit, services, and technology instead of land and that this process could go hand-in-hand with increased political control of the peasantry was very attractive for liberal technocrats in the agricultural bureaucracy.[121]

The PEP reportedly channelled over 100 million baht to 1.3 million households in 288 districts during the Fifth Plan Period (1981–86). In tandem with the PEP, the RECP employed thousands of farmers in labour-intensive construction work. At the village level, these antipoverty pro-grammes may have had some impact, but overall they could not arrest the accelerating trends marginalizing agriculture and immiserizing the rural population. Agricultural employment increased much more slowly in the period 1982–86 than in the 1970s, and the share of income from specifically agricultural occupations in total rural income fell from 49.7 per cent in 1981 to 26.9 per cent.[122]

'Participation' in projects by the intended beneficiaries of rural develop-ment was one of the buzzwords of the development bureaucracy in the 1980s, but it was clear that the participation intended was not the kind that was designed to encourage the autonomy of the producers, as was the case with the FFT, but a process organized by the state and dominated by local elites and representatives of the central state. The participatory process in projects of the Community Development Department in two communities in Uithaithani province in western Thailand is typical of the bureaucratic structuring of participation in rural Thailand:

> [T]hese *klum* [groups] have been used as a means of enforcing participation on the terms of outsiders and key individuals within the village … Control of the terms of participation is in the hands of state functionaries, who determine the standardized forms of such groups. Day-to-day running of and benefit from the group is controlled by a small minority of village 'society', while the only innovation related to production, the savings group, is limited to better-off members of the community, since the treasurer refuses loans to anyone of insufficient stature as to ensure prompt repayment.[123]

Despite the fact that rural development programmes were accelerated in the 1980s, overall the countryside remained, from the perspective of Bangkok-based policymakers, an area of relatively low priority, one that was important to pay attention to politically but not one that was to be seriously integrated into the reigning strategy of urban-industry-led development. Indices of physical and social infrastructure underlined this reality. While there were twelve telephone lines per hundred people in Bangkok, there were only two in every other region. Road investments in rural areas came to only 6 to 39 per cent of the value of investment in

Bangkok. Local governments depended entirely on central government for their financial resources, but the total budget for local governments came to only 3.5 per cent of the central government budget in 1990.[124]

The central government, in fact, continued in its traditional role as a gigantic suction machine drawing huge resources from the rural areas and returning very little. Figures for Samut Prakarn cited by Nipon Poapongsakorn, for instance, show that of the sales tax revenue worth 5.4 million baht collected by the central government in 1998, only 9 per cent was allocated back to the province.[125]

Aborted 'NAICdom': Thai agriculture in the late 1980s

In the mid-1980s, however, some economists and technocrats came to regard rural development not just as a political stabilization scheme but as a component of a modified development strategy for Thailand. In contrast to the urban-industrialization-led strategy of the NICs (newly industrializing countries) of Asia, the new paradigm was christened NAIC, or 'newly agro-industrializing country', since it envisioned a central role for export agriculture via the consolidation of the country's comparative advantage in traditional export crops and gaining comparative advantage in new agro-industrial exports, like broiler chickens.[126] While the strategy meant an even tighter integration of Thai agriculture into the world market, some of its advocates saw smallholders as beneficiaries since they could become growers on contract with big local or multinational firms.

But several developments in the late 1980s and early 1990s made the NAIC strategy a more difficult option for Thailand to pursue. These were the intensification of Bangkok-centred industrialization, the speculative boom associated with this process, the technological constraints on the development of non-traditional crops, the limitations of contract farming, and the country's water crisis.

Intensification of Bangkok-centred industrialization The massive wave of Japanese investment that swamped Thailand in the late 1980s, as Japanese corporations relocated labour-intensive manufacturing operations to Southeast Asian sites in response to the appreciation of the yen, consolidated the political economy of Bangkok-dominated industrialization and foreclosed the possibility of a pattern of development with a more prominent and more equitable role for agriculture. This development, which brought more Japanese investment to Thailand in just one year, 1987, than had come in during the previous 20 years, reinforced the policy of keeping down the price of rice and accelerated the outflow of able-bodied and young men and women from rural areas, particularly the northeast, to serve as workers in the proliferating factories of Bangkok. While, as noted earlier, migration to Bangkok and other regions has always been a feature of the northeastern labour force, the boom period of the late 1980s and early 1990s appeared to be unparalleled in its impact on the agricultural economy. The increasing gap between income from urban factory work and income from agriculture inclined more and more workers to permanent settlement in Bangkok rather than the more traditional pattern of seasonal migration. Money did flow back to the villages, but as Akin Rabibhadana notes: 'In a large number of villages in the Northeast, only old people and their daughters, children are left in the villages. The entire middle generation has gone to work in Bangkok.'[127]

The speculative boom The rapid expansion of industry, coupled with the absence of effective zoning laws, encouraged the conversion of more and more prime agricultural land into land for either real estate development or speculation. It is estimated, for instance, that almost one-third of the cultivable land in the Chiang Mai Valley has been bought by land speculators.[128] While in the late 1980s, widespread speculation was limited to areas within easy reach of urban centres, in recent years speculation has spread to the hinterland. As Charles Mehl has noted:

> It seems at times as though the entire country is being bought by the ever-growing wealthy, by the rapidly expanding middle class, and by foreign investors. The effects of this on social organization are not yet clear, but what can be stated with some certainty is that the relative independence, and indeed the existence, of the small-farm cultivators is increasingly threatened.[129]

Conversion of land for real estate or speculative purposes meant the displacement of tenant farmers and agricultural workers. It also made it difficult for ALRO to purchase private land for distribution to farmers as part of the land reform programme, and for small farmers to buy land to expand their holding to an economically viable size. With the spread of land speculation, small farmers in fact found themselves in competition with capital-rich national and even international land-buyers.[130] Indeed, it was not only small farmers who were affected negatively by the speculative boom but even agro-industrial enterprises, which were forced by high land prices to relocate from agricultural areas closer to Bangkok to the upper central region and the lower northeast.[131]

The vagaries of the international market Third, Thailand's export agriculture became increasingly threatened by developments in world trade. As noted earlier, in the 1960s Thailand diversified from rice into commodities for which there was growing international demand, like cassava, sugar, maize, kenaf, and sorghum. Especially in the north and northeast, much of the new land stripped of forest cover was devoted to the new crops, and in many areas raising cassava and other new crops was seen by farmers as a key income supplement to their rice production. Diversification was, however, limited to a few export crops, with 70 per cent of Thailand's farmland and more than 10 million farmers involved in the production of six commodities: sugar, rice, rubber, maize, cassava, and sorghum.[132]

The agro-export strategy paid off as long as the world prices of Thai agricultural commodities were rising. But in the 1980s, after years of expanding income from exports, Thai agriculture was exposed to the merciless dynamics of the world market and real export prices fell: rice 36 per cent, maize 29 per cent, rubber 44 per cent, and sugar 50 per cent.[133]

Aside from the sharp drops in commodity prices, Thai firms were suddenly confronted with effective competitors in world markets. Thailand was already being undercut in maize by other producers, and in kenaf, which was losing out to jute from Bangladesh. In the case of rice, the Vietnamese quickly moved into challenging Thai exports of low-grade rice in the late 1980s, a price-depressing development that hurt great numbers of Thai farmers hooked into world market production of low-grade rice.[134] And while it is true that Thailand maintained its leading edge in higher grades of rice, on the horizon lay the spectre of China, which, in the opinion of some specialists in Thai agriculture, would eventually be able to produce high-quality rice to rival and displace Thailand's.[135]

The dangers of dependence on the world market were illustrated by the case of cassava. Encouraged by preferential arrangements for Third World products adopted by the European Union (then the European Economic Community) in the 1970s, Thailand went for cassava production in a big way. But so successful were Thai cassava exports that the EU pushed Thailand to limit its exports, beginning in 1982. With the domestic market unable to absorb the cassava surplus, the government began a programme of reducing the area planted to cassava in the northeast by 50,000 hectares.[136] In the next few years, the inevitable revision of the EU's Common Agricultural Policy (CAP) would lead to the loss or reduction of Thailand's quota, prompting major cutbacks in cassava production and the loss of thousands of jobs, unless cassava could be shifted in significant quantities to domestic uses in the animal feed industry.

With traditional export crops under pressure, Thai technocrats and agribusiness interests began to move into the production of the so-called 'higher-value-added' commodities, which included shrimps, cut flowers, fresh vegetables, processed food, and broiler chickens. There were, however, several problems associated with this strategy. It was improbable, for one, that, even in the domestic market, Thailand would be able to maintain its edge in temperate crops, like cabbage, since this niche was likely to be filled by Southern China owing to cheaper production and labour costs.[137]

Moreover, in most of these new 'higher-value-added' commodities, technological innovation was central to maintaining competitiveness, and in this area Thailand was facing major constraints. The state was ill-equipped to step into the role of R&D coordinator and technological innovator. The public research infrastructure for agriculture was woefully underdeveloped, a reflection of the traditional government attitude towards agriculture as a sector to be milked of resources to be channelled into industry rather than a sector to invest significant amounts of capital in.

But it was an illusion to expect the private sector to step into the R&D vacuum. As Scott Christensen has pointed out, private firms are not likely to expend much R&D effort on open-pollinated crops like rice and corn, since the diffusion of technological innovation in these crops cannot be controlled owing to the natural reproduction of improved varieties.[138] Where private firms would find investment attractive would be in those hybrid plants and livestock whose mass reproduction necessitates specific biotechnological processes that can be monopolized and patented. Most innovation in biotechnology, however, has been done by US firms, and it is unlikely that they will allow Thai agro-industrial firms to make use of these processes without exacting significant royalty payments and imposing very restrictive conditions, especially now that their position has been bolstered by the intellectual property rights regime of the GATT–WTO (General Agreement on Tariffs and Trade/World Trade Organization), to which Thailand is a signatory.

But even if technological innovation improved Thailand's prospects in the new commodities, it was unlikely that large numbers of workers threatened with unemployment by the crisis of the traditional crops could be absorbed in their production. As a World Bank report pointed out:

> In 1980 the labor force employed in rice, maize, rubber and cassava amounted to about 13.8 million. By contrast, the labor force engaged in the cultivation of fruit, vegetables, livestock, fisheries, and other field crops amounted to only 1.6 million. Such numbers indicate that the additional amount of labor likely to be employed through the expansion of nontraditional commodities would be small, and smaller than the number of rice farmers who may decide to change activities in view of the low return to rice cultivation. In addition, since the most promising commodities are items such as fisheries, agriculture, poultry, and livestock, farmers who would benefit from an expansion of these activities may not be the same who are currently affected by the fall in the prices of traditional commodities. For these farmers, relevant alternatives would be to engage in off-farm activities or migrate.[139]

Technological innovation in the new crops could, in fact, lead to a reduction in those already employed in the production of fruits, vegetables, and some feedgrain crops, where the proportion of exports in total output was small and domestic demand was relatively unresponsive to downward price changes.[140]

The limitations of contract farming The one major institutional innovation of the 1980s was contract farming, wherein big corporations engaged small farmers to raise inputs that they processed into high-value commodities and exports like broiler chickens. Contract farming promised to keep small farmers on the land while making them efficient producers. The great success in contract farming was CP or Charoen Pokphand, a vast conglomerate that replaced the USA as the prime supplier of broilers to Japan. But by the 1990s the hope that contract farming was the solution to the employment and income problems of Thailand's agricultural population had been dampened.

Widespread exploitation of small farmers was one factor leading to a more sceptical view. In many cases, firms took the lion's share of the profits while making the smallholders take a disproportionate part of the risk.[141] Smallholders were often swindled into accepting unfair contracts, with many of them falling into debt with the company from purchases of seeds, fertilizers, and other inputs.[142] And there were also cases in which officials of ALRO, in exchange for financial arrangements sometimes disguised as 'consultancies', used their position to get farmers to grow crops for firms.[143] Another problem was that contract farming tended to reduce the entrepreneurial capabilities of farmers by converting them into workers in a vast agro-industrial assembly line who gained specialized production skills, like chicken raising, but could not apply this knowledge and experience to other types of agricultural enterprise.[144]

But the prospects for contract farming in Thailand were clouded most of all by the fact that, for a variety of reasons, many firms, including the pioneer itself, CP, were moving away from this method of production in favour of industrial farming. Partly responsible for the decreasing reliance on smallholders were the stricter quality control and hygiene requirements of key export markets like Japan. Also significant was the rising price of land in prime agricultural lands near urban centres. This was forcing many agribusiness concerns to relocate their operations to more distant sites, pushing them towards more direct farming to reduce the costs and uncertainties involved.[145]

Contract farming appeared to receive a boost, however, with the eucalyptus frenzy of the late 1980s. Owing to growing internal and external demand for pulp and paper products, many agribusinesses had originally moved to set up plantations of the fast-growing eucalyptus tree, which was seen as an ideal raw material. They were encouraged by the Royal Forestry Department's plans to use commercial forestry to 're-green' degraded forest land, especially in the northeast. But the eucalyptus boom was soon mired in controversies. Cases were registered where commercial firms chopped down virgin forests to plant eucalyptus.[146] The establishment of eucalyptus farms often involved the massive displacement and re-settlement of peasants and the conversion of many of them into labourers in the plantations. Eucalyptus enterprises would take over, via formal leaseholding arrangements with the state, lands that were already occupied by smallholders, intrude into properties belonging to small farmers, buy up small owner-cultivators, and privatize communal properties that peasants used for forage and hunting game.[147] The upshot was great insecurity and stress for peasants, especially in the northeast, and this provoked widespread opposition and attacks on plantations and nurseries by angry farmers.

Peasant resistance, which culminated in a massive march of northeastern peasants against the government's *Khor Jor Kor* 'Green Resettlement' programme in 1991 and 1992, forced the Anand government to ban commercial afforestation projects, including eucalyptus plantation schemes. This pushed agribusiness and pulp and paper firms like the Phoenix Pulp and Paper Company to explore alternative ways of obtaining raw material supplies, such as contract farming by smallholders. But while contract farming may have been more attractive to smallholders at first glance, it was doubtful whether it could escape some of the same problems that had made eucalyptus plantations controversial.

Foremost among these was the labour-displacing effects of eucalyptus in contrast to other crops. Eucalyptus was not a labour-absorptive crop – a Swedish study showed that it could be raised profitably by only 20 people per square kilometre and a Shell Thailand study showed that a 110 square kilometre plantation could support only 5,000 local people, or 45 people per square metre.[148] These absorption rates for labour were problematic in light of the high population density in both traditional farming areas and degraded forest lands. Indeed, Apichai Puntasen and his colleagues' observation on the employment impact of eucalyptus plantations were also applicable to smallholder contract farming: 'If replacement effect is taken into account, employment generated by the whole eucalyptus and related activities can be negative due to the capital-intensive nature of the plantation. If the negative net employment generation is the measure, eucalyptus plantations should not be a viable business from the outset as far as employment is concerned.'[149]

Added to this negative employment effect were the constraints that eucalyptus-raising could place on the ability of farmers to raise other crops, owing to the ecological effects of eucalyptus, particularly its high rate of water absorption, which could take away water from other crops.[150] This was especially of concern to the northeast, which is perennially plagued by drought.[151] A related problem was that a heavy layer of eucalyptus leaves apparently makes the soil less capable of supporting other crops, making it suitable only for really arid lands that have less potential to grow other crops.[152]

By the early 1990s, then, contract farming had lost its status as the answer to the interrelated problems of productivity, poverty, employment, and resource constraints that were plaguing the Thai countryside. The agriculture crisis was, in fact, deepened by another development : water shortage.

The water shortage In the early 1990s, it increasingly dawned on the public that owing to the short-sighted entrepreneurial and government approaches to the country's resources, Thailand was running out of water. With the degradation of watershed areas caused by deforestation and increasing water consumption in the north, where the watershed areas for the central plain were located, the water available for dams in the central plain breadbasket dropped from 11 billion cubic metres to 7 billion, at the same time that water demand in agriculture, industry, and Bangkok was skyrocketing. Although most of the dam-water had traditionally been used for irrigation, especially for the second crop during the dry season, agriculture was now being squeezed by competing demands from other sectors. Demands from bureaucracies servicing primarily urban-industrial interests, like the Electricity Generating Authority of Thailand (EGAT) and the Bangkok Metropolitan Water Authority (BMWA), increasingly took precedence over farmers' demands in the water allocation and water management plans of the Royal Irrigation Department (RID).[153] This brought to a head the underlying sectoral conflict that ran through the whole history of postwar economic policymaking, since the demand for water had concurrently skyrocketed in both agriculture and industry, in Bangkok and the countryside. The response of Bangkok-based bureaucrats to the crisis was consistent with the past.

To accommodate urban demands, the RID in fact reversed its 40-year policy of encouraging farmers to plant a second rice crop during the dry season – a strategy adopted at a time when water was relatively plentiful and the Thai government was pushing Thai rice onto the world market. In 1993, farmers in the central plain were discouraged from planting a second rice crop because of rice's great demand for water and told to plant vegetables or other less water-intensive crops. This was highly threatening to farmers, who had become dependent on the second crop to make ends meet following the low rice price policies implemented by the government. For many observers, this policy of discouraging a second or third crop was seen not simply as a short-term accommodation, but as the latest example of agriculture's long subordination to urban-industrial interests.[154]

Increasingly, many farmers took the view that the more successful the urban-industrial sector was, the more the government could turn its back on agriculture. This sentiment began to border on conspiracy theory in some – as one NGO worker saw it: 'It seems the more the farmers fail, the more satisfied the government will be because then the industrial sector will be able to obtain cheap labor.'[155] Such sentiments were understandable, since at the top levels of both government and business there were few new ideas on what to do with agriculture. A current at the agricultural bureaucracy, in fact, favoured doing nothing, since market forces would ensure that most of the agricultural workforce would eventually be absorbed into industry, and 'then, we won't have to worry about agriculture'.[156]

Such complacent free-marketeers were, however, in the minority. While the solutions were not clear, the strategic perils of a deteriorating countryside were clear to many experts and policymakers. To former Land Reform head Thaugsuban, for instance, lack of policy innovation in agriculture would eventually rebound on the city in the form of environmental deterioration and strains on the urban infrastructure as the rural poor moved to Bangkok in even greater numbers as the land frontier was reached and very little new land could be brought under cultivation.[157]

To agricultural expert Sompop Manarangsan, agriculture's downward slide prefigured a macroeconomic Waterloo. According to him, the NIC strategy of export-oriented manufacturing was increasingly running into difficulty owing to rising labour costs and increased protectionism in developed country markets. Increasingly, Thailand would have to depend on its domestic market to absorb its manufactures. 'But how can you have purchasing power for these goods, how can you have effective demand, if most of your population is impoverished?'[158]

Thus one of the central challenges to economic planning is increasing the purchasing power of people in the countryside, not only by channelling more capital to the rural areas but by making sure the appropriate institutional framework exists that will assure the effective use of financial resources. The reaching of the land frontier and a more competitive international environment has made the creation of such a framework imperative. Among the institutional innovations identified by experts as necessary and urgent are genuine land reform, land titling that would guarantee farmers' ownership and thus encourage them to make the land more productive, credit access, price support systems, a public R&D complex, an effective resource and environmental management system, and a tough regulatory and law enforcement apparatus.[159] The fate of Thailand's agriculture, in short, is increasingly a function of major reform in the social organization of production.

Down the road of NIC agriculture?

Despite some major differences, Thailand's experience is essentially similar to the experiences of two of East Asia's most successful cases of recent industrialization, those of Taiwan and South Korea. In all three cases, agriculture subsidized industry via a net transfer of resources and by serving as a reservoir of cheap labour. In all three, this process was a highly unbalanced one, where little capital was channelled back to agriculture, and the sector was subjected either to official neglect or to rural development programmes that did not change the essential relationship of subordination but served the objective of political stabilization. The end result was a high-cost agriculture that was on the verge of extinction in Korea and Taiwan. In Thailand, despite the low levels of capital being channelled back to agriculture, the sector was propped up for a long time by the presence of vast tracts of forest land that could be brought under cultivation, a factor that also kept a relatively large number of low-cost workers on the land by providing an alternative to migration to the cities. But by the beginning of the 1990s, the crisis of Thai agriculture was becoming more manifest as the land frontier was reached at the same time that levels of productivity remained low in land that had been brought into cultivation. This reality was seen in Thailand's becoming non-competitive in selected products like low-grade rice in export markets that the country's farmers had previously dominated.

Where Thailand differed from Taiwan and Korea was that in the latter two, the process of agricultural decline was, by the 1990s, irreversible, with the proportion of the workforce in agriculture down to less than 20 per cent and the protectionist wall surrounding high-cost agriculture about to be pulled down by either GATT or US trade pressure. In Thailand, there was still time to save agriculture, but this would mean striking a New Deal between industry and agriculture, in a strategy of development where the countryside would be critical not only as a source of capital but as a market. The question was: would Thailand's policymakers have the political will to forge the long-postponed institutional and social reforms that were necessary to avoid the sad fate of agriculture in the classic NIC countries?

Thai agriculture in the eye of the storm

Thailand's recent financial débâcle has underlined two things. First, the neglect of agriculture over the last few decades has weakened the ability of the country to deal with economic crisis. A healthy agricultural sector could have served to absorb industrial production for which demand was falling in foreign markets. It could also have been in a better position to absorb the workers expelled from the cities by the industrial recession.

Second, the policy responses to the crisis are likely to exacerbate the trends leading to the marginalization of the agricultural economy. The 'rescue package' of the IMF promises several years of economic stagnation through structural adjustment. The government will have to balance the budget, reduce government spending, privatize state enterprises and reduce corporate taxes. Through this difficult period, as the economy worsens and urban unemployment increases, there will be moves to keep food prices down to pacify the urban unemployed. This containment of food prices will be extraordinarily costly because rice yields will drop sharply in what is expected to be the worst drought in 50 years.

A decline in rice production was expected to hit the country in 1998.[160] Due to El Niño, rain was late in arriving for the rice-growing season, and was expected to fall only in May of that year. Reservoirs in the north and northeast which irrigate rice fields were drying up, as shown by water levels in the Bhumibol and Sirikit dams, which retained less than 50 per cent of their capacity.[161] Cloud-seeding and price controls were among measures to be taken. Within the context of the deepening financial crisis, the Commerce Ministry, which is responsible for intervening in the crop market, is charged with the monumental task of trying to keep the price of rice from soaring as rice yields decrease.

What this means for Thai agriculture is further impoverishment. The present dismal state of agriculture is likely to be exacerbated with the suppression of prices of agricultural commodities, especially that of rice. The rural population, with already little buying power, will be further deprived of income by price depressions and drought. The end of the boom could very well mark the end of 20 years of relative peace in the countryside.

Notes

1. Quoted in Paul Handley, 'Thought for food' *Far Eastern Economic Review*, 29 April 1993, p. 46.

2. Mehdi Krongkaew, 'Contributions of agriculture to industrialization: the case of Thailand', paper presented at the conference 'The Making of a Fifth Tiger?', Australian National University, Canberra, 7–9 December 1992, Table 1, p. 40.; Asian Development Bank, *Key Indicators of Developing Asian and Pacific Countries* (Manila: Asian Development Bank, 1996), p. 20.

3. Estimate by Sompop Manarangsan cited in Pravit Rojanaphruk, 'Farmers face uncertain future', *The Nation* (Bangkok), undated.

4. Amar Siamwalla, 'Land abundant agricultural growth and some of its consequences: the case of Thailand' (Bangkok: TDRI, 1991), p. 39.

5. A variable tax based on the value of a commodity.

6. Wattana Sugunnasil, 'The state and agrarian policy in Thailand, 1960–80', Ph.D. dissertation, University of Wisconsin at Madison, May 1991, p. 84.

7. Scott Christensen, 'Conditions and collective choice: the politics of institutional change in Thai agriculture', Ph.D. dissertation, University of Wisconsin at Madison, May 1993, pp. 196–7.

8. Christen Holtsberg, 'Rice pricing policy', in Peter Richards, ed., *Basic Needs and Government Policies in Thailand* (Singapore: Maruzen Asia, 1982), p. 176.

9. Mehdi Krongkaew, p. 16.

10. Wattana Sugunnasil, p. 86.

11. Mehdi Krongkaew, p. 25.

12. Amar Siamwalla and Suthad Setboonsarng, *Trade, Exchange Rate, and Agricultural Pricing Policies in Thailand: The Political Economy of Agricultural Pricing Policy* (Washington, DC: World Bank, 1989).

13. Wattana Sugunnasil, p. 76; Mehdi Krongkaew, pp. 40, 41, 49.

14. Quoted in Handley, p. 47.

15. Christensen, p. 218.

16. Ibid.

17. World Bank, *Agro-industrial Diversification: Issues and Prospects* (Washington, DC: World Bank, 1987), p. 23.

18. World Bank, cited in Christensen, p. 215.

19. Warin Wongchanchao, 'Agricultural development policy of Thailand', in Warin Wongchanchao and Yukio Ikemoto, eds, *Economic Development Policy in Thailand: A Historical Review* (Tokyo: Institute of the Developing Economies, 1988), p. 111. One hectare equals 6.3 rai.

20. Pravit Rojanaphruk, 'Farmers face uncertain future'.

21. Holtsberg, p. 162.

22. Charles Mehl, 'Culture, power, and history of resource management', paper presented at Ninth Biennial Conference of the Agricultural Economics Society of Southeast Asia on Poverty, Deforestation, and Resource Management in Asia, Bangkok, 22–24 June 1993, p. 8.

23. Amara Pongsapich et al., *Sociocultural Change and Political Development in Central Thailand, 1950–1990* (Bangkok: TDRI, 1993), p. 44.

24. Wattana Sugunnasil, p. 54.

25. Edward Bernard Fallon, 'The peasants of Isan: social and economic transitions in northeast Thailand', Ph.D. dissertation, University of Wisconsin at Madison, August 1983, p. 121.

26. Amara Pongsapich et al., p. 15.

27. Fallon, p. 126.

28. Amara Pongsapich et al., p. 49.

29. Ibid.

30. Wattana Sugunnasil, p. 99.

31. Christensen, p. 163.

32. Holtsberg, p. 163.

33. Mark Ritchie, prospectus for Ph.D. dissertation, University of California at Berkeley, 1994.

34. Anan Ganjanapan, 'The partial commercialization of rice production in northern Thailand, 1900–1981', Ph.D. dissertation, Cornell University, Ithaca, NY, January 1984, pp. 147–249.

35. Anan Ganjanapan, p. 201.

36. Ibid., p. 260.

37. Ibid., p. 274.

38. Ibid., pp. 300–1.

39. Suchai Trikat, cited in Chayan Vaddhanaputi, 'Cultural and ideological reproduction in rural northern Thai society', Ph.D. dissertation, Stanford University, Stanford, CA, p. 143.

40. Andrew Turton, 'The current situation in the countryside', in Andrew Turton, eds, *Thailand: Roots of Conflict* (London: Spokesman Books, 1978), p. 112.

41. Katherine Bowie, 'Introduction', in Samruan Singh, *Voices from the Thai Countryside* (Madison: Center for Southeast Asian Studies, University of Wisconsin, 1991), p. 10.

42. Anan Ganjanapan, p. 435.

43. Midas Agronomics Company, Ltd, *Study of Conservation Forest Area Demarcation, Protection, and Occupancy in Thailand: Vol. III: Occupancy Study* (Bankok: Midas, 1991), p. 133.

44. Larry Lohmann, 'Thailand: land, power, and forest colonization', in Marcus Colchester and Larry Lohmann, eds, *The Struggle for Land and the Fate of the Forests* (London: Zed Books, 1993), pp. 209–10.

45. Amara Pongsapich et al., p. 9.

46. Ibid., p. 15.

47. Holtsberg, p. 162.

48. Fallon, p. 242.

49. Ibid., pp. 239–43.

50. Ibid., pp. 180–1.

51. Ibid., p. 160.

52. Ibid., p. 155.

53. Charles Mehl, 'Land, agricultural labor, and development in rural Thailand: a study of variations in the socioeconomic structure of three villages in Nakhon Ratchasima province', Ph.D. dissertation, Cornell University, August 1985, p. 45.

54. Fallon, pp. 239, 241.

55. Peter Richards, 'Basic needs and government policies in Thailand: an overview', in Peter Richards, ed., *Basic Needs and Government Policies in Thailand*, p. 5.

56. Fallon, p. 258.

57. Ibid., p. 261.

58. Wattana Sugunnasil, p. 76.

59. Fallon, p. 215.

60. Ibid., p. 264.

61. Somchai Jitsuchon, *Alleviation of Rural Poverty in Thailand* (Bangkok: TDRI, 1989), p. 48; Amara Pongsapich et al., p. 17.

62. Amara Pongsapich et al., p. 17.

63. Mehl, pp. 60–1.

64. Ibid., p. 169.

65. Ibid.

66. Andrew Turton, 'Poverty, reform, and class struggle in rural Thailand', in S. Jones et al., eds, *Rural Poverty and Agrarian Reform* (New Delhi: ENDA and Allied Publishers, 1982), p. 20.

67. Victor Karunan, *If the Land could Speak, it Would Speak for Us: Vol. I: A History of Peasant Movements in Thailand and the Philippines* (Hong Kong: Plough Publications, 1984), pp. 35–40.

68. Turton, 'Poverty, reform, and class struggle', p. 34.

69. Karunan, p. 46.

70. Turton, 'Poverty, reform, and class struggle', p. 25.

71. Karunan, p. 45.

72. Wattana Sugunnasil, p. 142.

73. Holtsberg, pp. 178–9.

74. Richards, p. 10.

75. Ibid., p. 11.

76. Wattana Sugunnasil, pp. 164–5.

77. Anan Ganjanapan, pp. 396–7.

78. Richards, p. 9.

79. Identity of source withheld.

80. Bowie, p. 14.

81. Ibid.

82. Chayan Vaddhanaputi, 'Cultural and ideological reproduction in rural northern Thai society', Ph.D. dissertation, Stanford University, Stanford, CA, pp. 556–7.

83. Ibid.

84. Ibid.

85. Karunan, p. 50.

86. Ibid., p. 68.

87. Holtsberg, p. 178.

88. TDRI, *Policy on Agricultural Land Reform in Thailand* (Bangkok: TDRI, undated), p. 26.

89. TDRI, p. 65.

90. Interview with Suthep Thaugsuban, deputy minister of Agriculture and Cooperatives, Bangkok, 16 September 1993.

91. Tongroj Onchan, 'Natural resource and environment policy and institutional reform', paper presented at the Ninth Biennial Conference of the Agricultural Economics Society of Southeast Asia, Bangkok, 22–24 June 1993, p. 12.

92. Agricultural Land Reform Office (ALRO), *Briefing on Land Reform Implementation in Thailand*, Bangkok, undated.

93. Ibid.

94 CUSRI, *Master Plan Study of the Agricultural Land Reform; Vol. 2: The Main Report* (Bangkok: CUSRI, 1989), pp. 1–6.

95. Ibid., p. 114.

96. Somkiat Pongpaiboon, 'Powerful education through people organization: a case of movement against salt farming in the northeast of Thailand', paper presented to ICEA Sixth World Conference on Community Education on Developing the Global Village, Trinidad and Tobago, 29 July–2 August 1991.

97. CUSRI, pp. 1, 5–6.

98. Tongroj Onchan, p. 3.

99. Interview with Anan Ganjanapan, Chiang Mai, 10 September 1993.

100. Philip Hirsch, 'The state in the village: interpreting rural development in Thailand', *Development and Change*, vol. 20 (1989), p. 42.

101. Richards, p. 10.

102. Interview with Peter Cox, Bangkok, 31 March 1994.

103. Interview with Taweekiat Prasertcharoensuk, Bangkok, 18 June 1993.

104. Prasong Charasdamrong, 'Land reform: fighting over the fruits of the forest', *Bangkok Post*, 20 August 1995, p. 24.

105. 'This land is mine', *Bangkok Post*, 2 April 1995.

106. Matchima Chanswangpuwana, 'Politicking delays solution to land problem', *Bangkok Post*, 7 August 1995.

107. Ibid.

108. 'Ten more families to lose Sor Por Kor 4-01 papers', *Bangkok Post*, 29 August 1995.

109. 'Businessmen lose Phuket reform land', *Bangkok Post*, 23 February 1995.

110. Ibid.

111. Ibid. 'Spotlight falls on land issue', *Bangkok Post*, 23 November 1994.

112. 'New evidence may revive Phuket land reform cases', *Bangkok Post*, 29 July 1997.

113. 'Who will take over from rich owners?', *Bangkok Post*, 16 April 1995.

114. '400 recipients lose land rights as authorities correct errors', *Bangkok Post*, 29 April 1995.

115. 'Chart Pattana families given land, says Govt', *Bangkok Post*, 3 December 1994.

116. 'Cabinet revokes land reform resolution granting title deeds', *Bangkok Post*, 23 August 1995.

117. Matchima Chanswangpuwana, 'Politicking delays solution to land problem', *Bangkok Post*, 7 August 1995.

118. Interview with Andrew Turton, London, 1 December 1993.

119. Philip Hirsch, *Development Dilemmas in Rural Thailand* (New York: Oxford University Press, 1990), pp. 20–1.

120. Ibid., p. 202.

121. Wattana Sugunnasil, pp. 192–3.

122. Kosit Pampriempras and Ladawan Pawakaranond, 'Employment strategies for accelerated economic growth in Thailand', in Ismael Getubig and Harry Oshima, eds, *Towards a Full Employment Strategy* (Kuala Lumpur: Asian and Pacific Development Centre, 1991), p. 148.

123. Hirsch, *Development Dilemmas*, p. 202.

124. Nipon Poapongsakorn, 'Rural industrialization: problems and prospects', paper presented at the conference 'The Making of a Fifth Tiger? Thailand's Industrialization and Its Consequences', Australian National University, Canberra, 7–9 December 1992, pp. 34–5.

125. Ibid.

126. See, among others, World Bank, *Agro-Industrial Diversification: Issues and Prospects* (Washington, DC: World Bank, 1997).

127. Akin Rabibhadana, *Social Inequity: A Source of Conflict in the Future* (Bangkok: TDRI, 1993), p. 20.

128. J. Ruland, cited in Thomas Enters, 'The economics of land degradation and resource conservation in northern Thailand', paper presented at Fifth International Conference on Thai Studies, School of Oriental and African Studies, London, 5–10 July 1993, p. 10.

129. Mehl, p. 9.

130. Mark Ritchie, personal communication, 18 July 1994.

131. Sompop Manarangsan, 'Contract farming and Thailand's agricultural development', in Buddhadeb Chaudhuri, ed., *Our Lands, Our Lives* (Bangkok: ACFOD, 1992), p. 155.

132. Handley, p. 47.

133. Ibid.

134. Ibid.

135. Interview with Paul Handley, 4 March 1993.

136 World Bank, p. 112.

137. Interview with David Thomas, Ford Foundation Office, Bangkok, 2 January 1994.

138. See Scott Christensen, *Between the Farmers and the State: Towards a Policy Analysis of the Role of Agribusiness in Agriculture* (Bangkok: TDRI, 1992).

139. World Bank, p. 29.

140. Ibid.

141. Interview with Scott Christensen, 31 March 1994.

142. Interview with Taweekiat Prasertcharoensuk, Bangkok, 18 June 1993.

143. Ibid.

144. Sompop Manarangsan, p. 156.

145. Ibid., p. 155.

146. Interview, Peter Cox, Bangkok, 31 March 1994.

147. Ibid.

148. Larry Lohmann, 'Peasants, plantations, and pulp: the politics of eucalyptus in Thailand', *Bulletin of Concerned Asian Scholars*, vol. 23, no. 4 (October–December 1991), p. 8.

149.   135. Apichai Puntasen et al., 'The political economy of eucalyptus: a case of business cooperation by the Thai government and its bureaucracy', paper presented at conference 'The Political Economy of the Environment in Asia', Simon Fraser University, Vancouver, Canada, 11–13 October 1990, p. 37.

150.   Ibid., pp. 42–3.

151.   Interview with Peter Cox, Bangkok, 31 March 1994.

152.   Apichai Puntasen, pp. 42–3.

153.   Scott Christensen and Areeja Boon Long, 'Better water management needed', *The Nation*, 17 September 1993.

154.   Interview, Sompop Manarangsan, Bangkok, 17 August 1993.

155.   Kamol Sukin, 'A policy for poverty', *The Nation*, 10 March 1994, p. C1.

156.   Interview, Agriculture and Cooperatives Ministry official, anonymity requested, September 1993.

157.   Interview, Suthep Thaugsuban, Bangkok, 16 September 1993.

158.   Interview, Sompop Manarangsan, Bangkok, 17 August 1993.

159.   Christensen; Handley.

160.   'Action plan unveiled: worst drought in 50 years expected', *Bangkok Post*, 26 December 1997.

161.   Ibid.

CHAPTER 9

The Dynamics of Deforestation

Ecological degradation has been one of the hallmarks of Thailand's high-speed economic development. The crisis of the environment has many dimensions – deforestation, climate change, air and industrial wastewater pollution, depletion of marine life in coastal waters caused by overfishing. This chapter will focus on two activities that have contributed much to the environmental destabilization of the country – deforestation and dam-building.

Even as the country begins to confront the problem of massive water pollution triggered by uncontrolled industrialization, it continues to be burdened by the serious problems of deforestation and natural resource depletion that accompanied its earlier integration into the world economy as a natural resource and agricultural exporter.

The consequences of the country's massive deforestation problem were brought home in 1989, when flash-floods triggered by the lack of forest cover took 116 lives, destroyed 16,000 homes, and damaged one million farmlands in southern Thailand. A ban on logging by the Chatichai government was the outcome of the resulting popular outcry. But many people wondered: Was it too late? Would it make a difference?

Official estimates put the portion of Thailand covered by forests at around 26 per cent today. Less sanguine observers put the figure at 20 per cent or less. But whatever the actual figure, the situation is out of control, as underlined by the government's Thai Forestry Sector Master Plan (TFSMP):

> Over more than half a century, the forest administration has tried many strategies to curb the forest loss. Forestry laws were passed; protected areas were established; forests were patrolled; flows of forest products were regulated and checkpoints manned; trees were planted; many poor farmers who ventured into the forests were prosecuted; and many forest occupants were resettled. Deforestation proceeded at an average rate of almost 3 million rai per year in the last 30 years, but the actual [tree] plantations established covered less than 100,000 rai per year as an average.[1]

The Thai state, admitted the Master Plan, 'has proved incapable of managing or even protecting the forest because of inadequate manpower and financial outlay, which can never match the magnitude of the task'.[2]

Previously, the line of the Royal Forestry Department was that the deforestation problem was created mainly by the hordes of poor people who invaded forest areas belonging to the state. But the Master Plan admitted, at least rhetorically, that the problem was probably more fundamental, being rooted in the process of development itself:

> Virtually everyone would like to cash in on the economic boom. The drive for accelerated economic growth fosters environmentally detrimental land use, such as export-oriented but extensive agriculture. Rapidly changing national values place emphasis on quick extraction of whatever materialistic benefits from the forest, such as land and wood, instead of long-term benefits that can be obtained through conservation measures.[3]

Moreover, the state's forest policy was part of the problem, lacking as it did a 'long-term vision'. It tackled problems on an *ad hoc* basis, 'and although it was unable to protect the forests, it prevented other groups, such as communities, forest dwellers, and enterprises from engaging in forest management'.[4]

The Master Plan, as will be seen later, proposed a solution that did not match its effort to project a candid appraisal of the roots of the forest crisis. Nevertheless, its frank admission of almost total failure was bracing. How did the situation run out of control? A close look at the dynamics of the interaction between forest and people in three regions would reveal the complexity of a situation that the government had analysed and dealt with so inadequately.

Deforesting the north

The north of Thailand is an especially critical ecological zone, being the site of seven river basins that drain principally into the country's breadbasket, the central plain. While the most important and largest river basin is the Chao Phraya basin in the middle of the country, the headwaters of this basin are largely the Ping, Wang, Yom, and Nan rivers in the north.[5] Many of the remaining standing forests in the north thus constitute head watersheds, and, with their destabilization by rapid deforestation, the flow of water from these watersheds has become quite irregular: in the dry season, drought has become more severe; in the rainy season, flooding has become more devastating in its impact on lives, soil, and property. For instance, the flow of water into the Bhumibol Dam, one of the two large-scale dams supplying the central plain and Bangkok, has declined since 1975, mainly due to reduced flows from the Ping River. Moreover, soil erosion due to water runoff has not only decreased soil fertility and productivity in degraded forest areas converted into farmland, but has contributed to heavy siltation of waterways and reservoirs downstream.

Traditionally, the official explanation has been that poor peasants migrating from the lowlands and tribal people practising swidden agriculture in the highlands have been principally responsible for deforestation. However, a more honest attempt to understand the situation would come to the conclusion that while poor people and tribal people are involved in the dynamics of deforestation, they are both victims and agents, often unwilling and unwitting, of the process. The role of government bureaucracies in creating the situation they are now decrying must be taken into account.

The process of deforestation might, in fact, be said to have begun with the exploitation of the rich teak forests of the North by western firms operating under license from the Royal Forestry Department (RFD). Indeed, central to the early forest management philosophy of the RFD was the cutting and processing of wood for export to Europe. So central were foreign markets that the administrative head of the agency was always an Englishman from its founding in 1896 until 1932.[6] Most of the logging concessions distributed during this period went to foreigners as well. In 1927, for instance, out of 32 forests under concession, 17 were operated by British citizens, six by French, and one by Danes. As one scholar points out:

> In those concessioned areas, which contained a total of 1,313,396 teak trees, the British have 819,682, the French 216,614, and the Danes 110,312, while the Siamese managed to keep only 94,788 teak trees under their concessioned forests. Even though the Siamese were given concessions of eight out of 32 forests, the total number of trees was much less than in the one forest that had been given to the Danes. In short, it would not be wrong to say that deforestation in Thailand has its origin in the long history of colonial expansion in the region.[7]

Foreign concessions were phased out following the 1932 revolution, which disempowered the monarchy. However, commercial logging, now by Thai citizens, continued to serve as the spearhead of deforestation. Also, by cutting down the big teak trees, the concessions in the North facilitated the migration to the forests of peasants from the valleys and lowlands – a movement that would otherwise not have taken place owing to the migrants' lack of heavy equipment to fell the trees.[8]

The movement of small farmers to the forests in the north has usually been attributed to population pressure. While population growth was certainly a factor, probably even more instrumental was the fact that, as one key study put it: 'landless people who lived in the large plain areas were facing the problem of tenancy, because of the insufficiency of rice for household consumption after paying part of their total rice production to the landlords as rent'.[9] The deforestion of the highlands therefore cannot be understood without paying attention to the central role of the inequitable distribution of land in the plains and valleys, a condition captured in the statistics, which show that the proportion of rented land to total agricultural land rose from slightly under 14 per cent in 1981 to close to 18 per cent in 1991.[10] In absolute numbers of full-time and part-time tenants, the north outstripped other regions of Thailand. Indeed, in 1988, close to 418,000 tenant farmers – fully 26 per cent of tenant farmers in the whole of Thailand – were found in the north.[11]

Arriving in the forests, these peasants were influenced by the practices of the big concessionaires, who often abused the terms of their contract with the RFD by cutting in areas not allocated to them. Villagers in Lamphun, for instance, told interviewers for one study that 'they started doing illegal logging after they had seen the unlawful tree cutting of the concessionaires. They were competing in doing illegal logging. It was difficult to tell which timbers were legal or illegal.'[12]

Migrating poor people, moreover, entered into a structure of illegal logging dominated by local influentials. Many did illegal logging as work for these local powers, being 'recommended for work through the kinship network'.[13] While one could say that poor villagers did exploit the forest, they did it for subsistence. But the local elites, using the poor as hired hands, exploited the forests for profit, and this was probably greater in terms of its impact. As an in-depth study of one northern village showed:

> [L]ocal leaders and government officials exercise their powers to legitimize their use of forest resources in terms of land-use patterns and acknowledgement of rights, in controlling and providing conveniences for transportation of sawn timber wood out of the forests. In the village studied, sub-district chiefs (*kamnan*) and village headmen (*phuyaiban*) were very often the ones who allocated lands and acknowledged the right to utilize forest lands. In use and cutting of trees on forest lands, the local politicians were financial supporters; the police were timber transporters or convenience providers. Before the intervention of state power, forest communities joined local powers and illegally exercised their powers. As the law enforcers did not conform to the law themselves, state laws, thus, were meaningless for villagers.[14]

Another factor drawing lowlanders to forest reserves was the cash crop boom, which began in the late 1960s in response to export-oriented agricultural programmes promoted by the government, with strong support from the World Bank. Since many of these crops could be grown with relatively little water and on lower-quality soil than that used to grow rice, degraded forest land, valleys, and hillsides became objects of a scramble for land. Former logging concessions, in particular, became choice sites for the expansion of cash crops.[15]

Cash cropping was especially marked in the 1970s and 1980s. Among the key cash crops cultivated were maize, tobacco, ginger, and sesame.[16] Especially noteworthy was maize, which had its golden age in the 1970s, when corn enjoyed an export boom stimulated not only by international market demand but also by government policies, like extensive road construction in forest areas. Maize was planted principally in forest areas that had been cleared by extensive logging.[17] In the north, areas for maize cultivation rose from 127,790 rai in 1970 to close to four million rai betwen 1975 and 1980. Maize expansion thus emerges as one of the forces behind the destruction of 4.5 million rai of forest cover in the mid-1970s.[18]

Cash cropping became even more important in the 1980s, when non-paddy cash crop cultivation in the north went up by over 8,200 square kilometres, compared to paddy cultivation, which rose by only 1,644 square kilometres.

The battle for the highlands

This complex of forces contributed to creating a situation in which an estimated three million lowlanders ascended to the northern midlands and highlands, producing a situation of severe competition for increasingly scarce land and accelerated devastation of the increasingly constricted forest area. The lowlanders competed with the half-million or so minority peoples to whom the highlands were traditional, ancestral, communal, or open-access land.[19]

The hill peoples (*chao khao*) are communities of various distinct tribal groups that include the Lua, Karen, Lisu, Hmong, Akha, and Lahu. There are an estimated 2,000 communities, usually very small, interspersed through the forests. Many of these communities were, over the last 250 years, driven by wars from the lowland areas of southern China to the upland areas of Burma, Laos, and eventually northern Thailand.[20]

Most of these tribal groups practise swidden agriculture. There are two types of swiddening common among them. Shifting cultivation, or the felling, burning, and growing of biomass, raising crops on the cleared land for as long as soil fertility allows, then moving on to clear new land, is practised by the Hmong, Yao, Akha, and Lahu. Cyclical swiddening, on the other hand, clears land for planting but leaves it to regenerate for long periods before cultivating it again. This form of agriculture, which is practically sedentary and non-expansive, is found among the Karen, Lua, Htin, and Khamu.[21] Cyclical swiddening is regarded by anthropologists as a benign adaptation to the forest environment, in contrast to shifting cultivation, which is depicted as entailing constant movement and cutting down of new forest areas.

The Karen, in particular, have been positively cited for their sedentary economy – some of their villages are said to be 200 years old[22] – and for their irrigated terraces and conservationist practices. As one observer notes: 'Such features as complex intercropping, heavy labor expenditures on weeding and conservation measures, and fairly close specification of land rights of communities and individuals all indicate that the [Karen] can ill afford to be prodigal with their land.'[23] Their agro-technology is said to be remarkably environment-friendly. In clearing the swidden, for instance, the Karen:

> usually leave belts of trees intact on the slope above each swidden. Also, they avoid felling some of the larger trees that stand in the area of the swidden itself. Although the trees are lopped so that their foliage will now shade the crop, their recovery is usually rapid. By leaving some trees intact, the Karen, as they say themselves, 'help many trees to spring up,' causing satisfactory regeneration.[24]

The result is that there is a continuity rather than a sharp break between forest and swidden, with the swidden constituting, in the respectful words of a World Bank report on the Pwo Karen, 'a variegated ecosystem in itself by holding a mix of creepers, vines, sesame, cotton, chili, eggplant and rice besides numerous existing forest plants which are left in the field because of their valuable properties'.[25] The field would normally be used only for one or two years, then allowed to lie fallow for ten to thirty years.[26]

Unlike the Karen, the Hmong and other shifting cultivators have had a bad press, especially since they are associated with an unsustainable type of swiddening, opium-growing and, lately, pesticide-intensive vegetable production. It is important to place their activities in context, however. As the anthropologist Leo Alting Von Geusau points out: 'Swiddening has been done more by Thai peasants than by hilltribes. The five million Thai people who have moved into the mountains since the 1960s are an enormous force ... compared to the 250,000 to 300,000 mountain people.'[27]

This encounter betwen land-hungry lowlanders and desperate highlanders, both subject to forces beyond their control, has focused on the so-called 'middle zone' in the north, an area some 600 to 1,500 miles above sea level, where the conservation-conscious Karen live. Within this zone in the nine provinces of the upper north, Karen communities have been increasingly subject to what one analyst has called a 'sandwich-like condition' that has driven them into ever more marginal slopes and narrow valleys.[28]

Specific government policies toward the tribal communities helped create this middle-zone crisis. One of these was security policy. In the struggle against the Communist Party of Thailand in the 1960s and 1970s, the Thai military and development bureaucracy sought to extend their control among the highland tribes in a pre-emptive move to prevent the Communists from creating a base among them. The extension of effective coercive authority was promoted by a slew of infrastructure projects, especially road building, that were also justified as development-related. These projects made a tremendous contribution in opening up the highlands to population movements from below, as can be gleaned from the account of two former student activists who revisited in 1993 a Karen village they had stayed in in the late 1970s:

> We went back to visit Mae Hae Kee village ... at the beginning of 1993. The mountains have been destroyed to make a wide road which is wide enough for ten-wheel trucks to pass each other easily. This road is a military road built as part of the Mae Jaem-Mae La Noi national security project which resulted from the political situation in the forests and mountains of this area between 1976 and 1980. It is a road which was cut through very steep mountains the whole way. Some former traces can still be seen of the mixed forests, pine forests, and virgin jungle that existed along both sides of the road. We passed trucks transporting cabbage at various points. The journey from Mae Hae Kee village to Mae Jaem, which we used to walk in a day and a half, now takes only a little more than an hour and a half by car.[29]

While roadbuilding promoted migration from the lowlands to the middle zone, the government's programme to eradicate opium growing among some of the tribal groups had the effect of encouraging movement from the higher altitudes. For nearly a century before the 1970s, the Hmong and some ten other tribal groups had engaged, at least partly, in cultivating opium, a practice that stemmed from British and French demand for the product in order to sell it to China and other markets.[30] Opium production had been concentrated mainly at altitudes higher than 3,000 feet. When the Thai government, with the support of USAID and the United Nations, campaigned to stamp out opium production beginning in the 1960s, a key part of its strategy was to get the opium-growing groups to shift to cultivation of other crops, including cabbages and other vegetables. The government programme was successful, with the Hmong, for instance, largely withdrawing from poppy cultivation.[31] But this success had residential and ecological consequences not foreseen by the government, for cultivation of these crops could be productively undertaken only at lower altitudes. The middle-zone Karen way of life, in particular, was destabilized:

> A resettlement program and some highland development operations have created a flow of Hmong, Lisu, Lahu, and Yao into the intermediate areas. Some ethnic families who traditionally cultivate swidden crops, opium, and corn, have re-settled in the deserted villages of the Karen. The migration of these groups is a gradual process. After a few years, the migrants tend to change their pattern of forest/land-use. Many Hmong have bought irrigated rice fields from the Karen, and have eventually occupied whole villages.[32]

The resulting conflicts were caught in a microcosm in the Karen community of Ban Om-Long, which lay in a critical watershed area in Mae Hong Son Province. Hmong communities began to settle in the area beginning in the late 1950s and again in the late 1980s. The two groups then began to get locked into conflicts that stemmed principally from the differences in the shifting patterns of cultivation of the Hmong and the cyclical swiddening of the Karen. As one observer saw it, 'the Karen wanted to keep some land for cultivation and some for conservation. But the Hmong, who have different ways of life and different methods of cultivation, wanted to use the land conserved by the Karen without taking good care of future benefits.'[33]

But beyond the differences in agricultural technology was an even more basic difference in the motivations for production. While the Karen communities produced rice and vegetables mainly for subsistence, the Hmong were integrated into a commercial network that linked them to markets in Bangkok, Singapore, and Malaysia.[34] Indeed, so commercially integrated are the Hmong that they apparently have their own informal credit system and recently formed their own trading corporation to increase their bargaining power *vis-à-vis* other market actors.[35]

However, the Hmong are probably exceptional. The other tribal groups that shifted from opium growing to cash-crop cultivation, like the Lahu and Lisu, benefited far less because of their lack of access to good transport and lack of bargaining power *vis-à-vis* middlemen.[36] Indeed, the impact of the market on most of the tribal communities, be they cash-croppers like the Lahu or subsistence farmers like the Karen, are probably similar: communal disintegration, increasing social differentiation, and growing impoverishment of the less powerful sections of the community.[37] Addiction to both opium and heroin is now rife, particularly among the Akha, suicide rates are up, and the young and the promising leave the villages for the cities.[38] Prostitution has become endemic as families sell their women to pay off debts, with one experienced NGO worker claiming that among the Lahu and the Akha, almost all the young girls are becoming prostitutes.[39]

This growing impoverishment of the many tribal groups is invisible to many lowland Thais, who have seen mainly the successes of some groups, like the Hmong, in raising high-value temperate crops. On the one hand, this has increased antagonism between the highlanders and the lowlanders since the latter perceive the success of the highlanders as being achieved largely at their expense. Since vegetable growing is water-intensive and heavily dependent on pesticides, the downstream Thais complain that they are being starved of water and that what water flows to them is now heavily contaminated with pesticide residues. In many areas, this conflict has begun to unravel the traditional understandings around water flows that underpin the *muang fai* indigenous irrigation systems, in which the needs of downstream groups have primacy in claims to water. In most areas, this traditional cooperative relationship has weakened, in some cases leading to violence.[40]

On the other hand, the perceived success of the tribal groups in raising vegetables, coffee, lychees, and other crops have made the highlands more valuable in the eyes of the lowlanders. Property values in the highlands began to shoot up in the 1980s, leading lowland interests to begin pressuring the state to give the Thais, especially Thai business interests, greater access to the highlands. These pressures are said to have been as important as environmental considerations in the consolidation of a state policy toward tribal groups which aimed to relocate them from catchment and watershed areas. The new 'Masterplan for the Highlands', according to one NGO specialist, is really a plan to resettle tribal peoples because most of them live in the two types of communities targeted for resettlement: those categorized as 'problem communities' because of their impact on ecology or widespead drug use, or 'small villages' that have fewer than fifty houses, are peopled by people legally considered non-citizens, raise opium or cash crops, and are riddled with drugs.[41]

Despite their being declared state lands, there was an intensified buying and selling of property in the highland areas as their value increased in the eyes of commercial interests. This led to virtual landgrabbing in certain areas since tribal groups did not buy and sell land traditionally and thus could show no land titles for their community property. Indeed, tribal people were extremely disadvantaged in commercial transactions because only 35 per cent had identification cards issued by the state, and without ID cards, many of them found it difficult to buy or sell land since they could easily be tagged as aliens with no land rights.[42]

By the early 1990s, the situation in the north could only be described as a mess, with deforestation going on unabated, growing conflicts between tribal communities and lowland Thai interests seeking greater control of properties in the highlands, greater inter-tribal competition for land, with subsistence farmers like the Karen slowly but surely losing out, and the implementation of government policies that the many tribal groups and NGOs saw as rhetorically pro-environment but actually anti-tribal.

Ecological crisis in the northeast

The northeast has experienced one of the most devastating losses of forest in Thailand. In 1961, forest land in the region covered about 44.3 million rai, or 42 per cent of the total 105.5 million rai comprising the region. Today, however, the forested area is down to less than 14 million rai, or below 14 per cent of the total land area.[43]

The ecologically diverse and heavily forested region depicted in Kampoon Boontawee's famous *Child of the Northeast*, where forests could be traversed for hours on end with little sunlight penetrating the thick canopy of leaves and branches, has given way to a sterile landscape. Only pockets of forest remain, among them the 3,200-hectare Dongyai Reserve, a key watershed that constitutes one of the last remaining stands of primary forest in the region. Even this forest area, however, is a fragment of the great forest that Koon's family crossed on the way to Chi River.[44]

Most of the remaining forests are, in fact, in a sorry state, with surveys showing that the tropical evergreen forests, mountain evergreen forests, mixed forests without teak trees, and *shorea botusa* forests are entering a terminal state. What forest cover remains is largely secondary natural growth, or the crop of small trees that gain light and soil nutrients with the destruction of the previously dominant larger species. There are very few large trees with a circumference of more than 100 centimetres, noted one study, with the average being only one such tree per rai.[45]

Deforestation has been accompanied by the same consequences as in the north, including erosion and watershed destabilization. In addition, the land has been plagued by increasing salinity. The northeast has massive salt deposits owing to its having been submerged under the sea millions of years ago. In the past, forest cover helped prevent the salt from coming up to the topsoil. But in recent years, the fatal combination of accelerated deforestation and unrestrained dam-building has contributed to the dilution of underground salt deposits and the spread of salt through natural waterways. This has led to the dispersion of salt in the topsoil, negatively affecting soil fertility.[46] In recent years, the salt-dispersing effects of deforestation have been complemented by rock-salt mining in many provinces, which has pumped up brine in massive quantities for salt farming.[47] Salinity is a problem on approximately 17.8 million rai, with the problem quite serious on 3.7 million, where salt deposits can be seen on the surface of the ground. In these areas, according to one study, crop yields are less than half of what they once were and 'are not worth the farmers' efforts'.[48]

What forces were responsible for what can only be described as an ecological tragedy of the first order? Again, in many accounts the blame is laid on the poor. The argument is that the combination of population pressure and a climate inhospitable to agriculture had led the masses of the country's poorest region to invade the forests. These are the same forces, it is alleged, that have also led vast numbers of northeastern or *Isan* people to migrate to forests in other parts of Thailand, to Bangkok, and to the Middle East as construction workers.

But as in the north, the dynamics of deforestation in the northeast are complex. As in the north, the big logging concessions had a key role in touching off the migration to the forest areas of the now estimated 250,000 families found in the region's 352 forest reserves. Not only did logging concessions carry out minimal reforestation, as required by their licences, but their felling of big trees and their roadbuilding activities paved the way for the clearing of the degraded forest areas by impoverished peasants. These dynamics are captured by one fairly exhaustive study:

Roads built to facilitate logging and transportation of felled trees have made it easier for villagers to enter, occupy, and clear forest areas for agriculture, and enable them to transport their agricultural products to town markets.

The fact [is] that clearing of forest lands where big trees have been felled [can be done] with less expense than ... in the case of clearing dense forest lands ... Farming can be done without the help of fertilizer which contributes to the low cost of production. At harvest time, agricultural products can be transported to town markets or traders can come to buy agricultural commodities in the villages due to the existence of roads. A great number of villagers have migrated to occupy and clear forest lands where big trees have been cut down by concessionaires. This contributes to greater difficulty for forests to recover naturally.[49]

It is not accidental, the study suggests, that the period 1973–78, when most logging concessions were granted, was also the time that the forests were most rapidly depleted.[50]

Roadbuilding, however, was carried out not only by private concessionaires but also by the military, in this case to support counterinsurgency activities. With the Indochina War raging across the border and the Communist Party of Thailand (CPT) entrenching itself in the forests of the region, roadbuilding became one of the key instruments of anti-guerrilla warfare, as military units cut down trees and built roads to pursue and push guerrillas from their hiding places.[51]

In addition to their roadbuilding activity, the military launched another counterinsurgency initiative that had a negative impact on the forests. This was the practice of encouraging poor peasants to resettle in and clear the forests in order to set up farming communities that could serve as 'buffer zones' against the Communists.[52] This was the case with the communities that came to settle at the Dongyai Reserve in Buriram province. The villagers were encouraged by the Second Military Command's promise that they could continue to live in this national forest reserve if they assisted the government against the Communists.[53] It was a pledge that would entail tragic consequences after the Communist threat faded, as will be shown later on.

But it was not only the government side that made use of population policy for security purposes, with an impact on the surrounding forest. In establishing their base areas in the northeast, the CPT allotted forest land to villagers, which was cleared and turned into farmland.[54] Also, in some Communist-controlled areas, illegal logging operations would be tolerated by the guerrillas in exchange for food and medicine. Nevertheless, in terms of the impact of their policies on the ecology, the Communists came out ahead of the government since:

it appears that, in some areas where there were communist movements, capitalists dared not enter to conduct illegal logging. Even though the capitalists were granted logging concessions in those areas, they dared not go there for logging operations. At the same time, it turned out that the communists in those areas also had a policy to protect forests.[55]

To big-logging activity and counterinsurgency as a stimulus for migration to the forests must be added the government's failure to carry out land reform. While land distribution has been less unequal in the northeast than in other parts of Thailand, it has worsened in recent times. With increasing inequality, migration to the forests has increasingly been seen by government as an alternative to land reform in private landholdings in traditional farming areas. Thus, in 1974, part of the land reform declared by a weak reformist government was the granting of amnesty to millions of farmers residing in state forest reserves – a move that led to a 'huge upswing in forest clearance during the mid and late 1970s'.[56]

A fourth factor that precipitated the rush of farmers to the forests was, as in the north, the cash crop boom of the 1960s and 1970s. More than any other region, the northeast took to cash cropping in a big way, becoming the country's prime producer of kenaf and cassava. Land considered unfit for cultivation was seen as excellent for cash crops, leading to a greater commercial value placed on degraded forests, which could provide a few years of good yield even without the application of fertilizer. The linkages between world trade, government promotion of cash crops, road construction and deforestation in the northeast is caught in microcosm in the recent history of the Khao Phu Luang forest in Nakhon Ratchasima province:

> Although tree felling for the lumber industry was a major factor in the deforestation of the area, the promotion of maize as a major export commodity from the mid-1950s onwards was also critical. According to the Department of Business Economics (Ministry of Commerce), the value of maize exported by Thailand before 1957 was less than $5 million. By 1964, it had increased to $57.3 million. Pak Chong Hai began to emerge as a maize trading center in 1957, but the rapid expansion of maize growing began in 1964. Tractors were introduced in 1966. Construction of Highway 304 began that year and was completed in 1969. This highway considerably enhanced the importance of Pak Thong Chai as a trading center. A second trading center emerged on the highway at Ban San Chao Pao some 50 km to the south and became known as Kilometer 79 Market. Maize traders from other locations such as Muak Lek and Pak Chong on the Friendship Highway flocked to this market to set up maize buying depots.[57]

In the early years of maize growing in the Kho Phu Luang reserve, profits were high since the soil of newly cleared forest lands was rich and produced good yields even without the application of fertilizer. However, profits are said to have declined considerably as intensive planting impoverished the soil at the same time that the cost of fertilizer skyrocketed owing to the OPEC price hikes.

The maize boom triggered different waves of migrants to the cleared forests, as word spread from earlier settlers 'to their home villages that new fertile land was available in the Kho Phu Luang forest'. The result was 'a large influx of maize growers who came to settle permanently on land they purchased from previous occupiers or cleared themselves, mainly by burning whatever trees and brush remained'.[58] And because of the usual delayed demographic reactions to economic trends, the inflow of settlers continued way past the end of the maize boom in the mid-1970s.

In the northeast as a whole, land planted to maize, cassava, and other field crops rose from 1.7 million rai in 1961 to 10.5 million rai by 1989, an increase brought about not only by the conversion of traditional rice land but also by the massive clearing of forest land.[59] The spread of cash crops was also intensive. Other agro-export crops, including soy beans, black gram, and sesame were also planted, often being intercropped with maize.[60] Different crops were often planted in different years on the same land, depending on their current profitability. The results were predictable: loss of fertility and declining productivity. Combined with insecure land tenure owing to the lack of titles to cleared forest land, these factors induced many farmers to sell their lands to newcomers and move on to other recently cleared areas, sometimes in other parts of Thailand.

Disaster in the south

The ecological crisis in southern Thailand caught the attention of the world in November 1988, when three days of rain triggered floods and landslides that caused massive property damage and took over a hundred of lives.

The rapid expansion of rubber growing in the disaster area was identified by many people as the principal cause of the disaster. Rubber planting had steadily moved upslope from the plains, supported by government and World Bank programmes promoting more expansion. In places like the Khao Luang Mountains, planters eager to cash in on the state-supported rubber boom followed the roads made by big logging firms into the forest, where they cut down undergrowth and mature rubber trees, replacing them *en masse* with the new 'clonal' variety that was supposed to be more productive and profitable.[61] Minimal concern was paid to the erosion that could result from this process, with the World Bank assuring the local people that 'less than 10 per cent of the planted area would require terracing'.[62] The result is history. Heavy rains triggered massive erosion in recently planted areas, with floods, trees, and cut logs all crashing down on the lowland farms and communities.

What occurred in Khao Luang was a microcosm of a process that was drastically transforming the ecology of the south, where only nine million rai out of the 22 million rai of forestland in 1958 remained.[63] Logging firms, which were granted concessions beginning in 1968, led the way, eliminating not only large numbers of big trees but also, as in the north and northeast, building the roads that gave thousands of smallholders access to the interior. While the concession agreement stipulated that the companies take measures to prevent encroachment into the forest, in fact, according to one report:

> they often ignored both the proviso and the encroachers, because it was in their best interests to do so. Allowing encroachment was, in fact, beneficial to the companies, as they were in need of a regular supply of labor. The settlers' relatives and friends would often work for the companies, while at the same time clearing the land for agriculture. Indeed, trying to prevent encroachment would have been detrimental to the logging companies, who would then have had to bring all their labor from elsewhere.[64]

Although rubber cultivation existed prior to the granting of logging concessions, it was boosted tremendously by the opening up of forestland by the big loggers. Both smallholder plots and plantations were set up in degraded forest areas, and the area planted to rubber rose from 4.7 million rai in 1963 to 10.6 million rai in 1986.[65] About 35 per cent of the total area under rubber cultivation was located either in areas that had been designated national forest reserves or conservation forests.[66]

International demand and pro-agro-export government policies combined to create a boom in other cash crops in the south. Rubber expansion was accompanied by the introduction of palm tree plantations. Palm oil production was heavily subsidized by the government, which leased large tracts of intact or degraded forests to plantations. By 1985, there were over 500,000 rai planted to palm trees, with some 58 per cent of them controlled by 88 business enterprises and the rest by small businesses and approximately 5,600 households.[67]

As serious as the damage to inland forests was the impact of economic activities on the coastal mangrove or marshland areas. Between 1969 and 1989, mangrove forests decreased from 2.2 million rai to less than one million rai.[68] By the late 1980s, about 900,000 rai of this figure were found on the beautiful western coastline by the Andaman Sea, while no more than 100,000 rai were left along Thailand's eastern coast.[69] In the judgement of one report, 'it is doubtful if Thailand has any significant areas of intact mangrove remaining, certainly none that are of global significance when compared to the much richer and more extensive stands in neighboring countries such as Indonesia.'[70]

Several activities contributed to the degradation of the mangroves, including wastewater from inland factories and households, destructive methods of fishing, indiscriminate logging, and prawn farming. Perhaps the most destructive were logging by charcoal concessions in marshland areas and prawn farming.

Table 9.1 Loss of mangrove forest area, 1961–92 (in rai, where 6.3 rai = 1 hectare)

Year	Mangrove forest area	Total change	Annual change
1961	2,299,375	-345,500	24,678
1975	1,954,375	-158,700	39,675
1979	1,795,675	-568,001	81,143
1986	1,227,674	-99,180	33,060
1989	1,128,494	-32,326	10,775
1992	1,096,168		
Total change		-1,203,707	
Av. change			38,829

Source: Thanwa Jitsanguan, 'Natural resources and management policies of the coastal zones in Thailand', paper delivered at the Ninth Biennial Conference of the Agricultural Economics Society of Southeast Asia, Asia Hotel, Bangkok, 22–4 June 1993, p. 13.

Table 9.2 The rise of shrimp farming in Thailand, 1980–90

Year	No. of farms	Area (rai)[a]	Production (metric tons)	Area/farm	Production/ farm
1980	3,572	162,727	8,036	45.56	2.25
1981	3,657	171,619	10,728	46.93	2.93
1982	3,943	192,453	10,091	48.81	2.56
1983	4,327	222,107	11,550	51.33	2.66
1984	4,519	229,949	13,007	50.88	2.88
1985	4,939	254,805	15,841	51.59	3.21
1986	5,534	283,548	17,886	51.24	3.23
1987	5,899	325,929	23,566	55.25	3.99
1988	10,246	342,344	55,633	33.42	5.42
1989	12,545	444,785	93,495	35.46	7.45
1990	15,072	403,787	82,947	26.79	5.5

Note: [a] 6.3 rai = 1 hectare
Source: Natural Resource Management Programme, Thailand Environmental Institute, *Thailand's Trade and Environment* (study submitted to ASEAN Secretariat) (Bangkok: Thailand Environmental Institute, 1997), pp. 2–32.

Mangrove wood is especially desired for conversion into charcoal owing to its high calorific value, which results in little smoke when burned. Some 90 per cent of mangrove wood is, in fact, processed into charcoal.[71] With demand for charcoal rising, charcoal enterprises have adopted 'clear-cut' methods of logging, leaving vast tracts of marshland denuded because many concessionaires did not live up to their contractual obligation to reforest their areas.[72] The situation was aggravated by the fact that cutting down mangroves was exempted from the logging ban of 1989.

The takeover of land by prawn-farming enterprises has been exponential, with the area rising in just 13 years, 1977 to 1990, from 77,600 rai to 403,780 rai. And this was an underestimate, based only on registered farms – many shrimp farms are currently operated without being formally registered.[73]

Since seawater is essential to prawn farming, mangrove forests or beaches are prime locations, with many large investors cornering huge plots of land adjoining the mangroves.[74] Even when these entrepreneurs raise the shrimps on their own property, their activities inevitably encroach on the adjoining mangroves. Their latest methods of production are, in fact, very ecologically destabilizing. For instance, modern intensive processes involved in the cultivation of the black tiger prawn rely not only on high-nutrient food and antibiotic drugs but also on chemicals to kill undesirable marine life that 'hamper' the growth of the prawns.[75] Like agriculture, aquaculture in Thailand is increasingly chemical-intensive.

Mangrove forests must be seen as part of a larger, interdependent coastal ecosystem, encompassing seagrass forests and coral reefs. Thus, wastewater from prawn farms in mangrove areas have destroyed not only the mangroves but also adjoining seagrass forests and coral reefs. The complex relationship is described by one observer:

> The deterioriation of mangrove forests causes soil erosion, which causes siltation. The muddy water chokes and kills the seagrass and subsequently the coral reefs in deeper water. On the other hand, the deterioration of coral reefs and seagrass forests allows ocean waves to erode the coastal area where mangroves grow.[76]

With the deterioration of these three subsystems, the wealth of marine flora and fauna disappears, leading in turn to greater difficulties for people dependent on mangrove life for their subsistence. The sustenance provided by mangrove forests is not to be underestimated: there are at least 72 species of fish, 37 species of shrimps, 54 species of crabs, and 20 species of molluscs in Thailand's marshlands, and most of these are marine species of great value.[77] The destabilization of their habitat has translated into more precarious livelihoods for coastal communities, which have seen progressively smaller catches of progressively tinier fish and crustaceans.

In contrast, prawn farming has been an extremely profitable enterprise, with profit rates ranging from 79 per cent to 174 per cent.[78] And one of the reasons it is so profitable is that leases are, to quote one study, 'ridiculously low', with a five-year registration fee of only 100 baht.[79] Aquaculture can truly be said to be subsidized by government.

Shrimp farming has, in two decades, moved from the estuary of the

Chao Phraya river near Bangkok to the coastal provinces of Chonburi, Rayong, Chantaburi, and Trat in the eastern region, then down to the east coast of the southern region to the provinces of Songkhla, Nakhon Si Thammarat, and Surat Thani. It is now moving to the west coast to the provinces of Ranong, Phangnga, and Krabi, which contain the most developed mangrove forests. In this downward march, aquaculture has cut a swathe of environmental destabilization that has led to the disappearance of coastal forests and resources. After a decade of intensive farming, for instance, much of the land devoted to the industry in the Chao Phraya estuary is now barren.[80] And it is unlikely, says one observer, that the last frontier of mangrove forests will be able to escape the same fate: 'The same conflict of resource use of coastal resources will also be expected to occur in this last coastal zone and at even higher social cost than before.'[81]

Government: part of the problem?

An important variable in the crisis of the forest has been government. Indeed, the seeds of today's increasingly confused and ineffective policy were sown in the late nineteenth century, with the founding of the Royal Forestry Department. As noted earlier, the RFD was originally set up to manage the cutting of teak for export, trying to achieve the contradictory objectives of profiting from teak export while rationalizing the felling of trees. A fateful step that set the framework for future forest policy was taken in 1899, when full ownership and control of natural forests was assumed by the state, with administration vested in the RFD.

Backed by a 1937 law empowering it to declare protected forest reserves, the government has, since the 1960s, specified targets for the proportion of the country's total area that should remain under forest cover. Under the Seventh National Economic and Social Development Plan (1992–96), 40 per cent was designated for forest cover, with 25 per cent earmarked for 'conservation forests'. In the most recent formulation, by the government of Anand Panyarachun in March 1992, about 143,200 square kilometres, or 28 per cent of total land area, was declared a conservation area, where no commercial logging and farming would be allowed and mining concessions would be ultimately phased out.[82]

Conflicting property systems

A fundamental problem with this approach of decreeing protected areas from above is that it has clashed with the sense of property of people who established communities in the forest. For those who have studied the complexity of Thailand's people–forest relationship, the problem is contained in Prime Minister Chuan Leekpai's response to the bloody clash between police and villagers fighting eviction from the Dongyai forest reserve: 'The villagers have to be made to understand that the forest belongs to the state.'[83]

While people knew that 'the forest belonged to the kingdom', in practice communities evolved their own rules for landownership and land use. Thus, when government forestry officials arrived to enforce bureaucratic decrees, it was a case of a new property system being imposed on the existing informal system of landownership. Consequently, in frontier areas, two landownership systems existed, creating much insecurity about land tenure. This insecurity contributed to constant movement further into the forests, as people in possession but with no legal rights to land did not develop an attachment. Thus developed that lack of attachment to a particular piece of land noted among peasants on the frontier, a character-istic that was part of a mentality of exploiting the land as quickly and intensively as possible, and selling it off and moving on to clear new forest areas.

Government efforts to manage the deforestation problem included land-entitlement programmes in degraded forests, resettling of peasants, reforestation programmes, a logging ban, and experiments in community and social forestry. The results have not been favourable, the main proof being the disappearance of forests at the astounding rate of three million rai per year over the last 30 years. If the rate of deforestation has appeared to be slowing down somewhat recently, this is because there are fewer and fewer forests to cut down in most parts of the country.

Lack of political will

The failure of these efforts has been attributed to several factors, with weak government control over private interests cited as one of the most important. The fashionable term these days is 'lack of political will'. Private interests are influential throughout the government bureacratic apparatus that deals with the forests, and, aside from the RFD, there are about thirteen other agencies involved. Moreover, logging interests have been well represented in successive government cabinets. Logging lobbies have been even more influential at the level of provincial and local governments. In recent years, illegal loggers, through bribery and connections to pro-vincial and local governments, have practically neutralized government enforcement capability and subverted the ban on logging declared by the government in 1989, as a result of popular outcry over the floods in the south. 'In the north, for example, an intelligence report of the Thai Army revealed that:

> 50 police officers are involved in log poaching in Lampang, Lamphun, Phrae and Kamphangphet provinces, up from 40 in 1990. Six of them are chief

inspectors of district or village police stations. The bribes collected by the cops are reportedly divided 20–60–20. Lower echelon officers get 20 per cent, 60 per cent goes to the officers who provide protection, and their superiors skim the remainder.[84]

Army officers were also implicated by the report, as were village and sub-village heads. Local politicians, especially members of provincial councils, are said to be central in the chain of corruption forged by illegal loggers, for it is they who have contacts with national police and army authorities as well as national-level politicians who can provide the ultimate protection.

In contrast, local forestry units, even if they are serious about suppressing illegal logging, are terribly understaffed and underequipped. To cover two million rai of forest land in Lampang, for instance, the RFD had a total manpower of 50 forest officers and seven cars. The situation was as bad, weapons- and manpower-wise, in the Thung Yai Naresuan Wildlife Sanctuary. As one forest ranger asserted: 'With an unreliable gun and five knives, do you think we can match intruders with their modern weapons? Every time we go out patrolling, I feel I'm half-way to death.'[85] Rangers thoughout Thailand indeed had reason to be afraid, for in the last few years, a number of them had been shot or murdered by illegal loggers or poachers armed with high-powered rifles and electronic communications equipment.

The forest village and STK programmes

The government also initiated programmes that were ostensibly intended to improve 'man–forest interaction' in degraded areas. There were, however, few successes, and a major part of the problem is that the overriding concern of government agencies became the establishment of government control and authority over forest communities. In the 'Forest Village Programme' in the northeast, for instance, ecological concerns took a back seat to countering Communist influence.

Another major problem, in both the Forest Village Programme and the National Forest Land Allotment Programme (STK), was that plans were generally imposed from above, with little participation by the intended beneficiaries, who were already greatly suspicious of the government's motives. Probably typical was the government–villager relationship in a Forest Village Programme in the Khao Phu Luang National Forest:

A major problem with the project was that it was planned and imposed from the top on a population that was not consulted and which was not given a choice to accept or reject it. Although planned with the benefit of the people in mind, it was not so perceived by them. Initial reactions of the forest-land encroachers to the project were very negative, stemming from their perception of foresters as law-enforcement officers. They were naturally suspicious and fearful that the project would lead to their eviction and the loss of their livelihood.[86]

In many Forest Village and STK projects, the government's approach was viewed by peasants as making land use more insecure rather than more secure. For instance, the STK certificate, which gives villagers allotments not to exceed 15 rai per household, are not supposed to be divided or transferred except through inheritance, and violations of the rules would make STK certificates subject to cancellation by the provincial government, with no possibility of appealing the action in court. Many farmers who had divided or transferred some of their land thus felt that their status as landholders was at risk.

Moreover, obtaining land certificates was often a very slow process, owing to different requirements posed by different agencies with jurisdiction over forests, land registration, and land reform. The difficulty of obtaining certificates and the highly conditional character of the certificates led villagers to feel that they were being fooled by the state, which could take back the land whenever it wanted to. Not surprisingly, according to one study, 'whenever a chance to sell arises, villagers will hurriedly sell their land and use the proceeds from the sale to purchase land in another National Forest Reserve'.[87]

There were a host of other problems with these projects, including bureaucratic competition among the 14 agencies with jurisdiction over forests, land and land distribution; little attention paid to providing villagers with alternative occupations to exploiting the forest; lack of credit facilities to support farmers; and lack of personnel to administer the programmes effectively.

Not surprisingly, there was a lack of interest on the part of the local population. And most Forest Village programmes were failures, at least in the northeast, where most were implemented.[88]

Reforestation and resettlement

The fundamental problems with the government's approach to the forest crisis perhaps come out most clearly in its policies of commercial reforestation and resettlement, which were often tied together.

Commercial reforestation programmes involved, in the first instance, a great subsidy for private enterprises. Degraded forest lands have been leased to these businesses at a low price – 10 baht per rai compared to a market rental of 150–200 baht per rai. The bias towards the rich and powerful becomes more stark when one realizes that the bargain-basement lease prices are being quoted in areas where most villagers do not have land titles or documents.

Indeed, in many areas reforestation has become a big racket, where a web of corruption and intimidation binds together government officials, commercial interests, and local 'godfathers'. In Eastern Thailand, for instance, untitled land has been sold to influential interests for half to one-third of its full-title price. Moreover, most of the land on which eucalyptus trees have been planted was once controlled or owned by small farmers, many of whom were forced to sell the land to local influentials. An excellent description of the dynamics of this process is provided by Larry Lohmann:

> Businessmen anticipating the interest of plantation companies are sending their representatives to organize land transfers so that they can later resell at profits of up to several hundred per cent. Local villagers, who are often recent migrants indebted as a result of consumerism and increased dependence on commercial agriculture, generally end up accepting payments for land they are occupying.[89]

Several methods are employed to force the farmers to give up their land:

> The land around them may be bought up, cutting off their access. Forestry officials may attempt to clear out 'illegal squatters' on charges of 'forest encroachment.' Various schemes may be employed to get villagers further into debt or to play on their jealousy of neighbors who are temporarily flush with cash following recent sales. Violence and murder and threats thereof are also frequently used. Local officials, meanwhile, collect bribes for issuing land documents that will make it easier for the buyers to ask high prices of their customers. Once off the land, their cash running out, villagers often wind up encroaching on fast-dwindling forests in outlying areas ... many simply to await the next wave of land speculation.[90]

In many cases reforestation has become an engine of deforestation, because primary forest is not as valuable, in market terms, as a eucalyptus plantation. Many times, eucalyptus planters have encroached on and cut down adjacent virgin and community forests. In one of the most notorious cases, the Suan Kitti company encroached on 13,000 rai of natural forest between Chachoengsao and Prachinburi provinces.[91] Sometimes speculators are the ones who cut down natural forests, employing villagers to clear the forest of trees so that it can be categorized as 'degraded land' suitable for eucalyptus.[92]

Commercial reforestation has been a central consideration in the most controversial reforestation projects, the Dongyai Reserve resettlement scheme and the *Khor Jor Kor* programme. In the Dongyai Reserve case, the conflict focused on 3,200 hectares of forest that serve as an important watershed area and remain one of the few remaining stands of primary forest left in Thailand today. Thousands of villagers came to settle in the Reserve during the time when the government was struggling against the influence of the Communist Party. The government, represented at that time by the military, encouraged the formation of these settlements to contain the influence of the CPT and the guerrillas.[93]

However, by the beginning of the 1980s, with the collapse of the Communist threat, the former allies drifted apart as the government's concern became 'forest conservation', with an approach that saw people as obstacles to the commercial reforestation of degraded forest areas. Resettlement, as Phra Prajak Khuttajito, an activist Buddhist monk, saw it, 'is really a way of taking away land from people who have been there for years and giving it to private firms to plant eucalyptus'.[94] The fears of the villagers were not unfounded since resetttlement had barely begun when a private firm began to plant eucalyptus in parts of the reserve forest, a move that involved the expulsion of many villagers. When the military did try to resettle the villagers, it could find an adequate resettlement area for only 300 out of 1,200 families. There was simply no free land in other areas, and resettlement could be achieved only by clearing new forest land. Led by Phra Prajak, the peasants resisted the encroachment of eucalyptus, formed a forest conservation committee, and, in some instances, cut down eucalyptus trees in non-violent protest, evoking a punitive government response. Dongyai continues to be a problem area for the government.

Eucalyptus planting as a means of reforesting degraded areas became generalized under the Fifth Economic and Social Development Plan (1982–86). And perhaps the most ambitious and draconian effort to evict people to make way for eucalyptus was the *Khor Jor Kor* programme, which was projected to last five years, from 1991 to 1996. This programme was pushed principally by the army as the centrepiece of its 'Green Isan Project'. The programme meant to move 250,000 northeastern families from 14 million rai of land classified as degraded forest land. Some 4.9 million rai of this land was to be allocated for use for small farmers, and the remaining 9.1 million would be turned over to the private sector for reforestation.[95]

As in the Dongyai controversy, the ensuing events showed the utter inadequacy of the government's approach. With the land frontier having been reached, villagers were being settled from degraded areas to land that was already settled. For instance, 400 villagers from Baan Nong Yai in Nakhon Ratchasima were displaced to Baan Santisuk, only to find that much of the land was already owned by people from a neighbouring village. The solution of the RFD 'was to burn down and clearcut 10,000 rai of primary forest in Tab Larn National Park to make way for re-settlers'.[96] While tractors levelled the forest, 'RFD officials cynically moved the park's borders so that it no longer includes those 10,000 rai, but *does* include the expropriated land around Baan Nong Yai'.[97] *Khor Jor Kor* was soon satirized as 'destroying the forest in order to save it'.

Fighting for their economic survival, thousands of peasants from 17 provinces massed and marched to Nakhon Ratchasima city and Pak Chong district in June 1992, where they closed the highways until the government agreed to allow them to return to their original lands. The government backed down. It also issued a cabinet order suspending commercial reforestation. But in spite of the cabinet's announcement of a suspension, the farmers insisted on continuing the demonstration because they wanted an immediate cessation of *Khor Jor Kor*. Deprived of any signficant support, the programme was eventually shelved.

The Thai Forestry Sector Master Plan

By the end of the 1980s, the forest bureaucracy admitted the failure of previous efforts at reforestation. It proclaimed two new initiatives that it claimed took into consideration the flaws of previous approaches. One was the Thai Forestry Sector Master Plan (TFSMP), the other was a new forest conservation and biodiversity protection programme co-funded by the Global Environmental Facility, a window for environmental conservation in the Third World managed by the World Bank. Under pressure from NGOs, parliament also introduced the Community Forestry Bill, which was an attempt to give communities some control over forest resources.

The TFSMP was put forward as a plan to balance conservation and development through 'consensus building', Under the plan, Thailand's forest sector would be divided into a Protected Area System (PAS) of 'conservation forests'; 'multipurpose forests', which would be divided into several uses including community forestry; and degraded land designated for land reform or private use.[98]

While employing the language of community participation and conservation, the TFSMP was basically a document making a strong case for reforestation through commercial forestry, which had been suspended by the Anand administration in 1992. Its thrust was revealed in the discussion draft's statement that: 'On current trends, the Kingdom will be increasingly dependent on imports of wood and wood products. But the bulk of the Kingdom's products can be met from domestic sources, if that is what the Kingdom wants and works for.'[99] More specifically: 'Importation of wood products can be kept at less than 70 billion baht annually if enough trees are planted in the Kingdom, but would shoot up to 200 billion baht per year, or three times as high, on current trends.'[100] Some Thai NGOs went so far as to claim, in fact, that the Master Plan was a barely concealed effort to end the logging ban and resume logging in Thailand's natural forests under the guise of 'sustainable management of the natural production forest'.[101]

The kernel of the Master Plan was the creation of 20 million rai of man-made forest plantations, partly through forest land reform whereby millions of rai of deforested state land would be leased to the villagers now occupying them. While villagers, according to the plan, would be free to choose which crops to grow on their land, it was likely that the controversial, ecologically damaging eucalyptus tree favoured by the wood industry would be the crop of choice. Indeed, the Master Plan asserted:

> Medium-rotation crops of relatively fast-growing native species suitable for saw timber, and short-rotation crops of vast-growing exotics suitable for poles and pulpwood will be promoted. The two crops can be planted in alternate strips. With short-rotation crops, the farmer has to wait only a few years before harvest. Medium-rotation crops will provide higher revenue because of the higher price for saw timber. There are a number of ways to rotate the crops so that there would an annual stream of benefits. Ultimately, the short-rotation crops should be replaced with medium-rotation crops. A relatively longer crop rotation period allow for higher revenue, better soil conservation, and longer carbon retention.[102]

Given its commercial-industrial bias, the Master Plan, according to Thai NGOs, was likely to worsen rather than alleviate Thailand's forest crisis because it would increase encroachment into natural forests by commercial wood enterprises, whether run by small farmers or by big entrepreneurs. But even as small farmers were portrayed as beneficiaries, in fact, the driving force and main beneficiary of the plan would be the wood and wood-based industry. 'Rural communities will be further marginalized,' noted one NGO commentary, 'while their farm land and community forests are subordinated for tree plantations for the wood-based industry.'[103]

Thailand's forest crisis will actually be further exacerbated because plantations of eucalyptus, pine and acacia will cause ecological degradation, not enhance it. The rapid growth and extraction of commercial trees cause nutrient depletion of the soil. Given the short rotation of harvest, and the clearing of natural vegetation to plant the trees, the exposed soil will experience greater compaction and erosion. Plant and animal bio-diversity will also be reduced in the monocultures of treestands. Most damaging of all is the water deficit caused by the high and rapid intake of water by trees, and the loss of the regulation of natures water cycle by the previous vegetation of the area. Thus, in many commercial planta-tions that are close to primary watershed areas, the water table becomes severely reduced.[104]

Yet the strategic thrust of the TFSMP was probably not surprising since its author, the Finnish consulting engineer, Jaako Poyry, has been one of the main consultants for the global pulp and paper industry, having been engaged in promoting wood-based projects in Brazil, the Philippines, Indonesia, Australia, Burma, Sri Lanka, and other countries.

Despite widespread criticism of the Master Plan, the go-ahead for it was given in September 1993, when the Council of Economic Ministers of the Chuan Leekpai government decided to lift the ban on commercial reforestation that had been imposed by the previous administration.

The Forest Conservation Development Project

The other key new government initiative was the 'Forest Conservation and Development Project' funded by the World Bank-administered Global Environmental Facility. This was an effort to unite forest conservation and people's livelihoods in an experimental area, the Huai Kha Khaeng/ Thung Yai Naresuan Wildlife Sanctuary (HKK/TYN) in western Thailand bordering Burma, which had previously been designated a World Heritage Site for its extremely rich fauna and flora. Basically, the idea was to set up a protected conservation area, where there would be minimal human presence and activity, and surround it with a 'Conservation Buffer Zone' that was five kilometres in depth, where communities would engage in economic activities that were either designed to protect the conservation zone or were ecologically beneficial in their impact.[105]

There were several problems with the Forestry Conservation scheme. The first, which was forcefully pointed out by a group of Thai NGOs, was the project's reserving the option to forcibly relocate and resettle Karen groups living within the Conservation Zone.[106] The rationale was articulated thus by the consultancy group that prepared the proposal:

Decisions to resettle people, especially tribal peoples, are never easy. Such decisions should be made according to criteria of biodiversity and watershed protection. It is, however, a fallacy to insist that people, other than the most primitive hunter/gatherers, can live in harmony with forests and wildlife. Tribal peoples in Thailand's protected area network have had, and are continuing to have, significant impact on natural ecosystems, altering and simplifying habitats through unsustainable shifting agriculture and by hunting many large mammals and birds to extinction. The decision to resettle or allow tribal villages to remain in individual national parks and wildlife sanctuaries and pursue their existing way of life is a political decision and will depend on a host of factors, including history of settlement and demographic patterns. It is perfectly legitimate to manage a national park which includes tribal settlements as a man-affected ecosystem, but it must be recognized that in most cases human settlements and agricultural activities are incompatible with a primary objective of biological conservation. If RTG [Royal Thai Government] wishes to conserve Thailand's already depleted biodiversity some conservation areas will have to be protected from all human encroachment.[107]

Thus, 'removal and resettlement of occupants of protected areas may be necessary at selected sites and should remain an option for RTG.'[108]

What was especially problematic about the eviction option was that it would affect several Karen villages at Thung Yai Naresuan. As the Project for Ecological Recovery (PER) pointed out:

For the Karen people, the protection and regeneration of biodiversity is an essential characteristic of their agricultural system of rotational farming. Their sophisticated knowledge of plant and animal species, combined with their cultural beliefs and agricultural methods, have conserved their forests and its biological diversity for generations.[109]

Indeed, even a World Bank team had to detach itself from the forced resettlement option, although this was not, of course, binding on the government, which could take the option of forcible resettlement so long as it did not use foreign donor funds to pursue this. It is worth quoting the World Bank rationale in full:

[To] forcefully resettle the Pwo Karen from TYN is unlikely to be a feasible option. First, from a legal perspective, the Pwo Karen have been there all their life and prior to any gazettement. Second, there is practically no unoccupied land where they could be resettled except for nearby (fertile) conservation forest. Third, from a cultural and human rights perspective, resettlement may turn out to be detrimental. The values that would be lost are not only socio-cultural but intellectual as Pwo Karen knowledge of forest habitat is still more comprehensive than that of many scientists. Furthermore, from a biotechnological standpoint, certain varieties of crops (especially rice) grown by the more isolated villages ... are unique and could be potential genetic material for gene pools. Hence, there are cultural and technical heritage reasons for finding viable solutions for these communities to stay where they are.[110]

Related to the Karen relocation problem was the voluntary resettlement of people who lived in the inner 'Conservation Buffer Zone'. Would there be land available on which to resettle these people? As the World Bank mission report admitted: 'ALRO [Agrarian Land Reform Office] will face difficulty in finding sufficient land to settle all those who wish to move out of the inner part of the CBZ.'[111]

The resettlement issue reflected a fundamental problem with the project, which was its being dictated by a 'national parks philosophy' that sees the solution as keeping people away from the forest and taking care only of trees, lands, and wildlife, instead of viewing the relationship between the villagers and forests as a dynamic process based on 'trying to coexist in equilibrium'.[112]

A third problem had to do with the fact that the project could itself increase encroachment owing to the economic activities that would be set up in the outer CBZ, which would include agro-forestry and eco-agricultural enterprises. As the World Bank report itself pointed out: 'There is ... the risk that successful economic development in the buffer zone area would attract more people from outside the area and hence place increasing pressures on the land and natural resources.'[113]

Fourth, there was the danger that even a well-designed project could fall on its face without the political will to push it through against bureaucratic inertia and the ability of local influentials or mafia elements to subvert the project. Given the almost complete record of failure of the

Royal Forestry Department, including the enforcement of the logging ban, it was not surprising that the World Bank report remarked that 'the primary risk is that political will and official commitment remain weak in certain quarters and affected stakeholders (land speculators and big time wildlife poachers) would seek to thwart the project's initiatives'.[114]

Fifth, the programme did not take into consideration area developments that could undermine it, including the Royal Irrigation Department's plan to build a large dam, the Mae Wong dam, in an area adjacent to the GEF biodiversity project. This project would have severe ecological consequences on a wide area since it would flood at least 2,700 hectares of natural forest in the Mae Wong National Park, which is contiguous to the Thung Yao-Huay Kha Kaeng forest complex.[115]

Finally, there was the question of which interests the biodiversity programme served. Given the wide-ranging bioprospecting that transnational pharmaceutical firms engaged in, it was understandable that one Thai NGO warned:

> Thailand's forest dwelling communities possess wide-ranging knowledge of the health benefits of medicinal plants and herbs. The 'biodiversity research' proposed for these 'priority' areas could support transnational drug companies using the knowledge of forest village people to find genetic material to be patented and developed into commercial products.[116]

The Community Forest Bill

The debate over the relations of people to the forest that marked the Forest Conservation Project was reproduced during the discussions over the Community Forest Bill, which aimed to give control of forest resources to communities. However, various groups, including NGOs, were at loggerheads with the issue of allowing communities to use conservation areas. Groups such as Thammanart Foundation argued that forests should be best left alone, while the Project for Ecological Recovery maintained that villagers can live in harmony in forests. This conflict and parliamentary instability have delayed approval of the bill.

A working committee was set up in 1996 by the government of Banharn Silapa-Archa to resolve this issue. However, the process was halted when parliament was disbanded later that year. Then a new public hearing committee was set up by the new prime minister, Chaovalit Yongchaiyudh, to resolve the three controversial issues of how community forests should be defined, the type of activities allowed in conservation areas, and how management and monitoring should be conducted. The two groups with opposing perspectives were still in disagreement but the RFD gave its backing to the draft bill, which essentially allows communities to manage resources in their forests instead of the traditional way where only government officials have the mandate to do so. This draft bill also allows the creation of community forests within areas zoned as conservation forests.[117]

After three public hearings, on 16 September 1997 the committee of the public hearings presented its conclusions to the cabinet, which approved the bill. However, the bill has yet to be voted on by members of parliament, which is the final process. Besides this delay, the bill was subjected to many changes after the public hearings without any of the NGOs involved being consulted. One major change was related to the difficulty in creating community forests within conservation areas. The communities have to prove that they can conserve the areas for more than five years after the law allowing them to set up community forests takes effect. Community forests will also be subjected to inspections by four different government organizations.

Community forestry continues on its tortuous course, and while it is laudable in its aims, the chances that it will be able to reverse the country's slide into terminal deforestation, with the loss of biodiversity and other ecological disequilibria that this will bring, are not great.

Notes

1. Royal Forestry Department, *Thai Forestry Sector Master Plan: Discussion Draft* (Bangkok: Thailand, 1993), p. 15.

2. Ibid., p. 13.

3. Ibid.

4. Ibid.

5. Sacha Sethpura, Theodore Panayotou, and Vute Wangwacharakul, *Water Shortages: Managing Demand to Expand Supply* (Bangkok: TDRI, 1990), p. 15.

6. Midas Agronomics, *Study of Conservation Forest Area Demarcation, Protection, and Occupancy in Thailand. Vol. III: Occupancy Study*, p. 59. Hereafter referred to as *Occupancy*.

7. Shalardchai Ramitanondh, 'Forests and deforestation in Thailand: a pandisciplinary approach', in *Culture and Environment in Thailand: A Symposium of the Siam Society* (Bangkok: Siam Society, 1989), p. 32.

8. *Occupancy*, p. 120.

9. Ibid., p. 119.

10. Amara Pongsapich et al., *Socio-Cultural Change and Political Development in Central Thailand, 1950–1990* (Bangkok: TDRI, 1993), p. 15.

11. CUSRI, *Master Plan Study for the Agricultural Land Reform: Main Report*, vol. 2 (Bangkok: CUSRI, 1989), pp. 5–6.

12. *Occupancy*, p. 122.

13. Ibid.

14. Ibid., p. 134.

15. Ibid., pp. 130–1.

16. Larry Lohmann, 'Thailand: land, power, and colonization', in Marcus Colchester and Larry Lohmann, eds, *The Struggle for Land and the Fate of the Forests* (London: Zed, 1993), p. 206.

17. *Occupancy*, p. 123.

18. Ibid.

19. Lohmann, p. 209.

20. Mountain People's Culture and Development Educational Programs Founda-

tion (MPCDE), *Impact of Regional Development on Tribal Minorities in Southeast Asia* (Chiang Mai: MPCDE, 1991), p. 4.

21. Chantaboon Sutthi, 'Highland agriculture: from better to worse', in John McKinnon and Bernard Vienne (eds), *Hill Tribes Today* (Bangkok: White Lotus, 1989), p. 109.

22. MPCDE, p. 4.

23. Peter Hinton, 'Declining production among sedentary swidden cultivators: the case of the Pwo Karen', in Peter Kunstadter et al., *Farmers in the Forest: Economic Development and Marginal Agriculture in Northern Thailand* (Honolulu: University of Hawaii, 1978), p. 193.

24. Ibid.

25. World Bank, 'Thailand: forest area conservation and development project: preparation aide-mémoire', Washington. DC, 23 February 1994, Attachment 3, p. 3 of 5.

26. Ibid.

27. Discussion excerpts in Siam Society, *Culture and Environment in Thailand* (Bangkok: Siam Society, 1989), p. 555.

28. Uraivan Tan-Kim-Yong, 'Participatory land-use planning for natural resource management in northern Thailand', Rural Development Forestry Network Paper 14 b, Overseas Development Institute, London, Winter 1992.

29. Introduction by Kaulaya and Veerasak Todrabum to English translation of Paw Lay Pah, 'The Pwakanyaw: a Karen man's story', unpublished, undated.

30. Prasert Trakansuphakorn, interview, Chiang Mai, 9 September 1993.

31. Ibid.

32. Uraivan, p. 7.

33. Uraivan Tan-Kim-Yong, 'The Karen culture: a coexistence of two forest conservation systems', Social Forestry Research Series, Resource Management and Development Programme, Faculty of Social Sciences, Chiang Mai Univesity, p. 11.

34. Uraivan Tan-Kim-Yong, interview, Chiang Mai, 9 September 1993.

35. Anan Ganjanapan, interview, Chiang Mai, 10 September 1993; and Uraivan, interview, Chiang Mai, 9 September 1993.

36. Uraivan, interview, Chiang Mai, 9 September 1993.

37. Anan Ganjanapan, interview, 9 September 1993.

38. Leo Alting von Geusau, interview, Chiang Mai, 6 September 1993

39. Prasert, interview, Chiang Mai, 9 September 1993.

40. Uraivan, interview, Chiang Mai, 9 September 1993.

41. Prasert, interview, Chiang Mai, 9 September 1993.

42. Leo Alting Von Geusau, interview, Chiang Mai, 6 September 1993.

43. *Occupancy*, p. 76; 'Northeast forest, soil resource crisis examined', *Ban Muang*, 13 September 1992, p. 19; reproduced in *FBIS Environment*, 17 December 1992, p. 18.

44. Kampoon Boontawee, *Child of the Northeast* (Bangkok: Editions Duangkamol, 1994).

45. 'Northeast forest, soil resource crisis examined'.

46. Somkiat Pongpaiboon, 'Powerful education through people organization: a case of movement against salt farming in northeast Thailand', paper presented to ICEA Sixth World Conference on Community Education: Developing the Global Village, Port of Spain, Trinidad and Tobago, 29 July–2 August 1991.

47. 'Impact of salt mining operations felt in northeast', *Bangkok Post*, 10 March 1991, p. 8; reproduced in *FBIS*, 11 June 1991.

48. 'Northeast forest, soil resource crisis examined'.

49. *Occupancy*, p. 82.
50. Ibid.
51. *Occupancy*, p. 91.
52. Ibid.
53. Chaianan Samudavanija and Kusuma Sanitwong Na Ayuddaya, *Environment and Security* (Bangkok: Political Science Faculty, Chulalongkorn University, 1992). In Thai.
54. *Occupancy*, p. 91.
55. Ibid.
56. Lohmann, p. 215.
57. *Forestland for the People: A Forest Village Project in Northeast Thailand* (Bangkok: FAO, undated), p. 18.
58. Ibid. p. 19.
59. *Occupancy*, p. 85.
60. James Haffner, 'Forces and policy issues affecting forest use in northeast Thailand 1900–1985', in Mark Poffenberger, ed., *Keepers of the Forest: Land Management Alternatives in Southeast Asia* (West Hartford: Kumarian Press, 1990), p. 205.
61. John Hamilton and Pratap Chatterjee, *Food First Action Alert*, 1992, p. 3.
62. Ibid.
63. *Occupancy*, p. 163.
64. Ibid.
65. Ibid., p. 167.
66. Ibid., p. 165.
67. Ibid., p. 166.
68. Ibid., p. 157.
69. Ibid.
70. Midas Agronomics, *Conservation Forest Area Protection, Management, and Development Project: Final Report*, vol. 2 (Bangkok: Midas Agronomics, October 1993), p. 41; hereafter referred to as *Conservation Forest Area*.
71. Thanwa Jitsanguan, 'Natural resources and management policies of the coastal zones of Thailand', paper presented to the Ninth Biennial Conference of the Agricultural Economics Society of Southeast Asia, Asia Hotel, Bangkok, 22–24 June 1993, p. 7.
72. Phisit Chansanoh, 'Villagers should manage coastal resources', *Thai Development Newsletter*, no. 24 (1994), pp. 26–7.
73. Thanwa, p. 10.
74. *Occupancy*, p. 171.
75. Phisit, p. 27
76. Ibid., p. 26.
77. Thanwa, p. 9.
78. *Occupancy*, p. 169.
79. Ibid., p. 171.
80. Thanwa, p. 12.
81. Ibid., p. 13.
82. Claudia Sadoff, *The Effects of Thailand's Logging Ban: A Natural Resource Accounting Approach* (Bangkok: TDRI, 1992), p. 9.
83. Quoted in Nattaree Prachak, 'Natural resource management and the poor in Thailand', *Thai Development Newsletter*, no. 24 (1994), p. 9.
84. 'Out on a limb', *Manager*, January 1992, p. 42
85. Quoted in Pannachai Kongsanit, 'Hardship in the heart of the forest', Outlook Section, *Bangkok Post*, 27 July 1994, p. 32.

86. *Forestland for the People*, p. 74.

87. *Occupancy*, p. 105.

88. Ibid., p. 111.

89. Larry Lohmann, 'Peasants, plantations, and pulp: the politics of eucalyptus in Thailand', *Bulletin of Concerned Asian Scholars*, vol. 23, no. 4 (October–December 1991), p. 8.

90. Ibid.

91. Orawan Koohacharoen, 'Commercial reforestation policy', in Project for Ecological Recovery, *The Future of the People and Forests in Thailand after the Logging Ban* (Bangkok: Project for Ecological Recovery, 1992), p. 74.

92. Lohmann, 'Peasants, plantations and pulp', p. 9.

93. See Chai-anan and Sanitwong.

94. Interview with Phra Prajak Khuttajito, Dongyai, 9 January 1994.

95. 'Northeast forest, soil resource crisis examined'.

96. *The Nation*, 21 June 1992.

97. Ibid.

98. *Thai Forestry Sector Master Plan* (Bangkok: Royal Forestry Department, undated), p. 31. Hereafter referred to as TFSMP.

99. Ibid., p. 26.

100. Ibid.

101. 'Thai NGO statement on the Thai forestry sector Master Plan', Bangkok, 22 October 1993.

102. TFSMP, p. 41

103. 'Thai NGO statement on the Thai Forestry Sector Master Plan'.

104. Ricardo Carrere and Larry Lohmann, 'Pulping the South – the expansion of commercial tree plantations', *Watershed*, vol. 2, no. 1 (July–October 1996), pp. 17–18.

105. Midas Agronomics, *Conservation Forest Area Protection*.

106. Project for Ecological Recovery, 'Conservation Forest Area Protection, Management and Development Project, Thailand,' Bangkok, 9 December 1993.

107. *Conservation Forest Area*, pp. 47–8.

108. Ibid., p. 103.

109. Project for Ecological Recovery.

110. World Bank, Thailand: 'Forest area conservation and development project: preparation aide-mémoire', Attachment 3, p. 5 of 5.

111. Ibid., 2, p. 6 of 7.

112. *Occupancy*, p. 113; also interview, Larry Lohmann, London, 2 December 1993.

113. World Bank, 'Investment project initial project documentation', Washington, DC, undated, p. 6.

114. Ibid.

115. Project for Ecological Recovery.

116. Ibid.

117. Chakri Ridmontri, 'Information from Forestry Department now backs community bill: pressure from forum seen as key factor', *Bangkok Post*, 14 May 1997; Chakri Ridmontri, 'Groups slug it out over forest bills: first public hearing held at Govt. House', *Bangkok Post*, 16 May 1997; Pennapa Hongthong, 'Groups still split over forestry bill', *The Nation*, 23 May 1997; Pennapa Hongthong, 'Community forest bill wins cabinet approval', *The Nation*, 17 September 1997; Chakri Ridmontri, 'Community forest bill goes to Govt.', *Bangkok Post*, 17 September 1997.

CHAPTER 10

Damming the Countryside

Deforestation is one of the two biggest ecological threats to the Thai countryside. The second – a development that has itself contributed to accelerated deforestation – has been the construction of massive dams to harness the energy and water of the rest of the country to the needs of the minority of the population that lives in Bangkok.

The building of dams, whether for irrigation or for hydroelectricity generation, has increasingly been recognized as one of the prime ecological threats to rural Thailand. Since 1960, when dam-building in the country began in earnest, it is estimated that over 2,000 square kilometres of forest have disappeared under the reservoirs of hydroelectric dams.[1] In human terms, according to Malee Traisawasdichai, the costs have been great, with at least 24,002 families uprooted according to records of the construction of 13 dams. This includes 5,500 families from the construction of the Lam Prao dam, 4,000 from the construction of the Ubol Ratana dam, 3,300 from Sirikit dam, 2,363 from Bhumibol dam, and 1,800 from Khao Laem dam.[2]

EGAT begets resistance

The impetus for dam-building has come principally from the Electricity Generating Authority of Thailand (EGAT) and its inspiration was provided by the World Bank-inspired National Economic Development Plan of 1961, which sought to provide the infrastructure for urban-based rapid industrialization. EGAT took its task seriously, and by 1970 three large dams had been constructed. By 1980 there were ten large dams, and by 1991 there were 26 dams, with an installed capacity of 2,427 MW.[3] In the process, EGAT had become one of the leading dam-building agencies in the world, as well as an 'object of national pride and a model of modern technological development'.[4] But EGAT's forced march of dam construction would not have been possible without foreign loans, a significant portion of which came from aid agencies like the World Bank and the Asian Development Bank.

But even as EGAT became a model of efficient technocratic development, it also acquired a record of high-handed treatment of the concerns of communities that would be affected and an almost total lack of concern about the environment. The technocratic agenda of EGAT first came into sharp conflict with the emerging social and environmental agenda over the proposed Nam Choan dam, which would have been built on the upper part of the Kwae Yai river near the border with Burma. One of its impacts would have been to flood 223 square kilometres, a great part of which would have been located in the Thung Yai Naresuan wildlife sanctuary.[5]

In trying to push through the Nam Choan dam, EGAT tried to minimize publicity, conduct a pro forma environmental impact assessment, and avoid public debate. But when the project did become public, it generated such resistance from the community that EGAT was forced to shelve the project in 1982. An attempt to resurrect it in 1986, with the hope that there would be little opposition, triggered instead a coalition of environmentalists, NGOs, villagers, scientists, and students who waged a sophisticated local and international campaign that forced the project to be shelved a second time.[6] The struggle revealed the shoddy assumptions behind the big dam approach to energy provision, as well as the pathetic lack of serious environmental analysis behind the dam projects. It also demonstrated that, as in the case of Nam Choan, popular opposition, when well-informed and well-organized, could be more than a match for the bureaucrats.

The plan to build the Kaeng Sua Ten dam across the Yom river inside the Mae Yom national park in Phrae province had orginally been justified on the need for irrigation and diversion of water to the Chao Phraya river. Villagers, however, were suspicious and were very much aware of the record of unfulfilled promises of compensation, availability of water and electricity for them, and relocation to new fertile lands that had been the lot of communities displaced by earlier projects such as the Bhumibol, Sirikit, Sirindhorn, and Pak Mun dams. Most important for them was the fact that the forest, on which they depended for their livelihood, would be eliminated.

The ensuing struggle between villagers and the bureaucracy revealed that the dam's social impact had not been investigated, and that studies of the projects environmental impact had been very inadequate. For instance, environmentalists point out that the biodiversity of the Mae Yom national park would be most likely to be negatively affected. The park is home to the last golden teak forest in Thailand, the special mineral composition in the soil creating the golden hue on the leaves of the trees. The gene pool of this species would disappear for good if the forest were flooded. Many bird species would become rarer, with the green peafowl being especially threatened because it has been observed in only one other site. Many fish species in the Yom would disappear.[7]

Representatives of the villagers, backed by environmentalists, demanded a cancellation of all plans to construct the dam while proposing an alternative system of weirs controlled and managed by local communities. Protests in 1989 and 1991 had already caused the project to be shelved twice. As a result of ongoing negotiations between then Prime Minister Chaovalit Yongchaiyudh's cabinet and opponents of the dam, the cabinet decided to restrict itself to considering a progress report on the dam. An ad hoc committee was also appointed to settle this dispute and review the initial EIA.[8] The Royal Irrigation Department is conducting three EIAs on geology, ecology, and resettlement, to be completed in 1997 for appraisal by the National Environment Board, prior to parliament's vote on the issue. To ensure a favourable outcome, for over a month in April–May 1997, representatives of more than 2,700 families of the proposed Kaeng Sua Ten dam area united their issue with those of the 20,000 protesters assembled by the Forum of the Poor who camped outside Government House in Bangkok.[9]

The stakes are high in the construction of the Kaeng Sua Ten dam. Proponents of the dam have used advertisements, organized rallies, and distorted environmental studies to build the dam. If successful, the dam would flood the last reserves of the golden teak forest of Thailand, which, if logged, is worth 1,691 million baht or US$67 million[10] This would cause the loss of Thailand's largest natural teak gene pool. Furthermore, developers of tourist resorts, golf courses, and the planned Phrae industrial estate in the surrounding area are powerful elements that want the dam completed because it would mean access to cheap water.

The problem with dams ...

By the early 1990s, the costs of dam-building in terms of the flooding of now scarce primary forests and forced resettlement had become more widely perceived. By that time, too, the alleged benefits had become more questionable. For instance, while hydroelectric power generated from three dams accounted for about half the electric power in the country in 1970, the figure came down to 8 per cent of the national output in 1980, despite the fact that the number of dams had increased to ten.[11] In 1990, power from 26 dams accounted for only 10 per cent of national energy input, with the figure expected to go down to 5 per cent by the year 2006.[12]

The argument that big dams were a very good source and efficient generator of renewable energy was called into question by the record of Thai dams. Partly because of the destruction of watersheds by uncontrolled deforestation, the yearly flow into the Bhumibol and Sirikit dams was reduced from eleven billion cubic metres in 1983 to just seven billion in 1993. Since the two dams have a combined storage capacity of close to 24 billion cubic metres, there was a tremendous overcapacity problem.[13] Data also revealed that Thailand's big dams did not store water efficiently. It was estimated, for instance, that during the 1993 dry season, 500 million cubic metres drawn largely from the Nan and Ping rivers disappeared from the the Bhumibol and Sirikit reservoirs because of evaporation. And at the Nam Pong dam's reservoir in the northeast, 830 million cubic metres of water were lost to evaporation every year.[14] This extreme evaporation may cause salinity, which could contribute to the destruction of crops and aquatic organisms and corrosion of pipes and machinery.

The most serious problem faced is sedimentation, which reduces both the efficiency and lifespan of dams. Patrick McCully, author of the book *Silenced Rivers*, says that: 'Despite more than six decades of research, sedimentation is still probably the most serious technical problem faced by the dam industry.'[15] This leads to a reduced storage capacity, the deepening of riverbeds downstream as sediments remain stuck above in the dams, and accelerated coastal erosion. Already these effects are being seen in Thailand. For instance, the 30-year-old Bhumibol dam is now loaded with 620 million tons of sediment. One dam analyst, David Hubbel, claims that feasibility studies carried out by EGAT for the controversial Pak Mun dam in the northeast underestimated the silt load of the Mun river by at least 10,000 times, rendering the official estimates of a 30-year lifespan for the dam questionable.[16]

Dams are also frequently but falsely touted as a flood-control mechanism. McCully exposes this myth:

> Structural control such as dams and embankments, while they eliminate 'normal' annual floods, can also worsen the severity of extreme floods. Containing the river's sediment load within its banks raises the bed of the river, which means that the embankments must in turn be raised further to compensate. Not only is this constant rebuilding of levees extremely costly, but eventually the river level will rise above the height of the surrounding plain, providing the potential for disastrous flash-floods should the huge embankments break.[17]

A good example is the northeastern province of Nakhon Ratchasima, where frequent flooding is caused by the overflowing of dams when the rainfall is heavy. Massive evacuations of families have taken place when dams have overflowed due to their incapacity to drain excess water. The homes and farmlands of residents were flooded when Lam Takhong dam overflowed in October 1996 because it was designed to hold only 323.29 million cubic metres, but water had reached 344 million cubic metres. Water could be drained at 100 cubic metres per second, but this was not adequate during heavy rainfalls.[18] Floods have also occurred at the Lam Phra Ploeng dam, and in four districts of Petchaburi when the Kaeng Krachan and Phet dams overflowed following heavy rain.[19] Another key problem was that the bulk of the water generated by hydroelectric dams did not go to rural areas or to the uprooted populations. This was most evident in 1993, when the water available for dams in the central plain dropped from eleven billion cubic metres to seven billion. Demand from Bangkok's residents and industries was granted priority over the needs of agriculture in the ensuing crisis, and farmers were told by the RID to desist from planting a second or third rice crop and to raise vegetables or other less water-intensive crops instead.[20] All in all, 72 per cent of all power and electricity produced in Thailand goes to urban-industrial uses, although close to 68 per cent of the population is rural.[21]

Because of the expropriation of damwater for urban and industrial purposes, people living along rivers usually suffer from reduced water availability. As the water table gets lower through the desiccation of floodplains, and rivers downstream experience a drop in water levels, previously easy access to water is drastically reduced.[22] The experience of villagers living in the Mae Klong river basin illustrates this. The first phase of water diversion from the Vajiralongkorn dam on the Mae Klong river to Bangkok began in late 1995. Protests began soon afterwards, with the claim that this diversion by the Bangkok Metropolitan Water Authority (MWA) to meet the needs of Bangkok would destroy farmlands. This fear was confirmed in a study by Professor Decharat Sukkamnert of Kasertsart University, which showed that water shortages would increase from January to April/May each year. At present, water shortage is experienced in the dry season from March to about September/October annually. The diversion is almost certain to guarantee the destruction of farmlands along the Mae Klong as water disappears along the basin.[23]

The long-term social impacts on riverine villagers also contribute to the unpopularity of dams. Compensation is based only on direct impacts, meaning that only villagers whose houses and farmlands that are flooded will be compensated. The effects on the quality of life of resettled villagers, such as having to travel further to reach their farmlands, other social and opportunity costs, and the livelihoods and lifestyles of those indirectly affected by the construction of dams, are factors not considered by state authorities.

Villagers from the area affected by the Sirindhorn dam on the Lam Doi Noi river, a tributary of the Mun river, were resettled 25 years ago. However, at present not only are they hungrier due to the soil infertility and scarcity of water in their new farmlands, but the compensation of 300 baht per rai of farmland promised has not been fully paid. Many of the villagers, both old and young, have been forced to look for work in Bangkok, breaking up families and communities. Despite being beaten, imprisoned, and shot at by state officials in the past, the villagers are still determined to obtain what was promised them. In 1994, together with villagers affected by the construction of the Pak Mun, the resettled Sirindhorn villagers began their protest. Finally, negotiations with the government through the Assembly of the Poor (a coalition of poor farmers, villagers, workers, concerned individuals and NGOs) in April 1997, resulted in an agreement of 1.2 billion baht to be paid to affected families.[24]

Big dams are ecologically destructive projects causing the decline of animal and plant biodiversity wherever they are built. The clearance of large tracts of forests, often in watershed areas, for the construction of dams opens up previously inaccessible areas, resulting in uncontrolled deforestation activity such as logging. Pisit na Patalung, the secretary-general of Wildlife Fund Thailand, does not 'think the giant catfish will survive such a gigantic development plan [referring to the Mekong River Commission's plan to build a string of dams in Laos, Thailand, and Cambodia]'.[25] The migratory and little-studied giant Mekong catfish is endemic to the Mekong, with a lifecycle, breeding and feeding grounds spanning the four countries of Thailand, Laos, Cambodia, and China. The dams will hinder the movement of the catfish – more than two metres long and weighing between 200 and 300 kilograms – which have already declined in commercial catches from 69 in 1990 to just 18 in 1995.[26]

The loss of abundance in fish varieties is an acknowledged fact. A 1995 Kasertsart University study for the World Bank reports that 52 species of fish disappeared when the Rajaprabha dam in Surat Thani province was built.[27]

The Pak Mun face-off

All the problems associated with EGAT's technocratic approach surfaced in the biggest dam controversy Thailand has experienced: the struggle over the Pak Mun dam. The dam, built across the Mun river in the province of Ubon Rachatani, was designed to produce 136 megawatts, allegedly for agricultural and industrial uses in the northeast. At no point in the period leading up to the construction of the dam was there any consultation done with the villagers whose livelihoods would be affected. As one analyst pointed out:

> Since the late 1960s, at least 8 separate studies of Pak Moon were financed by the Interim Mekong Committee, a United Nations agency promoting the construction of large-scale hydroelectric dams throughout the lower Mekong basin. EGAT's proposal to the cabinet was based on its own feasibility studies completed in 1982 and 1984. None of these studies consulted the village people whose homes and fields would be flooded, whose communities would be divided by resettlement, and whose fishing-based means of livelihood would be destroyed.[28]

Instead of consulting the community and conducting thorough studies of environmental and resettlement impacts before construction, EGAT commenced operations after it had secured the approval of the region's political elite, including the twelve members of parliament from Ubon Rachatani. Predictably, the affected communities and the environmental community reacted to this initiative from above, and in the ensuing controversy the following points emerged:

1. EGAT had not conducted adequate studies on the impact of the dam on the biological life in the Pak Mun river. This was a major flaw since the river is, in the words of one ecologist, 'the largest and most biologically diverse river in Northeastern Thailand and the largest tributary of the Mekong river'.[29] The Mun intersects with the Mekong just six kilometres from the dam site, and the Mekong basin as a whole is the habitat for over 1,000 species of fish.[30] Fish migrate upstream from the Mekong to spawn in the Mun river, bringing up the impact of the dam on these migrations. These seasonal migrations were not studied.

While EGAT said that it would build a 'fish ladder' to facilitate migration, it was pointed out that only certain fish, like trout and salmon, which naturally swim upriver and jump obstacles, can use such a ladder. With over one hundred species of fish in the Mun river, 'to build a ladder suitable to all is just not practical'.[31] Or as one Thai villager put it: 'They are not trained circus animals. Thai fish don't jump.'[32]

In November 1996, two years after the completion of the dam, fishermen reported a drastic decline in fish species, despite the existence of a two million baht fish ladder; and that the few species remaining were not economic, resulting in a migration to the Mekong river for fishing.[33]

Dr Tyson Roberts, who has studied Mekong fisheries for over twenty years, has observed that 'a portion of migrating fishes [passing] a ladder is not sufficient evidence that the fishes will continue to return year after year to pass the ladder, as they must if fish populations are to survive. With each passing year the number of fishes … using the fish ladder on the Pak Mun dam will decline until finally no naturally occurring migratory species are left.'[34]

2. By not carrying out an adequate study of the impact of the dam on the fish population, EGAT also had no knowledge of the impact of the dam on people's livelihoods. Significant numbers of village people along the banks of the Mun were dependent on fish, molluscs, and snails as their chief source of protein, and many derived cash income from the sale of part of their catch.[35] Moreover, the health impact was hardly considered, yet the ecological conditions that would exist in the reservoir would be similar to those that had bred the snail *Neotricula aperta*, a key carrier of the dreaded schistosomiasis disease.[36]

3. But perhaps most controversial was EGAT's shoddy performance

on the issue of resettlement. The government agency had shifting estimates on exactly how many people would be affected by resettlement. When the project began in June 1989, notes David Hubbel:

> EGAT estimated that 379 families would be affected. In mid-April of 1990, less than two months after … massive protests in Ubon Rachatanee, Prime Minister Anuwat … and Minister Chaisiri … reported to the Chatichai cabinet that only 39 families would be affected by Pak Moon. EGAT Managing Director Poapat … confirmed that only 39 families would be affected by the Pak Moon project during a meeting with students and villager representatives on 23 April. Less than one month later, the Chatichai cabinet again approved the Pak Moon project and released EGAT's new estimate of 262 families affected by Pak Moon. In March 1991, two months prior to the commencement of dam construction, the estimate of families losing their homes and/or farmland was reported as 248 families. But by June 1991, following 2 months of construction work, EGAT's estimate of affected families jumped to 835 families. At this time, EGAT officials admitted that the previously released number of 248 affected families were those whose houses would be directly affected by the waters of the reservoir. In October 1991, EGAT again revised its estimate to 970 families affected by Pak Moon … [37]

However, by July 1995, EGAT reported an additional 2,506 families to be compensated, bringing the actual total to 5,438.[38] For the first time in its history, EGAT admitted that the people who depended on the free-flowing Mun river for their livelihood both upstream and downstream were severely affected and deserved compensation. At the time of writing, the compensation process continues.

Confronted with these shifts in estimates and standards for compensation, it is not surprising that the Pak Mun residents were provoked to wage a five-year struggle for justice. It was a rough five years though, for what many NGOs had predicted would happen to the Pak Mun communities with the construction of the dam occurred. A survey carried out by the Project for Ecological Recovery discovered that dependence on the river for food among families living in the eleven villages along the Mun river within striking distance of the Pak Mun reservoir plunged precipitously. By 1993, the number of families dependent on fishing for both subsistence and income fell by close to 30 per cent compared to 1989. A key reason was the drop in fish catches: whereas in 1989 and 1990, average fish catches for food were about 1½ kilograms per day per family, the figure had gone down to one kilogram per day per family by September 1993.

January is usually a month of plentiful fish in the lower parts of the Mun river. However, in January 1995, fishermen said that the catch totalled half a kilogram on a good day, or five grams or nothing at all. As one villager aptly put it: 'Finding fish in the Mun river is difficult. Finding a fisherman fishing in the Mun river is impossible.'[39] The protest took on international dimensions, provoking even a postponement of a World Bank loan of 550 million baht and forcing a site visit by executive directors of the Bank. But the Bank eventually went on to approve the loan in December 1991, over the opposition or the objections of three countries – the USA, Germany, and Australia – and an abstention by Canada. A key factor in the US decision was apparently a USAID report that recommended that no US funding be given because of 'probably irreversible ... potential environmental and social impacts'.[40] The same report characterized EGAT's environmental impact study as 'out-of-date, flawed and inadequate'.[41] By mid-1994 EGAT, despite continuing opposition, announced that it was ready to open the Pak Mun dam. But it was a Pyrrhic victory, since the well-publicized resistance of the communities had managed to win the sympathies of broad sectors of the public. Put on the defensive, EGAT put out advertisements in many Thai newspapers defending the dam. In one of its statements the agency, unwittingly perhaps, revealed its ideology of 'development from above':

> The most difficult element of any such project is reconciling the inevitable trade-offs between the interests of those affected by a project and those benefiting from it ... Such trade-offs are made in developing and developed countries every day and it is the function of governments to make them in what they perceive to be the best interests of the nation and its people.[42]

By mid-1996, the EGAT had ceased all advertisements and other tools of the campaign to sell Pak Mun as 'beneficial'. This silence came about because the intensifying social and economic problems caused by Pak Mun were too glaring to claim otherwise. The livelihoods of an increasing number of families were threatened as fish disappeared, causing rapid migration to Bangkok to look for jobs. Pak Mun had made the World Bank's and EGAT's plans to build more dams in the Mekong basin very unpopular, not just with the affected people but also with the general public in Thailand.[43]

Regionalization of Thailand's environmental crisis

Thailand's fast-track capitalism has, not surprisingly, outrun the capacity of its forests and rivers to provide it with the energy and other resources necessary to keep it going. It was therefore not surprising that Thai bureaucrats and businessmen turned to exploiting the natural resources of their neighbours. This was most evident in the case of forestry, when the logging ban adopted in 1989 pushed large Thai companies to Burma and Cambodia. In Burma, a visit in December 1989 of top Thai generals resulted in the granting initially of some 40 concessions to Thai companies, many of them with direct connections to the Thai military, to log along the length of the Thailand–Burma border. Similarly, following the signing of the 1991 Peace Accords, Thai loggers, again many of them linked to the Thai military, were granted large concessions along the Cambodian border by the Khmer Rouge to make up for their loss of assistance from China. With significant imports of timber coming from Vietnam and Laos into Thailand as well, both legally and illegally, what has resulted, according to Philip Hirsch, is that mainland Southeast Asia has developed a 'relatively integrated regional timber economy, with Thailand as the major importer and neighboring countries as suppliers'.[44]

The result has been a displacement of Thailand's forestry crisis into its adjoining countries, although, of course, Thai timber demand is not the only cause of the crisis of the forests in these countries. In Myanmar or Burma, according to the International Burma Campaign:

> [T]he last of the world's great teak forests is being devastated at a horrifying rate, with replanting almost nil. Burma now has the third highest deforestation rate on the planet, with 1.2 million of its tree cover disappearing each year. If the rate is not curtailed, Burma will be virtually denuded in fifteen years, with rainforests along the Thai–Burma border gone in five years. Thailand's soldier businessmen may not be entirely joking when they reportedly propose toasts to the 'last tree in Burma.'[45]

In Cambodia, the country's forest cover has been reduced from 13 million hectares to seven million, according to official estimates. More than 575,000 cubic metres of timber from Cambodia entered Thailand in 1992, and some 100,000 Thais were estimated to be felling timber in Cambodia, most of them working for Thai concessions along a 650-kilometre stretch of the Thailand–Cambodia border.[46] In neighbouring Laos, where Thai private interests are also active, forest cover is vanishing at the rate of 500,000 acres a day, leading to projections that only 26 per cent of the country's forests will be left by the year 2000.[47]

But it is not only in forestry that Thai companies and the Thai state have expanded their reach into neighbouring countries. Thai investors are actively involved in the mining or purchase of gemstones in Burma, Laos, Cambodia, and Vietnam, and the supply of gems from these areas has helped make Thailand the world's second largest exporter of processed gems.[48] And while Thailand is the biggest exporter of fish in the Southeast Asian region, very little of what is exported is actually caught in Thai waters, which are severely depleted due to overfishing; most exported fish are caught in regional waters. Thailand already has an agreement with Burma for Thai boats to fish in Burmese waters, and Thai fishermen continue to be granted access to Vietnamese waters, including a concession in the rich fishing grounds around Phu Quoc island.[49] The problem of illegal fishing is so severe that it strained Malaysia and Thailand's relationship when a Malaysian patrol boat shot at a Thai fishing trawler, and killed two fishermen.[50] The National Fisheries Association of Thailand estimates that there are 2,810 boats fishing illegally in Southeast Asia, Bangladesh, India, and Saudi Arabia.[51] And the devastation of Thailand's mangroves caused by prawn farming is being extended to Vietnam by Thai companies.[52]

It is, however, in the area of energy that in the long term Thailand's resource requirements may have their most severe impact. With industrial and urban growth continuing at current projections but with local water supplies becoming more and more unpredictable, partly due to the depletion of watersheds through deforestation, EGAT has sought to harness the water resources of neighbouring countries for its own use.

Along the border with Burma alone, for instance, there are some nine Thai or joint Thai–Burmese dam projects being studied.[53] The most important of these projects are the Upper Salween River Project, which would build a dam that could generate 4,540 MW of electricity and a reservoir storing 21 billion cubic metres of water, and the Lower Salween River Project, which would divert a maximum 10 billion cubic metres from the Salween river to the Mae Taeng river in Chiang Mai province.[54]

Laos has been a source of electricity for Thailand since 1970, with the latter accounting for two-thirds of the output of the 150-MW Nam Ngum dam, about 80 per cent of the output of the newly completed 45-MW Xeser dam, and most of the output of the recently finished 210-MW Theun-Hinboun dam. The country has a 'non-binding' agreement signed in 1996 to provide 3,000 megawatts to Thailand by the year 2006.[55] Laos' largest development project, the Nam Theun 2 dam, is meant to service Thailand's energy needs. More dams serving Thailand will be built in Laos if that country follows the recommendation of the Asian Development Bank to build, with Thai support, three new hydroelectric dams on the Nam Song, Nam Louk and Nam Man rivers just south of Vientiane.[56]

Laos is particularly attractive to Thailand, says David Murray, because it 'has immense water reserves but because of its mountainous terrain, has only 800,000 hectares of arable land. With its small population and low level of development, it can currently use only a fraction of the capacity of its hydroelectric potential, which is about one half of the lower Mekong's total potential output.'[57] The problem for Thai technocrats is that owing to concerns about environmental degradation, Laos is very cautious about plans to harness its hydroelectric resources.

Cambodia has also been eyed by EGAT, with a proposal to develop jointly a project that would build a dam in the Cambodian province of Battambang and a power plant in the Thai province of Trat. The idea would be to generate and supply electricity not only for western Cambodia but also for the eastern part of Thailand.[58]

But perhaps the most ambitious – and potentially most ecologically disruptive – is the plan to dam the Mekong put forward by the inter-governmental Interim Committee. Some eight major dams – making up the so-called 'Mekong Cascade' – would be built on the Mekong itself. One project would be the Pa Mon dam project, which in its initial draft plan foresaw the relocation of 250,000 villagers, a figure that was reduced in a later version to 42,000 people, three-quarters of whom would be from Thailand.[59] Notes Murray:

> [L]ocal resistance to forced resettlement, and the large numbers of people people involved, would suggest that this particular project could only be undertaken against a background of considerable conflict. Yet this is an option seen by some observers as an essential act of good faith for Thailand to demonstrate to its neighbors that it is prepared to make the sacrifices as they will be asked to to when dams are built in their territories.[60]

Perhaps equally controversial are plans to divert water from the Mekong to new or existing hydroelectric complexes in Thailand. The biggest of these projects would divert water from the Kok and Ing rivers, which are tributaries of the Mekong, into the Yom and Nan rivers, which are tributaries of the Chao Phraya river. This additional water would be used by a new hydro-power complex at Kaeng Sua Ten and supplement the water supply of the Sirikhit reservoir, which, as noted earlier, is operating far below capacity because of the water shortage. Another plan is to divert water from the Mekong itself to the Khong, Chi, and Mun rivers in Thailand to boost electricity generation at the Ubolrat and Lam Pao reservoirs and provide a new water supply for irrigation. 'Together,' notes Philip Hirsch, 'these schemes would result in a net loss of water to the Mekong.'[61]

The financial crisis and the environment

By the late 1990s, Thailand was in a fairly serious state of environmental degradation, a plunge whose speed was positively correlated to the relatively high GDP growth rates it was registering. Thus, when the financial crisis of 1997 developed into the great economic collapse of 1998, it was not certain in what way the developments would influence ecological trends in the country.

On the one hand, in an effort to keep foreign investors, the government might decide to dilute even further the already very weak enforcement of environmental regulations in industry. On the other hand, the slowdown of the Thai economy is likely to slow down the exploitation of natural resources not only in Thailand but in neighbouring countries as well. Construction has already been halted at two sites, the Xepian-Xenamnoy and Nam Ngum 2 dams while the concession of power purchase agreements at Nam Theun 2 are reported to have lapsed.[62] The terms of electricity purchase from the Houay Ho dam are no longer profitable, leading the contractor, Daewoo, to seek a renegotiation of the terms with

EGAT.[63] The concession and purchase agreements at Nam Theun 2 are also reported to have lapsed.[64] EGAT has reported that it would have to renegotiate the $0.0455 cent per kilowatt-hour previously agreed upon.[65] Norconsult, hydropower consultants for the ADB, has said that the buying power of hydroelectric power needs to be raised to six to eight cents per kilowatt-hour to generate a 20 per cent rate of return on investment.[66] As one report notes, many experts believe that by 2006 Laos will be supplying Thailand not with 3,000 MW of hydropower but with only about 700 MW.[67]

In any event, the crisis provides a golden opportunity for Thais to pause and ponder their future road to development, and with the collapse of the old model of strip-mine, fast-track capitalism, strategies with ecological sustainability as a central principle are likely to have a more receptive audience.

Notes

1. David Hubbel, 'Antithetical perceptions of development and environment: village people and the state in rural Thailand', Master's thesis, York University, Toronto, September 1992, p. 12.

2. Malee Traisawasdichai, 'Large dams Versus "Common Good" of People', *The Nation*, 25 January 1994.

3. David Murray, 'Dam(ned) conflicts in Thailand,' Occasional Paper no. 21, Indian Ocean Center for Peace Studies (Perth, 1992), pp. 4–5; Traisawasdichai.

4. Murray, p. 5.

5. Montree Chantawong, 'Infrastructure development policy: legalized deforestation', in *The Future of People and Forests in Thailand after the Logging Ban* (Bangkok: Project for Ecological Recovery, 1992) , p. 144.

6. Murray, pp. 6–7.

7. See, among others, Project for Ecological Recovery, 'Kaeng Sua Teng dam project: an update', Bangkok, 9 April 1991; Karuna Buakumsri, 'Another dam issue crops up', *Sunday Post*, 1 October 1995; Wasant Techawongtham and Kanittha Inchukul, 'Dam decision put on back-burner to avert immediate confrontation', *Bangkok Post*, 13 October 1995; 'Villages to sue Banharn government: Kaeng Sua Ten Dam approval aftermath', *Bangkok Post*, 1 December 1996; and Waraphorn Mungkornchai, 'The dam battle is on again', *Bangkok Post*, 15 December 1996.

8. Suebpong Unarat and Supara Janchitpah, 'Protestors hail go-slow on dam plans', *Bangkok Post*, 30 July 1997, p. 1.

9. Noel Rajesh, 'Local participation and the Kaeng Sua Ten dam controversy', *Watershed*, vol. 2, no. 3 (March–June 1997), p. 17.

10. Noel Rajesh, 'Local participation and the Kaeng Sua Ten dam controversy', *Watershed*, vol. 2, no. 3 (March–June 1997), p. 17.

11. Murray, p. 4.

12. Ibid.

13. Scott Christensen and Areeya Boon-Long, 'Better water management needed', *The Nation*, 17 September 1993, p. B3.

14. Dave Hubbell, 'Environmental and social impacts of large dams: experience from around the world', *Thai Development Newsletter*, no. 25 (1994), p. 23.

15. Patrick McCully, *Silenced Rivers* (London: Zed, 1997), p. 107.

16. Hubbell, p. 21.

17. McCully, p. 147.

18. 'Dam water exceeds danger mark', *Bangkok Post*, 7 October 1996.

19. 'Overflowing dams swamp Petchaburi: some 1.35 million affected nation-wide', *Bangkok Post*, 1 October 1996.

20. Christensen and Areeya.

21. Murray, p. 29; National Economic and Social Development Board, *National Urban Development Policy Framework*, vol. 1 (Bangkok: NESDB, 1993), p. 78.

22. McCully, p. 149.

23. 'The west bank project: taking water from the provinces, giving water to Bangkok', *Watershed*, vol. 3, no. 2, November 1997–February 1998, pp. 10–17.

24. 'Government reaches deal with villagers: Bt. 1.2 Bn compensation for Sirindhorn dam hit', *The Nation*, 29 April 1997.

25. Nantiya Tangwisutijit and Kamol Sukin, 'Giant catfish becomes the bait in a new era of regional unity', *The Nation*, 12 May 1996.

26. Ibid.

27. 'The fight for Kaeng Sua Ten: either side of the river', *Bangkok Post*, 17 January 1997.

28. Hubbel, p. 56.

29. Ibid., p. 46.

30. Ibid., p. 47.

31. Murray, p. 17.

32. 'Thai fish don't jump', *Thai Development Newsletter*, no. 25 (1994), p. 32.

33. 'Fish ladder ads said to be misleading: local fishermen told to register complaint', *Bangkok Post*, 16 November 1996, p. 2.

34. 'Can fish climb ladders?', *Watershed*, vol. 1, no. 3 (March–June 1996).

35. Hubbel, p. 50.

36. Ibid., p. 17.

37. Ibid., pp. 63–4.

38. 'Chronology of disaster: the growing costs of the Pak Mun dam', *Watershed*, vol. 1, no. 3 (March–June 1996), p. 21.

39. 'Pak Mun: the lessons are clear but is anyone listening?', *Watershed*, vol. 1, no. 3 (March–June 1996), p. 20.

40. Murray, p. 18.

41. Ibid.

42. Quoted in *Thai Development Newsletter*, no. 24 (1994), p. 18.

43. 'Pak Mun: the lessons are clear, but is anyone listening?', p.16.

44. Philip Hirsch, 'Thailand and the new geopolitics of Southeast Asia: resource and environmental issues', paper presented to Fifth International Conference on Thai Studies, School of Oriental and African Studies, University of London, London, 1–10 July 1993, p. 5.

45. International Burma Campaign, *Burma Today: Land of Hope and Terror* (Washington, DC: International Burma Campaign, 1991), p. 23.

46. 'Logging operators experience problems with Cambodian deals', *Bangkok Post*, 15 November 1992; reproduced in *FBIS Environment*, 30 December 1992.

47. 'Forest conservation policy outlined', *Dao Siam*, 26 May 1991; reproduced in *FBIS Environment*, p. 23.

48. Hirsch, p. 9.

49. Ibid., p. 8.

50. 'Mahathir expresses sorrow at deaths of Thai trawlermen', *The Nation*, 10 December 1995.

51. Yindee Lertcharoenlek, 'Thais fishing illegally black mark on nation', *The Nation*, 9 September 1996, A6.

52. Ibid., p. 12.

53. 'Three Thai companies submit bids for building dams on Salween river', *Thai Development Newsletter*, no. 24 (1994), p. 7.

54. 'Dam and reservoir projects studied', *Thai Development Newsletter*, no. 25 (1994), TDSC, p. 2.

55. '"Battery of Asia" may run flat', *Financial Times*, 6 April 1998, p. 3.

56. Murray, p. 33.

57. Ibid., p. 33.

58. Ibid.

59. Ibid., p. 34.

60. Ibid.

61. Hirsch, p. 7.

62. '"Battery of Asia' may run flat'.

63. Ibid.

64. Ibid.

65. Malee Traisawasdichai, 'A recipe for disaster', *The Nation*, 26 August 1997.

66. 'The rise and fall of EGAT: from monopoly to marketplace?', *Watershed*, vol. 2 (November 1996–February 1997), p. 23.

67. '"Battery of Asia' may run flat'.

CHAPTER 11

The AIDS Crisis

Since the mid-1970s, when HIV/AIDS was first detected in the United States, the virus has spread across the globe. According to the World Health Organization, as of 1996 over 20 million people worldwide were infected with HIV (human immunodeficiency virus), with over 7 million having already progressed to full-blown AIDS (acquired immune deficiency syndrome). An estimated 4.5 million people have already died from AIDS-related diseases and it is believed that everyday over 8,000 people around the world become infected with HIV.[1]

Thailand has one of the highest rates of HIV infection in the world, with an estimated 800,000 people infected. Thailand is considered one of the two countries most devastated by the virus, the other being Uganda. The dynamics of key factors in the spread of AIDS in Thailand – poverty, labour migration, gender inequality, and the sex industry – are analysed in this chapter. As a result of the country's present development model of export-oriented industrialization (EOI), labour migration has steadily increased. Most of the sex industry-related migrants are young women, many from the hills of Thailand's northeast or from Burma or China, who end up working in Thailand's infamous sex industry, which has served to commodify women and sex and greatly exacerbate the spread of HIV/AIDS. In 1994, it was estimated that 33 per cent of all commercial sex workers (CSWs) in Thailand were HIV-positive.[2] Although illegal, the sex industry has become a major source of income for the Thai economy and an integral part of Thai society. Commercial sex work provides young women and the families who depend on them with more income than any other unskilled job in Thailand.

In 1991, the Thai government set up a well-funded and highly participatory AIDS programme. The programme, touted as a model for other countries in the region, has succeeded in reducing the rate of HIV infection by promoting condom use and raising public awareness of modes of infection. The success of the programme is due to strong coordination between the Thai government and NGOs and support from foreign governments and agencies. Thailand is now seen as having passed through the AIDS crisis, and because of its status as a newly industrializing country,

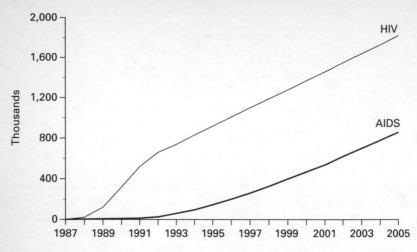

Source: NESDB Working Group, HIV Projections for Thailand, November 1994

Figure 11.1 Projection current HIV infections and cumulative
AIDS in Thailand, 1987–2005

cutbacks are expected from inter-governmental organizations such as the
EU and UNICEF. The UN and USAID, the largest funders, are phasing
out their support and bilateral government funding is on the chopping
block.[3]

But is Thailand really out of the red zone? For one thing, as a result
of the financial débâcle, the government will be hard pressed to cover the
cuts in multilateral and bilateral funds. But, more important, AIDS
researchers and activists are concerned about the scaling back of Thailand's
AIDS programme, because the key issue of women's empowerment has yet
to be effectively addressed and because Thailand's neighbours constitute
the new hotspot for the pandemic. More than 90 per cent of reported
HIV/AIDS cases in Asia are from India, Thailand, Burma, and Cambodia.[4]
With heavy cross-border labour migration, weak AIDS programmes in
neighbouring countries, and the lack of regional programmatic coordination, an escalation of AIDS in Thailand seems inevitable in the foreseeable
future. Drug treatments are far out of the financial reach of the vast
majority and a vaccine is still a distant hope. Until drug treatments are
widely available and effectively used, the only way to fight AIDS is through
prevention, by investing in women, education and health, and strengthening
cooperation.

AIDS in Asia

Often referred to as a pandemic, AIDS is more like a collection of distinct regional epidemics linking across the globe. Home to more than half the world's population, Asia is fast becoming the new epicentre for AIDS. Although it arrived relatively late in the region, it is spreading rapidly. In mid-1994 it was estimated that there were over 2.5 million HIV-positive people in Asia, nearly a 50 per cent increase from 1993.[5] Before the end of the twentieth century, the annual number of HIV infections in Asia is expected to exceed that of Africa.[6] The WHO and UNDP predict that by the year 2000 there will be 40 million people worldwide infected with HIV, and 40 to 50 per cent of these people will live in Asia.[7] Predictions by Harvard's 1992 Global AIDS Policy Coalition Report have been realized as India and Thailand are the hardest-hit by AIDS in the region. Including Burma, Cambodia, and Southern China, this subregion constitutes the epicentre of the Asian HIV/AIDS epidemic.[8]

In Asia some 50 to 70 per cent of AIDS-related deaths are due to tuberculosis. According to Dr Arata Kochi, tuberculosis programme manager for WHO, the rapid spread of AIDS in Asia threatens an even bigger epidemic of tuberculosis. An estimated 50 per cent of Thailand's population is infected with TB bacilli, and a smaller fraction usually comes down with the disease. But the numbers of those becoming infected are steadily increasing with the high incidence of HIV infection. WHO now estimates that those with TB bacilli are 30 times more likely to develop tuberculosis if infected by HIV.[9]

AIDS in Thailand

The first HIV case in Asia was reported in Thailand – in 1984. By 1989 in Thailand HIV had spread to the general population: from intravenous drug users to commercial sex workers, to sexually active heterosexual men, and soon after to non-high risk groups including married women, children, and newborns. Through heterosexual intercourse (accounting for 77 per cent of all AIDS cases[10]) two groups, sexually active heterosexual men and female CSWs, are now the primary agents in the pandemic's 'chain of transmission' in Thailand.[11]

If current trends continue, 3 to 6 million Thais will be infected with HIV by the year 2000, or about one in every 14 people. While more men than women were initially infected, now there is an equal number of men and women becoming infected. By the end of the twentieth century, women are projected to constitute the majority, not only in Thailand but worldwide.[12] As in many African countries, life expectancy rates have already begun to fall in Thailand as a result of AIDS. With an already low birth rate, Thailand stands out as the only country in the world whose population is actually expected to decline due to AIDS. The Census Bureau has reported that Thailand's population growth rate will change from 0.9 per cent in 1985 to negative 0.8 per cent by 2010. Furthermore, the Bureau has reported that Thailand's death rate is predicted to triple by the year 2010 because of AIDS, which, if trends continue, will become the leading cause of death, representing more than 30 per cent of all deaths in Thailand.[13]

Women are the most vulnerable group due to gender inequality and because women are biologically more susceptible than men to acquiring AIDS through heterosexual intercourse. Sex workers' male clientele fuel the cycle of infection in the country. More than 75 per cent of Thai males have had sex with CSWs, and 75 per cent of them patronize the cheapest brothels, where HIV is most prevalent and where many undocumented migrants work. Men then pass it to their girlfriends, wives and unborn children.[14]

Because AIDS is a social disease, economic and sociocultural practices determine the rate of spread and the socioeconomic groups AIDS will most likely effect. Poverty, labour migration, and the sex industry – each a cause or an effect of the other – have served as the key elements in the spread and intensity of AIDS in Thailand. Because labour migration, the strength of the sex industry, the increase in poverty, and a disparity in wealth are results of Thailand's development strategy, there is a need to reassess Thailand's export-oriented and rapid industrialization paradigm.

Poverty, labour migration, and AIDS

Population movement in the Mekong region has grown exponentially over the last decade. As such, the incidence of STD/HIV is growing rapidly as economic development and transportation links increase mobility within and between countries, and previously isolated rural people and ethnic minorities become more vulnerable to exploitation.[15] From rural areas and from across borders, people are working in Bangkok and other urban centres in nearly all sectors of the economy. According to conservative estimates 372,000 Thais are working abroad, while Thailand hosts 600,000 migrants.[16]

Labour migration to and within Thailand are both a response and a strategy to cope with unequal economic opportunities, and to feed industrial growth. Fleeing economic hardships and political strife, Burmese are migrating to Thailand in search of work. Chinese, Laotians, Cambodians, and other nationalities are also migrating to Thailand, but to a lesser extent. As Thailand is currently experiencing a shortage of unskilled labour in construction, fisheries, and agro-industry, the government and the private sector are looking favourably to migrants. Widening wage disparities between countries such as Thailand and Burma guarantee a steady supply of migrants prepared to take these jobs. There are an estimated 600,000 illegal Burmese migrants living in Thailand, many of them ethnic minorities with no rights.[17] This makes them the largest immigrant population living in Thailand. Many of the migrants are young women who end up working in Thailand's cheapest brothels, where HIV and STD prevalence are high. These migrants lack access to health care and education and because they are illegal, they also lack the power to negotiate for a better environment. According to the Public Health Research Centres in Thailand's northeast, 80 per cent of Burmese sex workers tested in the border areas are HIV-positive.[18] And a 1996 Thai study by the Epidemiology Division found a proportionately high rate of syphilis amongst migrant workers in Thailand.[19]

The desire for upward mobility and/or a mere strategy for economic survival are the two prime motivators in labour migration to/within Thailand. AIDS has struck with particular severity in communities struggling under the burdens of economic adjustment and crises caused by distorted internal production and widening disparities in wealth.[20] And so today, the vast majority of those who are becoming infected are people in the low socioeconomic bracket.[21]

While Thailand's AIDS programme has been successful thus far in reducing the rate of HIV infection, SLORC (Burma's military government) has done very little to control HIV. After Thailand and India, Burma has been identified as the third hardest hit by HIV/AIDS in Asia. Estimates of HIV prevalence in Burma are still crude, but the under-resourced Myanmar National AIDS Programme puts the figure at 750,000 to 1 million.[22] In fact, SLORC has deliberately repressed information about the spread of the disease. Until 1992, condoms were illegal in Burma. They are now legal, but they are expensive by Burmese standards.

Rural–urban migration is largely a result of the Thai government's export-oriented industrialization strategy. Thailand's economic boom has significantly increased the purchasing power of middle- and upper-class urban residents *vis-à-vis* the rural populace, and prospecting agents are buying up rural farmland at a fast pace. The land has been increasingly converted into export-oriented crop production and the amount of rural landlessness has increased dramatically. The result is an exodus of villagers, selling their land and migrating to urban areas in search of economic alternatives.[23]

As the market economy and its values encroach upon traditionally self-sustaining rural villages, people are becoming more dependent upon commodity markets. Commercial relationships involve the sale of agricultural produce to merchants and their brokers and also the purchase of a variety of inputs such as seed, fertilizer, pesticides, fuel, and consumer goods such as clothes, medicines, processed foods, television sets, and motorcycles. While crop prices fluctuate with the rise and fall of world demand, agricultural income becomes unstable, resulting in the need either to borrow money or to obtain it through family members migrating to urban areas to seek work. Today more than 50 per cent of CSWs come from farming families, demonstrating the severity of this phenomenon.[24]

Upon arrival in urban centres, the unskilled and poorly educated majority discover that they cannot find jobs that offer wages high enough to send money back home and keep themselves out of poverty. Because of Thailand's specialization in cheap labour, competing with other low-wage countries such as Indonesia, Burma, and Vietnam, wages in Thailand's factories fail to lift workers out of poverty. Women are the most exploited, as they are concentrated at the bottom of the skill and wage scale in Thailand's factories.

These heavy streams of people migrating or relocating from rural to urban settings are intimately linked with the diffusion of HIV. Studies indicate that Thai villages with a high degree of urban contact typically have a significantly higher rate of infection.[25] HIV is continuing to spread not only among CSWs but also among factory and construction workers, military conscripts, fishermen, and hilltribes – all highly mobile groups.[26] Along their migration paths and away from their familiar communities with their restrictive social rules, these migratory people, primarily men, become more promiscuous and often visit prostitutes. When they eventually return home, they frequently become agents of HIV transmission in their families and communities.

This is still true despite the fact that the percentage of men who frequent prostitutes has decreased significantly due to AIDS education. Some researchers have claimed that now less than 35 per cent of men visit sex workers – startling figures given that as early as the 1990s, some 90 per cent of men in certain areas frequented brothels – and that most of them use condoms. This sounds like a positive development except for the fact that two-thirds of men who visit sex workers patronize the cheapest brothels, where HIV/AIDS is most prevalent and where many undocumented migrants work.[27]

AIDS and the sex industry

There is a strong correlation between poverty and the sex industry, as CSWs are disproportionately affected by poverty and AIDS. Either by force or by choice, women and girls enter the sex industry to escape poverty or in hope of improving their economic situations.

In Thailand a web of cultural, historical, and economic factors has served to make the sex industry a booming sector of capitalist growth. For centuries, brothels and the practice of concubinage have existed in Thailand, but over the past few decades the sex industry has expanded rapidly and has become an integral part of the Thai economy and society. Today it is the primary cause of the spread of HIV.

Cultural factors Although lax government policies and regulation of the sex industry are important factors, the roots of Thai society's social acceptance of prostitution go further back into history.

The principal strain of Thai Buddhism (Theravada Buddhism) is a hybrid of the original Indian Buddhism and has been a powerful force in Thailand for over 700 years. Buddhist values and beliefs continue to influence the attitudes and values of most Thais, as over 90 per cent of Thailand's population is Buddhist.

The traditional emphasis on polygamy in Theravada Buddhist society is said to have fostered the widespread practice of commercial sex work in Thailand today. Polygamy was outlawed in 1935 but is still practised today – formally through men having more than one wife and informally through visiting CSWs.

Thailand's current economic development model has also served to institutionalize sex as a commodity and women's bodies as easily obtainable objects of consumption. The sex industry can, in fact, be viewed as a variant of polygamy, as both provide men access to the sexual services of more than one woman.[28]

The Vietnam war The enormous scale of Thailand's sex industry today is largely a result of the Vietnam war. In the 1960s US military bases began to proliferate in Thailand, and many young women were induced into the sex industry by their families and profiteers, as the high demand of US servicemen coalesced with the needs of Thailand's impoverished villages – eventually leading to the acceptance of prostitution as a source of income for young women.[29]

By the time the war ended in 1976, sex-industry establishments had expanded across the country and tourism was promoted in order to gain foreign exchange. Given that the sex ratio of tourists was 2:1, male to female, it was obvious that the main attraction was sex.[30] Thailand was advertised to male foreign tourists as a place where they could indulge in sexual services, while at the same time it remained common for Thai men to visit brothels. Thus commercial sex became a huge business in Thailand, and quickly evolved into a well-organized industry supported by powerful entities.

Dynamics of the sex industry today The majority of commercial sex workers in Thailand come from poor, rural families from the country's north and northeast, and more and more come from Burma and China. In the north, over 30 per cent of the rural population is landless, and another 20 per cent of farming families own less than one rai (two-fifths of one acre) – an insufficient amount to meet their needs. Women working as day-labourers on the larger export crop-producing farms are paid an average of US$1.40 a day. Similarly, in factories and working for golf courses – a new and booming business that primarily serves Japanese businessmen – they can earn between $.80 and $2.00 a day. Due to these substandard wages, female caddies often sell their sexual services after a round of golf and many factory workers engage in sex work after hours. CSWs can earn between $400 to $800 a month – and the more attractive ones in Bangkok can often average more than $20,000 annually.[31]

Tourism has had a particularly big influence on making the sex industry a common economic option for poor women in Thailand. 'Even though foreign men are a small portion [of the sex industry's total clientele], they generally pay more for commercial sex services.'[32] Thus sex tourists help fuel the fire by making sex work more profitable and glamorous. The Thai government has promoted tourism to become a major income-earning industry for the country. In 1987 tourism became the country's primary source of foreign exchange – surpassing rice and textiles.[33] Services within the tourism industry include restaurants, nightclubs, food and beverage stalls, hotels, and entertainment – all places where sex is sold. Thailand's Department of Communicable Disease Control and Ministry of Public Health have classified Thailand's sex service establishments into 19 categories including brothels, hotel/motels, tea rooms, nightclubs, beer bars, dancing bars, restaurants, coffee shops, cocktail lounges, pubs, massage parlours, beauty salons, barber shops, and others.[34] According to the Ministry of Public Health, these sex service establishments number nearly 6,000 – with unofficial estimates being much higher.[35]

Recruitment and human rights violations Despite Thailand's booming economy, in the 1980s and early 1990s many people in its poorest villages were becoming even poorer, as the wealth generated from Thailand's economic growth failed to provide sufficient economic opportunities for the population. At the same time, Thailand's capitalist growth has given birth to a cult of consumerism that has raised impossible expectations among the population. This fatal combination has contributed to the great expansion of the sex industry.

Girls and young women enter the sex industry largely to escape poverty, for themselves and also for their families, and to gain upward socio-economic mobility. Some migrate to Bangkok or other urban centres by themselves, but more often they are recruited. Girls as young as 11 and 12 are found working as CSWs all over Thailand.[36] Much of the recruitment into the sex industry is village-based. Men from the village – fathers, uncles, brothers – act as pimps for brothel owners. Middlemen give a flat sum, averaging around 5,000 baht ($200), to a relative of the young woman, who is often unaware of the nature or conditions of her employment. The money then becomes credit against future earnings that she must work off – with interest.[37] This practice is justified by many parents, as they feel that a job negotiated by a member of the family or community for their daughter would not be harmful.[38] However, many of these girls soon discover that the brothel owners use a combination of debt bondage, threats, force, and physical confinement to control them, forcing them to work in deplorable, abusive conditions, eliminating any possibility of negotiation or escape. The debt, often compounded with 100 per cent interest, is the cornerstone of control exercised by the brothel owners and procurers.[39]

The recruitment zone includes Thailand's borders and extends into Burma, Laos, Cambodia, China, and even post-Soviet Russia. One estimate claims that over 10,000 Russian women are working as CSWs in Thailand.[40] This phenomenon of girls and younger women entering Thailand's sex industry from the rural outskirts and abroad is stimulated by a high demand for 'newer' CSWs who are believed to be free of HIV.

Many of the minority ethnic groups living in Thailand's northeastern hills are engaged in opium poppy production, linked to the international trafficking of heroin, and many of their members are themselves often opium addicts. It is common for hilltribe parents to sell their daughters into the sex trade in order to get cash to maintain their opium habit. Some parents knowingly sell them into the sex industry, others are told the girls will be working in restaurants and are promised no harm will come to them. Many girls come illegally over the border with a relative, or, as is more common, in a group organized by recruiters. They are impoverished, poorly educated, often landless, and do not possess birth documents. They are an extremely vulnerable group, so they are easy prey for recruiters to lure or force into prostitution.[41] In the past few years increasing numbers of hilltribe girls – Tai Yai girls from the Shan state in Burma are the largest group – have been found in brothel raids and STD (sexually transmitted disease) clinics from the very north of Thailand to the far south. It is sometimes difficult to detect hilltribe girls, as racketeers make phony passports and Thai citizenship documents for their foreign recruits.[42]

The practices of forced prostitution, child prostitution, and debt bondage are flagrant violations of human rights. The lives of the girls and women who are forced into and held in prostitution have been taken away, as, according to Ron O'Grady, the effects of their nightmarish experiences are so traumatic they can never be completely rehabilitated.[43]

Regional differences in HIV prevalence   Because Thailand's regions are unique in their demographics, geography, culture, and economic situation, AIDS has taken on a different configuration in each area.

The highest prevalence of HIV is in Thailand's northern region. Here, commercial sex workers are the primary source of infection. In the cheaper brothels in and near the province of Chiang Mai, between 70 and 90 per cent of female CSWs are HIV-positive.[44] Why is this region plagued with the highest rate of HIV infection? First, the region serves as a passageway through which young women from Burma are recruited and sometimes forced into commercial sex work. There are some 20,000 Burmese women and girls, with 10,000 new recruits every year coming into Thailand.[45] The northern region also attracts many tourists and foreign investors who visit brothels. Compounded by an already high local demand for CSWs, sex tourism serves to increase the risk of infection. Because commercial sex work is a source of high income for uneducated and unskilled workers, it has become socially acceptable in rural areas for girls and young women to become CSWs, as they often sacrifice themselves to help support their family. According to Dr Teeranat Karnjana-Uksorn, professor of development economics at Chulalongkorn University in Bangkok, 'both the poor female farmer and the prostitute have no respect in this society, but at least prostitutes have money which can buy them freedom and security'.[46] Northern women represent the largest group of CSWs in the whole of Thailand, as many of them migrate to the central or southern regions of the country to work.[47] Often these young women return to the north infected with HIV.

The northeastern region is said to be the poorest region of Thailand, and also the region with the lowest incidence of HIV infection. This is something of a paradox, as poverty is a prime factor in the spread of the virus. The same December 1991 survey showed a median of 11.6 per cent of HIV-positive high risk groups in the northeast, including CSWs, intravenous drug users, and migrant workers. Other studies, however, have shown that HIV infection in the northeast is rapidly on the rise.[48]

The central region, or Bangkok Metropolitan Region (BMR), is characterized by high industrialization and urbanization with rapidly expanding service and manufacturing sectors.[49] This region has the second highest incidence of HIV infection. An average of 26 per cent of high-risk people, such as sex workers and intravenous drug users, migrants, and military conscripts, are HIV-positive.[50] Because prostitution is illegal, accurate figures of women engaged in this business are difficult to find. However, some studies have estimated that as many as 10 per cent of the employed females in Bangkok are working as CSWs.

The southern region is a major area of HIV contraction, but it is estimated that only 5 per cent of CSWs are from the south while 72 per cent come from the north and 15 per cent from the northeast. Intense manifestation does not occur in the south largely due to the average amount of time a young woman remains a CSW in the region: generally only 6–12 months, after which she either moves to another area to continue working in the sex industry or returns home to her rural community to get married and have children – passing the virus on to her family in the north or northeast. Also, when CSWs have been diagnosed as being HIV-positive or suffering from sexually transmitted diseases, brothel owners send them away and recruit new CSWs from the rural north and north-eastern provinces.[51] Ron O'Grady, international coordinator of ECPAT (End Child Prostitution in Asian Tourism) points out: '[T]reated as consumer items, [CSWs'] value decreases with usage until they are thrown away once they are of no further commercial value.'[52]

Exporting sex   Thai CSWs constitute a not insignificant portion of the foreign workforce in countries such as Germany, the United States, and Japan. As of 1988, approximately eight thousand Thai CSWs were based in Germany.[53] According to Japan's National Police Agency, between April 1995 and March 1996 nearly 60 per cent of CSWs in Japan were from Thailand. The remaining women were from South Korea, Taiwan, and the Philippines.[54]

Some women move abroad on their own, some go through agents, and others either apply or are induced into business-arranged foreign 'marriages'. Travel agencies, in cooperation with Thai tourist and business counterparts, often buy women in 'marriage' to be put to work as CSWs in the country to where they move. Those who do not re-enter the sex industry are still subject to labour exploitation – either through providing services that satisfactorily fulfil the fantasies that guided their new 'husbands' eastward or by entering the labour force in low-skill, low-wage employment.

Thai women's burden   In contrast to many societies, women in Thailand have historically played a central role as income-earners for their families and as financial supporters of their elders. In terms of social liberties, males in Thailand occupy a much more advantageous position than females. Young men are often given few responsibilities and allowed considerable personal and social freedoms. In contrast, young women must follow strict behavioural guidelines and must assume most of the family and household responsibilities, while sacrificing their own freedom.[55] Compounded by rural poverty and a lack of educational and economic opportunities, such heavy filial burdens push a large number of young women into the sex industry to earn income for their families. Performing their expected duties, young women from Thailand's poverty-stricken north and northeast often go willingly with employment agents to work in Bangkok's massage parlours and other sex industry establishments.[56] Commercial sex as a means for income has become standard for many rural communities in Thailand. It has been estimated that there are approximately two million commercial sex workers within the country. Overall estimates conclude that one in every five Thai women aged 13 to 29 is a sex worker.[57]

Although there is a clear predominance of single males in the over five million tourists who visit Thailand each year, the vast majority of the clientele in the sex industry are Thai men. The frequenting of CSWs has

become an institutionalized, socially acceptable practice for a very substantial part of the male population in Thailand. Approximately 70 to 80
per cent of all Thai males have visited CSWs and about 30 to 40 per cent
use their services regularly. And in certain areas of Thailand it is estimated
that approximately 90 per cent of Thai men are regular clients.[58] A visit
to a brothel has become a rite of passage for adolescent single males, and
by the age of 16, half of all Thai boys have visited a CSW.[59]

By 1989, the frequenting of CSWs by Thai males had become the
driving force of AIDS in Thailand. However, due to the AIDS programme's
promotion of condom use and public education targeting sex workers,
condom use has been high for the last few years in sex establishments.
However, in low-cost brothels, use remains inconsistent.

Because of Thai women's submissive role in society, and due to the
fact that many CSWs are young girls, sexual subordination of both wife
and sex worker is commonplace and continues to fuel the spread of the
virus. Some researchers and activists say the sex industry is shrinking,
while others believe it is as big as ever, but is going further and further
underground, putting women at more risk. Many AIDS experts say that
the new problem in Thailand is premarital or extramarital promiscuity.
Women and girlfriends do not ask their husbands or boyfriends to use
condoms. Thus even though they may not be visiting CSWs, men are
exposing themselves and their different sex partners to the virus. Thai
society has in fact helped to foster the belief that men have the right to
seek sexual gratification freely outside marriage, based on the myth that
the sexual urges of men are more compelling than those of women.

Legislation: aggravating the problem?

Commercial sex work is officially
illegal in Thailand, but because powerful vested interests are at stake,
there has been a tremendous lack of will to crack down on the sex
industry. According to Professor Pasuk Phongphaichit of Chulalongkorn
University, the money generated from the sex trade is higher than the
value of narcotics smuggled out of the country. A team of researchers
has estimated that the sex industry brings in approximately 450 billion
baht annually, or about half the fiscal budget for 1995.[60]

The Prostitution Prevention and Suppression Act of 1960 was strengthened in April 1996 to provide for harsher penalties for procurers, pimps,
and parents who sell their children into the sex trade. People who force
women and girls into prostitution now face life imprisonment if they are
seriously injured, and the death sentence or a life term if their actions
lead to death. Many organizations working to support sex workers are
concerned about the new legislation and stress that enforcement remains
weak and women and children remain unprotected. A specific concern is
the new provision under which parents will be punished for selling their

children into the sex trade, as parents are often victims themselves and are unaware or not fully aware of the fate of their children.

Even though the law states that the owners of the establishments will be penalized, bribes are made and accepted. Many politicians, officials (including those from Thailand's Tourist Industry Association), and policemen invest in and/or benefit from the sex trade in Thailand and some even own chains of brothels. Under the Thai Penal Code, punishments are stiffer and there are penalties against those who have sex with minors (the age of majority is in the process of being changed from age 15 to age 18). However, when arrests are made, they are rarely charged under this law. [61] The law gives the police the power to choose to prosecute either under the Prostitution Act or under the stronger criminal law. Under the proposed legislation, customers who have sex with children under the age of 18 will face jail sentences of one to six years, shorter than the four to twenty years in jail stipulated under the existing penal code.[62]

Many sceptics believe that, given the new legislation, law enforcers will demand more protection money from brothel owners and workers – which will lead to worse conditions for sex workers. Chanthawipa Apisuk of Empower, an NGO working to support sex workers, has said that stricter rules will be imposed on sex workers by bar and brothel owners. For example, the cost of protection money will be passed on to the sex workers.[63]

Over the years, a mutually beneficial relationship has been cultivated among the operators of sex-industry establishments, elites, government officials, the military, and police officers. Some sex service establishments are even located across the street or around the corner from police stations, yet they are rarely touched. Only infrequently will a raid be ordered due to complaints of forced prostitution, and in these cases, some girls will be arrested while the operators often escape legal action against them. In the 1980s, according to national records, brothel owners, procurers, and pimps were rarely arrested.[64]

The illegal status of sex workers in Thailand renders them particularly helpless and vulnerable to exploitation, for they have no recourse to any protection from law or society. Even if a CSW is brutally assaulted, her profession – the very situation in which she is assaulted – is in itself illegal, and therefore her punishment is seen as justified.[65]

While a downward trend in the number of brothel CSWs has been observed in the past few years, the scale of CSWs working in other more disguised sex establishments – such as nightclubs, karaoke bars and massage parlours – has escalated, especially in provinces other than Bangkok.[66] This is of great concern for the protection of women and for the potential spread of HIV, as it is more difficult to bring education and healthcare to them and to monitor abuses if they are in underground establishments.

Many activists argue that sex workers need to be protected under the labour law to provide them with recourse in the case of abuse, to ensure they receive at least a minimum wage and are guaranteed fair working hours. In practical terms, legalizing and regulating commercial sex work in Thailand would improve working conditions and the health and safety of CSWs. They would be able to organize more easily and could negotiate more safely with clients – knowing that the police would protect them as citizens rather than harass them as criminals.[67]

In a society and economy where prostitution has already become common and is the highest paid source of income for unskilled women, any attempt to suppress the industry without providing sound economic alternatives can only hurt them. The need to abolish child prostitution, forced prostitution, and trafficking is unquestionable, but hollow legislation fails to protect consensual CSWs from exploitation and puts them and the wives and children of their clientele at risk of HIV infection.

The economic impact of AIDS

The macroeconomic impact of AIDS in Thailand is quite large. Thailand spends more on AIDS prevention than any other developing country ($45 million in 1992, 75 per cent of which was from government funds).[768] And the extent of the epidemic will require a continuance of resources devoted to the healthcare system and popular education.

Nearly all of Thailand's productive sectors are affected. The productive sectors hardest hit are those employing migrant, mobile, and seasonal labour forces. Because these people are often away from their families and communities, they have more opportunities to have multiple sex partners and/or visit sex workers, which makes them more vulnerable to HIV infection.

Due to the government's successful family planning programme, Thailand's population growth rate has declined and this may cause a drastic reduction of the economy's labour supply. The country's annual population growth rate fell from over 3 per cent in 1970 to less than 1.5 per cent in 1990. The AIDS epidemic will worsen this situation. It is predicted that by the year 2010 the death rate will triple, with 30 per cent of all deaths being AIDS-related. Thailand's labour supply used to increase by an annual rate of 3–4 per cent, but as of 1990, the rate of increase has dropped to approximately 2 per cent.[69] Indirect costs to the economy resulting from the premature death of adults in their prime working years are conservatively estimated to average US$22,000 per death.[70]

Thailand's high incidence of AIDS threatens to use up a major portion of the rural and urban poor's already limited resources. When a family member falls ill from AIDS, often the infirm and others in the family must reduce work and pay for treatment. In rural communities, women serve as the primary providers of medical care for those with AIDS, which reduces their productivity and family income. The lost income from the reduction in work and increased medical expenses means that fewer resources are available for the rest of the family. Families may also fall deep into debt. To cover medical and death-related expenses, some households may sell assets such as land, reduce their consumption, and sometimes compromise future earnings ability such as taking children out of school.[71]

The high costs of treatment will severely strain Thailand's governmental resources. Individuals with AIDS are typically more prone to pneumonia, diarrhoea, and tuberculosis, and the cost of medical care is high even though there is no cure for AIDS itself. Healthcare costs for people with AIDS are conservatively estimated to be between US$658 and US$1,016 annually, which is roughly 30 to 50 per cent of annual household income for the average Thai family, or more than 25 times current annual government per capita health expenditure.[72] Most families will be unable to bear this financial burden. To avoid an increase in poverty, the government will have to fund healthcare costs with the help of private foundations and institutions.

The rate of HIV-infected pregnant women is expected to rise markedly. It is estimated that 3,000 pregnant women were HIV-positive in 1990, and this number is projected to increase to 96,000 by the year 2000.[73] Moreover, because of the general increase in premature mortality, it has been forecast that the cumulative number of orphaned children under 12 will be about 85,000 by the end of the decade.[74] Child mortality rates are also on the rise. At present, approximately 30 per cent of babies born of infected women are born HIV-positive. Most such babies survive their first year but succumb to opportunistic infections during their second or third year. Babies can also contract HIV through breast milk, creating difficult trade-offs between the risk of infection and the benefits of breastfeeding for child health.[75]

Increased premature death is leading to an increase not only in orphaned children but also in the infirm elderly. Daughters have traditionally cared for the elderly, and Thailand has yet to offer a social security programme to support people in their old age. The increase in mortality from AIDS is likely to create a generation of elderly without any form of support, leading to a large impoverished elderly population. Supporting the elderly will be yet another economic strain on the government.

Battling AIDS: the scorecard

Thailand's AIDS programme focuses on three objectives: to reduce sexual contact with different partners; to increase condom use; and to treat STDs quickly and effectively.[76]

Containment by condom   Due to Thailand's AIDS programme, condom use has increased and the rate of HIV infection and transmission of other STDs in some sectors has decreased. In probably the most glowing report, army recruits who tested positive for AIDS had dropped from 3 per cent in 1993 to 2.4 per cent in 1995. Furthermore, gonorrhea declined to 4 per cent in 1994, down from 18 per cent in 1995.[77]

It is estimated that within Thailand, 90 per cent of CSWs have an accurate knowledge of the mode of transmission of HIV and the use of condoms to prevent infection. However, because many CSWs are still forbidden to demand the use of condoms, and because many men feel it deprives them of their masculinity or full enjoyment of sex, it remains an inconsistent practice – especially in lower-class brothels. Many CSWs regard AIDS as only one among many social and health problems of their occupation.

In the case of sexual relations between steady lovers or between husbands and wives, condoms are practically never used, because it is a cultural taboo. Many women fear to ask their husbands/boyfriends to wear a condom, because it would imply that they do not trust them – even though male infidelity is common and socially accepted. It may also imply that the wife intends to be unfaithful or that she intends to restrict her husband's prerogatives. Wives' attempts to negotiate condom use may, in fact, lead to domestic conflict, loss of support, and even violence.[78]

Striving for 100 per cent condom usage in Thailand is important, but without breaking down deeply rooted social practices it will not be effective. Many researchers and activists believe that the problem with the condom campaign is that it focuses on prostitution and misleads men into believing they are safe as long as they are not sleeping with prostitutes. According to AIDS expert Katherine Bond, most people who are in a romantic relationship do not use condoms simply because condoms are linked with diseases and are perceived as a sign of distrust. Even though demand for commercial sex work might be down, premarital and extramarital promiscuity is up and condom usage between boyfriends, girlfriends, husbands, wives, and mistresses is rare. For men, their girlfriends and mistresses are 'good women', hence clean and virus-free. In terms of AIDS control, the notion of women's empowerment is central. Unless women have the power to negotiate condom use in romantic relationships, the risk of HIV infection will remain high.[79]

Further, the government's AIDS publicity campaign and educational materials have not been effectively extended to the ethnic minorities. Moreover, they fail to get at the roots of the problem: poverty, poor education, discrimination, gender inequality, and lack of economic alternatives.

NGO participation   Given the fact that Thailand has one of the strongest

NGO movements in Asia, with several hundred organizations playing an active and critical role in addressing social issues, there is great hope for Thailand's battle against AIDS. NGOs play a vital role in prevention, care, and community support programmes and are better able to reach those at highest risk. These groups have been highly effective in reaching individuals at the grassroots level, particularly by initiating peer education and media programmes that reinforce behaviour change and work to modify the perceived social norms.[80] At present, more than fifty community-based groups and national and international NGOs are involved in AIDS education and prevention efforts throughout the country. Their activities include research, education, counselling, provision of AIDS hotlines, and needle exchanges. The Daughters' Education Programme (DEP), based in Thailand's northeast, works to keep young girls out of brothels by sponsoring schooling and training for those whose families are too poor to fund their education. Founder Sompop Jantraka created DEP upon the belief that child prostitution will only end when the root causes are addressed. DEP currently supports about four hundred girls in primary and secondary school, vocational training, leadership training, and village development.

Others, such as the Association for the Improvement of the Status of Women, provide home services for infected prostitutes and vocational training. ECPAT (End Child Prostitution in Asian Tourism) provides the media with information and lobbies politicians. Empower, another women's organization in Thailand, provides health education for female CSWs with foreign clientele and teaches them how to read and write in Thai and how to speak English in order to minimize exploitation and enable them to negotiate safer sex in English. The International Labour Organization (ILO) started a project called the 'Campaign Against AIDS', which trains leaders of Thai trade unions on the realities of AIDS. Other more technical organizations, such as the Chulabhorn Research Institute, conduct biomedical research and train health personnel in educating and counselling techniques.[81]

NGOs, grassroots groups, and people's organizations are crucial in the fight against AIDS in Thailand, not only for the services they provide but for the pressure they apply on the government and international agencies for resources and for more effective joint AIDS programmes. In particular, Thai women's organizations have played a key role in bringing the problem of the sex industry to the forefront. Because of the strength of Thailand's women's movement, women's NGOs have been effective in vocalizing the need to improve the situation of poor women. They have also been effective in making the connections between impoverishment, lack of economic opportunities, and sex work.[82]

Conclusion

The basic health of Thailand's population is a major determinant of the spread of HIV. Because of widespread malnutrition, indigent living conditions, and migration of impoverished peoples, a large portion of the in-country population is disproportionately affected by AIDS. Over 25 per cent of Thailand's total population and 40 per cent of its rural population live below the official poverty level.[83] New drug treatments for HIV/AIDS are being developed in US labs, but they remain financially prohibitive for the poor and even the middle class. Improvement in health, education, and basic preventative measures continue to be the only realistic tools with which to fight HIV infection in Thailand. Furthermore, in order to maintain Thailand's progress in fighting AIDS, cross-border cooperation and support must take place to stave off a resurgence of the virus within the country.

The enormous size of Thailand's sex industry provides hard evidence of the real crisis in Thai agriculture and the rapid industrialization process. The sex industry is deeply rooted in the economy and the spread of HIV can be linked to the substandard wages paid to women workers and the continued demand for commercial sex. Poor education, low wages in factories, and insufficient income for farmers and farmworkers are all pivotal factors in pulling young women into the sex industry. Real educational and economic alternatives must be created. According to Mechai Viravai, chairman of the Population and Community Development Association in Thailand, 'girls who go on to secondary school have a 99 per cent chance of staying away from prostitution.'

With continued trafficking of uneducated, impoverished girls and women, from the borders of Thailand and beyond, the problem will not be resolved. In order to stop the trafficking of women into Thailand's sex industry, it will also be necessary for the government to reform – and enforce – its trafficking laws to make them non-discriminatory and in line with international human rights standards.[84] The reduction of the sex industry and AIDS will furthermore greatly depend on the creation of decent jobs that provide livable wages and benefits, as well as the shattering of traditional beliefs that hinder women's ability to make their own choices.

The social and economic conditions that have caused HIV to spread in Thailand must be confronted: poverty and powerlessness. The primary means to stop the spread is far-reaching prevention, which must include regional cooperation, economic alternatives for commercial sex workers and their families, appropriate and sufficiently funded education, and social support for all sectors of society – including the promotion of new sexual attitudes for men and women, the maintenance of a healthy population and, importantly, the empowerment of women to control their sexuality.

A key element in the effective control over AIDS is the elimination of the barriers that deny women control over their own political, social, economic, and sexual decisions. As Dr Teeranat has aptly stated, 'the only way to stop prostitution is to stop the man'[85] – in other words, men must educate themselves and participate in fostering change.

Notes

1. Various sources including World Health Organization (WHO) and papers presented to Eleventh International Conference on AIDS, Vancouver, July 1996.

2. Diane Bartz, 'Campaign for condom cuts fatal virus rate', *The Nation* (Bangkok), 12 July 1996.

3. Interview, Katherine Bond, World Bank and Red Cross consultant, Bangkok, 3 June 1996.

4. Cecile Balgos, 'AIDS-Asia: Thailand applies brakes; eyes now on India, Indochina', *Interpress Service*, 10 July 1996.

5. Seth Berkley et al., 'AIDS: invest now or pay more later', *Finance & Development*, June 1994.

6. Bencha Yoddumnern-Attig, *AIDS in Thailand: A Situation Analysis with Special Reference to Children, Youth and Women* (Bangkok: UNICEF, 1995), p. 6.

7. Paul J. Gertler, 'AIDS and the family: economic consequences and policy responses in Asia', paper presented at Study on the Economic Implications of the HIV/AIDS Epidemic in Selected DMCs Inception Workshop, Manila, Philippines, 8–10 September 1993, p. 2.

8. Rachel M. Safman, 'Projecting the effects of the AIDS epidemic for households and communities in rural Thailand', paper presented to Fifth International Conference on Thai Studies, School of Oriental and African Studies (London), 5–10 July 1993, p. 3.

9. Andrew Pollack, 'New drugs said to show promise in the fight against the AIDS virus', *New York Times*, 11 August 1994.

10. Sumalee Pitayanon, Wattana Sanjareon, and Sukhonta Kongsin, 'AIDS in Thailand', background paper presented at Commencement Meeting of the UNDP/ADB Economic Network on HIV/AIDS, Asian Development Bank, Manila, 8–10 September 1993, p. 1.

11. Yoddumnern-Attig, p. 10.

12. Ann Danaiya Usher, 'After the forest: AIDS and the ecological collapse of Thailand', *Development Dialogue*, vols 1–2 (1992), p. 25.

13. Steven A. Holmes, 'Child death rate for AIDS expected to triple by 2010', *New York Times*, 29 April 1994.

14. Steven Erlanger, 'A plague awaits', *New York Times Magazine*, 14 June 1991.

15. UNICEF Mekong Region HIV/AIDS Project Newsletter, vol. 1, issue 1, November 1996.

16. Pacific Economic Cooperation Council.

17. Nopporn Adchariyavanich, 'Use of foreign labor raises tough questions', *The Nation* (Bangkok) June 1996.

18. 'Burmese women sex workers in Thailand', paper prepared by 'Images Asia' for NGO-Forum on Women, Beijing, September 1995, p. 8.

19. 'Illegal immigrants bring in diseases', *Bangkok Post*, 30 December 1996.

20. Brooke Grundfest Schoepf, 'Gender, development, and AIDS: a political economy and cultural framework', in Rita S. Gallin et al., *The Women and International Development Annual Vol. 3* (Boulder, CO: Westview Press, 1993), p. 55.

21. Brian K. Murphy, 'The politics of AIDS', *Third World Resurgence*, no. 47 (Malaysia: Third World Network, 1994).

22. 'Out of control: The HIV/AIDS epidemic in Burma', report by the Southeast Asian information network, Thailand, December 1995.

23. Anchalee Singhanetra-Renard, 'Population movement and the AIDS epidemic in Thailand: some conceptual issues', paper presented at Fifth International Conference on Thai Studies, School of African and Oriental Studies, London, 5–10 July 1993, p. 11.

24. Yoddumnern-Attig, p. 73.

25. Safman, p. 7.

26. Singhanetra-Renard, p. 1.

27. Interview with Dr Chris Beyrer, director of AIDS Management Training Program, Johns Hopkins University, Boston, May 1996.

28. Khin Thitsa, *Providence and Prostitution: Image and Reality for Women in Buddhist Thailand* (London: Change International Reports, 1980), p. 16.

29. Shashi Ranjan Pandey and Darunee Tantiwiramanond, 'The status and role of Thai women in the modern period: a historical and cultural perspective', *Indian Journal of Asian Studies*, no. 1, 1989, p. 60.

30. Ibid.

31. Bruce Rich, *Mortgaging the Earth: The World Bank, Environmental Impoverishment, and the Crisis of Development* (Boston, MA: Beacon Press, 1994), p. 18.

32. Professor Teeranat spoke at the Foreign Correspondents Club of Thailand in Bangkok, 26 April 1995.

33. Usher, p. 21.

34. Bhassorn Limanonda, 'Female commercial sex workers and AIDS: perspectives from Thai rural communities', paper presented to Fifth International Conference on Thai Studies, School of Oriental and African Studies, London, 5–10 July 1993, p. 1.

35. Gordon Fairclough, 'No bed of roses: government tries to uproot prostitution from the economy', in *Far Eastern Economic Review* (Hong Kong: Review Publishing) 15 September 1994.

36. Limanonda, p.2.

37. Asia Watch, *A Modern Form of Slavery: Trafficking of Burmese Women and Girls into Brothels in Thailand* (New York: Human Rights Watch, 1993), p. 48.

38. Jennifer Gray, 'HIV/AIDS in the hills: a crisis just waiting to happen', paper presented at Fifth International Conference on Thai Studies, School of Oriental and African Studies, London, 5–10 July 1993, p. 12.

39. Asia Watch, p. 53.

40. 'Foreign women flooding in for prostitution', *The Bangkok Post* (Bangkok) 20 February 1994.

41. Gray, p. 5.

42. Mukdawan Sakboon, 'The Phuket brothel tragedy ten years after: child prostitution racket simply changes strategy', *The Nation*, 20 February 1994.

43. Ron O'Grady, 'Where have we been, where are we going?', *ECPAT Newsletter*, no. 10, September 1994.

44. Alan Beesey, 'Rural-based family and community care for HIV-infected people: a study in rural northern Thailand', paper presented at Fifth International Conference on Thai Studies, School of Oriental and African Studies, London, 5–10 July 1993, p. 5.

45. Asia Watch, p.1.

46. Professor Teeranat spoke at the Foreign Correspondents Club of Thailand in Bangkok, 26 April 1995.

47. Yoddumnern-Attig, p. 15.

48. Vichai Poshyachinda et al., 'Reappraisal of HIV/AIDS epidemic in Thailand', paper presented at Fifth International Conference on Thai Studies, School of Oriental and African Studies, London, 5–10 July 1993, p. 5.

49. Yoddumnern-Attig, p. 16.

50. Poshyachinda et al., p. 5.

51. Yoddumnern-Attig, p. 16–17.

52. O'Grady.

53. Nitaya Mahabhol, 'Commercial sex workers: their situation and health', in *Priority Issues for Women, Health and Development in Thailand* (Bangkok: National Committee on Women, Health and the Environment, National Commission on Women's Affairs), 1995.

54. 'Jail term for forced sex workers cut', *The Nation* (Bangkok), 17 July 1996.

55. Nicholas Ford and Sirinan Saiprsert, 'Destinations unknown: the gender construction and changing nature of the sexual lifestyle of Thai youth', paper presented at Fifth International Conference on Thai Studies, School of Oriental and African Studies, London, 5–10 July 1993, p. 33.

56. Maggie Black, 'Home truths', *New Internationalist*, February 1994.

57. Usher, p. 23.

58. Han Ten Brummelhuis, 'Do we need a Thai theory of prostitution?', paper presented at Fifth International Conference on Thai Studies, School of Oriental and African Studies (London), 5–10 July 1993, p. 5.

59. Poshyachinda et al., p. 20.

60. Mukdawan Sakboon, 'Prostitution bill is not the answer to the problem', *The Nation*, 9 April 1996.

61. Erlanger.

62. Teena Gill, 'Prostitution law misses the target, says activists', Gemini News Service, World Wide Web.

63. Chanthawipa Apisuk of Empower spoke at the Foreign Correspondents Club of Thailand in Bangkok, 26 April 1995.

64. Mukdawan Sakboon.

65. Thitsa, p. 14.

66. Nitaya Mahabhol.

67. Nikki van der Gaag, 'Prostitution: soliciting for change', *New Internationalist*, February 1994.

68. Berkley et al.

69. Mathana Phananiramai, 'Women's economic roles in Thailand', July 1993, p. 1.

70. Yoddumnern-Attig, p. 19.

71. Gertler, p. 9.

72. Yoddumnern-Attig, p. 19.

73. Ibid., p. 56.

74. Gertler, p. 14.

75. *World Bank Development Report*, p. 102.

76. Yoddumnern-Attig, p. 51.

77. Bartz.

78. Brooke Grundefest Schoepf, 'Gender, development, and AIDS: a political economy and cultural framework', in Rita G. Gallin et al. (eds), *The Women and International Development Annual*, vol. 3 (Boulder, CO: Westview, 1993), p. 57.

79. Interview with Katherine Bond, Bangkok, 3 June 1996.

80. *World Bank Development Report*, p. 105.

81. Pitayanon et al., p. 12.

82. Darunee Tantiwiramanond and Shashi Ranjan Pandey, *By Women, For Women: A Study of Women's Organizations in Thailand* (Singapore: Institute of Southeast Asian Studies, 1991), p. 159.

83. Poshyachinda et al., p. 21.

84. Asia Watch, p. 154.

85. Professor Teeranat spoke at the Foreign Correspondents Club of Thailand in Bangkok, 26 April 1995.

CHAPTER 12

Conclusion: Revisioning the Future

With the crash of the economy, the question of alternatives to the current economic model has become an extremely urgent one.

Emergence and dynamics of the NGO movement

The source of thinking about alternatives has been the vibrant NGO movement in Thailand. This movement, a rather diverse one, has several origins. One, of course, is the traditional movement of the left, which collapsed in the early 1980s, with the breakup of the Comunist Party of Thailand – partly as a result of the China–Vietnam conflict – and the return to above-ground life of many of the youthful cadres that had fled 'to the jungle' during the atmosphere of repression that followed the military coup of 1976. Many of the returnees, often after a period of professional education in pursuits such as law, resurfaced as activists in human rights and civil rights organizations as well as in movements around 'new' concerns such as the environment. Moreover, Marxism continued to be a significant influence in academic circles, though principally as critical theory.

Another source of new thinking – or rather, new approaches, since its emphasis was as much on process as on substance – was the non-communist movement stressing rural regeneration associated with Dr Puey Ungpakorn, who was also head of the Bank of Thailand. Ungpakorn and his associates had founded the Thai Rural Reconstruction Movement, which attracted many young Thais with its image as a non-partisan organization offering humanitarian services. The same activist humanitarianism was also institutionalized by Ungpakorn in the Thammasatt University Volunteer Service and this, in turn, became the model for the Thai Volunteer Service (TVS), which in the late 1970s and early 1980s was the seeding-ground for many social activists who were prominent in the environmental, social, and anti-AIDS struggles of the late 1980s and early 1990s.

In the same broad stream was a movement that came to be identified as activist or social Buddhism, one of whose principal exponents was Sulak Sivaraksa, a man of aristocratic descent who was twice arraigned on charges of *lèse-majesté*, or insulting the king. Sivaraksa, who won the Right Livelihood Award (the 'alternative Nobel Prize') in 1995, went on to become one of the country's most prominent social critics, in the forefront of developing a thoroughgoing critique of consumerism.

A dynamic source of new ideas and perspectives was the environmental movement, which included organizations such as the Wildlife Fund of Thailand, the Yadfon Foundation, and the Project for Ecological Recovery. The first began as a conservationist movement, the second arose as an alliance of environmentalists and communities in the south to preserve mangrove forests, and the third emerged in the struggle against big dams like Nam Choan in the mid-1980s and Pak Mun in the early 1990s. Important in linking environmental concerns such as deforestation and social issues such as the forced resettlement of forest dwellers were activist Buddhist monks like Phra Prajak Khuttajito, who helped lead the struggle to protect the Dongyai Reserve in the northeast.

An initial attempt to bring together the variety of groups that soon earned the description 'NGO network' was the NGO-CORD (or NGO Coordinating Committee), an effort supported by the National Economic and Social Development Board (NESDB), perhaps in a bid by technocrat reformers within the latter to co-opt what was seen as an extremely dynamic 'third force' to government and business.

The key features of the NGO movement, especially its preoccupation with the rural areas, its focus on issues rather than 'totalizing' programmes, its avoidance of hierarchy, and its emphasis on flat 'networking' cannot be understood without seeing it as a reaction to two developments: the marginalizing of the rural areas by the ideology strategy of urban-centred developmentalism and the increasing irrelevance and discrediting of both the programme of totalizing change proposed by the traditional left and its methods of top-down organizing.

In contrast to the elitist aims of the former and the hierarchical processes of the latter, NGOs, according to one prominent activist, 'have to study the kind of politics suited to ordinary people, which might be different from established political methods and may not require winning state power ... Such movements must be dynamic and avoid becoming institutionalized. Democracy must be both the aim and the means.'[1]

While the movement was avowedly 'non-political', it was a force that could influence political events via what Suthy Prasartsert calls its 'political-social infrastructure'. This included political information, resources, and facilities as well as 'modern information technology and telecommunications devices such as electronic mail, fax machines, mobile phones, and databases'.[2] This network became especially important during the May 1992 events:

As the struggle and campaign for popular democracy became more intense ... this socio-political infrastructure was further developed and strengthened, especially in the NGOs' participation in the Pollwatch Commission and establishment of the Forum for Democracy. Eventually at the time leading to the final confrontation, it had unfailingly provided ready support for political mobilization on a national scale to fight against the National Peacekeeping Commission.[3]

Even as Bangkok-based NGOs were playing a vital role in the process leading up to the deposing of the Suchinda dictatorship, farming communities, environmentalists, and social activists came together in the northeast to oppose the Khor Jor Kor commercial reforestation scheme pushed by the Thai military, the high point of this being the historic march by thousands of people from 17 provinces to Nakhon Ratchasima in June 1992. The same groups, fortified by lessons in community resistance learned during the struggle against the Pak Mun dam, came together to form the Forum of the Poor in Ubon Ratchatani in December 1995.[4]

Within 18 months of its founding, the Forum brought 12,000 people from the countryside to Bangkok to present 47 demands to the government covering forest-related problems, land questions, displacement by large dams, and toxic working environments. The rally lasted 28 days, from 25 March to 23 April 1996, and dispersed only when the cabinet of Prime Minister Banharn Silapa-Archa acknowledged the protestors' problems and promised to solve them.

Government inaction provoked another big rally that lasted for three weeks later that year, which was aborted when the Banharn government fell. Then, with the advent of the Chaovalit government, the assembly brought up to 30,000 people to a rally in front of Government House that lasted for 99 days. Here was rural Thailand 'besieging' Bangkok, as the protestors presented the Chaovalit government with 121 demands. After intense negotiations that saw the involvement of the prime minister himself, the cabinet 'agreed' to meet the assembly's demands and set up eleven committees to come up with solutions.

Critique of the system

The alternative movement was strong in terms of highlighting the flaws of the system. Economic development was seen as a process that achieved industrial growth at the expense of agriculture. The secondary status of agriculture, reflected in lower investment relative to industry and lower incomes relative to urban incomes, made the 58 to 60 per cent of the population that lived in the countryside effectively second-class citizens. Over time, with poverty concentrated in the countryside, agriculture became less and less attractive as an occupation and the rural population was converted into a reserve pool of cheap labour for industry. Extreme centralization was a characteristic of this pattern of growth: the subordination of the countryside to industry meant the subordination of most of Thailand to Bangkok since most of industry, about 90 per cent, was concentrated in the city.

The pattern of development followed in Thailand was also ecologically extremely destabilizing. A strip-mine type of development had accompanied the first phase of this process, which emphasized the export of natural resources, like wood, to raise the revenue necessary to finance industrial growth. The second phase – export-oriented industrialization – had also caused great damage, this being the result of a deliberately lax enforcement of environmental controls in order to attract foreign investment into the country, leading to massive air and water pollution.

A central factor contributing to both the crisis of agriculture and the crisis of the environment was the infrastructure building that accompanied this process of extractive development to facilitate the flow of resources and goods from the countryside to Bangkok and from Thailand to the outside world. The massive centralized projects, like the hydroelectric dams whose construction was accompanied by the clearcutting of huge tracts of forestland and the displacement of thousands of farmers and forest-dwellers, had paltry gains – as was underlined by the case of the Pak Mun dam, which generates only enough electricity to fuel one big Bangkok shopping mall for one day.

While the strategy favoured the urban population over the rural population, the principal beneficiaries of this pattern of centralized growth were in fact the political and economic elites of the country, as shown by the increasing inequality in income distribution as growth accelerated. In the early part of the period the role of the state in promoting industrialization and the continuing weight of the pre-industrial political elites (which allowed them to cut into the profits of the industrial elite by extracting 'rent') resulted in the primacy of the political elite in decisionmaking, but the industrial and financial elites gradually gained the upper hand. This was reflected by the increasing primacy of the market as state regulation was weakened – a process that was accelerated with the greater integration of Thailand into the international economy, for this meant the elimination of the state mechanisms that protected the Thai economy from the full impact of global market forces.

From a focus on the state as the main agent of 'development from above', with the greater integration of Thailand's economy into the global economy, the main concern of the NGO movement was becoming by the mid-1990s what it considered the disruptive forces unleashed by an un-regulated private sector, the global market economy, and transnational financial and corporate forces.

The crisis that overtook the Thai economy was seen as a vindication of the movement's critique of globalization. But like everybody else, it was taken aback by the suddenness of the financial collapse, for what had been projected was a gradual exacerbation of the contradictions of the economic and social structures. It was not surprising that it was not able to move into the vacuum – while its critique was strong, its articulation of the alternative left much to be desired.

Where the movement was strongest was in its long-term vision of the 'good society'. This was a decentralized system of communities engaged in largely self-sufficient production that was possible because its members had been weaned away from the multiple needs of consumer society. Change had both external and internal components; new strategies of productive organization had to be accompanied by a change in spirit. As Dr Prawase Wasi, one of the country's leading alternative thinkers, stated, the country had to end its preoccupation with 'chasing the *farang* [foreigners]' and to embark on a Thai path of development, one based on the Buddhist concept of *sammaditthi*, or right viewpoint, which 'focuses on goodness while interlocking the economy with mind, family, culture, and the environment'. Demanding that the country turn away from the disastrous Bangkok-oriented development process, Prawase promoted a small-is-beautiful, back-to-agriculture ideal of self-sufficient communities:

> A strong community is the one which can solve its problems by itself, be they about their own self-reliant economy or social, cultural, educational, environmental or public health matters.
>
> There are plenty of fundamental businesses that local communities can do. They include integrated or mixed farming, handicrafts, village businesses, cottage industries, and many other services …
>
> [C]ommunities can group themselves to work on community businesses together. For example, they can set up village-run gas stations or food businesses. Among the possibilities are chemical pesticide-free food, all sorts of preserved food, medicinal herbs, handicrafts, and many other tools or household wares that the villages can produce themselves.[5]

Prawase brought together, in a succinct way, the main themes of alternative thinking within the NGO movement prior to the crisis. Its strength was its clear articulation of a return to decentralized, community-based production and exchange. It had many weaknesses, however, not least of which were what some saw as its romanticizing a countryside that had vanished, its failure to specify the short- and medium-term measures necessary to bring the country nearer to what it envisioned as the long-term goal, and its not placing the process of economic reform in its regional and global context.

Fleshing out the alternative

Nevertheless, inspired by the crisis, efforts are being made not only in Thailand but throughout Southeast Asia to articulate the short term with the long term, the domestic with the regional and international. Although not yet operationalized in a 'hardheaded' fashion, the various themes and proposals in this agenda are coming together. What they add up to might be characterized as a selective or negotiated integration into the global economy, as opposed to the indiscriminate globalization and liberalization that marked the discredited model. Among the key points in this emerging programme are the following.[6]

- First, since the trigger of the crisis has been the unrestricted, herdlike movement of speculative capital across global financial markets, controls on the flow of capital are urgently needed. Thus the reformers are urging their governments to join in convoking a global conference, possibly sponsored by the United Nations, to devise mechanisms such as the Tobin Tax (after its proponent, the Nobel Laureate James Tobin), a transactions tax to be imposed on speculative capital not clearly earmarked for productive investment entering or exiting most countries.

- Also high on the agenda of many is the creation of an Asian Emergency Regional Fund, which would take the place of the US-controlled IMF in dealing with the financial crisis. The Fund would essentially bring together the massive dollar reserves of Japan, Taiwan, and China, deploy them to protect Asian currencies from speculative movements, and bring them back to realistic rates of exchange *vis-à-vis* the dollar.

- Also important as a regional element of the alternative economic programme is the working out of a common strategy among the Asian countries to bring to the table in negotiations with the Western governments and international financial institutions on the question of their foreign debt, which has become a crushing burden owing to the freefall of the local currencies. To be avoided at all costs is a repeat of the experience of the Third World during the debt crisis of the 1980s, in which the failure of the debtors to get together in a common front allowed the creditors to unite behind the IMF to pick them off one by one. The renegotiation of the debt must be done on the basis of the principle that a large part of the foreign debt is private debt and that both private debtors and private lenders must be forced to accept the penalties imposed by the market for making the wrong decision. The burden of servicing the debt must not be pushed onto the people, which is the IMF solution. Public money must not be used to bail out big private creditors and big private debtors. Coordination on foreign debt strategy must, in turn, be part of a broader effort that would include coordination of exchange rate, macroeconomic, and trade policies

These short-term measures are joined to several medium- and long-term proposals, among which are the following:

- While foreign investment of the right kind is important, growth must be financed principally from domestic savings and investment. That means good progressive taxation systems. One of the key reasons Southeast Asian elites relied on foreign capital for development was that they did not want to tax themselves. Regressive taxation is the norm in the region, where levies that cut deeply into the incomes of people at the low end of the scale are the chief source of government revenue. Meanwhile, only a tiny minority pays income tax. But progressive taxation would be just a start. Democratic management of national investment policies is also essential if local savings are not to be hijacked by financial elites and channelled into speculative gambles.
- Development must be reoriented around the domestic market as the main stimulus of development. The tremendous dependence on exports has made the region extremely vulnerable to the vagaries of the global market and sparked a race to the bottom that has beggared significant sectors of the labour force while benefiting only foreign investors and domestic economc elites.

  A 'Keynesian strategy' of enlarging the domestic market to generate growth must include a more comprehensive programme of asset and income reform, including the long-postponed land reforms in Thailand and other countries. There is in this, of course, the unfinished social justice agenda of the old progressive movement – an agenda marginalized by the regnant ideology of growth during the 'Asian Miracle'. Vast numbers of people in Thailand and the other Southeast Asian countries, in fact, remain marginalized because of grinding poverty, particularly in the countryside. Land and asset reform would simultaneously bring them into the market, empower them economically and politically, and create the conditions for social and political stability. Achieving economic sustainability based on a dynamic domestic market can no longer be divorced from issues of equity.
- While the fundamental mechanism of production, distribution, and exchange will have to be something more sensible and rational than the 'invisible hand' of the market, neither the interventionist hand of the East Asian state nor the heavy hand of the socialist state is a good substitute. Certainly, the state is essential to curb the market for the common good, but in East Asia the state and the private sector have traditionally worked in nontransparent fashion to advance the interests of the upper classes and foreign capital. While not denying that market and state can play an important and subsidiary role in the allocation of resources, the emerging view is that the fundamental economic mechanism must be democratic decisionmaking by communities, civic organizations, and people's movements. The challenge is how to operationalize such institutions of economic democracy.
- Ecological sustainability – the strong point of the Thai NGO move-

ment's vision – must be incorporated into this larger framework. Instead of 8 to 10 per cent growth rates, some progressive reformers now talk of 3 to 4 per cent or even less. This links the social and environmental agendas, since the elites' addiction to high growth is at least partly explained by their desire to take the lion's share of wealth while still allowing some to trickle down to the bottom for the sake of social peace. The alternative – redistribution of wealth – will clearly be resisted by the Thai and Southeast Asian ruling groups, but it is the key to a pattern of development that combines economic growth, political stability, and ecological sustainability.

In Thailand and throughout Southeast Asia, a key challenge for movements like the Forum of the Poor is to bring together such proposals into a credible and attractive programme for change that is both visionary and pragmatic. The other – even greater - challenge is how to wed such a programme to a political strategy for change that brings all those groups, strata, and classes negatively affected by the discredited strategy of 'fast track capitalism' into a broad alliance for change. Frozen during the years of the long boom, mass politics with a class edge is about to return to centre stage.

Notes

1. Witoon Permpongsacharoen, quoted in William Callahan, 'Oppositional consciousness and alternative organization: NGOs and nonviolent action as political forces', draft, Bangkok, undated.

2. Suthy Prasartsert, 'The rise of NGOs as critical social movements in Thailand', paper presented to conference on 'The Third World Today', Mexico City, 6–17 December 1993.

3. Ibid.

4. Wannida Tantiwatthayapitak, interview, Bangkok, 16 May 1997.

5. Prawase Wasi, 'The Thai path of development', *Bangkok Post*, Outlook Section, 14 January 1998.

6. These points are elaborated in, among others, the following articles by Walden Bello: 'The end of the Asian miracle', *The Nation* (New York), 9 January 1998; and 'The end of Southeast Asia's miracle economy', *Ecologist*, January–February.

Selected Readings

Many of the best works on Thailand have still to be translated into English. This selection is limited to those already available in English.

A good historical overview of Thailand's politics and economy is Pasuk Phongphaichit and Chris Baker's *Thailand: Economy and Politics* (Oxford: Oxford University Press, 1995). Accurate and fair reporting on Thai developments can be found in *The Nation*, *Bangkok Post*, *Far Eastern Economic Review*, and the *Financial Times*.

There are many excellent works on the political economy of pre-crisis Thailand. Among them are the following: Anek Laothamathas, *Business Associations and the New Political Economy of Thailand: From Bureaucratic Polity to Liberal Corporatism* (Boulder, CO: Westview Press, 1992); Kevin Hewison, *Power and Politics in Thailand* (Manila: Journal of Contemporary Asia, 1989); Akira Suehiro, 'Capitalist development in post-war Thailand: commercial bankers, industrial elite, and agribusiness groups', in Ruth McVey, ed., *Southeast Asian Capitalists* (Ithaca, NY: Southeast Asia Program, Cornell University, 1992); Nikhom Chandravithun, *The Social Costs of Becoming the Fifth Tiger*, Woodrow Wilson Center Asia Program Occasional Paper, no. 68 (Washington, DC: Woodrow Wilson Center, 1995); Ukrist Pathamanand, 'The Thaksin Shinnawat Group: a study of the relationship between money and politics in Thailand', *Copenhagen Journal of Asian Studies*, vol. 13 (1998); and Anek Laothamathas, 'From clientilism to partnership: business–government relations in Thailand', in Andrew MacIntyre, ed., *Business and Government in Industrializing Asia* (London: Allen and Unwin, 1994).

On the Thai and Asian financial crisis, two solid pieces that anticipated the débâcle are HG Asia, *Communiqué Thailand* (Hong Kong: HG Asia, 1996), and Jayati Ghosh, Abhijit Singh, and C. P. Chandrasekhar, 'Southeast Asian economies: miracle or meltdown?', *Economic and Political Weekly*, 12–19 October 1996. See also Walden Bello's 'The rise and fall of Southeast Asia's economy', *Ecologist*, vol. 28, no. 1 (January–February 1998), and 'East Asia on the eve of the great transformation', *Review of International Political Economy*, vol. 5, no. 3 (Fall 1998). On the International Monetary Fund and Thailand, see Nicola Bullard, Walden Bello, and Kamal Malhotra, *Taming the Tigers: The IMF and the Asian Crisis* (London: CAFOD, 1998).

A fine analysis of the economic and political dimensions of the crisis is provided by Amar Siamwalla's 'Why are we in this mess?', *Business in*

Thailand (undated). Siamwalla's findings parallel those of the report of the Nukul Commission, a body set up to investigate the financial disaster; as of the time of writing, the report was not yet available in English. The vicissitudes of industrial deepening, technology transfer, and technological innovation in Thailand are treated in a number of excellent works. The country's automobile industry is compared to those in neighbouring Asian countries by Richard Doner in his now classic 'Domestic coalitions and Japanese auto firms in Southeast Asia: a comparative bargaining study', Ph.D. dissertation, University of California at Berkeley, 1987. The electronics industry is analysed by Anupap Tiralap in his thesis available at the Bangkok-based Thai Development Research Institute (TDRI). Several studies conducted by TDRI in the late 1980s and early 1990s are among the most significant done on technology transfer; these include *The Barriers to and Strategies for Technology Acquisition* (1991), *The Development of Thailand's Technological Capability in Industry* (1992), and *Private Sector R&D: Lessons from Success* (1993).

A good analysis of the state of technology transfer from Japanese to Thai firms is Samart Chiasakul and Prasert Silalipat's 'The role of Japanese direct investment in developing countries: the case of Thailand', in *The Role of Japanese Direct Investment in Developing Countries* (Tokyo: Institute of the Developing Economies, 1992).

On the conditions of labour in Thailand, there are also many good reports and analyses, among which are Nikhom Chandravithun's *Thailand: The Social Costs of Becoming the Fifth Tiger* (see full citation above) and *Thai Labor: A Long Journey* (Bangkok: Thai Watana Panich, 1982); Sakool Zuesongham and Voravidh Charoenlet, 'Fragmentation of the trade unions: inevitable or not?', undated, unpublished manuscript; Andrew Brown and Stephen Frenkel, 'Union unevenness and insecurity in Thailand', in Stephen Frenkel, ed., *Organized Labor in the Asia-Pacific* (Ithaca, NY: ILR Press, 1993); and Stefan Chrobot, *Trade Unions in Transition: Present Situation and Structure of the Thai Labor Movement* (Bangkok: Friedrich Ebert Stiftung, 1996). Occupational safety issues are the subject of Bundit Thanachaisathavit, 'Situation of victims of occupational diseases/harm in Thailand', unpublished factsheet of Labour NGOs Network, undated; 'A painful way to go', *Thailand Times*, 12 December 1994; and 'Fire kills hundreds at Thai toy factory', *Asian Labor Update*, no. 12, July 1993. The conditions and struggle of women workers are analysed in, among others, Mathana Phananiramai, 'Women's economic roles in Thailand', paper prepared by the TDRI for the Conference on Women and Industrialization, Seoul National University, September 1993; Supawadee Petrat and Jaded Chaowilai, 'How to support the rights of women workers in the context of trade liberalization: a perspective from Thailand', paper presented to the Women Working Worldwide conference (date and location not indicated); *Young Women Workers in Manufacturing: A Case Study of Rapidly*

Industrializing Economies of the ESCAP Region (Bangkok: Economic and Social Commission for Asia and the Pacific, 1987); and National Commission on Women's Affairs, *Thailand's Report on the Status of Women and Platform for Action for the Fourth World Conference on Women* (Bangkok: Office of the Prime Minister, 1995).

On Bangkok and the dynamics of destabilizing urbanization, important data are presented in the two-volume *National Urban Development Policy Framework* published by the National Economic and Social Development Board in 1992. For insightful analysis of urban issues, see Anuchat Poungsomlee and Helen Ross, *Impacts of Modernization and Urbanization in Bangkok: An Integrative Ecological and Biosocial Study* (Bangkok: Institute for Population and Social Research, Mahidol University, 1992); Kraiyudht Dhiratiyakinant, 'Urbanization, inefficient urban management, and income inequality', paper presented to the Fifth International Conference on Thai Studies, London, 6–9 July 1993; and Mark Askew, *The Making of Modern Bangkok: State, Market, and People in the Shaping of the Thai Metropolis* (Bangkok: TDRI, 1993).

Urban transportation problems are treated in Ralph Gakenheimer et al., *Concept Plan for Bangkok: Metropolitan Development* (Cambridge: Massachusetts Institute of Technology, July 1993); 'Development of Bangkok's infrastructure: gathering momentum', in Bangkok Bank, *Annual Report 1996* (Bangkok: Bangkok Bank, 1996); and 'A ride on the skytrain: not for the squeamish while below a sick city chokes itself to death', *Thailand Times*, 21 August 1995.

The bias of urban land management policy against the lower classes are analysed in Yap Kioe Sheng, ed., *Low-Income Housing in Bangkok: A Review of Some Housing Sub-markets* (Bangkok: Asian Institute of Technology, 1992); while the efforts of the people of Klong Toey to stay on their land are described in S. Boonyabancha et al., *Struggle to Stay: A Case Study of People in Slum Klong Toey Fighting for their Homes* (Bangkok: Duang Prateep Foundation, 1988).

There is now a good deal of literature on the deterioration of the urban environment. A good sample of this includes Pitsamai Eamsakulrat, Direk Patmasiriwat, and Pablo Huidobro, 'Hazardous waste management in Thailand', *TDRI Quarterly Review*, September 1994; Tim Forsyth, 'Industrial pollution and government policy in Thailand: rhetoric versus reality', in Philip Hirsch, ed., *Seeing Forests for the Trees: Environment and Environmentalism in Thailand* (Chiang Mai: Silkworm Books, 1997); TDRI, *The Monitoring and Control of Industrial Hazardous Waste: Hazardous Waste Management in Thailand* (Bangkok: TDRI, 1995); and Thai Environmental Institute, *Thailand's Trade and Environment: Report Submitted to the ASEAN Secretariat* (Bangkok: TEI, 1997). Both of Bangkok's leading English-language daily newspapers *The Nation* and the *Bangkok Post* regularly carry stories on both urban and rural environmental issues.

Thailand's agrarian society and economy are very well studied. On the relationship of agriculture to the larger economy, see the now classic study by Amar Siamwalla and Suthad Setboonsarng on *Trade, Exchange Rate, and Agricultural Pricing Policies in Thailand: The Political Economy of Agricultural Pricing Policy* (Washington, DC: World Bank, 1989) and Mehdi Krongkaew's 'Contributions of agriculture to industrialization: the case of Thailand', Paper presented to the Conference on the Making of a Fifth Tiger, Australian National University, Canberra, 7–9 December 1992.

On the dynamics of capitalist penetration of the agricultural production system and its social and political consequences, see two works that are also now regarded as classic: Anan Ganjanapan's 'The partial commercialization of rice production in northern Thailand, 1900–1981', Ph.D. dissertation, Cornell University, Ithaca, NY, January 1984; and Chayan Vaddhanaputi, 'Cultural and ideological reproduction in rural northern Thai society', Ph.D. dissertation, Stanford University, Stanford, CA. Also very useful are Amara Pongsapich et al., *Sociocultural Change and Political Development in Central Thailand, 1950–1990* (Bangkok: TDRI, 1993); Charles Mehl, 'Land, agricultural labor, and development in rural Thailand: a study of variations in the socioeconomic structure of three villages in Nakhon Ratchasima province', Ph.D. dissertation, Cornell University, August 1985; and Scott Christenson, 'Conditions and collective choice: the politics of institutional change in Thai agriculture', Ph.D. dissertation, University of Wisconsin, Madison, WI, May 1985.

Rural class conflict in the late 1960s and early 1970s is the focus of Andrew Turton's 'Poverty, reform, and class struggle in rural Thailand', in S. Jones et al., *Rural Poverty and Agrarian Reform* (New Delhi: ENDA and Allied Publishers, 1982) and Victor Karunan's *If the Land Could Speak, It Would Speak for Us. Vol 1. A History of Peasant Movements in Thailand and the Philippines* (Hong Kong: Plough Publications, 1984). Rural development as a mechanism for containing the countryside, defusing social conflict, and advancing the interests of local elites is masterfully dissected by Philip Hirsch in *Development Dilemmas in Rural Thailand* (New York: Oxford University Press, 1990).

Light on the dynamics of the stalled land reform process is shed by TDRI, *Policy on Agricultural Land Reform* (Bangkok: TDRI, undated); Chulalongkorn University Social Research Institute (CUSRI), *Master Plan of the Agricultural Land Reform. Vol. 2: The Main Report* (Bangkok: CUSRI, 1989); and Agricultural Land Reform Office (ALRO), 'Briefing on land reform implementation in Thailand', mimeo, Bangkok, 1993.

The economic, social, and environmental impacts of recent efforts to modernize agriculture are the focus of the following works: Sompop Manarungsan, 'Contract farming and Thailand's agricultural development', in Buddhadeb Chauduri, ed., *Our Lands, Our Lives* (Bangkok: ACFOD, 1992); Scott Christensen, *Between the Farmers and the State: Towards a Policy Analysis of the Role of Agribusiness in Agriculture* (Bangkok: TDRI, 1992);

Larry Lohmann, 'Peasants, plantations, and pulp: the politics of eucalyptus in Thailand', *Bulletin of Concerned Asian Scholars*, vol. 23, no. 4 (October–December 1991); and Apichai Puntasen et al., 'The political economy of eucalyptus: a case of business cooperation by the Thai government and its bureaucracy', paper presented to conference on the Political Economy of the Environment in Asia, Simon Fraser University, Vancouver, Canada, 11–13 October 1990.

Deforestation and other forms of ecological destabilization in the Thai countryside are monitored and analysed in two superb periodicals, the *Thai Development Support Committee (TDSC) Newsletter* and *Watershed*, which is published by the Project for Ecological Recovery. Particularly helpful were the following works: Project for Ecological Recovery, *The Future of the People and Forests in Thailand after the Logging Ban* (Bangkok: Project for Ecological Recovery, 1992); Larry Lohmann, 'Thailand: land, power, and colonization', in Marcus Colchester and Larry Lohmann, eds, *The Struggle for Land and the Fate of the Forests* (London: Zed, 1993); Ricardo Carrere and Larry Lohmann, *Pulping the South: Industrial Tree Plantations and the World Paper Economy* (London: Zed, 1996); Midas Agronomics Company, *Study of Conservation Forest Area Demarcation, Protection, and Occupancy in Thailand* (Bangkok: Midas Agronomics, 1991); Shalardchai Ramintanondh, 'Forests and deforestation in Thailand: a pandisciplinary approach', in *Culture and Environment in Thailand: A Symposium of the Siam Society* (Bangkok: Siam Society, 1989); Thanwa Jitsanguan, 'Natural resources and management policies of the coastal zones of Thailand', paper delivered at the Ninth Biennial Conference of the Agricultural Economics Society of Southeast Asia, Asia Hotel, Bangkok, 22–24 June 1993; Phisit Chansanoh, 'Villagers should manage coastal resources', *Thai Development Newsletter*, no. 24 (1994); and the Thai NGO 'Statement on the Thai forestry sector master plan', Bangkok, 22 October 1993.

On the impact of development on the highland peoples, see, among others, Mountain Peoples' Culture and Development Educational Programs Foundation (MPCDE), *Impact of Regional Development on Tribal Minorities in Southeast Asia* (Chiang Mai: MPCDE, 1991); Peter Hinton, 'Declining production among sedentary swidden cultivators: the case of the Pwo Karen', in Peter Kunstadter et al., *Farmers in the Forest: Economic Development and Marginal Agriculture in Northern Thailand* (Honolulu: University of Hawaii, 1978); and Uraivan Tan-Kim-Yong, 'Participatory land-use planning for natural resource management in northern Thailand', *Rural Development Forestry Network Paper* 14b, Winter 1992.

Patrick McCully's *Silenced Rivers* (London: Zed Books, 1997) is a thoroughly researched indictment of big hydrodam projects and the technocratic mentality that propels them. The controversy over and resistance to hydrodams in Thailand are well documented and analysed in David Hubbel, 'Antithetical perceptions of development and environment: village people and the state in rural Thailand', master's thesis, York University, September 1992; David Murray, 'Dam(ned) conflicts in Thailand', Occasional Paper no. 21, Indian Ocean Center for Peace Studies, Perth, 1992; David Hubbel, 'Environmental and social impacts of large dams: experience from around the world', *Thai Development Newsletter*, no. 25 (1994); Noel Rajesh, 'Local participation and the Kaeng Sua Ten controversy', *Watershed*, vol. 2, no. 3 (March–June 1997); 'Chronology of disasters: the growing costs of the Pak Mun dam', *Watershed*, vol. 1, no. 3 (March–June 1996); and Philip Hirsch, 'Thailand and the new geopolitics of Southeast Asia: resource and environmental issues', paper presented to the Fifth International Conference on Thai Studies, School of Oriental and African Studies, London, 1–10 July 1993.

The AIDS Division of the Communicable Diseases Control Department of the Ministry of Public Health issues periodic updates on trends in HIV and AIDs infection in Thailand. A particularly useful compilation of papers is Asian Research Center for Migration et al., *Second Technical Consultation on Transnational Population Movements and HIV/AIDS in Southeast Asian Countries* (Bangkok: Asian Research Center for Migration et al., 1997). See also Bhassorn Limanonda, 'Female commercial sex workers and AIDS: perspectives from Thai rural communities', paper presented to the Fifth International Conference on Thai Studies, London, 5–10 July 1993; Bencha Yoddumnern-Attig, *AIDS in Thailand: A Situation Analysis with Special Reference to Children, Youth, and Women* (Bangkok: UNICEF, 1995); and Nitaya Mahabhol, 'Commercial sex workers: their situation and health', in *Priority Issues for Women, Health, and Development in Thailand* (Bangkok: National Committee on Women, Health, and the Environment, National Commission on Women Affairs, 1995).

There is an increasing number of studies on NGOs and the alternatives they present to the current model of development. Two, in particular, are recommended: Suthy Prasartsert, 'The rise of NGOs as a critical social movement in Thailand', paper presented to the Conference on The World Conditions and Alternatives, Universidad Autonoma de Mexico, Mexico City, 6–17 December 1993; and William Callahan, 'Opposition conscious-ness and alternative organization: NGOs and non-violent action as political forces', unpublished manuscript, Bangkok, 1994.

Index

Food First: The Institute for Food and Development Policy

The Institute for Food and Development Policy, also known as Food First, is a non-profit research and education-for-action centre working to expose the root causes of hunger and poverty in the USA and around the world, and to educate the public and policymakers about these problems.

The world has never produced so much food as it does today – more than enough for every child, woman, and man. Yet hunger is on the rise, with nearly 800 million people around the globe going without enough to eat.

Hunger and poverty are not inevitable. Scarcity and overpopulation, long believed to be the causes of hunger, are instead symptoms of the ever-increasing concentration of control over food-producing resources in the hands of a few. This deprives many millions of people of the power to feed themselves. Yet real change is possible once we understand the root causes.

In 55 countries and 20 languages, Food First materials help free people from the grip of despair, empowering them to work for a more democratic food system, so the needs of all can be met. To serve the public, activists, policymakers, the media, students, educators, and researchers, Food First produces books, reports, articles, films, electronic media, and curricula, and organizes interviews, lectures, workshops, and courses. Food First participates in activist coalitions and furnishes cogent, clearly written, and carefully researched analyses, arguments, and action plans for people who want to change the world.

Become a member of Food First Food First members join us in supporting our work. When you become a member, you receive:

- quarterly *Food First News & Views* and *Backgrounders*;
- a 20 per cent discount on most of our books and other educational material;
- an opportunity to receive *Food Rights Watch* by e-mail;
- a free one-year subscription to *New Internationalist* magazine with a donation of $40 or more.

Individual membership contributions provide more than 50 per cent of the funds for Food First's work. Because Food First is not tied to the government, we can speak with a strong and independent voice. The success of our programme depends on dedicated volunteers and staff, as well as financial support from our activist donors. your gift now will help strengthen our effort to improve the lives of hungry people around the world.

Become a Food First intern Interns, who come from around the world, are a vital part of our organization and make our work possible. There are opportunities for interns in research, advocacy, campaigning, publishing, computers, media, and publicity. Check our web page at www.foodfirst.org for information and application materials, or call 510-654-4400.

Zed Titles on Globalisation

Globalisation has become the new buzzword of the late 1990s. Despite the very different meanings attached to the term and even more divergent evaluations of its likely impacts, it is clear nevertheless that we are in an accelerated process of transition to a new period in world history. Zed Books titles on globalisation pay special attention to what it means for the South, for women, for workers and for other vulnerable groups.

Nassau Adams, *Worlds Apart: The North-South Divide and the International System*

Samir Amin, *Capitalism in the Age of Globalization: The Management of Contemporary Society*

Asoka Bandarage, *Women, Population and Global Crisis: A Political-Economic Analysis*

Michel Chossudovsky, *The Globalisation of Poverty: Impacts of IMF and World Bank Reforms*

Peter Custers, *Capital Accumulation and Women's Labour in Asian Economies*

Bhagirath Lal Das, *An Introduction to the WTO Agreements*

Bhagirath Lal Das, *The WTO Agreements: Deficiencies, Imbalances and Required Changes*

Diplab Dasgupta, *Structural Adjustment, Global Trade and the New Political Economy of Development*

Bjorn Hettne et al., *International Political Economy: Understanding Global Disorder*

Terence Hopkins and Immanuel Wallerstein et al., *The Age of Transition: Trajectory of the World-System, 1945–2025*

Jomo, K.S. (ed.), *Tigers in Trouble: Financial Governance, Liberalisation and the Economic Crises in East Asia*

H-P. Martin and H. Schumann, *The Global Trap: Globalization and the Assault on Prosperity and Democracy*

Harry Shutt, *The Trouble with Capitalism: An Enquiry into the Causes of Global Economic Failure*

K. Singh, *The Globalisation of Finance: A Citizen's Guide*

Henk Thomas (ed.), *Globalization and Third World Trade Unions*

For full details of this list and Zed's other subject and general catalogues, please write to:

The Marketing Department, Zed Books, 7 Cynthia Street, London N1 9JF, UK or email: sales@zedbooks.demon.co.uk

Visit our website at: http://www.zedbooks.demon.co.uk

Zed Titles in its Politics in Contemporary Asia Series

Asia has come to prominence in recent years because of its economic dynamism, despite the dramatic financial collapse of 1997–98. But the decade-long economic success of this highly diverse continent has been dependent on the maintenance of effective government. It can also lead, as the Zed Books Series on Politics in Contemporary Asia shows, to the downplaying of the region's many political problems in the areas of ethnicity, religious identity, democratic control and human rights.

For full details of this list and Zed's other Asia titles, as well as our subject catalogues, please write to:

The Marketing Department, Zed Books, 7 Cynthia Street, London N1 9JF, UK or email: sales@zedbooks.demon.co.uk

Visit our website at: http://www.zedbooks.demon.co.uk